WEST VIRGINIA HISTORY

**Flag of the United States
Flag of West Virginia**

WEST VIRGINIA HISTORY

Phil Conley, B.S., Litt.D., LL.D.
West Virginia Historian

William Thomas Doherty, Ph.D.
Chairman, Department of History
West Virginia University

Published by
EDUCATION FOUNDATION, INC.
Charleston, West Virginia
1974

Fourth Printing

Copyright © 1974

by Education Foundation, Inc.
Charleston, West Virginia

ALL RIGHTS RESERVED

ISBN: 0-914498-00-2

Library of Congress Catalog Card Number: 73-88729

4 5 6 7 8 K 4 3 2 1 0

Printed by C. J. Krehbiel Company
Cincinnati, Ohio

Photo, front cover, courtesy of Tom Evans,
West Virginia Department of Commerce

PREFACE FOR INSTRUCTORS

In writing this history of West Virginia, the authors have attempted to present such information as is necessary to show the political, social, economic, cultural, and intellectual development of the thirty-fifth state. Since these factors are best demonstrated in the lives of people, a prominent feature of the book is the inclusion of biographical sketches of West Virginians or friends of West Virginia believed to have played an important part in influencing the course of events both within and without the state.

Like the state itself, these individuals have engaged in a variety of endeavors, and their accomplishments have often transcended the boundaries of a town, municipality, county, state, region, or nation. Human effort has always exercised an important influence in determining history, and perhaps especially so in West Virginia where even the state motto suggests that the inhabitants therein will always be accorded an unusual degree of freedom and independence in achieving their particular destinies.

The liberties as well as the isolation of early Mountaineers were once protected by towering hills. But, because of new inventions and modern modes of transportation, these hills no longer serve as effective guardians of seclusion. Therefore this record relates the story of an awakening West Virginia to the history of the nation and of the world.

At the regional level, through comparison and contrast, West Virginia's kinship with Appalachia and with all states that surround its highly irregular borders has been noted here. An effort has been made to see that minority groups and persons receive their proper attention in their relation to the various events and movements in state and national history. This means, for example, that the Indians, the blacks, the women, and the children, as well as the prehistoric cultures, the labor movement, the Industrial Revolution, the movement in behalf of the preservation and conservation of the natural resources, the restoration of the natural beauty, and the restitution of the arts and crafts skills of the people are not merely grafted upon a bare-boned skeletal history of military and political facts, but stand as collateral entities worthy of equal study and consideration.

This history has been divided into three major segments: The Present and the Distant Past, From Nationalism to Statehood, and The Recent Period. The first introduces the state of West Virginia, its original inhabitants and first settlers, and considers border warfare and the American Revolution as events leading toward nationalism. The second examines life on the frontier, the divisiveness of sectionalism, and the political creation of a new state out of the Old Dominion. The third considers the impact of the Industrial Revolution, the creation of newer life-styles in answer to that significant revolution, and the response of West Virginians to war, government, politics, conservation, and recreation in the most recent period. Each segment contains its own three units.

Hopefully this story of West Virginia contributes to a better understanding of the human past and thus meets the test of historical values which Carl Becker has indicated as "liberalizing the mind, deepening the sympathies, fortifying the will." If such purposes are served, they will, according to Becker, "enable us to control, not society, but ourselves" and will prepare us "to live more humanly in the present, and to meet rather than to foretell the future."

Three scholars with a deep interest in West Virginia history have reviewed this book in manuscript form. They are Professors Maurice Brooks, Elizabeth Cometti, and Earl Core.

Dr. Maurice Brooks, noted author of *The Appalachians* and *The Life of the Mountains* and professor emeritus of wildlife management and forestry, West Virginia University, is an expert in all phases of West Virginia history. Currently a member of the West Virginia Antiquities Commission, he has also served as president of the Wilson Ornithologists Club and as an influential member of conservation, recreation, and forestry commissions at both the state and national levels.

Dr. Elizabeth Cometti, former professor of history at Marshall University and West Virginia University, has with Professor Festus

P. Summers coauthored *The Thirty-Fifth State*. She is a past president of both the West Virginia Historical Association and the West Virginia Historical Society. In addition, she has served as chairman of the Governor's Review Board of West Virginia to evaluate proposals of the statewide historic preservation plan.

Dr. Earl Core, curator of the Herbarium, West Virginia University, and former chairman of the Department of Biology, is the author of the multivolumed *Flora of West Virginia*, *Vegetation of West Virginia*, and many other works. He is a former president of the West Virginia Academy of Science, the Southern Appalachian Botanical Society, and founder of its journal *Castanea*. Professor Core is currently writing an in-depth history of Monongalia County.

Dr. Frank John Krebs, professor of history and sociology, Morris Harvey College, 1950-1973, and managing editor of Education Foundation, Inc., has been general consultant in the preparation of this history.

Dr. J. William Hess, archivist of the Rockefeller Foundation, New York, and formerly curator of the West Virginia Collection, West Virginia University, has also served as a manuscript reviewer.

In addition, Mr. Charles C. Wise, Jr., of the James, Wise, Robinson and Magnuson Law Firm of Charleston, West Virginia, and vice-president of Education Foundation, Inc., has reviewed the manuscript with special emphasis on the divisions relating to government and politics.

Mary Yost Sandrus, former editor for the San Diego City Schools, former editor of special readers for Scott, Foresman and Company, Publishers, and editor for Education Foundation, Inc., has done an outstanding job in the general editing of this book.

Mr. Rodney Pyles, assistant curator of the West Virginia Collection, West Virginia University Library, and staff members of the Library of Congress and the West Virginia Department of Archives and History have been most helpful in supplying basic materials and pictures for this state history. The West Virginia Departments of Commerce and of Natural Resources have been generous in providing many pictures for the book.

Phil Conley

William T. Doherty

TABLE OF CONTENTS

PART ONE *The Present and the Distant Past*

UNIT ONE INTRODUCING WEST VIRGINIA
Chapter 1	West Virginia Within the United States	3
Chapter 2	Inside West Virginia	15
Chapter 3	Natural Wonders and Mineral Resources	25
Chapter 4	West Virginia and Her Sister States	37

UNIT TWO FIRST FAMILIES OF WEST VIRGINIA
Chapter 5	Early Man in Western Virginia	45
Chapter 6	Historic Indians in Western Virginia	57
Chapter 7	Explorations of the Western World and Western Virginia	71
Chapter 8	Permanent Residency	83

UNIT THREE BORDER WARFARE AND THE REVOLUTION
Chapter 9	The French and the Indians	95
Chapter 10	Friends Into Enemies, 1763–1774	107
Chapter 11	Revolutionary Days, 1775–1783	125
Chapter 12	Frontier Policies, 1783–1796	137

PART TWO *From Nationalism to Statehood*

UNIT FOUR ON THE VIRGINIA FRONTIER
Chapter 13	Pioneer Home Life	153
Chapter 14	Religion and the Three R's	165

| Chapter 15 | Industrial Evolution: New Ways To Make a Living | 181 |
| Chapter 16 | Internal Improvements in Western Virginia | 195 |

UNIT FIVE SECTIONALISM IN VIRGINIA

Chapter 17	The Baltimore and Ohio Railroad	207
Chapter 18	East-West Conflicts	217
Chapter 19	Slavery: "A Firebell in the Night"	227
Chapter 20	Virginia: Union and Confederate	241

UNIT SIX AN OLD AND A NEW DOMINION

Chapter 21	The Civil War in Western Virginia	249
Chapter 22	Two Western Virginia Generals, Two Heroines	265
Chapter 23	The Thirty-Fifth State	273
Chapter 24	The Official "First Family" of West Virginia	283

PART THREE *The Recent Period*

UNIT SEVEN INDUSTRIAL EVOLUTION

Chapter 25	From "Reconstruction" to the Twentieth Century	293
Chapter 26	Inland Transportation	305
Chapter 27	Mineral Fuels: Coal, Oil, and Gas	317
Chapter 28	Developments in Labor and in the Coal Industry	329

UNIT EIGHT NEWER LIFE-STYLES

Chapter 29	The Farms and the Forests	341
Chapter 30	New Employment Opportunities	357
Chapter 31	Educational Development	375
Chapter 32	The Blacks in West Virginia	387

UNIT NINE MEN TO MATCH THE MOUNTAINS

Chapter 33	National and International Services of West Virginians	399
Chapter 34	State and National Politics: 1897 to the Present	415
Chapter 35	West Virginia Government	425
Chapter 36	In Celebration of the Mountain State	439

Appendix A	455
Appendix B	469
Acknowledgments	471
Index	473

WEST VIRGINIA HISTORY

Part One

The Present and the Distant Past

West Virginia Woods *(West Virginia Department of Commerce Photo)*

unit one | Introducing West Virginia

Chapter 1 WEST VIRGINIA WITHIN THE UNITED STATES

Land Divisions of the United States

There are four major land divisions of the United States. Two are flat, and two are mountainous. The two flat sections are the Atlantic Coastal Plain with its Piedmont Plateau in the East and the large North American Plain in the Mid-West. One of the two mountainous sections is the Appalachian Mountains, which includes the Alleghenies. This section is in the eastern United States. The other is the Western Mountains with its plateaus; it includes the Rockies, and it is in the far western United States. The Appalachians divide the Atlantic Coastal Plain from the North American Plain. The Appalachians are older than the Rocky Mountains and are generally more rounded and lower in elevation.

West Virginia in Appalachia

Appalachia is composed of the Appalachian counties as shown on the map. The state of West Virginia lies wholly within the Appalachian region. For this reason, it has acquired the nickname "Mountain State." Although its mountains are not the highest in the nation, they are often steep and rugged, and they rise and fall across the state in successive waves of ranges.

West Virginia is also called the "Panhandle State" because on a map it resembles a large pan with two handles. Four counties

(Hancock, Brooke, Ohio, and Marshall) between western Pennsylvania and northeastern Ohio form the Northern Panhandle. Eight counties (Jefferson, Berkeley, Morgan, Hampshire, Hardy, Mineral, Grant, and Pendleton) between western Maryland and Virginia comprise the Eastern Panhandle.

A part of the Eastern Panhandle is in a geographical area known as the Valley and Ridge Province. The remainder of the state, including its Northern Panhandle, is in the Allegheny Plateau. In the state this wide plateau's western boundary is the Ohio River, but the plateau extends across the Ohio River to the Cambridge-Zanesville region. Its eastern boundary is a steep mountain wall known as the Allegheny Front.

The Allegheny Front, separating the Plateau from the Valley and Ridge Province, extends irregularly and somewhat diagonally down the state from approximately the town of Keyser (on the

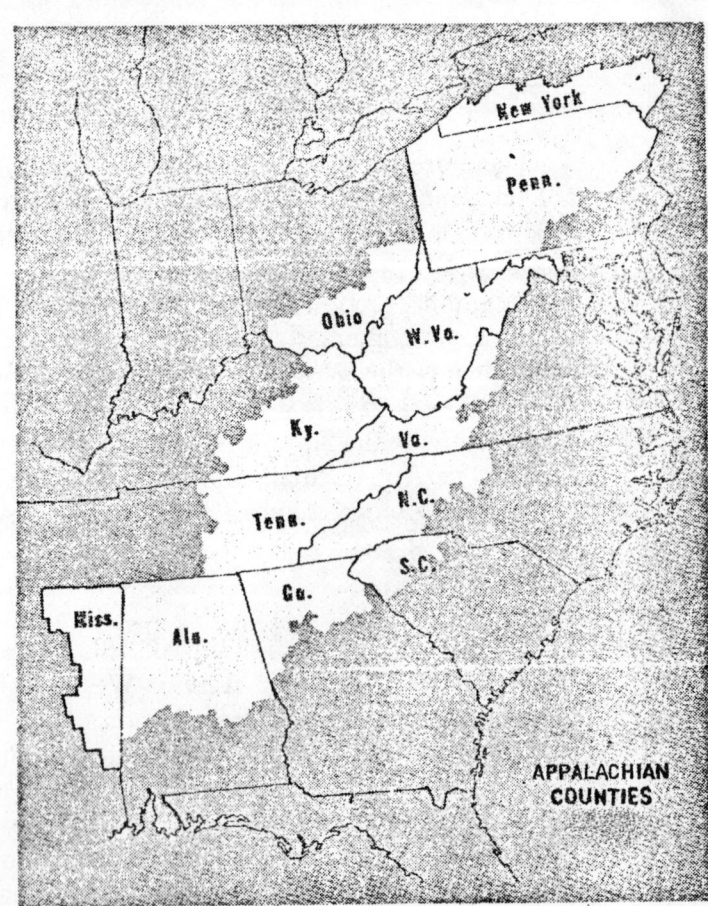

The Appalachian Counties Composing Appalachia *(Courtesy The Appalachian Regional Commission, Washington, D.C.)*

unit one / introducing west virginia

Spruce Knob, the Highest Point in West Virginia, as Seen from Route 33. Germany Valley lies in the foreground. (David P. Cruise Photo, West Virginia Department of Commerce)

West Virginia-Maryland boundary) to the town of Bluefield (on the West Virginia-Virginia boundary). Thus, about two-thirds of the state is a part of the greater Allegheny Plateau Province, which stretches from the state of New York to the state of Alabama.

Most of the eastern sector of the state lies in the Appalachians or in the Great Valley region and is a part of a large land province extending from Canada to central Alabama.

Position, Distances, and Elevations of West Virginia

West Virginia, the most mountainous state east of the Rockies, lies between 37° 12′ and 40° 38′ North Latitude and between 77° 43′ and 82° 38′ West Longitude. This makes the length of the state from north to south about 237 miles, and the width of the state from east to west about 265 miles. If one were to measure from Terrapin Neck of the Potomac River opposite Mercersville, Maryland, to a point on the Big Sandy River near Hewlet, Wayne County, West Virginia, he would arrive at an estimate of about 281 miles, the longest distance between two points in the Mountain State.

The irregular boundary lines of the state enclose more than 24,000 square miles or approximately 15,500,000 acres. A climber would have to prepare to scale West Virginia heights of almost a mile, for the Mountain State has an average elevation of about 1,500 feet above sea level. It is also a "Land of over Ten Thousand Valleys." Elevations in the state range from a low of 247 feet at Harpers Ferry to a high of 4,860 feet at Spruce Knob in Pendleton County.

Boundaries of the State

Almost the entire boundary line of West Virginia is defined by natural features such as rivers or mountains. Therefore, of all the American states, it has one of the most irregular shapes. Straight-line boundaries, typical of states west of the Mississippi River, form only small parts of the boundary lines between West Virginia and Pennsylvania, Maryland, and Virginia.

North and West. West Virginia is bounded on the northwest and west by Ohio, and the Ohio River serves as a natural demarcation line between the two states. The official West Virginia-Ohio dividing line is the low-water line on the western bank of the Ohio River. Consequently all of the islands in the Ohio River between the two states belong to the state of West Virginia.

North and East. West Virginia is bounded on the north by Pennsylvania and also on the north and northeast by Maryland. It is separated from Pennsylvania by the well-known Mason and Dixon Line. This line was established in 1763 when the British government commissioned Charles Mason and Jeremiah Dixon to survey and determine the boundary line between the colony of Pennsylvania and the colony of Maryland.

The Mason and Dixon Line has become famous in American history as symbolizing the division between the Northern and the Southern states during the American Civil War. Since West Virginia is south of this line, West Virginia can be thought of as a Southern state with three Southern neighbors to the east and south: Maryland, Virginia, and Kentucky; and two Northern neighbors to the west and north: Ohio and Pennsylvania. But because West Virginia was created as a Union state during the Civil War, it is hard to classify as either Southern or Northern. Sometimes it is difficult to classify as an Eastern state because of its name, West Virginia.

West Virginia is separated from Maryland by the Potomac River, the North Branch of the Potomac, and the headwaters of the North Branch. The West Virginia-Maryland line is the low-water line of the south bank of the Potomac and its North Branch to the source of the North Branch at Fairfax Stone. This line then proceeds from Fairfax Stone due north to the Mason and Dixon Line.

The Fairfax Stone was erected in 1746 to mark the western limits of the property of Lord Fairfax, an English nobleman who

Fairfax Stone, Most Noted Landmark in West Virginia and One of the Most Noted in the Nation   In 1746 the original stone was placed at the corner of Tucker and Grant counties to mark the western boundaries of the lands granted to Lord Fairfax by the King of England. The original stone was destroyed, and others have been erected to replace it. The stone in the picture is the most recent replacement. *(David P. Cruise Photo, West Virginia Department of Commerce)*

then owned what is now West Virginia's Eastern Panhandle and much of northern Virginia.

To describe West Virginia's northeastern boundary in another way, the state is separated from Pennsylvania and Maryland, in part, by meridians.

East and South. Generally, on the east and the southeast, the boundary line separating West Virginia from Virginia is formed by a crest of mountain ridges.

South and West. On the southwest, West Virginia is separated from the states of Virginia and Kentucky. The boundary line between West Virginia and Kentucky is formed by the Big Sandy River and the Tug Fork River.

Lakes, Rivers, Drainage and Navigational Systems

The official water area of West Virginia is confined mainly to a portion of the Ohio River. This limits the official water surface to a little over 100 square miles. The state contains a total of 24,282 square miles, of which 24,181 square miles represent land surface and the small remainder represents water surface.

Trout Pond This pond is said to be the only natural pond in West Virginia. It is located within the Rockcliff Lake Recreation Area, George Washington National Forest, near Wardensville. *(U.S. Forest Service Photo)*

Lakes. Although West Virginia was once a part of the bed of an ancient sea and still retains evidence of prehistoric lakes, it now is said to possess one two-acre natural lake, Trout Pond in Hardy County, whose great beauty makes up for its lack of size. The state has, however, made up for its loss of natural bodies of water by creating in recent times artificial lakes or reservoirs. These reservoirs are constructed on the New River, Cheat River, Tygart River, Elk River, and Gauley River. Constructed mainly for flood-control purposes and sometimes for power generation, the state's man-made lakes have also greatly increased opportunities for water-oriented recreational activities.

Rivers. *Western River System.* Three river systems serve West Virginia. One is in the western geographical division of the state, and two are in the eastern geographical division. The western river system consists of the Ohio River and its tributaries. In West Virginia these tributaries are located in the Allegheny Plateau and drain into the Ohio River. This river flows into the Mississippi River, which in turn empties its waters into the Gulf of Mexico.

Starting in the northern part of the state, the first of the West Virginia tributaries to drain into the Ohio River is the Monon-

Confluence of the Kanawha and Ohio Rivers at Point Pleasant *(David P. Cruise Photo, West Virginia Department of Commerce)*

gahela River. This river flows north. It leaves the state and crosses southwestern Pennsylvania before it joins the Allegheny to form the Ohio at Pittsburgh. Farther south, the Little Kanawha River enters the Ohio River at Parkersburg on the western boundary line.

Some forty miles below Parkersburg, the Kanawha River flows into the Ohio River at Point Pleasant. The largest of the West Virginia tributaries of the Ohio is the Kanawha River. Farther upstream the Kanawha is called the New River. In the southwestern portion of the state, the Guyandotte River and the Big Sandy River with its Tug Fork River complete the Ohio drainage system of West Virginia.

The Monongahela River flows in two states, helping at Pittsburgh to form the Ohio River. Except the Monongahela, all the West Virginia rivers emptying into the Ohio drain in a westerly direction.

Each of the rivers has its tributaries. The Cheat, Tygart, and West Fork rivers are tributaries of the Monongahela. The New

Boating on a Reservoir-Lake Boating is a popular sport on the man-made lakes behind the flood-control dams in West Virginia. (West Virginia Department of Natural Resources Photo)

River, Gauley River, Elk River, and Coal River are tributaries of the Kanawha River. The Bluestone River and the Greenbrier River flow into the New River. The New River is peculiarly named for it has been considered geologically the oldest river in the state.

Eastern River System. The eastern river system of West Virginia is in the Appalachian region. The parallel valleys here are drained by streams flowing northeast to the Potomac; and a part of Monroe County, in southeastern West Virginia, is drained by the James River. The Potomac River, forming the West Virginia-Maryland boundary line, flows eastward into the Atlantic. Important tributaries of the Potomac, running across the state's northern border from west to east, are the North Branch, Patterson's Creek, the South Branch with its own North Fork and South Fork, the Cacapon, and the Shenandoah.

Drainage and Navigation. As a result of these river patterns, West Virginia has an excellent drainage system. Nearly 21,000 square miles of West Virginia are drained directly or indirectly into the Ohio River. Nearly 3,600 square miles are drained into the Potomac River. About 80 square miles in Monroe County are drained into the James River.

These rivers have naturally quickened the commercial life of West Virginia. With the Ohio, Kanawha, and Monongahela river systems having a minimum depth of nine feet, waterborne commerce in West Virginia has increased each year. River commerce in the state approximates 200 million tons in the 1970's. Through the efforts of the United States Corps of Engineers, more than 350 miles of water in the state have been made navigable.

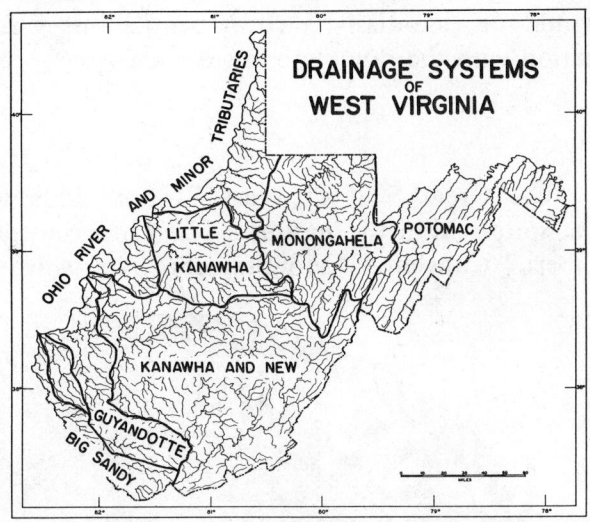

(West Virginia Geological and Economic Survey)

Historical Significance of West Virginia Geography

The rugged mountains provided a secluded and remote home where early West Virginians developed a spirit of individualism and independence. But the valleys and rivers eventually beckoned the mountaineers away from isolation and into interdependence with others.

Waterways and mountain gaps provided the original outlets to other neighboring states and population centers. Because much of West Virginia was drained by the Ohio River system, its economic and commercial developments were fashioned more in the Western and Northern patterns than in Eastern and Southern ones and were influenced by such cities as Pittsburgh, Pennsylvania, and Cincinnati, Ohio. Because most of the remainder of West Virginia was drained by the Potomac system, much of the state's business and political relationships were directed toward the Eastern cities, as Baltimore, Maryland, and Washington, D.C.

The geography of the state had determined that West Virginians could be physically self-supporting in a land of rugged beauty.

But geography also provided routes by which isolation could and would be broken. At a later time in West Virginia history, railroads and modern highways naturally followed the mountain gaps and the river systems, passages which Indians had marked out and traveled.

Geographical conditions determined that West Virginians would be essentially a rural people but would also furnish the nation with the raw materials for industry.

The State Seal

The Great Seal of West Virginia illustrates the working of the state within the nation. The Latin motto, "Montani Semper Liberi," translated "Mountaineers Are Always Free," circles the

The State Seal This side of the state seal is imprinted on official state papers. *(West Virginia Department of Commerce Photo)*

seal. A large stone in the center symbolizes strength. The date June 20, 1863 is inscribed on the stone. On this date West Virginia became a separate state in the Union.

On one side of the stone stands a farmer with his ax and his plow, signifying agriculture. On the other side of the stone stands a miner with his pick, signifying industry.

The other side of the seal has around its circumference a pattern of laurel and oak leaves. This wreath of leaves circles a picture of a log house, boats, and factories. In the background of the picture rise the hills of West Virginia.

Scholar, Researcher, Author

James Morton Callahan, Historian

Although born in Indiana in 1864, James M. Callahan, a noted historian, adopted the state of West Virginia as his home. He completed his studies at an Eastern university and his research in Washington, D.C. In 1902 Dr. Callahan joined the faculty of West Virginia University. He advanced the University in the disciplines of history and political science, and these areas of study became departments with appropriate courses and strong faculty members.

In 1916 Dr. Callahan was named dean of the University's College of Arts and Sciences. However, he continued to serve as professor of history until he retired in 1941. He was professor emeritus and dean emeritus until his death in 1956.

Diplomatic history was Dr. Callahan's original interest, and through his writings in that field he gained an international reputation. He edited *West Virginia University Studies in American History*, a series of monographs by faculty and students.

Of greater importance to West Virginia, however, were the advances made in the study of state and local histories under the leadership of Dr. Callahan. He saw the smaller units of local history as the building blocks to the study of national and international affairs. In particular, his interest was his adopted state. He completed the *Semi-Centennial History of West Virginia* in 1913, while serving as historian for the West Virginia Semi-Centennial Commission. Afterward, he wrote a *History of West Virginia, Old and New* and a book dealing with Morgantown.

In order to gain knowledge of the state and its inhabitants, Dr. Callahan traveled extensively. His contributions to historical literature in general and to that of his adopted state in particular have earned him a prominent place in the history of West Virginia itself.

Chapter 2 INSIDE WEST VIRGINIA

Geographical Sections of the State

West Virginia lies midway between the Atlantic Ocean and the Great Lakes. It has been called "the most northern of the southern states and the most southern of the northern states; the most eastern of the western states and the most western of the eastern states."

West Virginia may be said to consist of four major land divisions. These are, from west to east, the Ohio Valley Section, a lowland; the Allegheny Plateau, a hilly section, an extension of the Cumberland Mountains; the Allegheny Highlands, the mountain section; and the Potomac Section, another lowland area lying east of the Alleghenies and pointing toward the eastern United States. West Virginia lies wholly within the Appalachian region.

Boundaries. The Ohio Valley section gradually merges into the Allegheny Plateau. The Allegheny Plateau merges into the Allegheny Highlands. Separating the Allegheny Highlands from the Potomac Section is the Allegheny Front, a steep mountain wall.

Within the Potomac Section lying east of the Alleghenies is the Valley of Virginia. In the northern part of this valley, the Shenandoah Valley, lies a part of the two easternmost counties of West Virginia, Jefferson and Berkeley.

Ohio Valley. The Ohio Valley begins at the tip of the Northern Panhandle and extends southwest following the Ohio River as its western boundary line for the full length of the state. The counties in this section are, on the average, less than 2,000 feet above sea level and include approximately 8,000 square miles. The land is rolling, and beautiful hills to the east rise from the broad and fertile valleys. The section also contains oil, gas, salt, and coal deposits.

Allegheny Plateau. The Allegheny Plateau is high land which approximates 6,500 square miles. It passes through the central part of the Cumberland Plateau, which also extends across the states of Tennessee and Kentucky. This section is highly suitable for grazing. The Plateau consists of reasonably even horizontal beds of limestone, sandstone, and shales which include important seams of coal.

Millions of years ago the Plateau was broad, flat land and consisted of layers of solid rock. High above sea level, these layers of rock were folded in such a manner as to form long mountain chains. Rainfall caused streams to cut their ways in the direction of the Ohio River.

Allegheny Highlands. The Allegheny Highlands, consisting of about 6,000 square miles, is the mountain section of the state. The mountains were caused by huge layers of rock being folded over by great pressures. As some of the rocks were hard, they

Mountain Majesty, Smoke Hole Region, Grant County *(West Virginia Department of Commerce Photo)*

Restoration in Harpers Ferry National Historical Park In the foreground is Stagecoach Inn, built 1826–34, now serving as the National Historical Park visitor center. *(Gerald S. Ratliff Photo, West Virginia Department of Commerce)*

formed the long mountain chains. The soft rocks, worn down by rainfall and wind, formed the valleys. Where the highest mountains of hard rock are separated by the valleys of soft rock, many wonders of nature are found, and also numerous mineral springs, health resorts, and state parks. The lands are rich in timber and mineral deposits, and scattered land here is well adapted to grazing.

Potomac Section. The Potomac Section is made up of the eight counties of the Eastern Panhandle and comprises about 3,500 square miles. Much of the land is low and good for growing crops. Winds and rainfalls, which helped make a large part of the area into a valley, deposited lime, calcium, and other minerals here. These materials form a soil adapted to growing fruit and wheat.

Because the Potomac Section is near the Eastern cities and possesses a mild climate, it has become a favorite place for summer, or "second," homes. We have learned that it was an attractive and natural place for the early settlements in the state. Harpers Ferry

National Historical Park is in this section, and the early history of this region makes it of interest to visitors from every state in the Union.

Climate

The climate of West Virginia is continental; that is, its temperatures change in accordance with the seasons. It is similar to the climate of Ohio and western Pennsylvania and less like the climate of most of Virginia and Maryland.

Temperature. The average annual temperatures in the state range from about 56° Fahrenheit in the southwestern counties to about 48° in the higher parts of the mountain counties. This makes average yearly temperature in West Virginia approximately 53 degrees. The summer mean temperature averages 71.5°, and the winter mean temperature 33.6°.

One of the coldest temperatures ever recorded in the state was −37° at Lewisburg on December 30, 1917. One of the highest temperatures, 112°, was recorded at Martinsburg on July 10, 1936. The extremes may be explained in terms of elevation of the two communities. Lewisburg is at 2,200 feet above sea level, and Martinsburg only 435 feet above sea level.

Affected by the rains and the varying altitudes, the growing season in the various sections in West Virginia ranges from less than 120 days to more than 190 days.

Winds. Although the prevailing winds in the state are from south to west, and rarely from the east, West Virginia furnishes a setting where two wind systems confront each other and share each other's rains. Upon the ridges and slopes of the Alleghenies, clouds carried by eastern winds from the Atlantic meet and mingle with clouds carried by southern and western winds from the Gulf of Mexico and the Caribbean Sea or from cold British Columbia. Fortunately, hurricanes or tornadoes are rare in the state.

Rain. The average annual rainfall in the state ranges between 45 and 50 inches, distributed somewhat equally throughout the year. The Eastern Panhandle and Northern Panhandle receive from 35 to 40 inches, and the higher mountain counties receive well over 50 inches. The Allegheny Mountains in the eastern section, serving as a high barrier, catch the winds from the west.

The Rhododendron Maximum The rhododendron, or big laurel, is West Virginia's state flower. It was chosen by the schoolchildren of the state. It grows in nearly all parts of West Virginia. *(David P. Cruise Photo, West Virginia Department of Commerce)*

Before the water-laden winds and thick clouds pass over the mountains, they rise, grow cooler, and deposit most of their rain or snow on western slopes of the mountains before surmounting the peaks. Thus, the rainfall is heavier on the western side than on the eastern side. With the mountains stealing the moisture, the Eastern Panhandle reflects a drier and warmer climate.

Snow. Snow accumulations, which, on the average approximate 35 inches in the state, may vary in amounts from less than 20 inches in the southwestern portion to more than 100 inches in the mountains. Different years in West Virginia can bring very different weather. For example, the year 1930 was an extremely dry year, and the year 1950 was an extremely wet one.

Animal Life

Animals. Before European explorers entered West Virginia, large animals such as elephants, camels, and bison, likely roamed the state. Excavations across the state have revealed bones of the musk-ox, an arctic animal, and the peccary, a tropical animal. These remains of animal life indicate that, in millions of years past, extreme cold and, in turn, extreme heat must have prevailed in the land that is West Virginia, for here at some time lived animals which normally inhabit very cold areas and at other times animals that inhabit very hot regions.

Early explorers discovered deer, bears, elk, and wolves, along with the smaller forest dwellers such as foxes, skunks, squirrels, rabbits, opossums, raccoons, groundhogs, and chipmunks in the West Virginia area. With the exception of the protected deer and

The Black Bear The black bear is West Virginia's state animal. *(West Virginia Department of Commerce Photo)*

bear (hunting them being restricted by Virginia law as early as the year 1699), the larger animals are now extinct. Through bounties placed on wolves and the acceptance of the animal as tax payment, Virginia law encouraged the killing of wolves. By favoring deer and discouraging the existence of wolves, the state was protecting its domesticated animals, such as sheep, from slaughter by the more ravenous animal.

For the Indians and early settlers the forest wildlife provided food, clothing, coverings for beds and floors, and fur pelts for trading. Thus the supply of animals of the forest was reduced. Now protected by conservation regulations, smaller animals, including the otter and mink, still roam areas of West Virginia, primarily areas that have been reforested.

A few black bears and wildcats are present in the Allegheny Highlands, and in 1955 the Conservation Commission (now the Department of Natural Resources) adopted the black bear as the state animal of West Virginia.

Birds. About 300 species and subspecies of birds are found in West Virginia, and the cardinal is designated as the state bird. Selected by vote of students in all the schools of the state, garden clubs, civic organizations, and sportmen's clubs, the cardinal was victor in a close contest with the robin. Other songbirds of the state are the tufted titmouse, woodthrush, brown thrasher, and the scarlet tanager.

Game birds are the wild turkey, the ruffed grouse, and the bobwhite. Birds of prey are the hawks and owls. Field sparrows, catbirds, blackbirds, and crows are found in large numbers, as are woodpeckers, swallows, and warblers. Although undoubtedly

The Cardinal The cardinal is West Virginia's state bird. *(West Virginia Department of Commerce Photo)*

violated by hunters, a law of 1869 made West Virginia the first state in the Union to pass conservation legislation protecting all kinds of insectivorous birds.

Fish. Wastes from the mines and sawmills emptied into the streams of West Virginia have destroyed an amount of fish life. But in certain unpolluted mountain streams and in waters stocked by government agencies, trout, bass, pike, and other game fish may be found.

Over one hundred species of fish have been found in the state. Of special interest to fishermen have been the large- and the smallmouth bass and brook and rainbow trout. West Virginia at one time was able to supply almost all of the principal food fishes: the walleyed pike, the blue cat, mud cat, channel cat, rock bass, white perch, and the various members of the sucker family.

Other Animal Life. Frogs, turtles, and snakes abound. Poisonous native snakes are rattlers and copperheads.

Plant Life

Trees. Hilly terrain and ample rainfall have contributed to the spectacular growth of trees in West Virginia. With almost three-fourths of the land area of West Virginia forested, the state has more than one hundred native trees and has added still others through importation.

Originally, the entire land area of West Virginia was covered with a forest of large trees. The cone-bearing trees (hemlock, pines, balsam fir, and red spruce) were located in the deep river gorges

The Sugar Maple Tree The sugar maple is West Virginia's state tree. *(David P. Cruise Photo, West Virginia Department of Commerce)*

and on the banks of the cool mountain streams and on cold mountain ridges and plateaus. On the hills and river bottoms and within the coves were the broadleaf trees (giant oaks, hickories, maples, yellow poplars, and black walnuts).

Most of these trees, along with the magnolia, mulberry, and birch, were species unknown in Europe, and thus West Virginia was a novel producer of native timber. Hardwoods now make up 95 percent of the total cubic foot volume of West Virginia timber production. Oaks account for more than 40 percent of the volume. The more-desired species, the white oak and the northern red oak, represent half of that amount. As with the animal life, the plant life of West Virginia calls for conservation. Fortunately, more wood (370 million cubic feet) is currently being grown in West Virginia than is being cut (120 million cubic feet).

Shrubs and Vines. Blackberry, black and red raspberry, gooseberry, huckleberry, hazel, grape, and elder are among the West Virginia shrubs and vines. Likely the seeds of the sumac, yew, hemlock, violet, honeysuckle, raspberry, mountain maple, oxalis, and holly, as well as box-huckleberry, originated in Canada. These species may have been transplanted into West Virginia by glacial force or deposited here by birds.

University Professor and Lover of Nature

Alonzo Beecher Brooks, Naturalist

Alonzo B. Brooks, noted forester and naturalist, was a member of the well-known Brooks family of French Creek, Upshur County, West Virginia. He was born on May 6, 1873 and grew up in a rural environment which helped develop his interest in animal and plant life. As a boy he began explorations into the woods, never ceasing these excursions when he later took up the occupation of farmer and surveyor.

In 1912 he was awarded a degree in agriculture at West Virginia University and accepted a position with the West Virginia University Agricultural Experiment Station. He became a member of the State Department of Agriculture and served as the state's chief game protector from 1921 to 1928. Brooks moved to Oglebay Park at Wheeling and served as the park naturalist until 1942. He died at French Creek in 1944.

Between 1911 and 1929, A. B. Brooks wrote at least sixteen reports for the West Virginia Geological Survey. One of his best-known and most-respected works, written for the West Virginia Experiment Station Bulletin in 1920, was entitled "West Virginia Trees." This was a study of more than one hundred varieties of trees native to the state.

Mr. Brooks was also an amateur historian. He organized the Ohio County Historical Society in 1929 and, in addition, served as president of the Upper Ohio Valley Historical Society.

Mr. Brooks gained a wide reputation for his development of the natural beauty of Oglebay Park. He was instrumental in establishing the Oglebay Park Nature Training School, a summer program which taught the wonder of the wilderness and a love of nature. In the following quoted lines Alonzo B. Brooks was honored on the occasion of his retirement in 1942: "He lives in every tree, every flower, every bird and every scampering furry creature at Oglebay Park, for into the development of Oglebay, as it is today, he poured the richness of his great soul."

Chapter 3 NATURAL WONDERS AND MINERAL RESOURCES

Natural Wonders: A Result of Topography

The rugged gaps, the canyons, the rivers and streams provide West Virginia with some of the most magnificent scenery and most interesting natural wonders east of the Mississippi River. The picturesque mountains, woodlands, hillsides, coves, valleys, and lakes afford visitors a variety of attractions seldom found within a single state.

Rock Formations. In the southern and northeastern counties of Fayette, Mercer, Grant, Pendleton, and Hampshire, a number of rock formations are found near the gorges made by the rivers. With their amazing shapes, their heights, their awkward positions, and unusual sizes, these formations never cease to fascinate the inhabitants and the visitors.

Hawks Nest. One of these rock formations is Hawks Nest. This towering precipice of rocks located in Fayette County, juts out 585 feet above the New River Gorge. This stream rises in North Carolina and flows 85 miles through West Virginia to Gauley

Seven-Mile Panorama of Horseshoe Bend of New River This bend of New River is some miles south of Hawks Nest and in this view is seen from the Main Overlook in Grandview State Park, Raleigh County. *(Arnout Hyde, Jr., Photo, West Virginia Department of Natural Resources)*

Bridge. There New River joins the Gauley River to form the Kanawha River. The New River drops 850 feet on its way through the state, cutting through one of the longest, deepest, and most beautiful canyons or gorges in the United States. The sides of the mountains along which the river carves its path vary in height from 700 to 900 feet.

Hawks Nest was once known as Marshall's Pillar. The earlier name was given in honor of John Marshall, Chief Justice of the United States Supreme Court, who visited the rock in the year 1812.

In honor of the scenic wonder, West Virginia has set aside 237 acres to create Hawks Nest State Park. In this park is located a modern 31-room lodge overlooking the New River Gorge. Visitors may enjoy boating, picnicking, hiking trails, exceptional fishing opportunities, swimming, and browsing in a museum. In addition, an aerial tramway sweeps to the bottom of the canyon and offers unusual views.

Burning Rock, Castle Rock, Peter's Mountain, and Pinnacle Rocks. Also in the southern part of the state, Burning Rock and

Pinnacle Rocks near Bluefield, Mercer County *(West Virginia Department of Commerce Photo)*

Castle Rock in Wyoming County arouse wonder. Burning Rock seems to conserve heat perpetually, for snow melts here as quickly as it falls. In Monroe County, Peter's Mountain ridge stretches for forty miles in a straight line against the sky, providing a lengthy panoramic display.

In Mercer County, near Bluefield, are the Pinnacle Rocks, tall slender peaks that stand like ruins of an old temple. The Pinnacle Rocks extend for half a mile along the ridge of Flat Top Mountain. Here also West Virginia has created a state park consisting of 250 acres where visitors may utilize picnic grounds and hiking trails.

Seneca Rock, Image Rocks, Hanging Rocks, and The Trough. In the Eastern Panhandle counties, in the northeastern section of the state, are other interesting rock formations. Seneca Rock in Pendleton County resembles desert scenery. This is especially true when its various colors are highlighted by the sun. This rock rises more than 900 feet above the river and at times resembles a ruined ancient castle.

In Grant County where the South Branch forces its way through Patterson Creek Mountain may be found Image Rocks. In Hampshire County the Hanging Rocks, rising to a height of nearly 300 feet, lean out over the South Branch in the shape of lofty towers.

The South Branch of the Potomac River in Hardy and Hampshire counties pleases the most exacting tourist. It flows for a distance of seven miles through a valley with overhanging banks known as The Trough.

Caves

Greenbrier, Pocahontas, Monroe and Pendleton counties, which border on Virginia, and neighboring Grant County have a number of caves.

Organ Cave. Near Lewisburg, in Greenbrier County, is Organ Cave. This limestone cave received its name because its rocks not only resemble the pipes of an organ but also, when struck by stone or other substances, render musical sounds. In the past, Organ Cave was sometimes called a fugitives' cave, for it served as a haven for early settlers and for Southern soldiers during the Civil War. The early frontiersmen and military personnel were attracted to the cave because it contained saltpeter, a substance used to make gunpowder. Some hoppers used in separating the saltpeter from the earth are still preserved in the cave, one of the major caves in West Virginia open to the public.

Smoke Hole Caverns. In Grant County are located the Smoke Hole Caverns. From a main room called "The Room of a Million Stalactites," spectators enter broad, well-lighted pathways. In nearby Pendleton County is found a deep narrow valley of the North Branch of the Potomac called "The Smoke Hole." Here and in the nearby caves, in what still seems a remote section of the world, Indians and the early European settlers smoked their meat.

Seneca Caverns. In Pendleton County are found the Seneca Caverns. Extending for miles underground, they feature well-lighted corridors from which visitors may view such configurations as the "Ballroom," "Niagara Falls," and the pattern of a head of a young girl titled "Princess Snowbird."

Scenic Wonders: Falls, Valleys, and Glades

Three spots in West Virginia most visited because of their spectacular beauty are Blackwater Falls, Canaan Valley, and Cranberry Glades.

Blackwater Falls in Blackwater Falls State Park *(West Virginia Department of Commerce Photo)*

Blackwater Falls. Blackwater Falls is in Tucker County, one mile below the town of Davis. The falls deposit the waters of the Blackwater, a tributary of the Cheat River, from a height of 65 feet, into the narrow and deep Blackwater Canyon. This magnificent waterfall is the first in a series of falls and rapids in a river that drops steadily for a distance of ten miles. At Blackwater Falls, West Virginia has created a state park. This heavily patronized area consists of 1,688 acres and features deluxe cabins and lodge rooms. Boating, swimming in the lake, picnicking, hiking trails, fishing, and horseback riding are some of its recreational offerings.

Canaan Valley. Also in Tucker County is Canaan Valley, which was believed to have once been the bed of a prehistoric lake thirteen miles long and from three to five miles wide. West Virginia has set aside 6,014 acres here for a new park called the Canaan Valley Park. Along with Pipestem, it is one of two state parks that boasts a golf course and features winter sports.

Cranberry Glades. In Pocahontas County are the Cranberry Glades which cover about 700 acres. They are located in a high valley on an opening in the forest. This spot is the most southern point at which numerous northern birds nest. Birds of many kinds may be seen here. The Glades are a part of the Monongahela National Forest, and the United States government tract nourishes some plants similar to those found on the arctic tundra. Nearly half of the acreage is covered with shrubs, mostly speckled alder. On the open glades are found sedges, mosses, and lichens. The bog rosemary is also found in the Cranberry Glades, its only location in the state.

Dolly Sods. Dolly Sods, once owned by Johann Dahle, has become popular with informed visitors who enjoy its rugged grandeur, its growth of wild nature, and its air of loneliness. The sods, or area of native grasses and heaths, lies in the Monongahela National Forest. Curious plants, some common to the Far North, grow there. The treeless earth looks harsh, but it sustains a delicate and fragile ecology. The U. S. Forestry Service management will be directed toward "maintaining the scenic views, preservation of the diverse plant life, nature study, and enjoyment of the primitive values."

Oddities of Nature

Some of West Virginia's natural wonders perform seemingly magical tricks. The Ebb and Flow Spring near Petersburg in Grant County rises and falls like the tides of the ocean. At the Sinks in Randolph County, the Gandy River begins a passage of about a mile beneath the mountains. The Trout Pond in Hardy County is a deep natural lake with very cold water. The Ice Mountain in Hampshire County is a perpetual refrigerator.

In Hardy County is Lost River, which begins near Brock's Gap, widens, dashes against a mountain, and disappears into the earth under Sandy Ridge. Two miles away, it suddenly reappears as the

Lee's Cabin One cabin of the Lee family resort remains in Lost River State Park, Hardy County. *(Gerald S. Ratliff Photo, West Virginia Department of Commerce)*

beginning of the Cacapon River. Under the ridge from which the stream appears is Alum Rock, from which alum is extracted. Not far away is Lost River State Park, with an area of 3,680 acres. The state park contains lodge rooms, a restaurant, and a souvenir shop. It also offers visitors a swimming pool, picnicking grounds, a playground, game courts, hiking trails, and fishing.

At one time on the site of present Lost River State Park was located Lee's White Sulphur Springs, a summer resort. In 1796 the Virginia Assembly gave this property to "Light Horse Harry" Lee, the father of General Robert E. Lee, and the family built a hotel at the springs.

Mineral Springs

West Virginia contains many mineral springs, famous both as health resorts and as gathering places for prominent people of the state and the nation. These springs contain such minerals as salt, iron, and sulphur and have been considered to possess healing

"The Greenbrier," Facing North, at White Sulphur Springs

qualities. The springs in West Virginia have been favored by persons suffering from tuberculosis, arthritis, rheumatism, and the discomforts of old age.

Berkeley Springs. One of the most historic is Berkeley Springs in Morgan County, called "Warm Springs" by George Washington in 1748 and later named "Bath." These springs are located on lands once owned by Lord Fairfax. They became a favorite resort for American Revolutionary heroes and statesmen.

White Sulphur Springs. One of the most consistently popular of the mineral springs is White Sulphur Springs in Greenbrier County. Not only was it a social center for the Old South in days before the Civil War, but because of its nearness to Washington, D.C., it has remained to this day "the playground of the nation" for persons prominent in all activities and interests. Earlier owned and maintained by the Chesapeake and Ohio Railway, the Springs provided, in the elaborate "Greenbrier" resort, a general hospital for wounded and ill soldiers during World War II, but is again owned and operated by the railroad and open to the public.

Other Springs. Other important springs are the Old Sweet Springs, Red Sulphur Springs, and Salt Sulphur Springs in Monroe County; Borland Springs in Pleasants County; Shannondale Springs in Jefferson County; and Webster Springs in Webster County.

Mineral Resources

Professor Israel Charles White, noted West Virginia state geologist, many years ago stated that the column of rocks exposed within the state consists of sandstones, limestones, and shales. These geologic conditions produce the mineral fuels.

Mineral Fuels. It has sometimes been said that West Virginia with the nicknames of "Mountain State" and "Panhandle State" could add another title, "Fuel State." The state was probably originally endowed with more fuel resources — coal, oil, and gas — than any other single state in the Union.

Coal. Coal, used as a fuel both in home and in industry, is a vital resource. There are two kinds of coal — soft coal and hard coal. Only Pennsylvania possesses hard coal, which burns with less smoke and ash than does soft coal. Hard coal is called anthracite. The soft grade is called bituminous coal.

West Virginia and Kentucky are the leading bituminous coal producers in the nation. West Virginia accounts for more than one-fourth of the entire coal production in the United States, and, among all the states, West Virginia ranks eighth in the value of by-products of coal.

Although coal is principally a mineral fuel, it is also utilized as a raw material. Coke (of great importance to the steel industry), coke-oven gas, tar, light oil, and ammonia are coal's important primary products. Coal affords a bountiful source of synthetic gas. This gas serves as a source of energy additional to the available but ever diminishing deposits of natural gas and petroleum.

Of all West Virginia's mineral resources, coal is the most important; it accounts for over 80 percent of the state's total mineral output. It is present in 44 of the 55 counties. Twenty-eight counties have more than one billion tons of coal reserves, and 36 account for the 1,600 producing mines in the 1970 decade. Minable coal is located in more than 60 workable seams out of more than 100 seams which are distributed through nearly 5,000 feet of sedimentary rocks. Minable coal underlies about two-thirds of the total area of West Virginia.

Oil and Gas. Oil and natural gas are found in the rock layers of West Virginia which were subjected to tremendous pressures many years ago. When these pressures crushed the remains of animals and vegetation, they created the mineral fuels. Layers of oil and gas were formed about the same time as the beds of coal but are located much deeper in the earth.

The oil and gas belt of the state begins in the Northern Panhandle and sweeps in a southwesterly direction through the length of the state. The width of the belt is from the Allegheny Mountains to the Ohio River and contains 33 counties. The large chemical industry in West Virginia is dependent on petroleum and natural gas. This industry continues to expand rapidly in the Ohio River and Kanawha River valleys.

Oil furnishes power and also lubricates the nation's machines. Both petroleum (from Latin words meaning *oil from a rock*) and natural gas are now being used as raw materials in producing butane gasoline and numerous organic chemicals. In 1900 a total of more than 16,000,000 barrels of oil was produced in West Virginia. In the 1960's and 1970's production approximated 3,500,000 barrels, and proved reserves exceeded 50,000,000 barrels.

Natural gas, formed by nature in great pockets in the sands within the earth, is used by most of the cities and towns of West Virginia as a primary fuel. In the late 1960's and early 1970's production of natural gas jumped more than 200,000,000 cubic feet out of an estimated reserve of about 2,500,000,000 cubic feet. Production in natural gas liquids was close to 7,000,000 barrels out of a proved reserve of over 80,000,000 barrels. Liquid fuels are either gasoline or "bottled gas" for heating and cooking.

Other Minerals

Limestone. Limestone is used as a building material in the making of roads, and in the manufacture of iron and steel and glass. Farmers burn limestone to make lime for application on farming lands containing too much acid or clay, and miners use lime for dusting coal mines. Burned limestone is also useful for plaster, mortar, and other building materials.

Sand and Gravel. Extensive deposits of both sand and gravel are also found throughout West Virginia. Fine-quality glass sand is found primarily in the eastern portion of the state, but six of the seven leading producing counties lie along the Ohio River, the state's western boundary. Three are in the Northern Panhandle: Hancock, Brooke, and Ohio, and the other three are Pleasants, Wood, and Wetzel. The leading producer, Morgan County, is in the Eastern Panhandle.

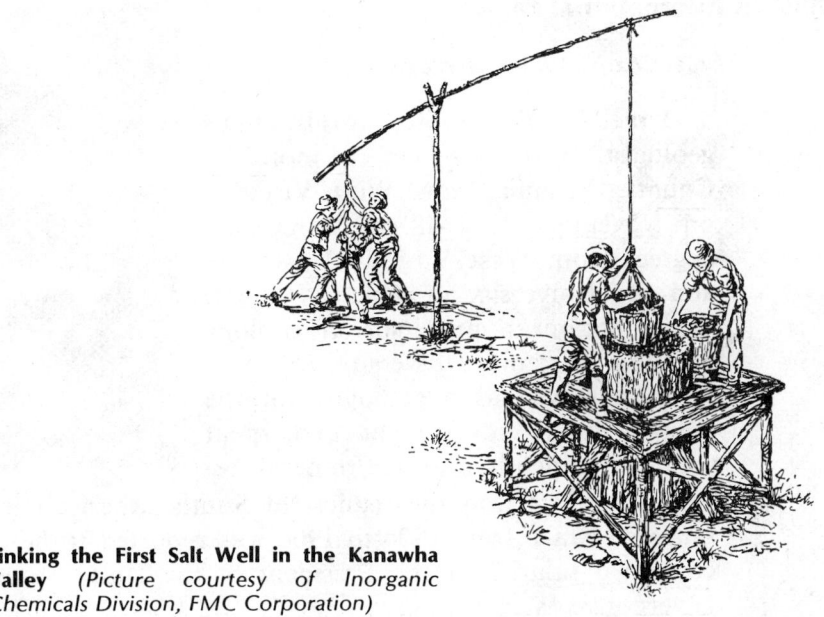

Sinking the First Salt Well in the Kanawha Valley *(Picture courtesy of Inorganic Chemicals Division, FMC Corporation)*

Clays. Inexhaustible supplies of clay are found throughout the state, but Berkeley County has the highest production of miscellaneous clays. The best clays are used for making high-grade china, and others in the manufacture of kitchenware, flowerpots, and such. Fire clays are used in making bricks, tiles, and sewer pipe. Kanawha, Cabell, Mercer, Lewis, and Taylor counties currently have the highest production of fire clays. Thick beds of fire clays are found in Marion, Hancock, Monongalia, and Preston counties and also in Cabell and Taylor.

Stone. West Virginia has large resources of both sandstone and limestone suitable for building purposes. Berkeley, Jefferson, Monongalia, and Greenbrier counties lead in limestone production; Kanawha, Wyoming, Harrison, Doddridge, Wayne, and Lewis counties lead in sandstone. Chert and quartz are collected from the Ohio River Valley terraces.

Salt. One of the first industries in West Virginia was the production of salt. Before the Civil War salt was produced in Kanawha and Mason counties, and in the early 1800's "Kanawha Salt" was much prized for curing and preserving meats and for domestic purposes. At least 27 counties in the state are capable of producing brine salt. The most important brine zones in West Virginia are the Salt Sand zone and the Big Injun Sand.

chapter three / natural wonders and mineral resources

Scientist of International Fame

Israel Charles White, Geologist

Israel Charles White, world-famous geologist, was born in Monongalia County, Virginia, now West Virginia, on November 1, 1848. He received degrees from West Virginia University and the University of Arkansas. Dr. White became a professor of geology at West Virginia University in 1877. He also served as a geologist for the United States government and spent two years identifying the mineral resources of Brazil at the request of South American leaders. His salary in Brazil from 1904 to 1906 was reported to be equal to the combined salaries of the President of the United States and the governor of West Virginia.

In his research Dr. White uncovered many useful and interesting facts about coal, petroleum, and natural gas, resources important to the economy of West Virginia. In 1882 he discovered scientific principles concerning deposits of oil and gas. These anticlinal theories, as they were called, made him world famous and marked him as one of the leading economic geologists of his time.

These theories were tested in the Washington and Taylortown, Pennsylvania, oil fields and in the Mannington, West Virginia, oil field. His abilities in the discovery of oil and gas also brought him a small fortune, which he used to a large extent for the benefit of the state of West Virginia and its first university.

Dr. White held many positions during his career, including an important conservation position to which he was appointed by President Theodore Roosevelt in 1906. As a representative of the United States, he attended two International Geological Conferences, one in Russia in 1897 and the other in France in 1900. From 1897 to his death on November 25, 1927, Dr. White served West Virginia as state geologist without salary.

Well liked as a teacher, Dr. White lived by a code which he invited his students to follow, a code which listed absolute honesty and truthfulness as the first essentials. At West Virginia University the building in which the geology department is housed is named in his honor.

Chapter 4 WEST VIRGINIA AND HER SISTER STATES

Forty-first in Area

West Virginia, admitted to the United States as the thirty-fifth state, is in area the forty-first state in the Union, totaling 24,181 square miles in land size. West Virginia is more than twenty times the size of Rhode Island, ten times the size of Delaware, five times the size of Connecticut, three times the size of New Jersey or Massachusetts, and nearly twice the size of Maryland. It is more than twice as large as the Kingdom of Belgium, twice as large as Holland, and half as large as England.

Thirty-fourth in Population

West Virginia, according to the 1970 census, ranks as the thirty-fourth state in population, with 1,744,237 residents. It has more inhabitants than Nebraska, Utah, New Mexico, Maine, or Rhode Island, and more than twice as many people as Hawaii, the District of Columbia, New Hampshire, Idaho, Montana, North Dakota, or South Dakota. Three times as many people live in West Virginia as in Delaware, Nevada, or Vermont, and four times as many reside in the Mountain State as in Wyoming or Alaska. Yet each of the cities of New York, Chicago, Los Angeles, and Philadelphia has a greater population than the state of West Virginia.

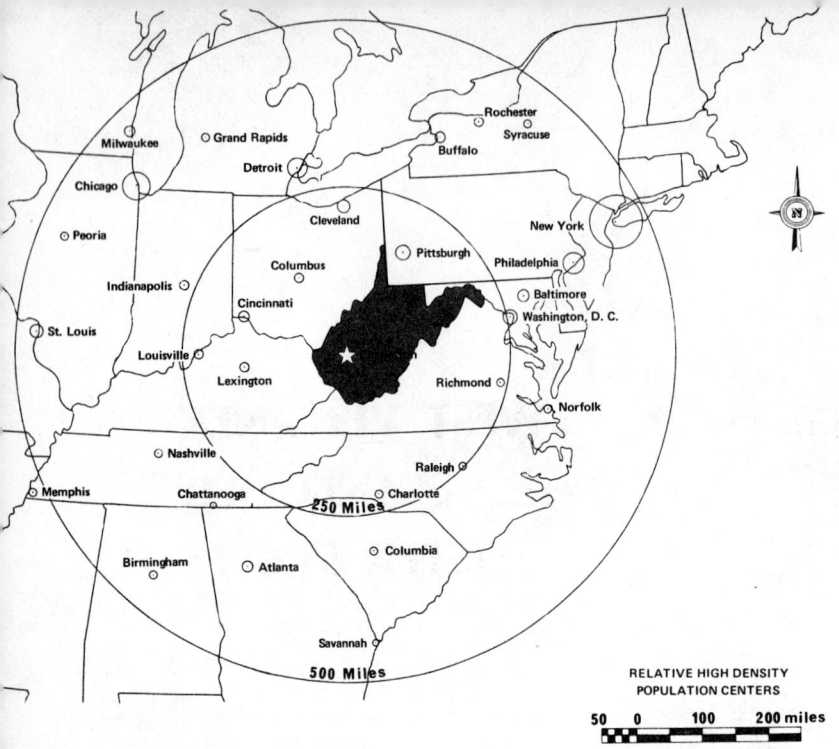

West Virginia's Geographic Location The map shows where West Virginia lies in relation to centers of high-density population. (Reprinted from "1973 West Virginia Economic Profile," West Virginia Department of Commerce, Industrial Development Division)

A Central Location

The center of population of the United States in the census years of 1820, 1830, 1840, and 1850 was near Moorefield, Clarksburg and Parkersburg, West Virginia. By 1970, however, the geographical center of the population of the nation had shifted west to Illinois. Yet in the 1970's West Virginia remained in a central location that was midway between the large population centers of the East and of the Mid-West.

Within a 500-mile radius of the state's geographical center, four out of five of the principal United States metropolitan market areas are located: New York, Chicago, Philadelphia, and Detroit. Within this area much more than half of the nation's people reside, and these people earn more than half of the nation's income.

Population Characteristics

Density. West Virginia, which was separated from Virginia on December 31, 1862 and admitted to the Union on June 20, 1863, first participated as a state in a national census in 1870. The census showed 442,014 residents. The state achieved its highest population count in 1950, with more than 2,000,000 people. In the 1960 and 1970 censuses, however, it experienced successive population losses.

Scene in a Greenbrier Valley in West Virginia Many people of the state live in rural areas. West Virginia has countless beautiful rural scenes, as fine as the view above. *(West Virginia Department of Natural Resources Photo)*

The number of births was approximately twice the number of deaths in West Virginia in the most recent decades. So migration of peoples to other states has been the explanation for population loss. In 1970, in addition to West Virginia, other states experiencing out-migration were New Mexico, North Dakota, and South Dakota, as well as the District of Columbia.

Yet West Virginia's population density — that is, the number of people per square mile — remains above the national average. In 1970 average population density in the United States was calculated as 57.4 persons per square mile. In West Virginia it is figured at 72.5 persons per square mile. But within Appalachia in West Virginia's border states, the number of inhabitants per square mile remains much greater. Per square mile, Virginia possesses more than 100 inhabitants, Pennsylvania and Ohio more than 250 inhabitants, and Maryland almost 400 inhabitants. Only Kentucky's density closely approximates West Virginia's, yet the former exceeds the latter by more than 80 inhabitants.

Urban-Rural. According to the 1970 census, almost three-fourths of the American people are counted as living in urban areas

—that is, in towns or cities of 2,500 inhabitants or more—and one-fourth are counted as living in rural areas. Almost two-fifths of the people of West Virginia are classified as living in urban areas, and three-fifths as living in rural areas. Among the South Atlantic states, in only West Virginia, North Carolina, and South Carolina do rural residents outnumber urban residents.

West Virginia possesses eight cities which range in population from a high of approximately 75,000 to a figure of approximately 25,000. These are, in numerical order, Huntington, Charleston, Wheeling, Parkersburg, Morgantown, Weirton, Fairmont, and Clarksburg.

TEN LARGEST CITIES
(1970 Census)

1.	Huntington	74,315
2.	Charleston	71,505
3.	Wheeling	48,188
4.	Parkersburg	44,208
5.	Morgantown	29,431
6.	Weirton	27,131
7.	Fairmont	26,093
8.	Clarksburg	24,864
9.	Beckley	19,884
10.	South Charleston	16,333

Ten West Virginia counties have over 50,000 people each. These counties are Kanawha, Cabell, Wood, Harrison, Raleigh, Ohio, Monongalia, Mercer, Marion, and McDowell. These more populous counties generally contain one or more of the larger West Virginia towns.

Population Areas

The Bureau of Census, in determining the numerical ranking of the major largest cities, uses a cut-off population figure of 100,000 persons. In that sense, West Virginia possesses no major cities. However, several government bureaus have invented the Standard Metropolitan Statistical Areas (SMSA's) which recognize that groupings of cities and counties reveal areas of population concentration more significant than listings of single cities. In some cases these groupings necessarily cross state boundary lines.

Charleston Civic Center The Grand Arena of the Civic Center seats 8,200 for stage events and 7,013 for basketball. The exhibit area contains 51,000 square feet.

West Virginia contains five areas of more than 140,000 people each. The Charleston area has almost 230,000 people living entirely within the state. The Wheeling area including Marshall and Ohio counties of West Virginia and neighboring Belmont County of Ohio, has almost 183,000 persons. Weirton with neighboring Steubenville, Ohio, approximates a population of more than 165,000. Parkersburg with its neighbor Marietta, Ohio, has almost 144,000 persons. The Huntington area reaching to Ashland, Kentucky, has more than a quarter of a million persons.

Majority and Minority Groupings. Almost all present West Virginians have been born in the United States. The state's foreign-born residents constitute only about 2 percent of the population. The first settlers of West Virginia were predominantly of Welsh, German, and Scotch origin. After the Civil War, in addition to the inhabitants from the British Isles, large numbers of immigrants to West Virginia were of Italian, Polish, and Hungarian descent.

In 1970 the census bureau determined the origin of state residents of first or second generations who either were foreign born or had at least one foreign-born parent. In West Virginia, 57,358 persons are of such parents, and 16,662 are foreign born. The principal countries of origin of these residents of West Virginia are Greece and the United Kingdom, followed by Germany and Poland. Other countries of origin are Ireland, Czechoslovakia, Austria, Hungary, Yugoslavia, Russia, Lithuania, Italy, and Canada.

chapter four / west virginia and her sister states

In the 1970 census American Indians show, across the nation, a greater than 50 percent growth since the previous census count. Yet in West Virginia, the number of American Indians more than quadrupled from 181 residents in 1960 to 751 in 1970. The Bureau of the Census also counts in the state 73,931 blacks, 368 Japanese, 373 Chinese, and 722 Filipinos.

Sex and Marital Status

In West Virginia and in the nation the number of females exceeds the number of males in the 14–70-year brackets. Across the United States there are 94.8 males for every 100 females. In West Virginia there are 90.5 males for every 100 females.

In determining marital status by sex, the Bureau of Census states in the 1970 report that of those over 14 years of age in the nation, approximately two-thirds of the males are married and one-third are either single, divorced, separated, or widowed. Of females, approximately 60 percent are married, and 40 percent fall into the categories of single, divorced, separated, or widowed persons.

West Virginia approximates the national findings, yet has a slightly higher percentage of those married as well as those widowed, and a slightly lower percentage of single, separated, and divorced persons of either sex. For example, the census bureau finds that in the nation more than 3 percent of the population are divorced, and in West Virginia no more than 2 percent of the population are divorced.

Per Capita Income

Annual per capita income in the nation, the 1970 census says, is $3,921; in West Virginia per capita income is listed as $3,021. West Virginia's per capita income approximates that of its neighbors Kentucky, Virginia, and Tennessee, and exceeds that of certain Southern states, including Alabama, Arkansas, Mississippi, and South Carolina. The per capita income of each of two other neighboring states, Pennsylvania and Ohio, exceeds the national per capita income, and Maryland is one of the top twelve states in the Union in per capita income.

The number of recipients of welfare per 1,000 population in the age group 12 to 70 in the nation is 67.1. West Virginia, with 72.4 welfare recipients per 1,000 population, exceeds in numbers the average for the nation, for all five of its bordering states, and for 33

National Computer Center at Martinsburg This center is the hub of the automatic data processing system of the United States Internal Revenue Service. All United States income tax returns are sent to the Internal Revenue Service. *(Photo courtesy of National Computer Center)*

other states across the country. But the average monthly payment for West Virginia welfare recipients who are classified as blind, disabled, aged, or qualified for aid to families with dependent children is below the average of monthly payments across the nation in all types of assistance by about one-third.

The average amount expended in monthly payments to persons on public welfare for each inhabitant of the United States is $61.90. In West Virginia it is $39.40, an amount that is still greater than residents of 21 other states received. In Pennsylvania, Maryland, and Kentucky persons on public welfare received payments exceeding the national average. In Ohio and Virginia they received amounts somewhat less than similar persons in West Virginia received.

Winner of the Nobel Prize

Pearl Sydenstricker Buck, Novelist

Pearl Buck, one of the best-known West Virginians, was born at Hillsboro, Pocahontas County, West Virginia, in 1892. She did not live there very long, however, for her parents were Presbyterian missionaries and were sent to China. It was in China that Pearl Buck spent her childhood, learning to speak Chinese even before she learned English. She taught school in some of China's cities from 1921 to 1931. She spent her later years in the United States, but China held a special place in her memory, as is revealed in her many books and magazine articles. Miss Buck returned to China a number of times.

As a child Miss Buck developed a nice command of words, and she became widely known as a writer. In her novels she incorporated word pictures of China and its people. In 1932 she was awarded the Pulitzer Prize for her book *The Good Earth*. The prize attracted much attention, and editors began to take notice of her writings. *The Good Earth* became a best seller and was translated into about twenty languages.

Other awards soon came to her. In 1935 she was given the Howells Medal for "the most distinguished work of American fiction published within the preceding five years." Most notable, however, is that she was the first American woman to win the Nobel Prize, given to her in 1938 for her achievements in literature.

Miss Buck wrote more than fifty books and delivered countless addresses and lectures. In addition to writing and speaking, she worked with many children's groups and fostered brotherhood among the various races of people throughout the world. This work is intended to continue beyond the life of the promoter through the Pearl Buck Foundation with its seven million dollar endowment garnered from Miss Buck's writings.

Pearl Buck, who died on March 6, 1973, was an outstanding example of the West Virginian as an American and as a citizen of the world. She always spoke fondly of her West Virginia birthplace. She said, "Had I been given the choice of place for my birth, I would have chosen exactly where I was born, my grandfather's large white house with its pillared double portico, set in a landscape of rich green plains and with the Allegheny Mountains as a backdrop."

For the past several years, Pearl Buck's West Virginia home has been undergoing restoration by the Pearl S. Buck Foundation, Inc.

unit two | First Families of West Virginia

Chapter 5 EARLY MAN IN WESTERN VIRGINIA

Entry of Man into America

Many of the American history books begin with Christopher Columbus's discovery of the New World in 1492. A reader of those books might gain an impression that the American continent was then one vast wilderness perhaps teeming with animals but with few human inhabitants. That is an incorrect picture, for it is known that many persons were present in America before the European explorers arrived. It is believed that man occupied the area as long ago as the year 40,000 B.C. (Before Christ).

The early Americans who roamed the continent have been named Indians. They received their name from Christopher Columbus who believed that the land he had discovered was the Indies. North of Mexico, these native Americans possibly numbered from one million to eight million people at the time of Columbus's discovery. They may have spoken over two hundred different languages. Throughout both the North American and the South American continents, their numbers ranged anywhere from six million to sixty million persons, and they spoke over five hundred different languages.

Origins. America's first inhabitants entered North America from Asia by way of the Bering land bridge, the stretch of land which then connected present-day Siberia with Alaska. This bridge no longer exists. About the year 9,000 B.C., the melting glaciers raised

Small Excavated Area at Buffalo Village Men observe their diggings. Holes made by posts show location of houses. *(Photo courtesy of West Virginia University Library)*

the sea, which covered the bridge, and the water which poured over this stretch of land separated the continents. The early people were in search of mammoths and mastodons (hairy elephants), bison (buffaloes), horses, camels, and wild pigs. They may have left Asia in search of a more plentiful food supply, or they may have been escaping from their enemies. They knew nothing about farming, and they moved from place to place in search of animal food.

Routes. The arrivals from Asia migrated far into North America, Central America, and South America. They made homes and developed varying degrees of civilization. The exact route they took across North America is not known. After migrating down the eastern slopes of the Rocky Mountains, they may have first settled in the southwestern part of the present United States and later moved east. Or they may have gone directly to the east and then moved to the southwest. West Virginia archaeologists study the past by examining artifacts (objects made or modified by man into tools and ornaments) and other relics excavated from the earth. Hopefully certain areas in the state may provide an answer to the question of routes. The scientists, in their diggings into the soil, seek artifacts as evidence of the early life in the region.

Time Periods and Locations of Prehistoric Man in West Virginia

Millions of years passed before man developed written records to tell of his history. This long period is known as prehistory. Scientists, such as archaeologists and anthropologists (who study the origin and nature of man), have established time periods which tell how man lived prior to his invention of writing. These time periods show differences in the kinds of tools man used, the animals he hunted, the ways in which he procured a living, and the manner in which he honored his dead kinsmen. These periods of prehistory are called the Paleo-Indian Period, the Archaic Period, the Woodland Period (with its Early, Middle, and Late subperiods), and the Late Prehistoric Period.

Paleo-Indian Period. The first of the prehistoric periods of early man is the Paleo-Indian Period. In this period, at least fourteen thousand years ago, Indians inhabited the Kanawha and Ohio valleys. They possessed fluted stone weapon points, a type of spear point, which they used to kill the large animals. Bones of these animals have been found in both valleys.

These early big-game hunters established kill sites, butchering sites, and camp sites as they organized themselves to procure the huge beasts. One of these camp sites for early hunters is believed to have been on Blennerhassett Island in the Ohio River near Parkersburg, in West Virginia. On this island, several fluted stone weapon points have been discovered. Peck's Run in Upshur County is also a Paleo-Indian site.

Archaic Period. The second of the prehistoric periods of early man is the Archaic Period. This period began at approximately the year 8,000 B.C. and lasted until 1,000 B.C. It started at about the time when the mastodons and other large animals disappeared. In the hunt for smaller game, the people during this period produced a greater variety of weapon points than the previous dwellers produced, and also made axes and spears. Some of these people were obviously skilled craftsmen and artists. The period closed with the introduction of pottery.

In the Archaic Period, perhaps as early as eleven thousand years ago, Indians entered the West Virginia valleys to hunt small game, to fish, and to gather nuts, roots, and berries. It is believed that these people first entered the state from the south, coming down the New River. They are known to have lived on the east bank of the Ohio River in the Northern Panhandle and throughout the Kanawha and Ohio valleys. There may also have been a few settlements in the Eastern Panhandle.

St. Albans in Kanawha County, Mill Pond in Monroe County, the Globe Hill Shell Heap in Hancock County, the Rhor Rock Shelter in Monongalia County, and East Steubenville in Marshall County are examples of archaic sites which are well distributed throughout West Virginia.

Woodland Periods. The third period of time when prehistoric people were in West Virginia is known as the Woodland Period, which lasted from about 1,000 B.C. to 1 A.D. In the Early Woodland Period, the people occupied the Ohio and Kanawha valleys and either were descendants of the people of the previous age or had migrated from Middle America. In the Middle and Late Woodland periods they were found not only in the valleys but also in the central and northern portions of West Virginia and in the Eastern Panhandle.

Grave Creek Mound, Cresap Mound, Natrium Mound, and Welcome Mound in Marshall County, the Murad Mound and South Charleston Mound in Kanawha County, the Lakin Mound and May Moore Mound in Mason County, the Camden Park Mound in Wayne County, the Doddridge Mound in Doddridge County, and the Half Moon Site in Brooke County are sites which contain archaeological evidence of the Early Woodland era.

Watson Farm Site in Hancock County, the Buck Garden Shelter in Nicholas County, Mount Carbon in Fayette County, the Hyre Mound in Randolph County, the Romney Center Mound in Hampshire County, the Mason City Mound in Mason County, the Golf Mound in Harrison County, Bens Run in Tyler County, and Hughes Farm in Ohio County are major archaeological sites of the Middle Woodland Period in West Virginia.

The people in the Woodland Period were among the first to construct burial mounds or earthworks for the dead. Most of the dead were cremated, but some of the important leaders were buried in tombs over which their people heaped dirt. Some earth mounds in central West Virginia were constructed half of stone and half of earth.

A few mounds found in northern West Virginia were located over a number of individual stone-lined graves. Often many burials were made in one mound, although some mounds seem to have been reserved for a few important leaders or chieftains.

Postmolds Showing Location of Palisades at Ancient Buffalo Village A palisade is a fence of stakes set up for defense.

Most of the Woodland people occupied their time by hunting and by practicing a simple agriculture, growing sunflowers and other plants. As time went by, they cultivated new plants such as corn, beans, and squash.

Although some lived close together in compact towns, others lived in scattered villages. Some constructed circular houses. Some camped out in rock shelters. They manufactured flint knives and hoes, bracelets, pottery tempered by clay, and pottery tempered with crushed rock and limestone. They also possessed drills, shell and bone beads, and notched projectile points (the tip ends of either spears or arrows).

Late Prehistoric Period. The period just before recorded history is known as the Late Prehistoric Period. It dates from about 1000 A.D. to 1700 A.D. Before this period concluded, the people were constructing large compact villages surrounded by circular stockades. Their houses were often of rectangular shape. The walls were probably covered with skins or bark, and the roofs with thatch or grass. These people, in addition to hunting and fishing, cultivated corn, beans, and squash.

Rock carvings, or petroglyphs, a pictorial feature of the Late Prehistoric Period, have been found throughout West Virginia. On rock the Indians engraved outlines of human figures, birds, fish, and animals, and sometimes scratched-in the tracks of deer, bear, wolves, turkeys, and other wild creatures. The West Virginia Geological and Economic Survey has listed the Indian Cave Petroglyphs in Harrison County, the Salt Rock Petroglyphs in Cabell County, and the Timmons Farm Petroglyphs in Ohio County, and named Hamilton Farm Site in Monongalia County as a prehistoric archaeological site.

These prehistoric people paid no special attention to their dead, who were often heaped together and buried in a single spot within the villages. The people smoked tobacco in pipes made in a variety of shapes, sometimes carved to represent birds or human faces. They possessed combs made of bone and such ornaments as pendants fashioned from the teeth of bear and elk. They used turtle shells for containers and manufactured pottery vessels with large strap handles. Archaeologists have uncovered tools such as drills, scrapers, blades, hoes, fishhooks, and pins made of bone.

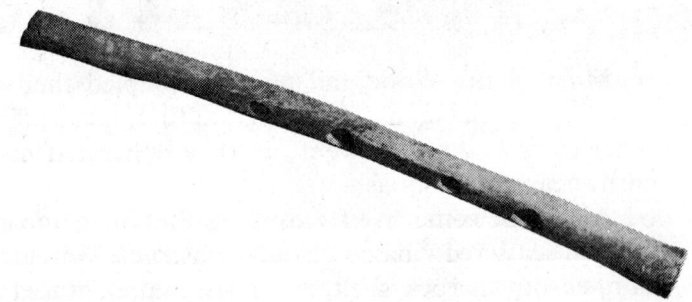

Flute Made from a Bird's Leg Bone The flute was unearthed at ancient Buffalo Village site.

Around 1700 the last of these men disappeared from West Virginia, an area which then became a hunting ground rather than an actual dwelling place for the various Indian tribes.

Appearance and Culture

Because these prehistoric people were not of one racial type, they varied greatly in appearance. In height they were tall, medium, or short. Their skin color ranged from very light to nearly black. Their builds were heavy or slender. Originally they all belonged to the

Mongoloid species of man, showing characteristics of the Chinese, the Japanese, and the Eskimo. Typical of this species, these prehistoric inhabitants of the continent had almond-shaped eyes, and the backs of their front cutting teeth were scooped out.

The people of this period are known by their cultures, and the names of the different groups are not the names of tribes. For example, in the Paleo-Indian Period they are sometimes referred to as Paleo-Indians and sometimes referred to as the Early Hunters. In the Archaic Period, they are known as the Archaic Foragers. In the earlier period of the Woodland era, they are known as the Adena people, and in the later period as the Hopewell people. In West Virginia the people in the Woodland Period represent a mixture of both Adena and Hopewell cultures. It is at the conclusion of the Late Prehistoric Period, when there was a noticeable absence of Indians in West Virginia, that one may begin to speak of certain tribes, such as the Iroquois or Cherokee.

Major Archaeological Discoveries

The Adena and the Hopewell peoples in the Woodland periods provide the major archaeological evidences of West Virginia's prehistoric habitations through the many mounds and earthworks found throughout the state. Some of these mounds have been investigated by trained archaeologists; many have been explored by individuals without special training in scientific excavation.

The Grave Creek Mound. The largest single earthwork in West Virginia and also the largest east of the Mississippi River is the Grave Creek Mound at Moundsville, now owned by the state of West Virginia. The state has established in the vicinity of the mound a park and a museum containing many articles from the mound. The mound originally measured 60 feet across its flat top, was 69 feet high, and at its base was 295 feet in diameter.

The mound was opened in 1838 by A. B. Tomlinson. When he and his neighbors started exploring the property, they dug a tunnel 10 feet high and 7 feet wide into a side of the earthwork. After penetrating into the mound 111 feet, they discovered in the center of the mound a burial chamber. The chamber contained two skeletons. Copper bracelets, shell beads, and mica surrounded one of the skeletons. Mica, a mineral sometimes called isinglass, probably came from North Carolina; so the Indians must have engaged in extensive trade.

Grave Creek Mound and Museum at Moundsville This is the largest conical mound built by prehistoric men on the North American continent. It is 69 feet high and about 900 feet around the base. *(West Virginia Department of Commerce Photo)*

The Tomlinson group then bored into the mound from the top. They discovered another room which contained one skeleton completely covered with about 150 pieces of mica. On one of the skeleton's arms were five copper bracelets. Around the skeleton lay 500 seashells.

The Great Kanawha City. In 1883 and 1884 Professor P. W. Norris of the Smithsonian Institution of Washington, D.C., directed the opening of a mound in South Charleston. This was the first investigation of West Virginia mounds by trained scientists. Professor Norris calculated that the original height of the South Charleston Mound had been about 35 feet and the diameter at the base about 175 feet.

Instead of tunneling in from the side, Norris and his associates began to excavate carefully from the top down. They first unearthed a stone vault, seven feet long and four feet deep, which contained a headless skeleton.

South Charleston Mound   This is the second-largest mound in West Virginia.

Six feet farther down they found a second skeleton. At nine feet below that discovery, they unearthed a third skeleton surrounded by the remains of a bark coffin.

At a depth of about twenty feet, they came across a burial vault constructed of walnut which held five skeletons. The skeleton in the middle of this vault, surrounded in a circle by the other four, measured in length an amazing seven feet six inches. His hands held three black flint spearheads and two hematite celts (chopping tools), and mica plates adorned his shoulders. On each wrist were six heavy bracelets, and on his breast was a copper gorget, an ornament which had probably hung from his neck. Surrounding the skeleton were other bracelets, spearheads, perforated shells, and shell beads.

The mound is now owned by the city of South Charleston and is surrounded by a small park.

Near South Charleston and Dunbar, Professor Norris also found about fifty more mounds ranging in height from 5 to 35 feet. Because of the great numbers, Professor Norris designated the area of many mounds as the Great Kanawha City.

chapter five / early man in western virginia

Other Mounds. Not all the West Virginia mounds have provided the exciting discoveries of the mounds near Charleston. Yet many have produced most interesting articles.

A whetstone in the shape of a turtle and an elk-antler headdress have been discovered in Cresap Mound in Marshall County. In another Marshall County mound, a tubular pipe containing the figure of a shoveler duck head has been uncovered. In Mount Carbon, in Fayette County, pottery of a distinctive orange-yellow color has been unearthed. This pottery collection, consisting of both large and small vessels, contains distinctively shaped earthenware. On the basis of the pottery, archaeologists have concluded that in earlier times a special cultural group maintained themselves in comparative isolation in this West Virginia area.

Walls, Fortifications, and Other Earthworks. At Bens Run, in Tyler County, two circular walls, about 120 feet apart, parallel each other and enclose an area of about four hundred acres, two small mounds, and a crosswalk south of the mounds. South of this area two additional curved walls about 300 feet apart parallel each other. In the neighborhood are more mounds and ancient burial grounds. At the end of two roadways are large flat rocks on the summit of a man-made mound of dirt and stone. The rocks may be the remains of a temple where prehistoric man worshiped the great sun god.

There are additional wall structures at Mount Carbon in Fayette County, at Pratt in Kanawha County, and at locations in Raleigh County. In the Kanawha Valley, about four miles east of Montgomery, Fayette County, ancient walls of loose stone appear around the top of a mountain which divides the waters of Loop Creek and Armstrong Creek. The walls are now in ruins and can hardly be recognized. In recent years strip mining has threatened almost to destroy them.

Six of these walls were probably built around the brow of the mountain about 300 feet from the top. They were perhaps eight or ten miles long, about six feet high, and built on bases six to eight feet wide. The builders and their purposes are still unknown. The walls may have been used as forts, or the area may have been designed as a sacred place for religious worship.

Buffalo Village. Buffalo Indian Village in Buffalo, Putnam County, West Virginia, is a unique archaeological site. Evidence indicates that the village was inhabited between the years 1600 and 1700, and contained a population between 500 and 1,000 Indians.

The village was surrounded by a large oval stockade, and was carefully plotted. A large ceremonial plaza, surrounded by ceremonial buildings, occupied the center. Three rows of houses circled these buildings, and beyond them, in the four corners of the fort, were the large lodge houses.

An archaeological and biological examination of bones found at the village has determined that the Buffalo Indian of West Virginia was an excellent food gatherer. The white-tailed deer was the primary object of his hunt, and bones of medium-sized furbearers, such as the beaver, opossum, gray wolf, black bear, raccoon, bobcat, mountain lion, and woodchuck, have been found. Evidence also indicates that squirrels, turkeys, fish, turtles, and all kinds of waterfowl in season were hunted.

Because of the numerous burials in a few grave sites at Buffalo, archaeologists have speculated that the Indians at Buffalo re-excavated the earlier graves, taking out earlier skeletons and putting in later ones.

The numerous mounds in West Virginia and the recent study of Indian villages give evidence that West Virginia was once occupied by Indians. Archaeological discoveries reveal that these early inhabitants made free use of the forest and river resources.

A Western-Virginia Frontiersman

Alexander Scott Withers, Chronicler of Border Warfare

One of the better-known frontier historians who wrote about the trans-Allegheny area was Alexander Scott Withers. His middle name, Scott, was chosen in esteem for Sir Walter Scott, a family relative. Withers was born October 12, 1792, in eastern Virginia. His parents, fairly well-to-do, had a plantation homestead called Green Meadows in Fauquier County. Alexander was the fourth of nine children.

He received an education excellent for the time and enjoyed reading whatever books were available. He studied at Washington College (later Washington and Lee University) at Lexington, Virginia, and then entered the law department at the College of William and Mary at Williamsburg, Virginia. By 1811, at the age of only eighteen, he was licensed to practice law.

When his father died in 1813, Alexander gave up his law practice in order to manage his mother's plantation. He was married in 1815, and, with a growing family, he and his wife moved west in about 1827.

Withers first settled near Bridgeport in Harrison County, but he later moved to Clarksburg. He was greatly interested in the history of the area and began to collect historical material for a book. Several other people also began to gather information on the Indian wars in western Virginia during the eighteenth century. A newspaper editor of the vicinity published a series of articles about the Indian wars, and others recorded notes and statements about the period.

In 1831 Withers published his book *Chronicles of Border Warfare, or a History of the Settlement by the Whites, of Northwestern Virginia: and of the Indian Wars and Massacres, in that Section of the State, with Reflections, Anecdotes, etc.*

The author presented an interesting history of early days in western Virginia based on accounts given him by those who had actually participated in the events and by their descendants. Withers' book was basically about settlers in what is now West Virginia and their relationships with the land and with the French and the Indians. His descriptions give a dramatic picture of what life was like on the frontier in the latter half of the eighteenth century.

Following publication of the *Chronicles* Withers moved to Missouri, but he soon returned to West Virginia and made his home near Weston. During the Civil War, Withers supported the cause of the Union. He was a boyhood friend of Joseph Andrew Jackson Lightburn, the "Fighting Parson," and knew Thomas J. "Stonewall" Jackson. Withers died on January 23, 1865 near Parkersburg.

Chapter 6 HISTORIC INDIANS IN WESTERN VIRGINIA

The Indian Language Families

Since so many thousands of Indian tribes constantly migrated from one location to another on the American continent, scientists have had great difficulty in determining the various locations of the "families." Difficulty has been encountered also in describing the various ways in which they were organized. The most satisfactory method has been to classify Indians on a language basis. When this technique is employed, Indians are described as belonging to so-called stocks or families, with each stock possessing members who speak languages having common characteristics. West Virginia has been inhabited at different times by four of these major Indian language groups.

Algonquin. One such language family was the Algonquin, whose members were to be found all over the United States. In the eastern section, the Algonquins located primarily in Virginia and New England. From this important Indian stock, the early white settlers gained knowledge which helped them survive in the New World.

The Algonquins were a religious people. They worshiped the "Great Spirit." Of the European nations which established colonies in America, the French were particularly favored by the Algonquins. Pocahontas, Pontiac, and Tecumseh were among important Algonquin leaders.

Logan, Chief of the Mingos *(From "Logan, The Mingo" by Franklin B. Sawvel)*

Iroquois. Another major language group was the Iroquois. The Iroquois, too, had great leaders. Cornplanter, Hiawatha, and Logan were among their heroes. They were particularly friendly toward the English in the early colonial period and became enemies of the French and the Algonquin Indians. The Iroquois had their headquarters in the present state of New York, but they soon extended their control throughout the Appalachian region, covering a large part of western Virginia. The Iroquois were particularly noted for their talent in political organization.

Muskogean. Closely related to the Iroquois in language was the Muskogean family. Located in the southern part of eastern

Red Jacket Chief Red Jacket (Sagoyewatha, "he who keeps them awake") was an orator, advocate of old Indian customs, and one of the prominent Seneca chiefs. He opposed "taking the hatchet" against the colonists but was overruled by the majority of his tribesmen. In both the Indian war of 1790–95 and that of 1812–15 he sided with the Americans. *(Permission of the State Historical Society of Wisconsin)*

America, they were also found to the west and in the Great Plains area of the country. Those who remained in the east lived primarily in the present state of Florida.

Siouan. For years the principal language stock in western Virginia was Siouan. The Siouans also occupied the central area of the United States. The Great Plain states of Arkansas, Missouri, and Iowa as well as the Dakotas held innumerable Siouans. In early history, Siouan territory in western Virginia was surrounded by the Algonquin nations to the east, by the powerful Iroquois to the north and west, and by the Muskogeans to the far south.

The various Indian stocks contested among themselves for control of the western Virginia forests and the plentiful game animals.

Nations. Indian stocks or family groups may be subdivided into nations. The Muskogees included the Creek, the Choctaw, and the Chickasaw nations. Sometimes aligned to the Muskogee was the Cherokee nation, but the Cherokees were actually a detachment of Iroquoian stock.

The Iroquois included the nations of the Miami, the Susquehanna, and the Tuscaroras. The Iroquois developed a political organization which incorporated the Mohawks, the Oneidas, the Cayugas, the Onondagas, and the Senecas. The organization was called the Five Nations but was renamed the Six Nations when the Tuscaroras joined the group.

The Algonquin included the Powhatan, the Illinois, and the Shawnee. Residing in Algonquin territory for a time were the Delawares who were later controlled by the Iroquois.

West Virginia in the 1700's

As has already been stated, the early hunters, the Archaic Foragers, and the Adena and Hopewell people, who were noted for their mounds and other earthen works, were Indians. Once the Mound Builders were believed to be of another race that achieved prominence before the Indians came. They were even considered to have been Egyptians and Phoenicians who had wandered far from home. Other guesses as to their origin were made. The Mound Builders were thought to have no connection with the eastern Indians of the United States, who were considered to be too primitive to have established such a civilization as that unearthed in West Virginia. But as we have seen, archaeological research established

A Variety of Indian Pipes Most pipes were artistically fashioned and highly polished. *(From the collection of Roland E. Barnett)*

that the Mound Builders were the true ancestors of Indians, such as the Algonquin or Iroquois, whom Europeans encountered in the age of discovery and exploration of America.

Hunting Grounds. Around 1700 most of the Indians had left the present area of West Virginia with the possible exception of the Eastern Panhandle. Formerly possessing a heavy Indian population, the present state of West Virginia later served primarily as a hunting ground for the Algonquin, Iroquois, Muskogean, and Siouan Indian language families.

Reasons for the Disappearance of Indians. With the appearance of European traders in the area, Indians were introduced not only to new trade goods but also to new diseases. Since they had no natural immunity to these new diseases, large Indian populations could have been wiped out as a result of epidemics of smallpox, measles, and other diseases. Intertribal warfare and emigration have also been suggested as reasons for the disappearance of the Indians. Certainly famine was not the cause, for game was plentiful.

An important historical explanation given for the emigration of Indians from West Virginia is the Iroquois conquest of the entire Ohio Valley. The conquest was undertaken to control the fur trade, first with the Dutch and later with the English. The League of Iroquois, an alliance of the Cayugas, Oneidas, Onondagas, and Mohawks, and later expanded to include the Tuscaroras, was a league of warlike nations. They had survived attempts of both the French and neighboring tribes to destroy their power. They used the area of western Virginia as a buffer between settlements of the French and the English.

One of the chief competitors of the Iroquois was the Cherokee nation which resided in western Carolina and eastern Tennessee. Here, too, the area of western Virginia was used as a buffer between two groups, helping to make West Virginia a no-man's-land. Occasionally these two competitors fought for control of western Virginia. At Packhorse Ford on the Potomac River and at Hanging Rocks in Hampshire County, the two nations engaged in fierce battles.

The English were relatively friendly with both the Iroquois and the Cherokee. In 1722 the Iroquois ceded to the English most of their lands in the Valley of Virginia. In 1744 the tribe gave up claims to land south of the Ohio River, an area that now includes most of West Virginia. In 1768 the Cherokees ceded to the English their claims to the region south and east of the Ohio River as far as the Kanawha River.

In the early 1700's West Virginia was relatively free of both Indians and the new white Americans.

The Border Indians. At the time of the first white advance into western Virginia, several Indian nations were located in the future state. To the north were the Susquehanna and the Delaware

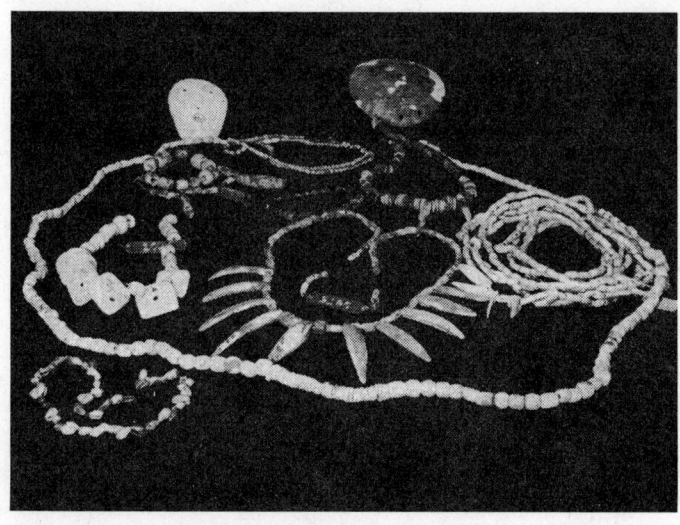

Indian Necklaces These necklaces were found at grave sites in Mason County. The ornaments are of seashells, bears' teeth, wolves' teeth, and animal bones. *(From the collection of Roland E. Barnett)*

Clay Pots Unearthed in Mason and Kanawha Counties Designs decorate the pots, and handles were applied to some. *(From the collection of Roland E. Barnett)*

nations, which were largely controlled by the Iroquois political organization. To the east were the Tutelo, Powhatan, Pamlic, and Tuscarora Indians, representatives of both Algonquin and Iroquois stock. To the south were the Shawnee, who frequently terrorized the Virginia frontier, the Yuchi, the Cherokee, and the Catawba, also of the Iroquois family. To the west were the Miami, the Illinois, and the Erie, nations of the Alonquin family.

These national groups often moved from place to place. Their locations were never permanent over any length of time during the period of European exploration and settlement.

Within western Virginia, small numbers of Indians wandered through or temporarily occupied certain sections. In the Eastern Panhandle, the Tuscarora settled briefly on the Potomac in their long trek from North Carolina to join the League of Iroquois in New York. Also present were the Susquehannocks and the Canoy. Shawnees settled near the Kanawha River, and Delawares on the Ohio River in the Northern Panhandle.

The Senecas frequently traveled through the state in their raids upon the Cherokee and the Catawba nations. In meeting the competition, Cherokees probably also intruded into southern West Virginia. Also present in the state were the Mingo, an aggregation of Shawnee, Delaware, and Seneca nations.

Indian Way of Life

The Indians of the eastern United States are probably less well known to science than any other Indians in the American hemisphere. Perhaps this is because their civilization was the one most thoroughly destroyed by the white man. However, a general idea of their way of life in the forested area can be reconstructed.

Appearance. In appearance, they often presented a broad, rather than heavy, face dominated by high cheekbones. Their skin color ranged from yellow-brown to red-brown, which caused some observers to characterize them as copper-skinned, and to very dark. Why Indians were often referred to in literature as Redskins is not certain, but it may have been because of the widespread practice of painting their skin red. Generally, they had straight black hair and brown eyes. Because of their active life in the air, their chests and backs were straight and well developed. Many had small hands and feet. However, one Indian skeleton found in the South Charleston mound measured seven feet six inches in length and nineteen inches between the shoulder sockets.

Although the men sometimes shaved their heads except for a scalp lock, women wore their hair long, fashioned in braids or tied in a "bun" at the back of the neck. Both sexes generally went bareheaded. In order to protect their legs against brambles and thorns, they wore leggings of deerskin. In order to move silently through the forests, they adopted soft leather moccasins.

Life-Style. With hunting grounds such as western Virginia, the Indians seldom moved because game had become scarce. The eastern Indian's life-style contrasts with the nomadic life of the Indians of the Great Plains whose migratory patterns were completely tied to the buffalo. In fact, the eastern Indian maintained fairly well-defined national boundaries. As illustrated by the Buffalo Village in West Virginia, they developed a home life, cultivated their crops in common, and protected their settlements with stockades. Their religion was a worship of nature, and some believed in magic powers which dwelt in, or protected, men, animals, or objects. Festivals were held in honor of harvests of corn or fruit. Ceremonies gave thanks for bountiful crops or for game. Life after death was often thought to be in a happy hunting ground.

The men and women performed different tasks in daily living. Men made the weapons and tools and hunted and fished. Women

Sketch of a Mohican Village Early Indian villages may have resembled the one in this sketch. There was a Mohican camp at Kanawha Falls when the first white explorers came into that section. *(From "Rhododendron Jungle, The Story of West Virginia Indians," published by The Conservation Commission of West Virginia. Photo courtesy of Kanawha County Public Library, Charleston)*

were occupied with household and agricultural duties, such as grinding the corn, dressing and curing the meat, and tanning the hides for moccasins.

Cleanliness was difficult in early times. Soap and cleaning fluids were unknown. Fleas were abundant. From evidence at Buffalo Village it is believed that stench from the animal and human decay and other garbage must have been powerful for such remains were not deeply covered.

The eastern Indians depended largely on hunting and fishing for their livelihood and used agriculture as a secondary source of food supply. Warfare was a condition of human existence. Prisoners taken in war were either adopted into the nation or tortured and killed. Sometimes heads became the trophies of war. Scalps were important prizes, particularly in the Appalachian region. To provide the victor with courage for future conflicts, he was sometimes required to eat the heart of a particularly valiant fighter he had captured.

Contributions to the White Man. In agriculture, the eastern Indians showed the white man methods of growing corn, white potatoes, sweet potatoes, tobacco, tomatoes, and peanuts. They also furnished the pioneer with many kinds of beans and squash and with varieties of cotton plants. They taught him the art of canoe building and gave him ideas for constructing homes and fortifying villages.

Attitudes of the White Man and the Indian. The white man's attitude toward the Indian was strongly affected by differences which the two races held regarding the land. To the Indian, land was possessed by all members of his tribe; to the white man, land was owned by the individual. When the European settlers in America traded guns, liquor, beads, or other trinkets for land, they believed that they had purchased the land and that it was now their private property. The Indian failed to comprehend this, although he enjoyed the gifts he had received, and he continued to trade his land or his furs for the white men's gifts because the gifts made his life easier.

With guns supplied by the white man, the Indian rapidly killed much of the wildlife he had before been careful to conserve. Because of whiskey and rum, he often signed treaties which he did not understand. When he had fulfilled the white settler's demands either in land transactions or in fur trade, both he and the white settler seemed to agree that it was best that the Indians now move to the west, away from the lands they had sold.

Some Indians did not agree, however, and rebelled against moving farther west. The white man interpreted the Indian's acts of violence as a breaking of their agreement. The Indians, in return, saw the white man as a cunning and deceitful trader.

Indian Trails in West Virginia

Western Virginia was crisscrossed by Indian trails which had probably been originally made by the buffalo. Generally these trails followed the watersheds or highlands rather than the streams. By taking to the higher land, the pathfinder avoided swamps and dense underbrush and probably also escaped ambush from the mountain gaps. Generally the western Virginia trails moved from east to west. They crossed each other many times or joined in such a way as to create a network of paths throughout the entire state. East-west paths were often considered paths of peace, because they seemed to have served for purposes of trade. North-south paths were viewed as paths of war for they were most frequently used by raiding parties.

Monument to the Mingo Indians This monument was erected by the Wood family at Mingo, Randolph County, in 1920. *(Photo by A. B. Brooks)*

Seneca, or Shawnee, Trail. The Seneca, or Shawnee, Trail, one of the most important passageways through the state, illustrates the network of paths. From the South Branch of the Potomac, the Seneca Trail followed the North Fork of the South Branch to Seneca Creek and to Seneca Rock in Pendleton County. At this point, a branch starting at the Rock crossed east over the mountains into Virginia, then turned back over the mountains into western Virginia to the headwaters of the Greenbrier River.

But the main part of the trail continued from Seneca Rock by way of the Cheat Mountain and Shavers Fork of the Cheat River to what is now Elkins in Randolph County. At Elkins, the trail turned both north and south. In its passage north, it crossed to Belington in Barbour County, to Parsons in Tucker County, across the state line to Oakland, Maryland, where it followed Nemacolin's Path to the forks of the Ohio, and then followed the Allegheny River to the land of the Senecas. [Nemacolin's Path, named for a Delaware chief, ran across most of southern Pennsylvania to the Monongahela River.]

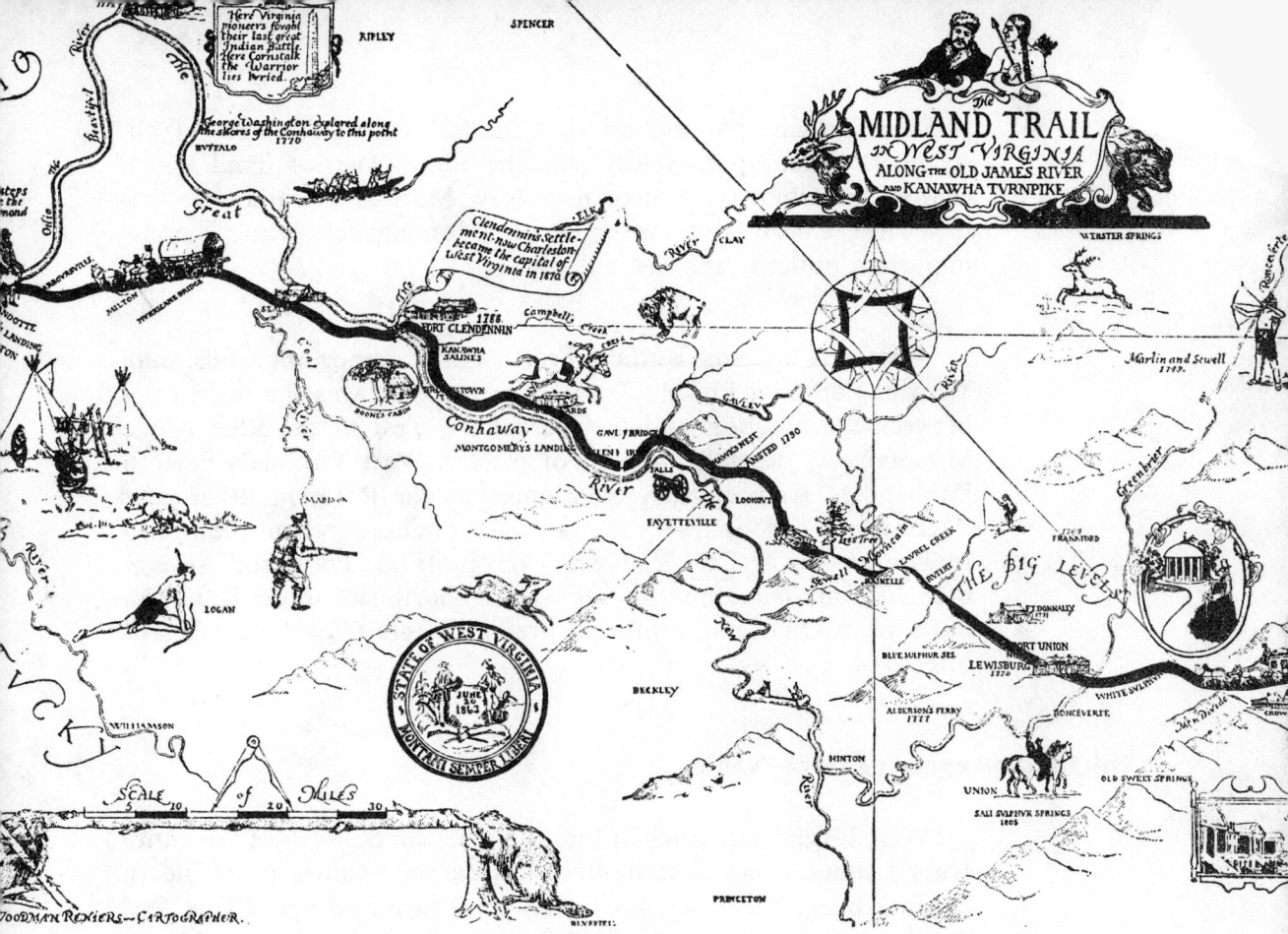

(Drawing by Ashton Woodman Reniers for "The Midland Trail," copyright 1926, 1954. Reproduced by permission)

At Elkins, the Seneca, or Shawnee, Trail dropped south to Mingo Flats in Randolph County, where it again divided into new western and southern branches. As it turned west, it followed along the Little Kanawha Trail. As it turned south, it proceeded from Mingo Flats to Marlinton in Pocahontas County, to Lewisburg in Greenbrier County, and then to Bluefield in Mercer County, following somewhat the outline of present Route 219.

Trails of the Monongahela Valley. Trails centering in the Monongahela Valley also illustrate the network of paths. One of the valley's western outlets was the Scioto-Monongahela Trail, connecting Indian villages on the Scioto River in central Ohio with both the Little Kanawha and the Monongahela valleys. A branch of the Scioto-Monongahela Trail was the Little Kanawha Trail, which followed the general course of the Little Kanawha River

chapter six / historic indians in western virginia

and also provided a junction with the Seneca, or Shawnee, Trail. Another western passageway was the Little Warrior Trail which crossed the Ohio River at or near New Martinsville and then followed the Cheat River to enter the Monongahela Valley's most important outlet to the east.

Warrior Path and Buffalo Trail. Other important trails were Warrior Path and Buffalo Trail. Warrior Path was the main road between the Iroquois and the Cherokees, west of the Blue Ridge Mountains in the valley region of present West Virginia's Eastern Panhandle. As previously mentioned, on the Potomac at or near Packhorse Ford an early battle was fought between these two Indian groups. The Kanawha, or Buffalo, Trail had several branches, but its main route followed the north side of the Kanawha River from Ohio and paralleled present Route 60 into the Greenbrier area.

The Indian Legacy of Place-Names

West Virginia abounds in Indian place-names, as does the entire United States, in which more than half the state names are of Indian origin. West Virginia towns such as Logan, Mingo Flats, and Buckhannon bear an obvious Indian heritage. Logan and Mingo counties received Indian names as did Pocahontas, Monongalia, Ohio, and Kanawha counties. Rivers such as Potomac, Cacapon, and Opequon and the Tuscarora Mountains point to early Indian occupation in the Eastern Panhandle.

But particularly rivers and mountains which border and cut into the state provide Indian names with interesting translations. Allegheny, "place of the foot," and Appalachia, "the endless mountain range," are conspicuous examples.

Rivers important to West Virginia sometimes have truly poetic names. Shenandoah, "daughter of the stars"; Ohio, "the white foaming river" or "the river of whitecaps"; Monongahela, "the river of caving or falling banks"; Kanawha, "the place of the white stone" or, in Shawnee terms, "the river of evil spirits"; Pocatalico, "the river of plenty of fat doe" are particularly descriptive. The Big Sandy was once the "Chattarawha," the Guyandotte was once the "Seconee" or "the narrow-bottomed river," and the Elk was the "Tiskelwah" or "the river of the fat Elk."

Greenbrier Pioneer and His "Memoirs"

John Stuart, Frontiersman of Many Abilities

John Stuart was born in 1749 near Staunton, Virginia. His parents were Scotch immigrants. Visiting the Greenbrier Valley of present West Virginia in 1767, Stuart resolved to settle in its broad rich lands after the Indian treaties of Fort Stanwix and Hard Labour were concluded. When Indian unrest along the Ohio led to Dunmore's War in 1774, Stuart joined the southern force under Colonel Andrew Lewis as a captain of militia and fought at Point Pleasant.

County Clerk's Office *(Drawing by Ashton Woodman Reniers from "Greenbrier Pioneers and Their Homes," by Ruth Woods Dayton. Reproduced by permission)*

Frontier defenses became important as the Revolutionary War progressed, and Stuart contributed his part in building Fort Spring near his home. When Indians, with the aid of the British, attacked Fort Donnally in May 1778, Stuart and Captain Matthew Arbuckle led a relief of 68 men from the Lewisburg area and prevented a major disaster for the residents of the Greenbrier region.

When he was not actively defending the frontier, Stuart was strongly backing the creation of a new county to establish better government for the growing district. He was successful in his efforts to form Greenbrier County in 1778. The first meeting of the county court was at Stuart's home a few miles south of Lewisburg. Stuart served the government as county clerk from 1780 until 1807. In 1799 in Record Book Number One he wrote several pages recording occurrences under the title "Memorandum."

When the town of Lewisburg was incorporated in 1782, John Stuart was named one of its eight trustees.

He also exercised influence in the county in matters of religion and education. He served as a delegate to the Virginia Convention which considered ratification of the new United States Constitution.

Through the years, Stuart accumulated much land, and his business interests multiplied. By the time of his death, he had an estate valued at more than $250,000, a very considerable sum at the time. Stuart was elected to the prestigious American Philosophical Society in 1797. He died on his estate near Lewisburg on August 23, 1823.

One of Stuart's contributions which has lived in the history of the trans-Allegheny settlement is his *Memoirs of Indian Wars and*

Other Occurrences. The *Memoirs*, written in 1819, was an expansion of Stuart's "Memorandum" and was published in 1833. It contains an account of the early settlement of the Greenbrier Valley and the activities of the Indians, English, French, and Americans along the frontier. Of particular interest is the section dealing with Dunmore's War, in which Stuart took part.

Stuart Manor John Stuart built his permanent home, "Stuart Manor," in 1789. The original native-limestone structure was long and low. The taller addition, also of stone, was erected a number of years later. Its interior beautifully finished and exquisitely furnished, "Stuart Manor" is now the oldest home in Greenbrier County and is certainly the most historic. *(Drawing by Ashton W. Reniers from "Greenbrier Pioneers and Their Homes." Reproduced by permission)*

Chapter 7 EXPLORATIONS OF THE WESTERN WORLD AND WESTERN VIRGINIA

Exploration Centuries, 1492–1700

When, in the fifteenth century, Christopher Columbus sailed west across the Atlantic Ocean and discovered America instead of a shorter route to Asia, he was acting as a representative of Spain.

Other explorers also continued to believe that by proceeding westward they could discover a way to the riches of the Far East. Even when, in the seventeenth and eighteenth centuries, certain English explorers reached inland to present West Virginia, they imagined that a route to Asia possibly lay just beyond the Appalachian Mountain barriers.

Spain and Portugal. In the sixteenth century, additional explorers in the name of Portugal and Spain concentrated upon sea routes to the west. Amerigo Vespucci, for whom America is named, Pedro Cabral, and Ferdinand Magellan, who circled the globe, passed by areas of Central America and South America. They were the forerunners of still-later explorers in the pay of Spain and Portugal who established claims to land in what is now the southern United States, Central America, and South America. Prominent

Robert Cavelier, Sieur de La Salle La Salle discovered and explored the Ohio River in 1669.

among these men was Hernando de Soto who visited the region north of the Gulf of Mexico and chanced upon the Mississippi River.

France. France also began exploration and colonization in competition for new lands and new routes to the Far East. By the sixteenth and seventeenth centuries, through the activities of Verrazzano along the Atlantic Coast, Samuel de Champlain in Quebec, Marquette, Joliet, and Robert Cavelier, Sieur de La Salle in the Mississippi area, France established an overseas empire for herself in Canada and the Mississippi Valley.

England. In the sixteenth century, to advance the claims of the English, other explorers, as Sir Humphrey Gilbert and Sir Walter Raleigh, commanded expeditions to the Atlantic Coast of America.

By 1606 King James of England issued charters to two companies in the hope of populating the eastern coast of America with his own subjects. One charter instituted the Plymouth Company, whose organizers were responsible for the development of the Massachusetts Colony. The other charter, of particular concern in West Virginia history, was issued to the London Company, whose developers were responsible for the Virginia Colony.

Results of Exploration and Colonization. In their struggle for colonial empires, all of these countries and others such as Holland appropriated land in the western hemisphere, made new routes to interior lands in search of riches, and established different policies and relationships with the Indians. In the beginning, Spain was the most successful in finding riches. France was particularly skillful in profiting from the fur trade and fishing. England directed her energies in the direction of fur trade, farming, and fishing.

In their relationships with the Indians, the Spanish tended to enslave the American natives for work in the mines. The French made allies of the Indians (except the Iroquois and the Cherokees) because of the Indians' assistance in the fur trade. The English, who became the agriculturalists, tended to push the Indians farther westward or to exterminate them in local battles and skirmishes as the settlers prepared their lands for farming.

Exploration of Western Virginia, 1607–1674

In the name of England, the London Company made its first settlement at Jamestown, Virginia, in 1607. We know that in the year 1607 there was no West Virginia. Land west of the mountains was, first, a part of the Virginia Colony and, then, a part of the state of Virginia, for a period of more than 250 years after the founding of the first English settlement at Jamestown. Until 1863 we cannot speak accurately of "West Virginia." We shall continue to speak of "western Virginia."

In 1607 Christopher Newport explored the James River thirty miles westward from the present site of Richmond, Virginia. Believing he could gain information about a short route to the Far East and about the inhabitants there, Newport became one of the first of the English explorers to venture into the interior of America.

During his years of service to the London Company, Newport made five voyages from England to Virginia. Serving as an intermediary between the colonists and the company as well as between the colonists and the Indians, he helped to keep the struggling first settlers alive. He negotiated with the Indians for a supply of corn, and he helped enlist skilled craftsmen from England to seek their fame and fortune in the New World.

Abraham Wood. Newport's belief that gold lay in the western lands of Virginia was, of course, proven false. But he and other promoters like him developed enthusiasm for what was believed to be another quick and easy source of wealth, the fur trade. In order to secure and defend their trading in the west, the Virginians were forced to establish a string of forts along the rivers and paths into the interior. Early forts were constructed on the present sites of Petersburg, Richmond, and Fredericksburg along the Appomattox,

Indian Family (From the Kanawha County Public Library Picture Collection, Charleston)

James, and Rappahannock rivers. The forts afforded protection against Indian attack upon the coastal settlements and also developed into important fur-trading centers. Commanders of these forts became promoters in far-ranging fur-trading opportunities.

One of the most important of the early commanders was Abraham Wood. Possibly an indentured servant when he first arrived in America, he became in time an important Virginia legislator and military officer. For maintaining a fort and garrison at Fort Henry (at Petersburg, Virginia), he was given the fort with its buildings and six hundred acres of land. From his headquarters he traded with the Indians and dispatched agents on expeditions into the western country.

One of these expeditions occurred in 1650 when he and Edward Bland, a merchant, led a small expedition from Fort Henry into the Roanoke Valley, the land of the Occaneechee Indians. Bland later published a narrative of this adventure, which in the years ahead kept alive Wood's enthusiasm and stimulated other people's interest in the western fur trade.

John Lederer. In addition to Abraham Wood, several governors of Virginia, including William Berkeley, promoted expeditions into the interior of the Virginia Colony. Governor Berkeley, because of his connection with an important trading concern known as the Hudson's Bay Company, was particularly active. Among those he encouraged to find a passage through the mountains was John

Lederer, a physician, traveler, and professional explorer who came to Virginia from Germany in 1668.

According to Lederer's published account, he made three journeys into western Virginia. His first venture was from the head of the York River due west until he reached the top of the Blue Ridge Mountains. He chose, however, not to descend their slopes.

Lederer's second expedition was from the falls of the James River through a part of North Carolina. The third was supposedly from the falls of the Rappahannock River west to the Blue Ridge Mountains. Although his accounts are not considered completely trustworthy, he is still considered to be the first known white man to have looked upon the Shenandoah Valley.

Lederer's companions deserted him on his journeys and spread reports that he had spent public tax moneys improperly in behalf of his wanderings. Lederer fled from Virginia into Maryland to save his life. To vindicate himself, he published an account of his travels, which is considered one of the first scientific reports upon the geology, plant life, animals, and native tribes of the interior.

Besides claiming he was the first of the explorers to reach the top of the Appalachian Mountains, he also asserted that those who thought they could cross the American continent from the Atlantic to the Indian Ocean in eight or ten days were in error.

Batts and Fallam. Abraham Wood also turned to Thomas Batts and Robert Fallam, professional explorers, to continue the work initiated by himself, Bland, and Lederer. Batts and Fallam were commissioned in 1671 to find "the ebbing and flowing of the Waters on the other side of the Mountains" which would lead to "the discovery of the South Sea." The men outfitted their party of scouts. They probably got as far west as the present West Virginia boundary line opposite Giles County, Virginia.

Fallam kept a journal of the expedition, recording on September 8, 1671 that the explorers came upon a tree inscribed with the initials M. A. N. I. These letters, marked with coal, seemed to indicate that unknown persons had preceded Fallam's group in their journey west. On September 16, 1671 Fallam indicated that his party had been helped rather than hindered by the natives in the interior. He recorded that the Indians had furnished the white explorers some "exceeding good grapes, two turkies" and a deer. Perhaps the explorers had been rewarded in their relationships through Perecute, a friendly Appomattox Indian who accompanied the exploring party.

View from Spruce Knob in Present Monongahela National Forest The mountains presented a formidable barrier as explorers sought passages to western Virginia. *(Gerald S. Ratliff Photo, West Virginia Department of Commerce)*

The journey of Batts and Fallam is considered important for three reasons. First, it provides the first day-by-day record of a passage across the Appalachian Mountains. Second, the expedition is considered the first whose members found a stream flowing west. And, third, it was an expedition upon which England later based her claim to the entire Ohio Valley region.

The explorers themselves must have been aware of the significance of their findings because in a ceremony across the mountains they marked four trees for identification of their claim, one for the king, one for the governor, one for Wood, and one in honor of themselves.

Needham and Arthur. In 1673 Abraham Wood commissioned another expedition, selecting James Needham, an Englishman, as its commander. Needham's company included eight Indians and a companion by the name of Gabriel Arthur, an uneducated but intelligent lad who was probably an indentured servant of Wood. One objective of Needham and Wood was to establish direct trade relations between Virginia and the Cherokee Indians. Another objective was to discover a passage by water to the southwest.

Their first departure was foiled by Occaneechees who were encamped on the Roanoke River and whose hostility forced the explorers back to Fort Henry. The Occaneechees enjoyed a monopoly of the trade with Virginia, and they opposed the white man's contact with the Cherokees. But the expedition's second effort proved successful. Needham and Arthur crossed the Blue Ridge Mountains and the headwaters of the New River and came into the valley of the Kanawha and Cumberland rivers.

Needham made a treaty with the Cherokees and returned to Fort Henry to lay plans for another trip in September 1673, but Arthur remained to learn the Indian language. Needham, on his way to return to the Cherokee village from Fort Henry, was murdered by his guide, an Occaneechee Indian.

Wood, quite naturally, was angered by the Occaneechee treachery. He vowed revenge upon all Indians, and it is believed that this forced the Cherokees into holding Arthur as hostage. Remaining with the Cherokees throughout the year, Arthur accompanied some of their war parties into west Florida, South Carolina, and Ohio.

In one of their excursions, Cherokee warriors took Arthur through western Virginia, probably following the Coal River to the Kanawha River for battle with the Shawnees. As a result, Arthur is credited with being the first white person known to have visited the Kanawha Valley.

Here the Cherokees found a village of Moneton Indians, a village very likely at present Saint Albans or Buffalo, West Virginia. Some say Arthur was captured by the Shawnees. In time, he returned to the Cherokee towns and was eventually returned to Fort Henry. This action may have cemented trade relationships between the Cherokees and Virginia and may have broken the usefulness of the Occaneechees as middlemen in the Indian trade. It also signified that the Spanish colonists in America no longer held a monopoly on Cherokee trade.

Western Exploration, 1674–1710

From 1674 to 1710 the English undertook little exploration west of the Allegheny Mountains. Partial explanations of the slow progress in these years were a series of colonial wars between the French and the English and the death of Abraham Wood. Also British officials in London who had been enthusiastic promoters of the fur trade retired, and interest in Virginia diminished. Nathaniel Bacon, who had led frontiersmen into a successful war against the Indians, died, and the Virginia governor had twenty-three of Bacon's followers, suspected of revolting against eastern authority, hanged.

In the period of inactivity by the English on the frontier, France strengthened its hold on inland America from the Great Lakes to the mouth of the Mississippi River.

Alexander Spotswood. In 1710 Alexander Spotswood became lieutenant governor of Virginia. Spotswood recognized that the French were surpassing the English in the occupation of the trans-Allegheny area. The governor, therefore, recommended that Virginians occupy the mountain passes and contest with the French for settlements on the Great Lakes. Also aware that the Spanish were making inroads into America in the south, Spotswood wanted to take possession of Florida.

To dramatize his interest in the west, he arranged in 1716 for an exploring party of colonial gentlemen, rangers, Indians, and servants to cross the Blue Ridge Mountains into the Valley of Virginia. He bestowed the Order of the Golden Horseshoe upon the members of his expedition.

We shall read more about Governor Spotswood and his expedition to the west.

Alexander Spotswood, Governor of Virginia
Governor Spotswood led an exploring party westward in 1716. The Knights of the Golden Horseshoe were the men who accompanied him. *(From an old painting in the Virginia State Library)*

Howard and Salling (Salley). In 1742 the governor of Virginia authorized John Howard and John Peter Salling (or Salley), a German emigrant from Pennsylvania, to travel westward to the Mississippi River in accordance with a petition they had made to the Virginia legislature. In a boat covered with buffalo hide, they ascended the South Branch of the Potomac; they crossed a divide to New River and another divide to Coal River. They followed the Coal River to the Kanawha River to the Ohio River.

From the Ohio they descended the Mississippi to New Orleans at the mouth of the Mississippi River. French authorities in New Orleans arrested them and carried Howard to France as a prisoner. But Salling escaped and after two years made his way back to Virginia. From him, Virginians gained their first information about the lower courses of the Ohio and the Mississippi rivers and about the Frenchmen who lived there.

Thomas Walker. Many of the early explorers had a variety of occupations, but few were so versatile as Thomas Walker. Walker, who kept a general store and carried on importing and exporting activities, was also a physician and soldier. Becoming chief agent of the Loyal Land Company in 1749, he inspected a part of the 800,000-acre grant on the southern frontiers of Virginia, a grant made to the company by the Council of Virginia. In a circular direction, he traveled by way of southwestern Virginia through the Cumberland Gap, proceeding north to the Kentucky River and then eastward to the Tug and New rivers. From there he ascended the

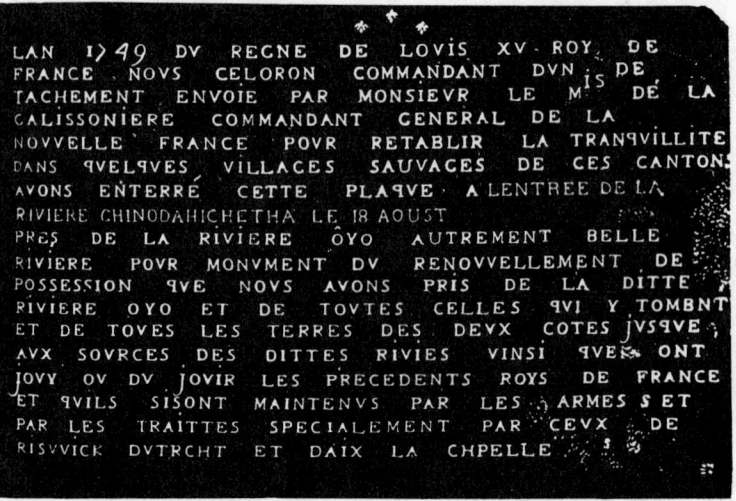

A Plate Buried by Celeron de Bienville French claim to western lands was strengthened when Celeron de Bienville led a company of Frenchmen and Indians down the Ohio River and, at the mouths of streams, buried lead plates inscribed in French. The plate shown here was buried at the mouth of the Kanawha in 1749 and was found by a small boy in 1846.

Greenbrier River and the lands of the Greenbrier Valley in order to render his report to the land company.

Celeron de Bienville. In the year in which Walker was exploring the present state of Kentucky and the Greenbrier area of western Virginia, the governor of Canada ordered Captain Celeron de Bienville, in the name of Louis XV, king of France, to take possession of all lands drained by the Ohio River. Leading a detachment of several hundred men, including Iroquois and Abenaki Indians, de Bienville buried leaden plates at strategic points on alternate banks of the Ohio to assert French control over the valley. One of these plates was buried at the site of present Point Pleasant at the mouth of the Kanawha River, and one was buried at the mouth of Wheeling Creek, both in what is now the state of West Virginia.

Christopher Gist. The following year Christopher Gist was appointed by the Ohio Land Company to explore Ohio River lands in behalf of the English. Gist, who was the son of the surveyor of the western shore of Maryland and one of the commissioners who plotted the town of Baltimore, came from a line of experienced surveyors. Starting from Cresap's post near Cumberland, Maryland, on October 31, 1750, Gist reached Pittsburgh, crossed the Ohio, and examined Ohio country to the mouth of the Scioto River. He then crossed into Kentucky, making his way back to Yadkin in northern North Carolina.

On his next journey he explored the country south of the Ohio from the Monongahela to the Great Kanawha. His reports showed he was well informed as to the topography of the country and the natives. Actually, in his exploration of lands in southern Ohio and northeastern Kentucky, he preceded the better-known explorer Daniel Boone by eighteen years.

By the middle of the eighteenth century, both English and French explorers were contesting for the control of the trans-Allegheny region. Although by far the larger number of explorers represented the English colony of Virginia, both the English and the French were determined to have the lands drained by the Ohio for their own. With the Indians siding first with one and then the other of the two competitors, western Virginia was early becoming a battleground in the European contest for America.

A Virginia Governor-Explorer

Alexander Spotswood, Chief Executive of the Colony

Until the early part of the eighteenth century, settlement in Virginia, as well as in other English colonies in America, was confined to the area east of the Appalachian Mountains. As population expanded, the land across the mountains was viewed as a possible area of settlement. In addition, promoters of the trans-Allegheny area believed the interior region would provide knowledge of the sources of the eastern rivers, open up trade with the Indians, and serve as a buffer region against the French and Spanish who might have designs upon the Piedmont and Tidewater areas.

Celebrating the Success of Governor Spotswood's Expedition

With these several possibilities in mind, Lieutenant Governor Alexander Spotswood of Virginia desired to explore the mountain areas.

Alexander Spotswood came of an illustrious Scottish family. Born at Tangier in Morocco in 1676, he eventually served as an officer in the British army. In 1710 he was sent to Virginia as lieutenant governor of that colony, a post which had been vacant for about four years. Spotswood had the blood of an adventurer in his veins and early interested himself in the lands to the west. He settled at a place called Germanna, not too distant from the frontier of the time.

Spotswood gave assistance to North Carolina and South Carolina in their difficulties with the Tuscarora and the Yemasee Indians. He established compact communities of friendly Indians in the western lands. Thus he sought to offer peace and security to those who ventured west. For such reasons, he negotiated with the Iroquois in New York a treaty whereby they were to remain north of the Potomac River and west of the Blue Ridge.

Spotswood requested the Virginia council to allow a party to proceed westward on a trip of discovery. The council approved.

Spotswood led a group from Williamsburg, the Virginia capital, to his estate and then to the foothills of the Blue Ridge. The party ascended the mountain, discovered one source of the James River, and drank to the health of England's King George I and the royal family. Descending the opposite side, they came upon a river which the governor named the Euphrates. This river was the Shenandoah.

In memory of the expedition, Spotswood at a later time gave each of his followers a small golden horseshoe. His companions styled themselves "Knights of the Golden Horseshoe." The state of West Virginia, in recent years, has recognized the students who have become most proficient in the knowledge of the history of the state, as worthy modern-day recipients of a golden horseshoe, a memorial to Spotswood and his party.

On his return east to the capital, Spotswood had visions of English settlement to the Great Lakes. Although he was unable to fulfill his plan of controlling the area beyond the mountains, he was responsible for creating an interest which impelled later pioneers to go west. For arousing this interest Alexander Spotswood is important in West Virginia history. The governor left office in 1722. He died in 1740.

Chapter 8   PERMANENT RESIDENCY

After the explorers had made their discoveries and the fur traders had proven that profits were to be made on the frontiers, government agencies in England and Virginia faced the problem of attracting permanent settlers into the western areas. By insuring protection and by providing financial rewards to both the speculator and the settler, could Virginia convince people to move beyond the mountains? Could Virginia convince those in the coastal area or those just arriving on American shores that western lands could produce a better life for the pioneers? It was to England's and Virginia's advantage to do so. Otherwise, the French or the Spanish would defeat the English in the effort to stretch the lines of empire from the Atlantic Coast to at least the Ohio and Mississippi rivers.

Some officials in Virginia, closer to the problem, recognized the situation more clearly than did those in England. None was more farsighted than William Byrd.

Colonel William Byrd, the Elder, of Virginia occupied a position much like that of Abraham Wood who had promoted so many explorations into western Virginia. Byrd commanded a fort near the present site of Petersburg on the Appomattox River. Byrd, like Wood, was a capable frontiersman. He deplored the colonial activity of the French in inland America. So also did his son, William Byrd, the Younger, who in 1729 told of his displeasure as to the delay in the English colonists' westward movements:

Our country has now been inhabited more than one hundred and thirty years and still we hardly know anything of the Appalachian Mountains, that are nowhere above two hundred and fifty miles from the seas. Whereas the French, who are later comers, have ranged from Quebec southward as far as the Mouth of the Mississippi, in the Bay of Mexico, and to the west almost as far as California, which is either way above two thousand miles.

To Byrd, permanent settlement under the auspices of the English colonies was essential. The mountain regions must be occupied or the English would sooner or later lose control of America to the European rivals.

Conditions Favorable to Western Settlement

Peace existed from the early 1700's to the outbreak of the French and Indian War in 1754. The peace provided a favorable half-century for encouraging movement west by those now residing in the east and those coming to America from the Old World. The number of people in the coastal areas had increased. This increase in population in the east discouraged later immigrants from settling in that area and quickened their interest in the unpopulated back country.

View of the South Branch Valley
This valley lies in the Eastern Panhandle. From these lands frontiersmen pushed across the Allegheny Mountains.

Newcomers also discovered that the earlier arrivals enjoyed a monopoly on the better farmlands in the east. Also in some cases, unscientific farming on the part of the original settlers had resulted in a loss in soil fertility. Expected land grants and fertile soils in the west were enticements for going farther inland.

Incentives to Settlement. To interest people in moving west, the government of Virginia offered certain incentives. When new counties were formed in the western regions, they were often exempted from paying taxes for ten years. In addition new counties often received special consideration of problems unique to frontier life. When Frederick and Augusta counties were created in western Virginia, a law required that no award be made to any person for killing wolves. But when the western settlers protested, the Virginia legislature authorized the payment of six shillings as the reward for killing an old wolf and two and a half shillings for killing a young one.

In 1772 the government of Virginia permitted families to live on state land without paying rent provided they occupied the land for ten years. A new land policy after 1730 provided that any speculator would receive 1,000 acres of land for each family he brought to settle in the wilderness. If he could convince 100 families to settle in western Virginia, he might receive for his efforts 100,000 acres of land.

Creation of New Counties. Virginia recognized that local government must be brought closer to the settlers in the western lands. Slowly but surely new political units were created for those settlers. In 1734 Orange County was formed, including all the lands of Virginia west of the Blue Ridge Mountains. Since Virginia's westernmost boundary was defined to reach to the Mississippi River and the Great Lakes, Orange County included the entire present state of West Virginia and other states to the west and northwest.

Because of the spread of population, by 1738 Orange County between the Blue Ridge and the Allegheny Mountains was divided into the County and District of Frederick and the County and District of Augusta. When the actual operation of county government began, between the years 1743 and 1745, Winchester was named the county seat of Frederick, and Staunton the county seat of Augusta.

chapter eight / permanent residency

Sandstone Falls of New River near the Site of the Present City of Hinton Travelers seeking a home place in western Virginia often found nature hostile and violent. *(Arnout Hyde, Jr., Photo, West Virginia Department of Natural Resources)*

After the establishment of Frederick and Augusta, the remaining part of Orange County west of the Allegheny Mountains was known as the "District of West Augusta." By 1754 Hampshire County was formed from the western parts of Frederick and Augusta. The area of Hampshire County was in present West Virginia. Thus, Hampshire County, in the Eastern Panhandle, is the oldest county in West Virginia, more than a hundred years older than the state itself.

Promotional Activities

In some instances, the task of promoting settlement was entrusted to single individuals who might be expected to locate families upon the land. In other cases, land companies were granted large tracts in the west and were expected to locate families in the area. Boundary lines of properties, however, were not definite, and so one person's claim to land might overlap another's claim. Uncertainty over title to western Virginia land often caused individuals to go farther west beyond the settlements of western Virginia, for in new lands the pioneers believed their claims to property would be secure.

The Fairfax Lands. One of the largest land grants in the Virginia Colony became, in time, the possession of one English nobleman, Lord Thomas Fairfax. In 1649 King Charles II of England granted approximately 5,000,000 acres of land in Virginia to six noblemen who had supported the king's father, Charles I, during a revolutionary period in English history when the monarchy was forced into exile.

On the map, said one of the owners, the grant looked like a neck protruding out from the colony of Virginia. In a way it did, because it included most of the land of northern Virginia and extended into the Eastern Panhandle of present West Virginia. For this reason it became known as the Northern Neck Proprietary.

By 1719, long after the English monarchy had reestablished itself, control of the property belonged only to Lord Fairfax. In 1735 Fairfax visited America to see and to measure his land. A survey that Fairfax had ordered indicated that his property began at the South Branch of the Rappahannock and extended in a straight line to the place believed to be the origin of the Potomac River. The Fairfax Stone was placed at this point. As we noted in an earlier chapter, the Fairfax Stone was utilized in determining boundary lines of Maryland, Pennsylvania, and Virginia.

As a young man, George Washington served as a surveyor on Fairfax property. Washington's journals indicate that he was surveying along the South Branch of the Potomac in 1748 when he was sixteen years of age.

In 1747 Fairfax returned to America and remained as a landlord on his vast estate until his death in 1781.

After the American Revolution, estates of English noblemen were confiscated. In 1785 the Virginia legislature abolished the proprietary system in Virginia. This means that quitrents, fixed rents charged individuals who lived on these estates, could not be collected. In 1786 the Virginia courts recognized that other persons had more valid claims to ownership of certain Fairfax lands than the Fairfax heirs had.

A Pioneer Home This was the home of the parents of Lewis Wetzel, Indian fighter, about whom we shall read later. The cabin was built on Wheeling Creek in Marshall County in 1764. *(From "Lewis Wetzel, Indian Fighter," by C. B. Allman)*

Ohio Land Company. In 1747 the Ohio Land Company, an association of Virginia gentlemen including several members of the Washington family, was organized for the purpose of promoting settlement. In 1749 the English government granted the company 200,000 acres in the vicinity of the forks of the Ohio, where the Monongahela and Allegheny rivers meet to form the Ohio River. In accepting this grant, the company agreed to build a fort and settle 100 families in the area within seven years. If they settled 300 more families within the next seven years, the company would be granted an additional 300,000 acres. Christopher Gist served as surveyor for this company.

Greenbrier Company. In 1745 John Robinson, speaker of the Virginia House of Burgesses, received a grant of 100,000 acres on the Greenbrier River in present West Virginia. In 1751 the Greenbrier Company was formed to develop these lands, and the company was expected to settle one family for each 1,000 acres it received. John Lewis and his son Andrew were agents for this company.

The Loyal Company. About 1751 the Loyal Company was organized and given a grant of 800,000 acres on the southern frontiers of Virginia. As noted in an earlier chapter, Thomas Walker served as agent for the Loyal Company.

Location of Early Settlements

East of the Alleghenies. Although most of present West Virginia lay beyond the difficult Allegheny Mountains, its Eastern Panhandle lay to the east. A part of the Panhandle was in the Valley of Virginia, within easy range of such centers as Philadelphia and Baltimore.

Because of easier access, the section east of the Alleghenies was the first to gain permanent settlers. The first wave of migrants came from New York, Pennsylvania, New Jersey, and Maryland (colonies to the north) rather than from Virginia (the mother colony to the east and south). It was not until about the time of the American Revolution that migration from the south and east countered migration from the north. The Eastern Panhandle was settled by Germans, Scotch-Irish, and English.

West of the Eastern Panhandle and the Great Valley, French control of some of the mountain passes and the mountains themselves slowed settlement. Nevertheless, permanent settlers were on both sides of the mountains in western Virginia before the French and Indian War began. For all practical purposes the settlements were limited to the Potomac and Greenbrier rivers and their tributaries.

In addition to being an easier area to enter, the eastern region had received a certain amount of advertising prior to actual settlement. Louis Michel in 1706-1707 led a party from Annapolis to a point near the forks of the Potomac where he skillfully sketched a map of the area. In 1711 Baron de Graffenreid, who had encouraged Michel in his efforts to call attention to the area, planned to settle several Swiss families at the forks of the Potomac. But land title disputes prevented settlement at this time.

By 1730 John Van Meter and Isaac Van Meter of New York and west Jersey were given grants in the region of the lower Shenandoah River. In 1731 Joist Hite and Robert McKay purchased some of the Van Meter land and added still more. By 1731 or 1732 Morgan Morgan, acknowledged as the first permanent resident of present West Virginia, established his home in the area. In the early eighteenth century, settlers, as Reese Reese, Evans Evans, William Snodgrass, Nicholas Henshaw, Edward Mercer, Robert Harper, Irah Friend, along with Van Meters, Hites, Morgans, and many other first families of West Virginia, settled the Valley areas.

West of the Alleghenies. West of the Alleghenies Andrew Lewis, who was surveying lands for the Greenbrier Company, came across

Monument in Beverly, Randolph County, Commemorating the Files and Tygart Indian Massacres, Westfall's Fort, and the Battle of Rich Mountain *(Photo courtesy of Donald L. Rice, President, Randolph County Historical Society)*

a settlement made in 1749. On the Greenbrier River he found Jacob Marlin, for whom the town of Marlinton was later named, and Stephen Sewell, for whom Sewell Mountain was named. Although all alone in this area, they maintained separate dwellings. Marlin lived in a cabin which had been built by both men. Sewell lived in the hollowed trunk of a large sycamore tree. They had quarreled over matters of religion.

Marlin and Sewell were known as "long hunters," a frontier term which meant that they had undertaken an expedition whose time lengthened from days into months into years.

By 1753 Andrew Culberston had located in Summers County, and other families were locating along streams flowing into the Greenbrier River.

From the South Branch and the Potomac valleys other frontiersmen pushed over the Allegheny Mountains. Robert Files and David Tygart settled near the present town of Beverly in the same year in which Culbertson settled in Summers County. Like Marlin and Sewell, their names were bequeathed to local geographic sites, Files Creek and Tygart Valley River. In 1754 the three Eckarly brothers settled at Dunkard Bottom in what is now Preston County. But defense in the far western settlements of Virginia was inadequate, and Files and two of the Eckarly brothers were killed by Indians.

Nationalities

Early settlers in present West Virginia were mainly German and Scotch-Irish. There were also English, Welsh, and Dutch settlers. Many came directly south from the colony of Pennsylvania, a few in later years crossed over from Virginia, and some came directly from Europe. They were thrifty and industrious farmers, and, although some opposed any kind of warfare, others proved themselves to be excellent fighters. All were highly individualistic and became effective promoters of frontier democracy.

Germans. A good many of the Germans coming to America in the early period had left their home country which had been ruined by the Thirty Years' War (1618 to 1648). Many of the early German migrants were from the Rhine Valley. They had been displaced by Louis XIV of France, a monarch who was interested in making the Rhine River a boundary line of his own country. Not only had population there been uprooted, but agriculture, industry, and trade had been ruined. As a result, taxes were burdensome.

The leaders of the many small states in Germany also practiced severe religious persecution. Many of the people there were opposed to warfare. Upon coming to Pennsylvania, some became Quakers, and some would not fight in the French and Indian War or, later, in the American Revolutionary War because of their peaceful inclinations.

Scotch-Irish. The Scotch-Irish were Scots who had settled in Ireland. Primarily they had gone to the northern counties, called Ulster. As Protestants in a Catholic country, they were considered outsiders. Mostly Presbyterians, they were considered outsiders even by Englishmen who were Episcopalians. So the Scotch-Irish, too, came to the New World in search of religious freedom. They also sought political freedom, for in Ireland they had been denied important civil and military offices. They had suffered economically by being denied the right to export dairy products and, later, wool.

Others. The Welsh, the English, and the Dutch also made up a percentage of the early population. In the earlier period, the Welsh came in significant numbers. Many of them were Quakers who had originally located near Philadelphia. Generally, they spoke their

Christ Episcopal Church, Formerly Morgan's Chapel, at Bunker Hill, Berkeley County Morgan's Chapel was the first regularly organized church in what is now West Virginia. Morgan Morgan, who was Welsh, helped to establish the Chapel before 1740. Services are still held in the church.

native language, but when their sons and grandsons were absorbed by the English, they surrendered their native tongue. Like the Germans, many were skilled farmers. Most of them were not so wealthy as the Germans, and many gave up farming. A few became doctors. In the 1730's a large-scale migration from Pennsylvania into the frontier areas of Virginia occurred.

A Representative Type. Joist Hite is a notable example of an early immigrant interested in the Virginia frontier. He was an Alsatian who sailed from Holland in 1710, bringing with him sixteen Dutch and German families. First he settled in New York. Between 1716 and 1730 he relocated several times in Pennsylvania. By 1731 he contracted for 40,000 acres of land in western Virginia which was designated the Van Meter tract. In association with Robert McKay he made an additional contract with Virginia for the settlement of 100,000 acres, known as the Hite-McKay tract. Sixteen families were brought to the Opequon in 1732 by Hite.

By 1740 there were 6 Van Meter-Hite tracts in present Berkeley County and 28 Van Meter-Hite tracts in present Jefferson County. Five more tracts in Berkeley and 8 located in Jefferson had been surveyed, but grants had not then been made. Within a few more years, Hite colonized both the Van Meter tract and the Hite-McKay lands with additional family units.

Hite ran into difficulty with Lord Fairfax over boundary lines. Fairfax declared that the Virginia Colony had no right to grant Hite lands within the Northern Neck Proprietary. After a long series of lawsuits and after both Fairfax and Hite were dead, the courts decided in favor of Hite.

Settler in the Wilderness

Morgan Morgan,
First Resident in Present West Virginia

Monument to Morgan Morgan Near Christ Episcopal Church

Although the mountains on West Virginia's eastern boundary presented a natural barrier to settlement in the early period of American history, by the year 1720 routes through valleys and mountain passes allowed the opening of the area that today is referred to as the Eastern Panhandle. From Pennsylvania, New Jersey, and Delaware, many moved their families and belongings into the easternmost part of present West Virginia. Among these was Morgan Morgan, possibly the first white man to settle permanently in what is now the thirty-fifth state.

Morgan Morgan was born in Wales on November 1, 1688 and came to the colony of Delaware in 1713 or 1714. There he married and became a notable citizen of New Castle County, serving as county coroner. About 1730 he moved his family across Maryland, and possibly into Pennsylvania, and down the Virginia valleys, to settle along a creek near what is now Bunker Hill in Berkeley County, West Virginia. He had received a grant of 1,000 acres from two land promoters, Alexander Ross and Morgan Bryan.

By 1734 he was well established. In that year Orange County was created by the Virginia government, and it embraced the area of Morgan's settlement. He was appointed a justice of the peace and captain of militia in the new county. With an increase in the number of inhabitants and the need for proper government, Morgan Morgan led the fight for a more compact county to serve the north central section of Virginia. This was accomplished in 1738, when Frederick County was established, comprising what is now the Eastern Panhandle and part of Virginia around Winchester. In 1742 Morgan was named a justice of the peace and a militia officer of Frederick County.

Morgan served the community in a variety of ways in addition to his roles as administrator and military leader. He helped in the movement to build the first roads in the area. He established the first church in the community. The church continues today as Christ Episcopal Church at Bunker Hill. Morgan operated an "ordinary" (a place of lodging where meals were served) to accommodate travelers moving across the mountains and through the valleys.

Morgan Morgan died on November 17, 1766 at his homestead. In 1924 near the church he founded, the state of West Virginia erected a monument to honor him for his many contributions. In succeeding years in the state of West Virginia, the descendants of Morgan Morgan have played leading roles.

unit three | Border Warfare and the Revolution

Chapter 9 THE FRENCH AND THE INDIANS

The American Conflict as a World Event

The beginnings of settlement west of the mountains by the English colonists did not escape the notice of either the Indians or the French. Since the early days of exploration and colonization, competition among the three had been intense. The struggle progressed from formal protests to the erection of forts and from the establishment of settlers to actual warfare.

By the middle of the eighteenth century, the rivalry of the French, the English, and the Indians for the control of the Mississippi and Ohio Valley regions reached a climax. The Indians, on the whole, preferred to be independent and peaceful. But the French and English who were occupying the Indians' lands were more powerful than the Indians. The Indians recognized that they were in less danger from the French, who were primarily concerned with fur trading and not with actual residence. The Indians had greater fear of the English who were actually settling and farming the land.

Yet the Indians occasionally switched sides in the conflict; sometimes they supported one superior force and then the other. To the time of the American Revolution, the Indians thus changed allies; so they were unable to protect their interests in final peace settlements. Their indecision in alliances made easier their removal from the east to the west.

French Claims. France was in a good position to assert its claims in the contest for America. France based its right to control the Ohio Valley upon discovery by La Salle, who, France contended, had found the Ohio River before the English discovered it. France also cited its occupation of middle America by its control of the Illinois territory and its fort-like settlements on the Mississippi River.

Through trade with the Indians and by the evidence of Celeron de Bienville's leaden plates and marked trees along the Ohio River, France insisted that the American interior belonged to France. French claims upon Canada as well as on the Mississippi Valley region were also strengthened by early discovery, exploration, and some colonization.

English Claims. England, as did France, emphasized its early discovery, exploration, and colonizing activities. In extending control from the Atlantic Coast to the American west, England used the colony of Virginia as its advance agent. England called attention to the original Virginia charter which defined the colony's western boundary lines as extending at least to the Mississippi and Ohio rivers, if not to the Pacific Ocean. England made propaganda of the Batts and Fallam expeditions into western Virginia. The activities of the Ohio Land Company, the Greenbrier Company, and the Loyal Land Company in promoting settlement and English participation in the fur trade also enhanced English credentials of ownership.

Indian Claims. France and England were in positions to counter each other's legal claims to territory. But neither had better ownership rights than the Indians, who were the original occupants. To minimize Indian claims, England resorted to land deals with several of the Indian nations. By treaty agreements, England concluded that it had purchased title to land occupied by the Indians, who had accepted payment. The English looked upon the contracts concerned with western Virginia as binding on all parties. In 1722 the Iroquois ceded to the English all lands in the Valley of Virginia, which included the Eastern Panhandle counties. In 1744 the Iroquois surrendered their claims to land south of the Ohio River, which included most of the present state of West Virginia. In 1752 Christopher Gist, principal agent of the Ohio Company, concluded the Treaty of Logstown with the Delaware and Shawnee Indians. The Logstown agreement recognized Virginia's claims to land west

Thomas Hughes Hughes was a pioneer of Lewis and Harrison counties. He was killed by Indians on Hackers Creek, Lewis County. Notice his long gun, knee-length hunting shirt, high leggings, and moccasins. *(From a sketch by J. H. Diss Debar based on a description given by old settlers)*

of the Allegheny Mountains to the Ohio River. Later the Iroquois endorsed this same treaty.

Yet treaties as answers to questions of land ownership satisfied few of the Indians. Doubt whether all Indians had agreed to such treaties, or whether just a few chiefs of Indian tribes had concurred, caused continued uncertainty over land titles. Another legal perplexity was whether the Indians truly recognized the value of the lands they were surrendering. For example, the Ohio Valley territory was given up in the 1744 treaty at a purchase price estimated at only $2,000.

Another concern over the validity of treaties was that many Indian nations claimed title to land in western Virginia. If the Iroquois, Delawares, or Shawnees surrendered their rights to the territory, other neighboring tribes did not necessarily recognize such acts as binding upon themselves.

Strengths and Weaknesses of the Contending Parties. Despite the variety of legal claims of all parties to the western lands, the strength and weaknesses of the various parties prolonged the struggle as well as determined the final outcome. In the New World the population of the English colonies was fifteen times greater than the population of the French provinces. But the people in the French provinces were distributed over much greater distances, whereas the English were concentrated upon a smaller land area.

chapter nine / the french and the indians

France maintained centralized control over its provinces and had its own military officers stationed in America. The English possessions were more independent, and it was very difficult for the colonies to act as a unified body in a military contest.

The British colonies provided enough food supplies for their own people. The French did not produce enough food either for their settlers or for their soldiers, leaving them dependent on importation or upon their Indian allies.

The French had more Indian allies than the English. However, English allies at this time were the Iroquois, and the Iroquois had fashioned one of the strongest confederacies ever formed by any Indian nation.

In many ways France and England were equal competitors in the New World.

A New Governor and a New Program. In 1751 Robert Dinwiddie was appointed lieutenant governor of Virginia. He was not a stranger to the colonials, for at an earlier time he had served as surveyor-general for the southern part of America with jurisdiction over the Carolinas, Virginia, Maryland, Pennsylvania, and certain southern islands.

Dinwiddie was deeply interested in land speculation in all parts of America but particularly in the Ohio region. He had brought with him in 1751 gifts for the Indians so that they might respond favorably to English intentions. The governor also gave his strong approval and support to the land schemes of the Ohio Company of which he became a member. He protested the fact that the French not only were claiming the Ohio Valley but also were erecting forts along the rivers.

Dinwiddie tried to interest other colonies than Virginia in protesting French expansion, but although other colonies were willing to criticize the French, they were unwilling to furnish necessary troops for battle against France.

A Diplomatic Assignment for George Washington. In 1753 Governor Dinwiddie sent George Washington, 21 years old and an officer in the Virginia militia, on a long journey into the American interior. Washington's mission was to gain the consent of the French to withdraw from the Ohio Valley. Leaving the Virginia capital, Williamsburg, Washington proceeded to Alexandria and Winchester and then to Wills Creek, the site of present Cumberland, Maryland.

Colonel George Washington as Pioneers in Western Virginia First Knew Him *(From a painting by C. W. Peale, made in 1772 and now owned by Washington and Lee University)*

Crossing into Pennsylvania, he used the Nemacolin Path and other Indian trails to reach the forks of the Ohio. He moved on to Logstown, the site of the earlier Indian treaty, and finally reached Fort LeBoeuf. Fort LeBoeuf, a French stronghold, was located on a tributary of the Allegheny River and was very close to Lake Erie.

Accompanied by Christopher Gist and a French translator, Jacob Van Braam, Washington made contacts with Indian tribes along the way. In trying to persuade the Indians to the English cause, Washington enlisted Half-King, an Indian chieftain, as a guide. Half-King was invaluable to Washington. But at LeBoeuf, the French tempted the Indian chieftain with ample supplies of food and strong drink, and Half-King almost deserted the American cause during the negotiations.

When the French firmly refused the English request to remove themselves from the Ohio Valley, Washington, Gist, and Half-King with a bad hangover left LeBoeuf. Along the return journey to Virginia, Washington continued his diplomatic work among the Indians, stopping at the present site of Connellsville, Pennsylvania, to pay his respects to Queen Aliquippa.

In his diary of the journey, he recorded his observation that a fort at the forks of the Ohio would gain command of the area for its owner. He also made note of exciting experiences on the way home. Traveling by rafts through icy waters in temperatures below zero, Washington and Gist were tossed overboard. They spent the night with their clothes frozen to their bodies. Washington was also fired

chapter nine / the french and the indians

upon by Indians, but against the advice of his companions, he refused to return fire upon men who could be possible future allies.

Military Defeat in 1754. In January 1754 Dinwiddie sent Captain William Trent to build an English fort at the forks of the Ohio. The French, however, seized the outpost at the junction of the three rivers and named it Fort Duquesne. Under the leadership of Pierre de Contrecoeur, the French drove Trent and his men from the site.

Dinwiddie had also ordered a small band of soldiers under Washington to serve as Trent's back-up forces. Many of the men were from the Berkeley and Hampshire areas of western Virginia. Proceeding toward the Ohio River along the Nemacolin Path, the Washington command met Trent's original party in retreat. Nevertheless, Washington pressed forward toward the French fort.

Beyond the main ridge of the Allegheny Mountains in the general area of Great Meadows, Half-King, again serving as an Indian guide, informed Washington that the French were nearby and preparing to ambush the Virginians. Washington scouted the area and discovered a force of thirty-one men. On May 28, 1754 the

Fort Seybert, in Pendleton County (according to Wills De Hass, 1851)

colonials attacked, killed ten of the enemy, including Jumonville, their leader, and captured the remaining twenty-one who were sent to Williamsburg as prisoners.

The French looked upon the skirmish as provocative and unnecessary. They termed the death of Jumonville an "assassination." In retaliation a force of Frenchmen and Indians from Fort Duquesne, under the command of Coulon de Villiers, sought the immediate defeat of the Virginia troops commanded by Washington. Again informed of an approaching enemy, Washington quickly constructed Fort Necessity at Great Meadows in order to withstand the attack.

The forces faced each other at the site of the improvised fort on July 3, 1754. The American command of about 300 soldiers was low on ammunition, perhaps about one-third of the men were sick, and the command was outnumbered by the French command of 1,600 men. The battle was brief and decisive. On July 4, 1754, twenty-two years to the day before American independence was declared, Washington surrendered.

Washington agreed to three terms: He would leave the Ohio Valley at once; he would not enter the territory for one year for the purpose of building forts; and he would return all prisoners captured in the battle which had resulted in the death of Jumonville. However, the French also agreed to withdraw to their fort at the forks of the Ohio and not to build other forts in the upper Ohio Valley.

General Braddock in Command. Washington's failure in his negotiations with the French at LeBoeuf and his military defeat at Fort Necessity had involved the Virginians against the French stationed in America. In December 1754 the English government dispatched troops from England to Virginia under the command of General Edward Braddock, a trained English soldier. By spring Braddock was preparing at Alexandria a combined army of British regulars and colonial soldiers to march into the interior. Washington served as his aide.

Advancing along the Potomac River and the Nemacolin Path, Braddock and his heavily equipped forces had to widen the road on their march. The French, who had been preparing to withdraw, decided to make a last stand a few miles east at Fort Duquesne. On July 9, 1755 the Battle of the Monongahela River took place.

Braddock had been taught to march his men into battle with drums sounding the advance. His soldiers, in perfect order, were lined up row after row. At first they were able to drive back the

chapter nine / the french and the indians

Fort Ashby (Restored) Inscription on the road marker at the old fort reads: Fort Ashby, only standing unit in chain of Indian forts that Col. George Washington built along Virginia frontier, 1755. Sharp fighting here, 1756. In 1794, troops under Gen. Daniel Morgan camped here on way to suppress Whiskey Rebellion. *(William C. Blizzard Photo)*

enemy. The French and Indians, silently regrouped, opened fire from behind trees and rocks on both sides of the narrow road.

The British regulars were so confused that they even shot their own companions, but the Virginia militia rushed to cover behind the trees and rocks in order to fight in Indian fashion.

The French commander was Pierre de Contrecoeur. The French, who had expected defeat, to their surprise killed and wounded hundreds of the British troops, including General Braddock, himself. Washington assumed command and was able to lead the troops in retreat to a supply camp. Braddock hovered near death for only four days. Washington buried him in the middle of the roadway and had wagons driven over the grave so that the enemy could not find the body.

Washington, in further retreat, brought the army back to Virginia. Considerably frightened by the conspicuous failure of the British regulars, the colony of Virginia was nevertheless proud of the military abilities of its own men. Among the colonials who participated were Daniel Morgan, William Darke, Horatio Gates, Adam Stephen, Charles Lee, and William Henshaw. These were men from the Eastern Panhandle counties of future West Virginia. The Battle of the Monongahela River served as a training ground for later battles.

Andrew Lewis and an Offensive Position. In 1756 Governor Dinwiddie dispatched Major Andrew Lewis to move against the Shawnees on the Ohio River. Leaving Fort Frederick in Augusta County in February 1756 Lewis's expedition of about 340 men passed down the New River, through Draper's Meadows, in the general direction of the Big Sandy River, into a part of present West Virginia.

The expedition was a failure. It had been poorly planned, was badly provisioned and poorly led. Heavy rains made the journey difficult, and in the flooded streams Lewis lost most of his supplies and stores of food. William Preston, who kept a journal of this campaign, recorded the hunger of the men, their intention to desert and mutiny, and efforts of the officers to urge them forward in search of food if not in search of the enemy. Otherwise, they would either perish or be reduced to having to eat their own horses. However, the discontent of the men prevailed, and Lewis was forced to turn back without reaching the Shawnee towns.

Defending the Frontier. By 1755 Virginia frontiersmen shifted from an offensive to a defensive position. Washington assumed the task of guarding the frontier. He believed that the responsibility of protecting western settlements would be met best by local men, the sons of farmers, young, active, and entirely acquainted with the woods, men who would be defending their own homes. Also, these frontiersmen knew how to fight Indian style. Experienced with rifles, they were also skilled in using hunting knives and tomahawks. In their frontiersmen's garb of hunting shirts, breeches, leggings, and moccasins, they were not so conspicuous as were the British soldiers, uniformed in red.

Taking advantage of victory in the Battle of the Monongahela, the Indians made attacks upon the western settlements from many directions. In 1756 the Indians sent forays into the present counties of Hardy and Berkeley. Sometimes the settlers were able to resist successfully. Fort Evans (about two miles south of Martinsburg), which had been constructed in 1755, was saved by Polly Evans who enlisted women and children to take up arms while the men of the community were away fighting. In 1756 the Battle of The Trough, near the present site of Moorefield in Hardy County, occurred. A military company under command of Captain John Mercer was almost annihilated. In 1758 Killbuck, a Delaware warrior, attacked Fort Seybert and Fort Upper Tract in Pendleton County.

Washington joined with Dinwiddie in posting advertisements in which they tried to counteract the rumors of Indian destruction which might cause the pioneers to abandon their homes and return to the east. Nevertheless, many settlers were killed, and many were taken prisoner during the final conflict between the English and French for the control of the Ohio Valley.

Colonel William Preston kept a record of the captives and the casualties of the French and Indian War in Virginia. In 1754 he listed seven deaths of persons who lived on the Monongahela River; in 1755 he counted eleven deaths on the New River and nineteen deaths on the Greenbrier River; in 1756 four deaths on the New River; and in 1757 fifty-three deaths on the South Branch. All of these casualties were in addition to prisoners taken or persons wounded.

English Victories in 1758 and 1759. In the remaining five years of the French and Indian War, the English defeated the French at many points. These victories coincided with William Pitt's assuming the direction of the war effort. On November 25, 1758 General John Forbes, with a force of 7,000 men, most of whom were Virginians and Pennsylvanians, captured Fort Duquesne. Renaming the stronghold Fort Pitt, the Forbes command broke the French control of the Ohio Valley area of which present West Virginia was a part. In the same year the English were able to cut off the Great Lakes forces from those of the St. Lawrence River.

Peace Terms. However, final peace terms were not completed until 1763. They were truly decisive. England became dominant in America by gaining all territory east of the Mississippi River

Battle of Point Pleasant, 1774 (From "History of the Early Settlement and Indian Wars of Western Virginia," 1851, by Wills De Hass)

except the area around New Orleans. France was left with two tiny islands off Newfoundland and her sugar islands in the West Indies, only tokens of her former colonial empire in America. Spain surrendered Florida to England but gained France's Louisiana territory west of the Mississippi River.

The people in western Virginia had suffered much but also had contributed much to the English victory. They now looked forward to sharing in the spoils of war. To eastern Virginians the western lands beckoned more strongly.

Soldier and Statesman

Andrew Lewis, Defender of the Frontier, Continental Army General

Andrew Lewis was born of Scotch-Irish and Welsh parents in 1720 in the British Isles. With his family he moved to America in 1732, first settling near Staunton, Virginia. As an early frontiersman, he helped organize Augusta County in western Virginia. He and his wife moved west with the advancing frontier, and Andrew served in county offices and in the Virginia state legislature. He played an important role in the advancement of local government in areas far removed from county seats and from the colonial capital.

Lewis himself was a nationalist as were many original frontiersmen. He served as a member of the Revolutionary colonial conventions of March and December 1775. As an officer of the Augusta County militia, Lewis accompanied Washington on his unsuccessful expedition against the French at Fort Necessity. In other engagements of the French and Indian War, Lewis was captured and later released. He also took part in drawing up the Indian Treaty of Fort Stanwix in 1768.

When border problems between whites and Indians reached a climax in 1774, Governor Dunmore of Virginia organized two forces to attack the Indians along the Ohio River. Lewis was placed in command of the southern forces. He and his men marched from Camp Union (now Lewisburg, West Virginia) to Point Pleasant. In the Battle of Point Pleasant in Dunmore's War (about which we shall read later), the then Colonel Lewis's army of more than 800 was attacked by an Indian force led by Cornstalk. Lewis's forces proved victorious and helped set the stage for peace in the back country for the first three years of the Revolutionary War.

Andrew Lewis was made a brigadier general in the Continental Army on March 1, 1776 by appointment of the new Congress. He took command of American forces at Williamsburg, Virginia, the colonial capital, during the early part of the Revolutionary War and helped drive the British Governor Dunmore, his former commander, out of the colony.

Lewis resigned his military commission in April 1777 because of the demands of his private interests. One of these interests was the famous Burning Spring, near Malden in Kanawha County. The spring and approximately 250 acres surrounding it were owned jointly by Andrew Lewis and George Washington. Until his death on September 26, 1781 Lewis continued to serve Virginia in Governor Thomas Jefferson's executive council.

We shall read more about the Burning Spring. On the spring's bubbling water a flame could be lighted, and here in West Virginia, natural gas was discovered.

Chapter 10 FRIENDS INTO ENEMIES, 1763–1774

Attitudes toward Western Lands in 1763

The Treaty of Paris which ended the French and Indian War created an enlarged empire for England. In America, these new colonial lands were largely acquired at the expense of the French and the Spanish. The English opinion was that the new American property had to be surveyed and cleared of land title disputes with the Indians before being opened to settlement. In opposition to the English view, the colonists believed the new lands should be made available to them in return for their contribution to English victory in the wars from 1689 to 1763. The Virginians claimed that the fort at the forks of the Ohio and most of the Ohio Valley were within the boundary lines of the colony of Virginia. They believed that this land should be awarded to Virginia.

In competition with Pennsylvania for the control of the gateway to the West, Virginia was almost prepared to fight her sister colonies at the conclusion of the French and Indian War.

To the Indians, the English victory meant the departure of their ally, France, and the loss of the great rivers and valleys of mid-America. The Indians' hope of stopping the westward advance of the American frontiersmen appeared desperate, and the time to act seemed now or never.

A Pioneer Log Cabin (Restored) The restored cabin is one of the historical features at Jackson's Mill, Lewis County. *(Richard Mathews Photo, West Virginia Department of Natural Resources)*

Pontiac's War of 1763 and Bushy Run

In defense of their lands across the Allegheny Mountains, the Indians, particularly the Delawares and the Shawnees, decided to fight. In contrast to their earlier unorganized methods of resistance, they formed a league of all available Indian tribes to drive the British and American forces back to the Atlantic. Pontiac, the great Ottawa chief, became their leader and strategist.

Choosing an offensive rather than a defensive position, Pontiac decided to strike against all frontier outposts in the summer of 1763. His plan almost succeeded. Most of the western forts fell, including Fort LeBoeuf, where Washington had delivered his message to the French several years before. But Fort Pitt, the scene of so much recent fighting, as well as Detroit and Niagara, managed to withstand the Indian onslaught. As before, western Virginians were called upon to defend the frontiers, and Colonel Adam Stephen and Major Andrew Lewis were appointed commanders.

Colonel Henry Bouquet, who had been second in command to General Forbes in the capture of Fort Pitt in 1758, met the Indians on August 5, 1763 at Bushy Run, thirty miles southeast of Fort Pitt. Colonel Bouquet saved the day. Pretending to retreat, Bouquet split his forces into two groups and on the following day completely surrounded and routed the Delawares and the Shawnees in one of the decisive Indian battles in American history. The gateway to the West had been secured.

In 1764 the British sent two expeditions into the Ohio country, one under Colonel Bouquet which resulted in Shawnees and Delawares suing for peace and one under Colonel Bradstreet. These military expeditions shattered Indian resistance in Ohio. In the Illinois country, the British with George Croghan, the Pennsylvania Indian trader, as mediator made peace with Pontiac. These activities ended the possibilities of a major organized Indian war in eastern United States.

Proclamation of 1763

In the same year of the Indian uprising, the English king issued his Proclamation of 1763. The proclamation forbade settlements west of the crest of the Allegheny Mountains for the time being. To the colonials this regulation was as disturbing as the Indian uprising. Both seemed efforts to prevent occupation of the west.

The proclamation also created three new royal English provinces in the west: to the north, Quebec, and to the south, East Florida and West Florida. The territory between the northern and southern provinces was set aside as Indian territory. William Johnson was put in charge of the portion north of the Ohio, and John Stuart was named administrator of the portion south of the Ohio River and south of Pennsylvania. Indian trade was to be regulated, all traders were to be licensed, and individuals were forbidden to settle on the lands until proper titles had been obtained.

Indian Treaties

For the next five years, the administrators worked on achieving legal title to the Indian territory. In 1768 William Johnson concluded the Treaty of Fort Stanwix. By its terms the Iroquois ceded to Pennsylvania and the English crown all the lands claimed by the Iroquois and their allies east of the Allegheny and south of the Ohio rivers. This included the hunting grounds of the Shawnees and Delawares and some of the lands of the Cherokees. The boundary line of this land extended west to the Tennessee River, which meant that the territory incorporated nearly all of the present state of West Virginia.

In the same year of the Treaty of Fort Stanwix, the English were able to obtain other Indian lands in the Treaty of Hard Labour. In this treaty the Cherokees surrendered all their known lands between the Kanawha and the Kentucky rivers. Actually the Cherokees may have been claiming land of the Iroquois as well as lands belonging to the Shawnees and the Delawares. The Virginia Colony, of course, claimed that such land was Virginia's.

A Decade of Settlement

The lands ceded by these treaties in 1768 were declared opened to the settlers. The king's Proclamation of 1763, modified by these agreements, now seemed less harsh, if not absolutely meaningless, to the westerners, and settlements in western Virginia increased rapidly as news of the Indian treaties circulated throughout the back country.

In western Virginia beyond the ridge of the Alleghenies, a decade of settlement occurred from 1764 to 1774. The new western homes could be described as forming a circular belt around a large wilderness of heavily forested land. Most of the settlements were made along the rivers. These areas became meeting places for land speculators who were interested in promotional schemes for lands on the borders of Kentucky and Ohio.

Mainly, the new settlers were from the nearby colonies of Maryland and Pennsylvania as well as from Virginia. First, they secured tomahawk rights, blazing trees along the lands' boundaries by tomahawk, and then they secured settlement rights, clearing land, building cabins, and actually residing on the property. Although Virginia took no steps to sell land until after 1779, the colony respected the rights of settlers. If they erected any kind of cabin and if they could prove that the land they settled on was free of previous claims, the pioneers could expect to obtain title to a minimum of 400 or 500 acres if not more in the years ahead.

Year by year pioneers made inroads into the wilderness. In 1764 John and Samuel Pringle, brothers who had deserted garrison duty with the British army at Fort Pitt and had hidden temporarily in Maryland, created a makeshift forest camp at the mouth of Turkey Run on the Buckhannon River. Living in a hollow sycamore tree near the site of present Buckhannon in Upshur County, they opened their lands to others in the year of the two Indian treaties. The same year in which the Pringles moved to western Virginia, John Simpson, a trapper, established a camp at the mouth of the Elk Creek near the present site of Clarksburg.

Zackquill Morgan, the son of Morgan Morgan, settled at Morgantown in Monongalia County in 1768, and David Morgan ventured into what was to become Marion County. The next year new families located in many parts of present West Virginia. Ebenezer Zane and his two brothers selected a site at Wheeling Creek on the Ohio River in 1769, and by 1770 at least five more families had joined the Zane settlement. In 1769 John Stuart,

Tree Home of John and Samuel Pringle The Pringle brothers lived in a hollow sycamore tree near the present site of Buckhannon, Upshur County, from 1764 to 1768. The home tree fell many years ago; another sprang from its roots; and still another rose on the spot. *(Photo courtesy of R. L. Westfall)*

Zackquill Morgan *(Photo courtesy of West Virginia University Library)*

Robert McClanahan, Thomas Renick, and William Hamilton settled in Greenbrier County, and the Woods family founded Peterstown in Monroe County. A dozen or more families soon joined the Woods settlement. Several families also settled near Clifton Mills and Bruceton Mills in Preston County.

By 1770 the Tomlinsons had settled at the mouth of Grave Creek on the Ohio River, and new families joined them in 1772. Others had located on most of the land in the Tygart River Valley by 1772. A few settlers entered Brooke County in 1772, with more following in 1774. In 1770 Lewisburg in Greenbrier County and Montgomery in Fayette County were being settled. Having come by mule from Alexandria, Virginia, Levi Morris built his home at Montgomery, and he was followed by William Morris in 1774.

In 1773 Walter Kelley settled at Cedar Grove in Kanawha County, and the next year Thomas Bullitt settled at Charleston. In 1774 sons of James Parsons located at Horseshoe Bend on the Cheat River in Tucker County.

New Towns and Counties

From the king's Proclamation of 1763 to the Declaration of Independence in 1776, western settlement broke through the mountains. Services of municipal and county governments became necessary. In 1762 Shepherdstown and Romney in present West Virginia were incorporated as towns. Berkeley County was created in 1772. Ohio and Monongalia counties quickly followed in 1776. In Ohio County, Fort Fincastle, which had been constructed in 1774, received the name of Fort Henry in 1776 in honor of the new Virginia governor.

George Washington in the West

For those who had seen service in the French and Indian War, the Virginia government promised payment in the form of western lands. Of all the war veterans entitled to such benefits, none was more distinguished and none had greater expectations of a landed estate than George Washington. In addition to his own land claims for prior military service, he had purchased the claims of other soldiers.

In 1770 Washington prepared for a trip to the west to locate the best possible properties. Going by a route long familiar to him, he traveled past Fort Necessity on the old Braddock Road to Fort Pitt. He journeyed to Logstown and then on the Ohio River all the way to the mouth of the Great Kanawha. In one canoe were Washington and his party, and in another canoe were the customary Indian escorts.

Marking trees as beginning points for surveys, Washington went up the Kanawha about fourteen miles, and others of his party proceeded four or five miles farther upstream. On a part of Wash-

West Virginia Highway Marker This marker is on State Route 17 in Mason County.

ington's journey, his physician, Dr. James Craik, accompanied him; on another part, Colonel George Croghan joined him; and Kiashuta, an Indian chieftain, also became a traveling companion.

On this trip, Washington killed several buffalo. Believing these animals would furnish the future supply of meat for America, he undertook experiments in crossbreeding. Among his livestock at Mount Vernon, he produced a buffalo-cow.

At a later time, Colonel William Crawford, a boyhood friend of Washington, completed the surveys of the lands Washington had inspected on his trip.

Washington Properties. Washington's efforts on his western trip netted him almost 70,000 acres. At the time of his death, he held title to over 3,000 acres in Ohio, 5,000 acres in both Pennsylvania and Kentucky, and approximately 55,000 acres in the present state of West Virginia.

The major portion of Washington's western Virginia property was in the southern portion of the present state. His tract in Mason County bordering the Kanawha amounted to almost 11,000 acres, and in Putnam and Kanawha counties his tracts approximated 34,000 acres. He possessed about 10,000 acres along the Ohio River and tracts located at Round Bottom below Moundsville, at Washington Bottom below the mouth of the Little Kanawha, and near the present sites of Ravenswood and Millwood.

He also held property in Berkeley Springs in the Eastern Panhandle of the state. This property was close to the estates of his brothers Charles and Samuel who had established their homes, "Happy Retreat" and "Harewood," in what is now Jefferson County.

A Western Virginia Settlement. After Washington returned home, he advertised his western lands for settlement. At first, he planned to settle Germans on his land, but he could not interest Germans as prospective settlers. Later he found persons in England and Ireland who were willing to work as indentured servants on his land in Mason County in western Virginia. He appointed as overseer James Cleveland, a trusted employee at Mount Vernon.

Having been located on the tract in Mason County, half of the twenty indentured servants ran away. By 1776, however, Cleveland and his work party had cleared twenty-eight acres, constructed buildings (including four houses, a barn, and ten cabins), and planted 2,000 peach trees. The local assessor valued the improvements upon

"Harewood," Home of Samuel Washington This historic home near Charles Town, West Virginia, was built about 1771 by Samuel Washington, brother of George Washington. *(Photo courtesy of Dr. John A. Washington)*

the Kanawha property at more than $5,500, a considerable sum for that time. Yet, possible Indian forays as well as the American Revolution caused the original inhabitants of the settlement to disperse.

After Washington's death, his nephew, Lawrence Augustine Washington, took up residence on his Kanawha property in present Putnam County, West Virginia. Later this branch of the family moved to the Wheeling vicinity in Ohio County. Lawrence Augustine Washington, Jr., lived for a time in Charleston, West Virginia, before seeking his fortune farther west.

"Happy Retreat," Home of Charles Washington Charles Washington, brother of George Washington, built his home on a site at the edge of the present city of Charles Town.

Vandalia, A Fourteenth Colony

In 1769 the Vandalia Company was organized by a number of prominent men, including Benjamin Franklin, George Croghan, William Trent, and Sir William Johnson. This company was a combination of the Indiana Company, a land company whose members were primarily Pennsylvanians, and the Ohio Company, a land company whose members were primarily Virginians, veterans such as Washington who held land certificates, and English officials. The newer company was sometimes called the Grand Ohio Company and sometimes the Walpole Company after an official in England, but more often in America it was called Vandalia, a name which honored the Queen of England who imagined she was descended from the Vandals.

The company requested originally 2,500,000 acres of land in the west, but it shortly increased the request by many thousands of acres. Its holdings incorporated all of present West Virginia west of the Allegheny Mountains and eastern Kentucky. The promoters sought to form a fourteenth colony here, to be called Vandalia. The capital was to be at Point Pleasant. By 1772 the project was given tentative approval; by 1773 the final papers had been drawn up; and by 1774 the project had almost been approved. Uncertain land titles in the west, inadequate military protection on the frontiers, and distances from the seat of government were factors in its favor. Had not reports of disturbances in America been circulated in England, the king would undoubtedly have approved.

Revolutionary sentiment in America doomed chances for the new colony. Then those interested in Vandalia tried to create enthusiasm in another project, a fourteenth state to be named Westsylvania. Its territory was even larger. It included all of trans-Allegheny Virginia, Kentucky, and parts of western Pennsylvania. But it conflicted with the interests of too many speculators, land companies, and colonies, and the project failed.

Virginia-Pennsylvania Boundary Dispute

In September 1767 Mason and Dixon were completing their original survey of the Mason and Dixon Line between Virginia and Pennsylvania. For a time the men had had an escort of Indians representing the Six Nations and had proceeded a little farther than the site of Mount Morris when the Delaware and Shawnee Indians stopped them at the crossing of the Warrior and Great Catawba Indian trails. The boundary line remained undetermined for the next seventeen years.

Virginia wanted possession of the forks of the Ohio, and claimed that its territory extended as far north as the fortieth degree of latitude. Pennsylvania claimed that Penn had been granted land at the thirty-ninth degree of latitude. If Virginia had had its way, it would have obtained a part of two present counties of Pennsylvania, Fayette and Greene; if Pennsylvania had had its way, it would have taken a part of the Monongahela region.

If Dunmore's War and the Revolutionary War had not intervened, a bitter fight between the two colonies would probably have taken place.

By 1779, however, both colonies had agreed to appoint commissioners to solve their boundary dispute. They resolved to extend the Mason and Dixon Line five degrees from its beginning point and to accept the meridian passing through its most western point as the western boundary of Pennsylvania. This action accounted for the creation of the Northern Panhandle of West Virginia when it became a state. Location of line, however, was not finally determined until 1784, and the survey was not accepted until 1786.

Lord Dunmore   John, Earl Dunmore, was the last royal governor of the colony of Virginia. *(From a painting in the gallery of the State Library at Richmond, Virginia)*

Dunmore's War

Cresap's War. During the French and Indian War, Pennsylvania gained control of Fort Pitt. In 1773 Governor Dunmore of Virginia sent Dr. John Connolly to the Ohio River forks to secure the fort for Virginia. Having accomplished his assignment, Connolly changed the name of the fort to Fort Dunmore.

John Connolly, from his vantage point at the forks of the Ohio, called upon the settlers along the Ohio River to prepare to defend themselves against the Indians. Some of the pioneers fled from the area, and some prepared for war.

In the vicinity of Wheeling, a command of volunteers was first offered to George Rogers Clark, but was finally accepted by Michael Cresap, who had recently come into western Virginia from Maryland. Cresap undertook an attack upon a Shawnee camp at Captina Creek. In this encounter several Indians were killed. Two Indian canoemen were also killed. Although Cresap returned to Wheeling, the attacks were interpreted as a declaration of war by the Indians.

The Murder of Logan's Family. Believing that Chief Logan's brother and sister and other members of his tribe were planning revenge for the murders, white men under the leadership of Daniel Greathouse lured Chief Logan's family and other members of the tribe to a grogshop kept by Joshua Baker. The shop was on the Ohio River in western Virginia, opposite Logan's home at the mouth of Yellow Creek about fifteen miles above present Steubenville. After the Indians were intoxicated, they were murdered. The murder was deplorable and was foolhardy, for Logan had lived among the whites and was friendly to them.

When Logan heard of his family's fate, he went on the warpath in the summer of 1774, taking no less than 30 scalps and prisoners.

The whites committed other outrages. Bald Eagle, an old Delaware chieftain, was murdered and his body set afloat on the Monongahela River. Silver Heels, a Shawnee chieftain, was shot. The Iroquois, ready to forsake their alliance with the English, were preparing to spring into action in defense of their fellow Indians. Only the diplomacy of Sir William Johnson prevented the formation of an all-Indian alliance.

McDonald's Expedition. During a period of assaults by both sides, Major Angus McDonald, in command of 400 militia, marched from Fort Fincastle (at Wheeling) due west to the Muskingum River in the late summer of 1774. With the aid of an Indian chieftain, White Eyes, and Christian missionaries living on the Tuscarawas River, McDonald decisively defeated the Shawnee Indians living on the Scioto River. On his return by way of Greenway Court, a hunting lodge that had been built by Lord Fairfax not far from Winchester, Virginia, he joined the forces of Lord Dunmore preparing to bring the Indian conflict in the Ohio Valley to a close.

Dunmore's Strategy. Lord Dunmore had become governor of Virginia. He was originally a very popular figure in the colony. He had visited the northwestern frontier in 1773 and was ordering surveys made of the area. But within the year, he had twice dissolved the Virginia House of Burgesses when it had proposed a committee to consider colonial grievances and when it had set aside a day of fasting in an expression of sympathy with Massachusetts whose port of Boston had been closed because of the Boston Tea Party. Then his popularity rapidly vanished.

Perhaps to divert the attention of Virginians from their grievances against him or perhaps because of his strong interest in western lands, he prepared for major warfare upon the Indians and proposed to drive them from the Ohio Valley.

He proposed to defeat the Indians by the creation of two armies. One would proceed from the north and one from the south, and both would combine against the Indians at the Ohio River. Commanding the northern army, Lord Dunmore, himself, traveled by way of Fort Cumberland to Redstone where one division of his forces continued directly to Wheeling and the other went to Fort Pitt.

Dunmore gave command of the southern army to Captain Andrew Lewis. Two regiments of these armies were under the command of Captain John Stuart from the Greenbrier Valley and Colonel Adam Stephen from Berkeley County, areas now in West Virginia. The combined forces numbered about 2,500 soldiers, Captain Lewis commanding an army of about 800 men.

Cornstalk's Strategy. Lewis's army left Camp Union, at present Lewisburg, West Virginia, and in 19 days marched 160 miles across the Allegheny Mountains to Point Pleasant, the junction of the Kanawha and Ohio rivers. Dunmore's army did not stop at the Ohio River but crossed it near the mouth of Hocking Springs and pushed toward Pickaway Plains.

Cornstalk, chief of the Indian forces, spied out the movements of both armies. Cornstalk decided to strike at Lewis's army before it joined Dunmore's forces.

The advance guard of Lewis's army reached the mouth of the Kanawha on October 9, 1774. That night Cornstalk crossed the Ohio and located his forces of perhaps 1,200 men about three miles above Point Pleasant. The next day the Indians, discovered by two hunters, had no choice but to make an immediate attack.

The fight has been described as a succession of single combats, one white man against one Indian. The superiority of the backwoodsmen in the use of the rifle evidently turned the tide. The whites were victorious. In Lewis's army, 81 were killed and 140 were wounded; in Cornstalk's army 200 Indians were killed, and twice as many wounded.

Treaty of Camp Charlotte. On October 9, Dunmore had sent a message to Lewis to join him on the Pickaway Plains. After the Battle of Point Pleasant, Lewis was able to obey the order on October 11. However, Dunmore had already entered into peace terms. The Indians, members of Delaware, Shawnee, and Mingo tribes, agreed to surrender all white prisoners, to return all stolen

Tu-Endie-Wei Park at Point Pleasant The monument in the park commemorates the Battle of Point Pleasant fought in 1774. The house, a hewed-log structure, was built in 1796. *(West Virginia Department of Commerce Photo)*

horses, and to give up all claims to land south of the Ohio River (which would include the present state of West Virginia). As a pledge, they were willing to leave hostages.

Dunmore's Troubles with Lewis and Chief Logan. Two problems marred Dunmore's efforts. When Lewis and his soldiers marched to join Dunmore, the Indians became alarmed, fearing an attack against their towns. Dunmore instructed Lewis's army to halt and to return to Point Pleasant. The men who had been victorious in battle were angry that they had not been involved in the peace terms.

Dunmore also desired that Logan, one of the Indian chieftains, be present at the peace negotiations. Logan refused, and in his reply accused Michael Cresap of having murdered the chieftain's family.

Although Cresap's involvement remains unproven, Logan's address has become an example of Indian eloquence:

> I appeal to any white man to say if he ever entered Logan's cabin hungry and he gave him not meat; if ever he came cold and naked and he clothed him not. During the course of the last long and bloody war, Logan remained idle in his camp, an advocate for peace. Nay, such was my love for the whites that my countrymen pointed as they passed, and said, "Logan is the friend of white men." I had even thought to have lived with you but for the injuries of one man. Colonel Cresap, the last spring in cold blood and unprovoked, murdered all the relations of Logan, not even sparing my women and children.
>
> There runs not a drop of my blood in the veins of any living creature. This called on me for revenge. I have sought it. I have killed many. I have fully glutted my vengeance. For my country, I rejoice at the beams of peace. Yet, do not harbor the thought that mine is the joy of fear. Logan never felt fear. He will not turn on his heels to save his life. Who is there to mourn for Logan? Not one.

But despite his difficulties in these two instances, Dunmore was successful in his final peace terms.

Fort Gower Address. On November 5, 1774 the returning officers of Dunmore's forces met at Fort Gower and adopted a patriotic resolution. This was during the meetings of the First Continental Congress of September and October of 1774 when delegates were debating the relationship between England and the American colonies. However, the Dunmore army had heard no news from either Boston or Philadelphia, the storm centers of the revolutionary spirit.

The resolution of the officers expressed allegiance to his majesty King George III and respect for Lord Dunmore, but the men pledged to fight only "for the honour and advantage of *America* in general, and of *Virginia* in particular." The point they were making was that although they represented an already assembled army in the field, they would be available only for American rather than British purposes if war should come.

Results of the Battle of Point Pleasant

The Battle of Point Pleasant, taking place half a year before the Revolutionary battles of Lexington and Concord, was not a battle of the American Revolution; the Americans and the Englishman who was governor of Virginia were on the same side. However, the Battle of Point Pleasant was helpful in producing certain results relating to the Revolutionary War. It created peace with the Indians that lasted the first three years of the Revolutionary War and prevented the Indians from attacking the colonials.

The Battle of Point Pleasant also opened the way to rapid western expansion and was a forerunner of the George Rogers Clark campaign of 1778–79, which was intent on destroying British power in the West and securing additional lands for Americans.

Brave and Tragic Chieftain

Cornstalk, Chief of the Shawnees

Cornstalk, a Shawnee Indian chief, was born about 1720. His English name was a translation of his Indian name, Keigh-tugh-qua, which meant the blade or stalk of the maize plant. Little is known of Cornstalk's early life, but he lived with his people near the Scioto River in present Ohio after 1730. He first became known to the English on the frontier in 1759, when he made a raid against settlers during the French and Indian War, a disastrous attack.

Monument to Cornstalk

In 1763, during the great Pontiac uprising against white settlers encroaching upon Indian areas, he raided settlements along the Greenbrier River in present West Virginia. When Colonel Bouquet marched against the Indians in 1764, Cornstalk was one of the hostages taken to insure peace, but he was released.

From 1764 to 1774, there was an uneasy peace along the frontier. Cornstalk remained inactive, a condition of his release from serving as a hostage. In spite of his neutrality, however, his brother was seriously wounded by traders or settlers. Cornstalk asked for an end to growing hostilities, but peace did not follow.

At a meeting on the Pickaway Plains in Ohio, the Shawnee, Delaware, Wyandot, Miami, and Ottawa tribes with Cornstalk as leader formed a confederation to hold back the whites. A few Iroquois and Cherokees also joined the confederation. By 1774 the situation led to Governor Dunmore's calling the militia to suppress Indians of the Ohio region.

Cornstalk was pressured into action at the Battle of Point Pleasant where the Indians suffered great losses and, although they fought bravely, they had to retreat.

Dunmore and the Indians of the Scioto area made the Treaty of Camp Charlotte. Cornstalk, one of the principals of the treaty, returned all prisoners as he had agreed to do.

In 1777 the chief went to a fort in the Point Pleasant area to warn the settlers that the Shawnees, at the instigation of the British, were going to take up arms against the newly created United States. At this time a soldier was shot from ambush, presumably by Indians. Cornstalk was held at the fort and later was killed by enraged settlers.

The chief was brave to the end.

The attitude of the white settlers toward the Indians was such that the murderers of Cornstalk were not legally charged with the crime.

A monument to the memory of the Indian leader now stands in a park at Point Pleasant.

Chapter 11 REVOLUTIONARY DAYS, 1775–1783

In the struggle against England the Continental Congresses chose George Washington as commander-in-chief of the armies. In Washington they had chosen not only a Virginian but also an officer and former land surveyor who knew western Virginia.

Washington, with Congress, determined upon two great objectives for which the American colonies fought in the Revolutionary War: first, to confine the British armies to the east coast and, second, by thus preventing the British and their Indian allies from breaking through the Appalachian Mountain barrier, to protect the American West.

For the most part, Washington assigned to the men of western Virginia the duty of guarding the rear. Yet he and Congress designated some men of the Eastern Panhandle for major roles in guarding the area along the Atlantic Coast.

The war in western Virginia was a series of raids and counter-raids, of assaults upon forts and their defense, of countless massacres, and of individual heroism by both men and women on both sides of the conflict.

Generally the western Virginians occupied defensive positions in protecting home and family. But on rare occasions, they took the offensive, acting as far west as the Mississippi River in an effort to break large-scale Indian operations which were largely conducted from a British command post at Detroit.

A Western Virginia Wilderness Home of This Period *(Photo courtesy of West Virginia University Library)*

British and Indian Activity in the West

The Battle of Point Pleasant, occurring before the American Revolution, gave the colonists definite advantages. The fighting gave them valuable experience in battle, and also the Treaty of Camp Charlotte had brought peace to the western frontier. But westerners, to their dismay, learned that Governor Dunmore was returning the hostages of the battle, was calling off final negotiations with the Indians, and was abandoning the important forts at Pittsburgh, Wheeling, and Point Pleasant.

Treaty of Pittsburgh, 1775. Both the Continental Congress and the Virginia General Assembly, after getting rid of Dunmore as royal governor, hurried to restore the western defenses and revive the previous land settlements. Dr. Thomas Walker, an early surveyor of western Virginia lands, opened negotiations with the Indians. A new treaty, known as the Treaty of Pittsburgh, was quickly concluded in 1775. By its terms, the Ottawa, Wyandot, Mingo, Shawnee, Delaware, and Seneca Indians agreed to a policy of neutrality and peace and friendship with the Americans. This treaty made the pioneers feel that their frontier homes were now more secure, and it freed many westerners for enlistment in the Revolutionary War armies.

But the peace was again disrupted in 1777. Western Virginia was invaded by large numbers of Indians on so many occasions that the year became known as "the bloody year of the three sevens."

Indians may well have been tricked into destroying the peace by Governor Henry Hamilton, British commander at Detroit. By offering the Indians rum and bounties for scalps and for prisoners, Hamilton encouraged the Indian raids upon the frontier settlements. He became known as the "hair buyer."

Fortified Centers. During the war there were several main centers of fighting in western Virginia, from 1777 to the coming of peace in 1783. For the most part, these centers were located along the Ohio, the Monongahela, the Kanawha, and the Greenbrier rivers. Possession of the forts at these points was the objective of each side in the fighting. Among the more important of these strongholds were Fort Pitt, Fort Henry, Fort Randolph, and Fort Donnally. The forts withstood the great assaults of 1777.

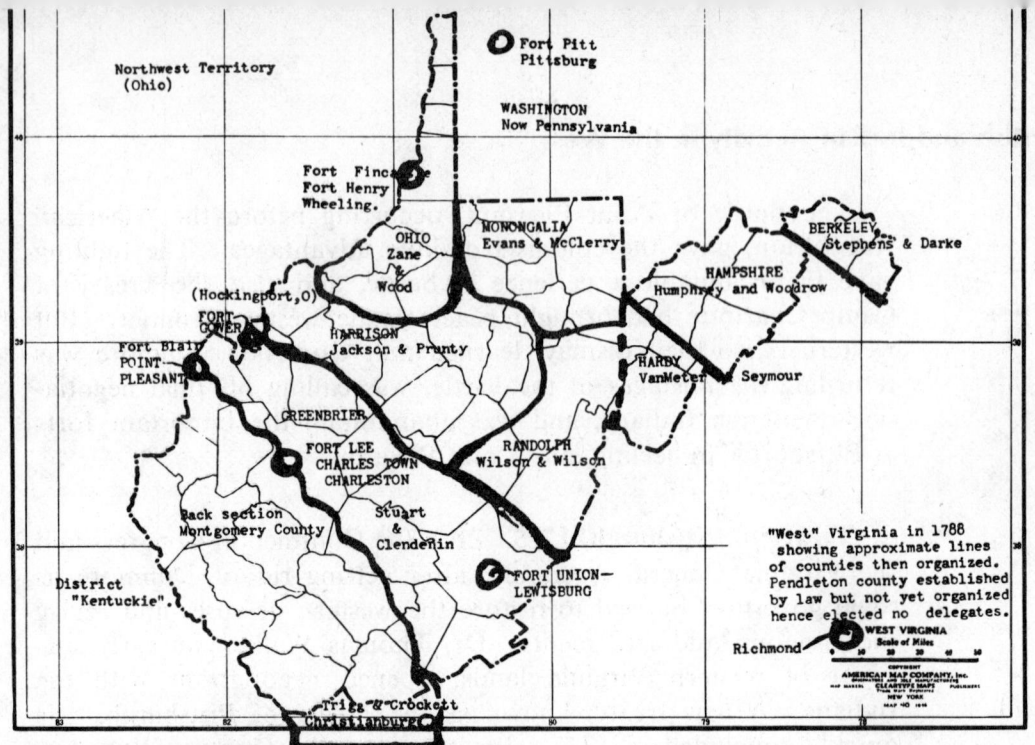

Map of Forts in Western Virginia The map shows the forts serving western Virginians in the mid-1700's; also the counties established there at the time; and the names of delegates from the counties to the convention held in Richmond in June 1788 to ratify the Constitution of the United States. Fort Christianburg in the south was in Virginia, not in what is now West Virginia.

Fort Pitt. Fort Pitt stood at the confluence of the Monongahela and the Allegheny rivers as they form the Ohio. The original fort, built by the French, as we have learned, was named Fort Duquesne. When the French lost control of the fort, it was renamed Fort Pitt in honor of William Pitt, an Englishman who had planned the English campaign in the French and Indian War.

When Virginia won control of the area from Pennsylvania, the fort was named Fort Dunmore in honor of the Virginia governor. When Dunmore gave up control of the military forces of Virginia, the fort again became Fort Pitt.

During the Revolution, under the direction of the Continental Congress General Edward Hand assumed control of Fort Pitt. Under his authority other forts were restored and new ones constructed. General Hand planned an attack on the British at Detroit. However, his plans to move the war so far into enemy territory failed, and in time he was followed by three other commanders, one of whom was General Daniel Brodhead.

Fort Henry. Fort Henry at Wheeling was first called Fort Fincastle, taking that name from one of the family names of

Lord Dunmore. In 1774 the fort was renamed Fort Henry in honor of Patrick Henry, the governor of Virginia.

In September 1777 a force of about 200 Indians and British rangers attacked Fort Henry. The Indians included members of the Wyandot, Mingo, Shawnee, and Delaware tribes. About 60 men were defending the fort. Some white settlers enticed outside the fort were killed.

The siege lasted three days and three nights. But the defenders inside the fort were expert riflemen and were able to prevent the Indians from battering down the gate.

Events which in time became frontier legends occurred during the siege of Fort Henry. Major Samuel McCulloch, an Indian fighter, trying to bring relief to the fort, was trapped by Indians on the steep slopes overlooking Wheeling Creek. Forcing his horse over a cliff, to the amazement of the Indians McCulloch leaped to safety and escaped.

Captain William Forman of Hampshire County, with a force of forty-six neighbors, also attempted to aid the fort. But about halfway between present Moundsville and Wheeling, the Indians mounted a surprise attack, killing twenty-one of the Forman party.

On September 10, 1782 Fort Henry was again attacked by Indians. The fort contained a small fighting force plus a larger number of women and children. The battle raged two days and two nights. According to a Philadelphia newspaper account in 1782, the fight was a classic frontier battle out of which emerged a genuine frontier heroine, Elizabeth "Betty" Zane.

At the outbreak of the battle Colonel Ebenezer Zane, commander of the fort, was in his fortified dwelling house which served also as a warehouse for ammunition and as a second outpost. His brother, Silas, and his sister, Elizabeth, were in the fort. Silas assumed command, and Elizabeth volunteered to run to the house for a supply of powder.

At first, the Indians did not fire on her because she was a "squaw." But as soon as they understood her mission, they opened fire as she dashed back to the fort with the gunpowder. She reached the fort in safety. In her dress one bullet hole was found.

This engagement is sometimes called the last battle of the Revolution.

Fort Randolph. An early fort at Point Pleasant was named Fort Blair. In the summer of 1775 the Indians burned Fort Blair. The fort was rebuilt and was named Fort Randolph in honor of

Old Fort at Morgantown *(From "History of the Early Settlement and Indian Wars of Western Virginia," 1851, by Wills De Hass)*

Peyton Randolph, Virginian and first president of the Continental Congress.

In September 1777 a series of murders occurred at the garrison at Fort Randolph. According to John Stuart's eyewitness account of the events of that year, Chief Cornstalk had told Captain Arbuckle, commander of the fort, that although the chief and his wife were opposed to joining the war on the side of the British, the rest of the Indians desired to take part in the conflict. This information caused the commander to detain Cornstalk at the fort either to prevent him from joining the Indians in battle plans or to protect him from Indian tribesmen.

During Cornstalk's confinement there, two white men, Hamilton and Gilmore by name, crossed the Kanawha to hunt deer. Gilmore was killed and scalped by a party of Indians. This atrocity so excited the men at the fort that they threatened their officers with death if the officers did not permit the murder of Cornstalk, his son Elinipsico, and Red Hawk. These latter two were visiting the fort. The officers stood aside, and the slaughter of the three Indians took place.

Governor Henry now expected the Indians to take revenge. On April 3, 1778 he ordered Colonels Fleming and Preston to express his regret to the Shawnees. Nonhelema, Cornstalk's sister, who was a friend of the settlers and lived at the fort, delivered the message. But the Indians were not satisfied.

In May 1778 about two hundred Indians struck the fort to avenge the murders. The siege lasted a week but was not successful.

Fort Lee Fort Lee was erected by George Clendenin on a site now within the city of Charleston, which is on the Kanawha River. *(Photo courtesy of West Virginia University Library)*

The Indians now moved up the Kanawha River in the direction of settlements in the Greenbrier Valley. From Fort Randolph, Commander William McKee dispatched two white messengers, John Pryor and Philip Hammond, to warn the Greenbrier residents of the threatened attack.

Pryor and Hammond were disguised as Indians. Their dress and coloring were perfected by Nonhelema, who was known as the "Grenadier Squaw." She obviously did not resent the death of her brother. Possibly her love for a white man also influenced her to cast her lot with the settlers.

Fort Donnally. Fort Donnally in the Greenbrier area had been an important objective of the Indians. The disguised messengers from Fort Randolph were able to slip through the Indians' lines and warn the settlers in time to save the fort and the many lives depending on it for safety.

The battle for control of the Kanawha and Greenbrier settlements took place here at Fort Donnally. So successful were the settlers in this engagement that never again did the Indians appear in the upper Kanawha Valley in large numbers, and the battle was known as the Second Battle of Point Pleasant. The settlers' victory in this engagement greatly favored the increase in frontier settlements.

chapter eleven / revolutionary days, 1775–1783

Richard Henry Lee for Whom Fort Lee Was Named Henry "Light Horse Harry" Lee was a distinguished officer in the Revolutionary War, governor of Virginia, and father of General Robert E. Lee.

Defectors in the West

It has been said that at the outbreak of the American Revolution, about one-third of the people supported the cause of the colonies, about one-third supported the British cause, and about one-third were totally indifferent to the outcome. The defectors — those who supported Great Britain — were Tories or Loyalists. In western Virginia, both Tories and Loyalists were present. After the Indian attacks of 1777 Colonel Zackquill Morgan enlisted five hundred men to put down the Loyalists in the Monongahela area.

In March 1778 a Tory band left Fort Pitt to join the British in the west. The most famous member of the group was Simon Girty. Simon Girty was known as the "white Indian" or the "white renegade." He was born in Pennsylvania. He learned the Indian language as a young boy and in time became an interpreter for Lord Dunmore on his march against the Indians in Ohio. From 1778 to the end of the American Revolution, he lived among Indians, often directing and leading their attacks against the colonists. After the Revolution, Girty escaped to Canada. There he died in 1818.

Major Walter Crockett suppressed a Loyalist plan to seize control of the lead mines in Montgomery County. In 1780 Colonel Charles Lynch, with the aid of the local military authorities, crushed still another conspiracy in the same area.

In 1780 General Daniel Morgan defeated a group of Loyalists led by John Claypole, a Scotsman, in Hampshire County. Most of the Loyalists were Germans who had been led by John Brake.

They refused to give loyalty to Virginia, to pay taxes, and to enter military service against the British.

Activity in the Far West

In 1778 George Rogers Clark, 24 years of age, with a force of less than 200 riflemen from the Monongahela area and some from the Shenandoah Valley, undertook an offense against the British and the Indians in the West. Descending the Ohio River, Clark marched to and across the southern part of Illinois and seized the frontier posts at Kaskaskia and Vincennes. This was the only successful American campaign in 1778. Governor Hamilton, moving down from Detroit, recaptured Vincennes, but Clark wrested the fort from Hamilton in 1779, sending the "hair buyer" back to Virginia as a prisoner.

Although Clark never mustered a force large enough to capture Detroit, he constantly kept the British alarmed with small skirmishes in the West.

Activity in the East

Early in 1775 the Continental Congress requested sharpshooters to harass the enemy behind the British entrenchments at Boston. George Washington secured Hugh Stephenson, from Berkeley

General Daniel Morgan General Morgan was the commander of Morgan's Riflemen. He lived in Berkeley County during the French and Indian War and served as a wagoner in Braddock's expedition. Later he moved to Winchester. Many western Virginians fought under his command in the Revolutionary War.

chapter eleven / revolutionary days, 1775–1783

County, and Daniel Morgan, from neighboring Frederick County, to head the Virginia riflemen.

Stephenson's men were from Berkeley County; Morgan's men were from Frederick, Hampshire, and Berkeley counties. The two groups struck "a bee line" for Cambridge and Boston. Morgan's men arrived first. The sharpshooters wore buckskin suits, moccasins, and usually coonskin caps with a bucktail on the side. They carried minimum equipment, such as rifles, tomahawks, and scalping knives. Their emblem was a coiled rattlesnake. They were highly successful in tormenting the enemy.

A long list of American Revolutionary War generals from the Berkeley area became famous, including Adam Stephen, Horatio Gates, Charles Lee, Daniel Morgan, and William Darke.

New Counties, Towns, and Settlements

The counties of Hampshire and Berkeley had been formed before the Revolutionary War, and the counties of Ohio and Monongalia were formed during the Revolutionary War. Six other counties in present West Virginia were created prior to George Washington's taking office as President of a new nation. They were Greenbrier, Harrison, Hardy, Randolph, Pendleton, and Kanawha.

In addition to Romney and Shepherdstown, which were designated as towns before the Revolutionary War, Lewisburg, Clarksburg, Morgantown, Charles Town, Frankford, and West Liberty were incorporated before the new United States government was organized.

In the southeastern part of present West Virginia, in the present counties of Mercer, Monroe, Greenbrier, and Summers, settlements were made by Mitchell Clay near Princeton in 1775; by Rev. John Alderson, Baptist minister, in Alderson in 1775; by Thomas Ingle near Bluefield in 1778; by the Peters family at Peterstown in 1783; and by the Davidson and Bailey families on the Bluestone, tributary of the New River, in 1780.

In Lewis and Harrison counties, Henry Flesher and Henry McWhorter settled in Weston and McWhortersville in 1784; along the Ohio James Wood made a home at Belleville and Captain James Neal constructed a blockhouse at Parkersburg in 1785. Daniel Boone arrived at Point Pleasant in 1788. George Clendenin purchased the Bullitt lands at Charleston in 1787 and constructed Fort Lee in 1788.

Patriot in Many Roles

Adam Stephen, Revolutionary War General

Like many of the first settlers on the American frontier, Adam Stephen was born in Scotland. Unlike most early colonials, Stephen was an educated man, a graduate of the medical school at the University of Edinburgh. He served as a surgeon during the English wars in the 1740's and moved to Virginia about 1748.

Adam Stephen's Martinsburg Home (Restored) *(Gerald S. Ratliff Photo, West Virginia Department of Commerce)*

In 1754 he accepted a commission in the militia and served under George Washington at Fort Necessity. He also participated in Braddock's campaign against Fort Duquesne in 1755. He received an appointment as a lieutenant colonel and became commander at frontier posts near Winchester and Cumberland.

Following an Indian campaign in South Carolina in 1757, he served in the Forbes expedition to the forks of the Ohio in November 1758.

While living in Frederick County, Stephen ran for the Virginia House of Burgesses in 1761. He was defeated by George Washington. With the outbreak of Pontiac's War in 1763, Colonel Stephen was called upon once again to lead a militia detachment to the Ohio region. By 1768 he had reached the rank of brigadier general in the state militia and decided to retire from active service.

Stephen was successfully elected to the Virginia House of Burgesses in 1769. In 1772, while serving as a justice of the peace for Frederick County, he was instrumental in the creation of Berkeley County as a distinct unit from the former county. He was the new county's largest landowner, one of the first justices of the peace, and sheriff. His lands soon became the site of Martinsburg, the seat of the county's government.

With the beginning of Dunmore's War, Stephen once again became an active soldier and served as a major general, second in command to Lord Dunmore. He led the northern group into Ohio and was instrumental in making the peace treaty with the Indians.

With the coming of the Revolutionary War, Stephen was a representative to the House of Burgesses which Dunmore dissolved. At the second Virginia Convention, he favored the raising of colonial forces for the cause of the American patriots. Commissioned a colonel of the Fourth Virginia Regiment about the beginning of 1776, he served in the campaign to oust Dunmore from Virginia.

When his unit was transferred to the regular Continental Army in February 1776, Stephen maintained command and was promoted to brigadier general. For his service in the Battle of Trenton in 1777, he was advanced to major general.

In the Battle of Germantown near Philadelphia, he was accused of drunkenness and conduct improper for an officer. Although he denied the charges, Stephen was relieved of his command and dismissed from service on November 20, 1777.

Stephen returned to his Berkeley County estate and held various local offices while maintaining his interest in business. After playing an important role in the incorporation of Martinsburg in 1778, he became one of the leading Virginia supporters of the new United States Constitution. Adam Stephen died in July 1791.

Chapter 12 FRONTIER POLICIES, 1783–1796

Official Policy

During the American Revolutionary War and with the conclusion of peace, resolution of the Indian problem in the East first passed to the Confederation government and then to George Washington as President of the new national government. A problem which was once considered local had now become national in scope. By treaties with the Indians, by the development of a national land policy, and by diplomatic negotiations with the British, the individual white settlers had won lands at the expense of the Indians.

Articles of Confederation. During the Articles of Confederation (1781–89) the government for the colonies and for the new states experienced some successes and some failures in dealing with the Indians and the trans-Allegheny lands. Between the years 1784 and 1786 the Congress concluded a series of three treaties (Treaty of Fort Stanwix, Treaty of Fort McIntosh, and Treaty of Fort Finney) whereby it hoped that the new western land was permanently and equitably divided between the Indians and the American settlers.

In the first treaty, the Six Nations and the Delawares and Shawnees were apportioned land divisions. In the second treaty, the Wyandots, Delawares, Chippewas, and Ottawas were given specified areas. In the third treaty, a boundary line between the lands of the Shawnees and the American settlers was drawn. The treaties dealt with land boundaries and not, however, with establishing a long-range peace or stopping western advance. The land allocations to the Indians were much too small to permit the tribes to follow their old conservation policies of alternating, over large areas, their hunting and trapping activities.

National Land Policy. The Confederation government was also responsible for identifying how land was to be organized and put into the possession of Americans. First, it secured agreement that the western lands belonged to all the states rather than to a few, such as Virginia. In the Ordinance of 1785 Congress determined the method of survey and sale of western land.

In the Ordinance of 1787 the Congress provided for the creation of a specified number of new states out of the western territory, guaranteed civil and religious liberty to the settlers and underwrote the opportunity of Americans to education. It also declared that slavery and involuntary servitude should not exist in federal territory.

The British and the Frontier Posts

In the final 1783 treaty the Revolutionary War government also secured agreement that the British would evacuate the frontier posts. The American government also conceded that the British would encounter no trouble in securing payment of debts owed them by Americans. Since the Confederation government could not prevent the states from creating difficulty in the matter of collecting payment, the English refused to evacuate the frontier posts in the Northwest. From these frontier posts the English encouraged the Indians as well as the earlier French and Spanish settlers to do everything possible to disrupt the western advance of the Americans.

Washington's Administration

When George Washington became President of the new national government, he devoted a good part of his two terms to solving the western problem. He felt that, if he could not satisfy western demands, the new nation might be unable to hold together. As commander-in-chief of the armed forces, he sought military victories in the West. The early military efforts were never truly decisive. In the beginning they were total failures because of undisciplined troops, poor leadership, and inadequate supplies.

George Washington in His More Mature Years *(From the collections of the Library of Congress. Photo courtesy of West Virginia University Library)*

In 1790 General Josiah Harmar was defeated by the Indians at the headwaters of the Maumee River, although the general was able to destroy a few dwellings and crops along the Maumee Valley. In 1791 Washington doubled the number of troops he had provided Harmar and entrusted the command to General Arthur St. Clair. St. Clair, leading a force of about 3,000 men, experienced a loss of about one-third of his troops, either dead or wounded, when he met the Indians along the upper Wabash River. His army was routed.

In 1794 General Anthony Wayne, in the Battle of Fallen Timbers, finally achieved success. Taking a lesson from the earlier generals who had not properly trained the men, he spent two years in drilling and teaching the arts of forest warfare as well as in building forts as adequate supply bases. With 1,000 regular soldiers and 1,600 mounted militiamen from the Kentucky area, he defeated the Indians in the very sight of Fort Miami (near modern-day Toledo) which was being held by the British.

Jay Treaty, Pinckney Treaty, and Treaty of Greenville — 1794–1795. Now that Washington had finally secured a general to produce the necessary victory, he was able to achieve through diplomatic efforts a lasting peace involving both the English and the Indians. By Jay's Treaty the English agreed to surrender all their frontier posts. By the Treaty of Greenville the Indians, who had been abandoned by the English, agreed to surrender most of the present state of Ohio. This really was a cession much like the earlier treaty agreements, 1784–1786. This represented the removal of the Indian menace in the Ohio River area and part of Indiana. In the Pinckney Treaty with Spain, Washington secured navigation rights to the Mississippi River. By satisfying demands of the frontiersmen, Washington was able to hold all sections of the nation together and secure American jurisdiction over approximately half of the American continent.

Frontier Heroes

The winning of the West was not accomplished merely by treaties between nations. The West had to be secured, in the final analysis, by individual actions of men and women. Some of these performances were of heroic proportions, and others were portrayals in greed and cruelty. But taken together, the ordinary men and women on the frontier gave the necessary meaning and substance to the western policies formulated in the nation's capital.

The American frontier hero will forever remain Daniel Boone. Although other men did more to win the West, Boone captured the imagination both in the United States and abroad. He became the legendary frontiersman in constant search of new lands who in his settlements further enabled the United States to expand its boundary lines.

Daniel Boone in Western Virginia. Born of Quaker parents in 1734 near Reading, Pennsylvania, Boone lived for a time in that state, in the Shenandoah Valley of Virginia, in North Carolina, and in Kentucky before residing in western Virginia. He was well acquainted with western Virginians, however, because he had served as a teamster and blacksmith in the Braddock campaign.

One of his greatest feats was blazing the Wilderness Road by way of the Cumberland Gap for the North Carolinians moving to Kentucky. In the fall of 1788 he quit his Kentucky lands because of dispute over title and moved to Point Pleasant in western Virginia. He later moved up the Kanawha River near the site of Malden. During part of his residency in the present state of West Virginia, he served as lieutenant colonel of Kanawha County, and in 1791 he was chosen the county's legislative delegate to the legislature of Virginia.

Shortly before 1800 he moved west to Missouri, where he made his home. Of his total lifetime of 86 years Boone spent about a decade in western Virginia, perhaps enjoying most his hunting of wildlife in the Kanawha Valley. We shall read more about Daniel Boone.

Simon Kenton, Scout and Ranger The fame of this pioneer of Kentucky, Virginia, and Ohio is second only to that of Boone. Kenton, with two companions, spent the winter of 1772 in camp on Elk River near Charleston. They were the first white men to live there. *(After a painting by L. W. Morgan)*

Simon Kenton. One of Boone's frontier companions was Simon Kenton, another legendary woodsman. Kenton, who had learned the art of scouting from Boone, saw service in Dunmore's War and in Clark's expedition to Kaskaskia. When Boone left Kentucky for western Virginia, Kenton was participating in the hunts along the Ohio, the Great Kanawha, and the Little Kanawha rivers. Kenton, like Boone, moved farther west when settlements began to destroy the wilderness. At different times Kenton lived in Kentucky, Ohio, and Illinois.

Frontier Heroines

Whereas the men who were captured by the Indians were often scalped and put to death, often the women were imprisoned by the Indian tribes and forced into menial labor. They witnessed the murders of their husbands and children. A few lived through their captivity to make another life, and a smaller number bested the Indian in mortal combat.

Mary Lewis Kinnan. None of the pioneer women faced greater hardship than Mary Lewis Kinnan. From 1787 to 1791 Mary Kinnan, her husband Joseph, and their daughter lived in peace in a log cabin at the mouth of the Elkwater on the west side of Tygart Valley River in Randolph County. When the Shawnees attacked the Kinnan homestead, they murdered Joseph Kinnan and the daughter. Mary Kinnan was taken away with the Indians. She was first imprisoned in an Indian village on the Maumee River and later made a servant of a Delaware squaw near Detroit.

Tormented by being shown her daughter's scalp, at times she lost hope. But after three and a half years she escaped. She cared not to return to western Virginia but went to live among friends and relatives in New Jersey, the area in which she had been born and reared. She later recounted her adventures in a pamphlet in Elizabethtown, New Jersey, in 1795.

Margaret Hanley Pauley. Mr. and Mrs. John Pauley, with their children and other relatives, were attacked by Indians near the mouth of East River in 1779 on their way from the Greenbrier section to Kentucky. Mrs. Pauley and her sister-in-law were taken into captivity, but the men and the children in the party were killed.

Monument to the Pioneer Mothers (at Wheeling)

For seven years Mrs. Pauley was held by the Indians. Luckier than Mary Kinnan, she was adopted by Chief White Bark and was treated as a member of the family. She was even given an Indian name, "Yellow Gold." Later she was ransomed by her family in Greenbrier, and she and the son born to her shortly after her Indian captivity were permitted to return home. Her route home was long and arduous as she and eight other ransomed captives traveled through the wilderness by way of Pittsburgh to the Greenbrier area.

Mrs. John Bozarth. Mrs. John Bozarth, living near the site of the present town of Core in Monongalia County, was called upon to defend her log cabin against an Indian attack in April 1779. Unable to get her children into the house, Mrs. Bozarth was forced to watch Indians murder them in the front yard. As the Indians proceeded to enter her home, she was able to prevent her own murder by slaying three Indians with an ax.

Mrs. Andrew Davidson. In 1791 Mrs. Andrew Davidson and her children were captured at their home at the head of East River, near the site of the present town of Bluefield, while her husband was away on a visit to see his father. On the way to Indian villages in Ohio, Mrs. Davidson gave birth to a child whom the Indians drowned the next day. The other Davidson children were shot. Mrs. Davidson was held in captivity until after Wayne's victory at Fallen Timbers.

Isabella Stockton. During the French and Indian War Isabella Stockton was captured by Indian raiders. She was later sold by the Indians to a wealthy Canadian trader who brought her up as his daughter in Montreal. Falling in love with a Frenchman, Jean Baptiste Plata, she and her fiancé returned to western Virginia to seek her father's permission to marry. When the family objected, the two planned an elopement. In their attempt, Plata was killed. As a result of the misadventure Isabella remained an invalid in her father's house for the next ten years. Later Isabella married William McCleery, and they moved from the William Stockton home in Berkeley County to Morgantown.

Frontier Families in Fighting Units

The Morgans. The present state of West Virginia was home to entire families of Indian fighters and hunters. Prominent among them were the Morgans, the Poes, and the Zanes, all of whom came

Home of Zackquill Morgan, Son of Morgan Morgan and Founder of Morgantown. This house stood on University Avenue in Morgantown. *(Photo from "The West Virginia Review")*

originally from northwestern Virginia, an area often infiltrated by Indian raiders.

David Morgan was the son of Morgan Morgan, officially recognized as the first settler in West Virginia. David was a noted Indian fighter. Finding two Indians looting his home near present Fairmont in 1799, Morgan took on both single-handedly, shooting one and knifing the other. Four of his children also became Indian fighters and served in the American Revolutionary War.

Two nephews of David Morgan became scouts and Indian fighters. One, Levi Morgan, was said to have killed almost one hundred Indians in his swift attacks. Most of his daring acts occurred in Wetzel County, where he and his brothers had constructed a fort on the Ohio River.

The Poes. Andrew and Adam Poe were Indian fighters in western Virginia. The Poes had located their home near Wellsburg in 1744. In 1781 Andrew scouted two Indians resting on the Ohio River bank near present New Cumberland. One was a huge fellow named Big Foot. Andrew attempted to shoot him, but the gun "flashed" too soon. Both Indians sprang at Andrew, and he jumped Big Foot. The smaller Indian tried to scalp Andrew, but Andrew grabbed a gun and shot him.

Big Foot and Andrew, struggling, slid into deep water, and both turned toward the shore. At that moment Adam Poe and a friend came along the river bank. Mistaking Andrew for an Indian, they shot him, wounding him in the shoulder. Realizing their mistake, they then shot Big Foot, who pushed himself back into deep water and was drowned.

chapter twelve / frontier policies, 1783–1796

Betty Zane Betty is preparing to carry powder back to Fort Henry during the siege of 1782. *(From an early painting. Reproduction courtesy of Jim Comstock)*

The Zanes. Under the leadership of William Zane, the Zane family, of Danish origin, first settled in Philadelphia. Breaking their religious ties with the Society of Friends, they moved into the South Branch Valley. During the years 1769 to 1772 Ebenezer, Jonathan, and Silas moved to Wheeling. As already noted, in the second siege of Fort Henry, September 1782, Ebenezer was in charge of the outpost, Silas was acting commander of the fort, and Elizabeth bravely brought gunpowder from the outpost to the fort. Two other brothers, Jonathan and Andrew, were also important frontier fighters. Andrew was killed by the Indians, and another brother, Isaac, at the age of nine was captured. Isaac lived as an Indian and desired to remain with the tribe in which he had grown up. He married an Indian maiden, sister of a chieftain, and had eight children. Ebenezer Zane's wife was a sister of Major Samuel McCulloch, who made the great leap.

Ebenezer Zane was given the contract in 1796 to construct a post road from Wheeling, Virginia, to Maysville, Kentucky, across southeastern Ohio. He had to locate the safest crossings of the Muskingum and Scioto rivers. Later at these river crossings the towns of Zanesville, Lancaster, and Chillicothe developed.

The Vengeance Seekers

Some frontiersmen had happy relationships with the Indians, married into Indian families, and adopted the Indian way of life.

But many white settlers had bitter experiences with Indians and avoided as best they could any contact with the original holders of the land. Others with cunning and cruelty sought out their adversaries as prizes.

Jesse Hughes. Another soldier in Dunmore's War and a resident near present Jane Lew in Lewis County was Jesse Hughes, master scout. With eyes described as like those of a mountain panther or a rattlesnake, Jesse was reported to be able to see at night as well as a wild animal, to outrun any Indian prowling in the forest, and to enjoy the killing of any Indian, young or old. For each Indian scalped, he notched his gun barrel. Next to Indian killing, Jesse excelled in snake kills.

Hughes massacred the Indians at Bulltown, an Indian village located on the Little Kanawha River in Braxton County. Those killed were a friendly tribe of Delawares under command of Captain Bull. For the killing Hughes made the feeble excuse that the Indians had murdered the Stroud family, but this murder had been committed not by the innocent Delawares but by Shawnees.

An old story of Jesse's use of his wits in the sounds of the forest concerns a time of trouble at a settlement near Clarksburg. Fearful of attack, the pioneers had gathered inside their fort. Jesse saw a boy fixing his gun and preparing to leave the stockade. Jesse questioned the boy, who explained that he was going to shoot a turkey he heard gobbling over the hill. Jesse convinced him that Jesse, himself, should go after the turkey. Secretly moving up the hill, Jesse found an Indian imitating turkey calls. Hughes shot him and presented the Indian's scalp to the boy.

Jesse later departed for Vincennes, now in Indiana; resided in eastern Kentucky for a short time; and then moved on to Jackson County in present West Virginia, where he spent the remainder of his days. He died in 1829.

Lewis Wetzel. Lewis Wetzel came from a family of Indian fighters who traced their origin to ancestors in the Netherlands, Switzerland, and Pennsylvania. The family settled near Wheeling in western Virginia. In 1777 Lewis and his brother Jacob were captured by Indians but managed to escape. Another of the five brothers was killed by Indians.

Wetzel prepared himself for border warfare as an athlete would prepare himself for a contest. He studied woodcraft, became an expert marksman, and learned to load his rifle while running. Al-

Anne Bailey, Heroine of the Frontier *(From the Kanawha County Public Library Picture Collection, Charleston)*

though he never enlisted in the regular militia, he followed the Indian movements on the frontier with the precision of an intelligence officer.

Twice he was criticized by his fellow frontiersmen, once for murdering an old Indian who had secretly released Lewis from captivity by the Indians, and once for unnecessarily killing a prominent Indian at Fort Harmar in 1789. This killing led to Indian reprisals upon nearby villages.

A conspicuous figure on the frontier, with his long black hair, his ears slit and decorated with silk tassels, Wetzel often served as a fiddler at country dances. He later moved to New Orleans, and perhaps lived for a time in Missouri and Arkansas and near Natchez, Mississippi.

Anne Bailey. For her daring adventures against the Indians, Anne Bailey became known as "Mad Anne Bailey." She was born Anne Hennis. The Hennis family, natives of Liverpool, England, came to America in 1761. Anne Hennis married Richard Trotter, who served in Braddock's expedition and at the Battle of Point Pleasant. He was killed in the latter battle. Forsaking the role of a woman and a widow, Anne adopted male costume and hunted for Indians. Not only did she become an excellent shot, but she also excelled as a horsewoman. She once claimed to have hit two Indians with one bullet. She later married John Bailey, a border leader and also a scout. She was so clever and so successful that the Indians were convinced that good spirits protected her.

In 1791 Fort Lee was besieged by Indians. The supply of ammunition ran low, and Anne volunteered to ride the hundred miles through dense forest to Lewisburg for powder. She returned safely with her burden.

When scouts were no longer needed, Anne Bailey became a mail and parcel carrier and is said even to have delivered a flock of geese over the road.

After her second husband's death she lived with her son. She died in Ohio in 1825. But her body was removed to a grave in the Tu-Endie-Wei Park at Point Pleasant.

The hardships and griefs of many early settlers on western Virginia's frontier reflect the courage, the ingenuity, and the stamina expended in opening up the land to provide suitable dwelling places.

Famed Trailblazer

Daniel Boone, Frontier Scout

Daniel Boone was born at Oley in the Schuylkill Valley of eastern Pennsylvania on November 2, 1734. He was the son of Quakers, Squire and Sarah (Morgan) Boone. As a boy he was very fond of hunting, and he had ample opportunity to practice all the frontier skills after his family moved to North Carolina, to a remote area called Buffalo Lick, in 1750.

Daniel Boone *(After a painting by Chappel. Photo courtesy of West Virginia Department of Commerce)*

During General Braddock's march to Fort Duquesne in 1755, Boone accompanied a North Carolina contingent attached to the British regular army. On the expedition he met a hunter who told him stories of the Kentucky wilderness. Boone desired to see the land for himself, but his journeys into the area were postponed because of his marriage to Rebecca Bryan in 1756. However, he did travel to back-country areas in the South. In 1765, following a visit to Florida, he resolved to settle in that territory, but his wife disapproved, and the project was given up.

In the fall of 1767 Boone and several companions ventured into the Kentucky wilderness. They returned east the next spring. He and a party of five others went back to Kentucky in 1769 and lengthened their visit into the spring of 1771. Feeling the area was ready for settlement, Boone convinced a land company to locate a group of settlers in Kentucky under his leadership. When the group arrived in April 1775, its members erected a fort called Boonesborough.

In the early fall, Boone returned to North Carolina to bring his family and a group of potential settlers to the new lands. He blazed the Wilderness Road by way of Cumberland Gap in order to move these North Carolinians into Kentucky.

When Kentucky was organized as a Virginia county in 1776, Boone was made a captain of militia. He was captured by Shawnee Indians in February 1778 but escaped in June and fought to defend Boonesborough in September. His difficulty in producing solid claim to his land there led to his moving to Boone's Station.

When Kentucky was divided into three counties, Boone was appointed a lieutenant colonel for one county, Fayette, and was chosen delegate to the legislature. After serving his area in various ways, however, he lost his lands because his claims were not properly registered. In the fall of 1788 he left Kentucky, moving to Point Pleasant in present West Virginia.

While at Point Pleasant, Boone became active in explorations up the Kanawha River. As population in the area grew, a new county of Kanawha was created. It included the towns of Fort Lee (the site of the future city of Charleston) and Point Pleasant. Boone eventually established residence in the Fort Lee vicinity and was elected a delegate to the Virginia legislature in 1791. In the same year he was named a lieutenant colonel of militia for Kanawha County.

The area became too well peopled for Boone, and he decided to move farther west. Some time in the late 1790's he reached Femme Osage Creek, Missouri, where he obtained land and lived near his son. He died on September 26, 1820 and was buried in Frankfort, Kentucky.

Part Two

**From
Nationalism
To
Statehood**

unit four | On the Virginia Frontier

Chapter 13   PIONEER HOME LIFE

In the pioneers' lives the problems of providing shelter and food and clothing for the family were first considerations. But maintaining health, caring for the sick, law and order, and recreation were necessarily of great concern also. A frontier family's success in meeting the demands of the rough country was determined by the resources they found in the forests, by their own skills, and by their circumstances of poverty or wealth.

Until the Civil War, life in western Virginia was an experience of the poor contending with their hardships or occasionally of the wealthy. Life was a story, too, of patriotism and devotion to the new country.

Early Buildings

Cabins. For pioneers, shelter might be provided in a hollow tree (as we have learned), or a cabin, a fort, a cottage, or rarely a mansion. Certainly on the distant frontier, a cabin located near a spring or a river was the normal abode. Although many frontiersmen in the early days were from the British Isles, the cabins they called home were often of Swedish or Finnish style. Most cabins had only one room, which combined kitchen, dining room, living room, bedroom, and in winter a simple workshop. A fireplace at one end served for cooking and heating and, to some extent, for lighting the cabin.

Interior of a Pioneer Home Note the gun on the wall with the powder horn below. Note the cooking pot, the water bucket and the gourd dipper hanging above, the spinning wheel, and on the wall the flax or wool yarn to be woven. *(From a sketch by J. H. Diss Debar)*

The log walls of the cabin were perhaps fifteen to twenty feet long and ten to twelve feet high. The logs were held together by wooden pegs because nails were very difficult to get and very expensive.

The cracks between the logs were filled with stones and pieces of wood and daubed with mortar. The roof was sometimes covered with brush or was shingled with clapboards, which were split pieces of oak, cedar, or cypress. The floor was often of earth, or sometimes the ground was covered with puncheons, which were split logs, with the smooth side up.

The windows seldom had glass; they were ordinarily covered with oiled paper. Often the windows were not much more than holes from which to shoot Indians. The cabins were unpainted, although the inside might occasionally be whitewashed with a mixture of lime.

Blockhouse. The blockhouse, or fort, was generally an oversized cabin of two stories, with the second story extending beyond the first. The spaces between the planks in the floor of the second story were not tightly closed. Rifles could be fired through the cracks if intruders reached the outside wall or succeeded in entering the first story, or boiling water could be poured on those below. The blockhouse might be surrounded by a log fence, or palisade, which would convert it into a major fort.

A Type of Blockhouse (From a sketch by H. L. Thompson)

Cottages. Cottages, copied from those in England, were often found nearer the east. Frequently they were begun as two-story dwellings made of hewn logs which were both squared and notched. Later, they could be enlarged because of an increase in the family and in wealth. A cellar might be dug, and a wing constructed to convert the original house into an L shape. Porches might be attached on the front and side, and a kitchen constructed separate from the original structure or as a lean-to against it.

Stockade Defense The log house is surrounded by a heavy wall of logs set on end. Notice the passage between the parts of the house. There were also openings in the wall for rifle fire. *(From a sketch by H. L. Thompson)*

chapter thirteen / pioneer home life

Blennerhassett Mansion Harman Blennerhassett built his mansion on an island in the Ohio River near Parkersburg in the year 1800. *(West Virginia Department of Commerce Photo)*

If circumstances were favorable, as they were for many settlers who lived on the fertile lands of the lower South Branch River or in the Eastern Panhandle counties, other buildings might be constructed near the main house. Chicken houses, barns, and even cottages for slaves could make an imposing frontier establishment.

A Mansion. On an island in the Ohio River there arose in 1798 one of the finest mansions in western Virginia if not the greatest house west of the Appalachians. It was built by Harman Blennerhassett, an Irishman and European traveler, for his bride, Margaret. The house was in the style and splendor of a "Persian pavillion." The main unit of the mansion was two stories high and sixty feet square. Two wings were connected to the main unit by semicircular verandas covered with myrtle vines. The grounds on the island were laid out with grassy lawns, walks, and shrubbery bearing flowers and fruit. Only a pioneer of great wealth could afford such an establishment.

In the east, however, many fine homes were built in the 1770's.

Home Furnishings. For the average pioneer, furniture included a few stools, possibly some long benches and crude tables, and beds were probably mattresses of leaves, corn husks, or straw, laid on the floor. Homemade candles or pine knots furnished light.

Bed covers consisted of animal skins (usually buffalo and bear skins) and homemade quilts.

Kitchen utensils were in short supply. Many "dishes" were made of wood and were shaped by the pioneer himself. A wooden plate was called a trencher. A cup was called a noggin.* Pioneer Joseph Doddridge, about whom we shall read later, recorded that bowls and drinking cups were sometimes simply hollowed gourds or the hard shells of squashes.

A family of moderate means might have dishes and spoons of pewter which had been made by the local blacksmith, or the family might have utensils of iron brought from the east. Silverware was not an accustomed article of pioneer life.

A spinning wheel and a loom for weaving cloth were a necessity, for the women commonly made clothing for all the members of the family.

On Blennerhassett Island and in comparable homes of the rich in the east, the furnishings were of the finest. Walls were hung with costly pictures, and furniture was imported from Paris and London. Mirrors, carpets, curtains, and quantities of large silver pieces adorned the many rooms. Foreign artists painted the ceilings of mansions. A large library might fill one wing of the house, and scientific apparatus another wing. Musical instruments, harps, harpsichords, and spinets, were an important part of the furnishings.

Food

Joseph Doddridge recalled that the pioneer dinner in western Virginia was mainly "hog and hominy." and that supper fare was often "mush and milk." Very often milk was lacking, and sweetened water was poured on the mush. Meat was not hard to obtain, for the forests abounded in deer, elk, bear, squirrel, rabbit, and other game. The rare items in winter were vegetables and fruit.

In summer most pioneers had small gardens of corn, pumpkins, squash, beans, and potatoes, and a few possessed fruit trees. Wild berries were a help. Yet the staple foods of the frontier were corn bread, hominy, and pork.

The wealthier pioneers fared better in diet. As early as 1774 George Washington directed the planting of an apple orchard in Berkeley County, and in 1786 Jacob Nessly in Hancock County planted fifty acres of apple and peach trees on lands bordering the Ohio River. For the well-to-do, vegetable gardens tended by servants were an essential part of the plantations.

chapter thirteen / pioneer home life

A Bear Trap Built of Logs Bears were important to the first settlers. The animals furnished meat and also thick fur for clothing and for bed and floor coverings. *(From a sketch by J. H. Diss Debar)*

Tobacco was widely used, either smoked or chewed. The richer members of society developed "taking a pinch of snuff" into an art. Hard liquor was consumed in large amounts.

Not only was whiskey, which was distilled from corn, important for the pioneer's personal use, it was also significant in trade with the west.

In 1795 the federal government placed a tax on whiskey. Westerners were outraged, and disorders broke out. To restore peace President George Washington had to send an army of more than twelve thousand militiamen against a few farmers in Pennsylvania. Despite the victory in that state, federal revenue officers who attempted to collect the whiskey tax were under frequent attack in western Virginia. In Berkeley County a small celebration was staged to honor the Pennsylvania rebels in their contest with the federal officers.

Clothing

The outer garb of a frontiersman consisted of a hunting shirt, breeches, coonskin cap, and moccasins. In the early days moccasins and hunting shirts were generally made from deerskin, and, in time, the hides of animals were tanned, and tanned leather boots were made. These were much more practical than the soft moccasins. Hunting shirts were made of linsey-woolsey and were often worn over leather underclothes. Linsey-woolsey was woven of linen threads and wool threads.

Linsey-woolsey was the common material for women's and girls' dresses. Headwear for women and girls was the cloth sunbonnet tied under the chin.

The few slaves on the frontier were scantily clothed in summer, the males sometimes wearing only breeches, and the females wearing loose dresses of the coarsest cloth.

But wealthy pioneers were well clothed in Virginia. They imitated the high fashions of England. Men had long frock coats of imported broadcloth, and tight-fitting knee-length breeches made of velvet or silk brocade. Silk stockings and slippers with large buckles completed the costumes. Wives and daughters wore dresses of calico, muslin, silk, and satin. Hoopskirts were the fashion, and high hats to which were attached feathers or plumes. Gloves were worn on every occasion. Fans not only stirred the breezes but also served as signals in the games of love and coquetry. The women wore rings, bracelets, lockets, and other ornaments. Portraits of the Blennerhassetts show their splendid costumes.

Health

Few early Virginia families were blessed with really good health. Epidemics of smallpox, measles, and diphtheria were frequent, and dysentery (particularly common among the military troops) reached every settlement. Rheumatism, arthritis, and tuberculosis were common.

Frontier medicines were usually made from herbs gathered in the woods. Joseph Doddridge recalled a favorite remedy for a rattlesnake or copperhead bite: A large quantity of chestnut leaves was boiled in a pot; the area of the bite was wrapped in a piece of chestnut bark; and the fluid from the boiled leaves poured over it. Boiled leaves were later bound to the wound. Occasionally a frontier doctor sucked the poison from the wound, and sometimes he made deep cuts into the flesh, filling them with salt and gunpowder.

Doctors trained in medical schools were virtually unknown. There were only two medical schools in America in the early colonial period, one at Philadelphia and the other at New York. Men who expected to practice medicine gained their training while serving as apprentices to the older doctors. Such training included a little reading in medical books and the gathering of different kinds of herbs for medicine.

Helpful Neighbors   *(Photo courtesy of West Virginia University Library)*

The wealthy and sometimes the poor who could travel to the warm springs might find relief from pain there. In 1776 the Virginia legislature established Warm Springs, also called Bath. Residents at the springs were encouraged to build conveniently located houses to accommodate those who came seeking recovery of their health. George Washington was a firm believer in the recuperative powers of the waters of the springs and perhaps was one of those most responsible for establishing health resorts.

Social Affairs

Because of the enormous amount of work to be done at the frontier home, recreation often took the form of sharing the labor. If a family needed their grounds cleared of trees or logs or were constructing a house, they invited their neighbors to help them. Clearing the woods, house raisings, log rollings, corn huskings, hog killings brought men, women, and children together socially and at the same time accomplished frontier tasks beyond the power of a single individual. Payment to the friends was made by furnishing dinner for them and standing ready to return the favor when a neighbor had similar needs.

Very special days were wedding days, and they were frequent. Pioneers married young. Frontiersmen were likely to remarry after the deaths of their wives.

Doddridge recounts the marriage customs in western Virginia. On the morning of the wedding day, the groom and his attendants assembled at the house of his father in order to reach the bride's home by noon, the usual time for the ceremony. The groom's party marched along the road and were subject to tricks along the way. Sometimes the road was mischievously blocked by felled trees or grape vines. Occasionally two young men of the party raced for a prize, a bottle of whiskey, which the winner of the race was compelled to share with all others.

A big wedding dinner was served, and there were fun and laughter and practical jokes. After dinner, the dancing began and generally lasted until early morning. During the dance the bride and the groom were kept separated from each other.

No social activity was more popular than dancing. Banjos, guitars, and fiddles were the common musical instruments. Fiddlers who were particularly good were always in demand.

Law and Order

In a frontier society most of the families were serious-minded, orderly, and law-abiding. There were, however, some who committed crimes. Minor crimes were acting inappropriately on Sunday and swearing. More serious crimes were drunkenness, selling liquor without licenses, and fighting. Major offenses were stealing, murder, and treason. The last was most difficult to prove.

Punishments were made to fit the crimes. Thomas Jefferson, in his *Notes on Virginia*, described some offenses and punishments. If murder was caused by poison, death by poison was decreed. If murder was the result of a duel or if manslaughter was a person's second offense, death by hanging was decreed.

Years of hard labor were common punishments. The number of years varied with the seriousness of the crime: seven years for first-offense manslaughter, six years for counterfeiting money, five years for setting fire to a building, and four years for robbery or burglary. Stealing a horse and breaking into someone else's house brought the offender a sentence of three years at hard labor. If he practiced heresy in religious matters, he was "merely to be pitied but not to be punished."

Blennerhassett Island in 1858 as Seen by George Washington and Other Early Visitors
(Sketch from "The West Virginia Review")

Treason. The wealthy Harman Blennerhassett was the outstanding example of a western Virginian accused of committing the high crime of treason against the United States. In their island home the Blennerhassetts had as their guest Aaron Burr. Burr was the former vice-president of the United States. He had killed the famous American statesman Alexander Hamilton in a duel. Burr had become very unpopular in the country and was believed to be plotting to create a separate country in western America, including sections of United States and Mexico. Burr would have headed this new country.

But westerners were satisfied to remain in the Union, which was meeting their needs. In an extension of the frontier, President Thomas Jefferson had purchased Louisiana in 1803 and had secured additional western territory and control of the Mississippi River all the way to its mouth.

When Blennerhassett learned that he had failed to recognize the patriotism of the people of the West, he fled to Natchez, Mississippi. Then the militia from Wood County looted his mansion and ruined the grounds.

Later, Blennerhassett was arrested and sent to Richmond where Burr was being tried for treason against the United States. Because Burr was found not guilty of treason, Blennerhassett also escaped the charge against him.

Although Blennerhassett tried to restore his island property, his wife would not live there. In a few years fire and floods had completely devastated the mansion. Until their deaths the Blennerhassetts moved from place to place. For a while they lived in Mississippi, then in New York, in Ireland, and in Canada. Following the death of her husband, Mrs. Blennerhassett requested the United States government to restore the island place. She died before the government took any action.

Today Blennerhassett Island is owned by the Du Pont Company, and efforts are being made to restore the property to its former splendor. Although floods in the Ohio River cover a small portion of the island at times, large parts are affected only once in a century. One problem was created by the rise in the normal pool stage of the river when the Belleville Lock and Dam was completed in 1968. The United States Corps of Engineers has reported, however, that no significant part of the island will be under water. The island was approved for inclusion in the National Register of Historic Places September 7, 1972.

Preacher, Physician, Historian

Joseph Doddridge, Frontier Observer

Joseph Doddridge was born at Friend's Cove, near Bedford, Pennsylvania, on October 14, 1769. His family moved to southwestern Pennsylvania when he was four years old, and as a young man, Doddridge settled at present Wellsburg in Brooke County, West Virginia. From his father, Doddridge received a strict and religious childhood education.

With but little formal schooling and after several years of work on his father's farm, Joseph became a circuit preacher in the Methodist Church at the age of eighteen. At the age of nineteen, he traveled across the frontier with the famous preacher Francis Asbury. After his father's death in 1791, he studied a year at Jefferson Academy in Canonsburg, Pennsylvania, and later was ordained a Protestant Episcopal clergyman, the first minister of this church to serve in trans-Allegheny Virginia.

For the remainder of his life Joseph Doddridge rode throughout northwestern Virginia, Pennsylvania, and eastern Ohio, spreading religion throughout the advancing frontier.

About 1795 he married and soon found it necessary to find a means to supplement his minister's income. He studied medicine under the direction of the noted Dr. Benjamin Rush of Philadelphia. This training enabled him to preach the gospel and also to heal the sick on his frontier excursions. He never was in the best of health himself, however, for his frontier travels required him to ride horseback over long distances in all kinds of weather.

Even with his duties as clergyman and physician, Doddridge found time to write. Besides a *Treatise on the Culture of Bees* and a biography entitled *Logan*, he composed his most famous work, *Notes on the Settlement and Indian Wars of the Western Parts of Virginia and Pennsylvania from 1763 to 1783, Inclusive*.

Pioneer House with Stockade   This home with its protecting stockade was built in western Virginia, in the Kanawha Valley, some miles above Charleston by Leonard Morris during the time of the Indian wars, about which (1763–83) Joseph Doddridge wrote. The drawing was made from an old faded picture of this unusual type of home place. *(Drawing by Naomi S. Hosterman from "Pioneers and Their Homes on Upper Kanawha," by Ruth Woods Dayton. Used by permission)*

His own life on the frontier, his habit of observation, his lifelong interest in the history being made around him, and his custom of recording the manners and events of his day prepared him well to write his book. He portrayed characters, related incidents, and recited the political history of the area. Doddridge noted the habits of the Indians, changes in the weather, and varieties of birds, animals, and serpents.

Doddridge died on November 9, 1826 at his Brooke County home.

Doddridge's work, according to Theodore Roosevelt's *Winning of the West*, was a basic contribution to records of the American frontier. It also won for its author a place in the larger history of the United States.

Chapter 14 RELIGION AND THE THREE R'S

Until the outbreak of the Civil War, religious worship and education developed together in western Virginia. Providing churches and schools first required a sufficiently large population to support them, and the necessary public support for these institutions came only after the pioneers had completed their homes, cleared their lands, and begun a settled way of life.

The ministers of religion and the schoolmasters cooperated with one another. Often the same building served as church and schoolhouse. Frequently the minister was also the schoolteacher. The few early colleges and academies originated with church support. Churches and schools usually appeared together in an area of the state or in the same town.

Early church and school buildings were rough log cabins furnished with hard wooden benches. Children of all ages were taught in one room by one teacher. The instructor aimed to teach the pupils to read the Bible, to learn to write a letter, and to add, subtract, and multiply. In the early days, teaching was considered a man's work, and, above all else, the schoolmaster was expected to maintain stern discipline.

Hard frontier life did not encourage interest in religious creeds and also produced little enthusiasm for classical education. Pioneer living called for a democratic religion and a practical education that

Old Rehoboth Church
This log church was one of the cradles of the Methodist Church in western Virginia. It was built near the present site of Union in Monroe County in 1786, a year before the Constitution of the United States was written. The weight poles on the roof held the boards in place. *(Photo courtesy of Ross B. Johnston)*

was of reasonably short duration. For these reasons, established religion, such as the Anglican faith, failed to gain many adherents on the frontier, just as the University of Virginia at first failed to attract large numbers of students from west of the Allegheny Mountains.

Protestant Episcopal Church

In England the established church was the Anglican Communion, and it was also known as the Church of England. After the colonies separated from England and established a new nation in 1789, the Anglicans in America adopted the name of the Protestant Episcopal Church. In England the government supported this church and placed restrictions on all other churches. The same conditions held true in Virginia while it was a British colony. The English officials and most of the wealthy persons in America were Episcopalians.

In 1740 Morgan Morgan, an influential official whom we have already met, built Morgan's Chapel, an Episcopal church, one of the first churches west of the Blue Ridge Mountains. In 1765 an Episcopal church was established at Shepherdstown. Most early Episcopal churches in present West Virginia were in the Eastern Panhandle, just as were the estates of most of the high-ranking officers of the American Revolutionary War. George Washington and most other Virginians who became President of the United States were Episcopalians. Thomas Jefferson, who did not belong to any church, was the famous exception.

The Episcopal Church had certain advantages of membership for early settlers, but it gradually lost its special privileges. In order to encourage western settlement, Virginia ruled that western pioneers who were not Episcopalians need not pay taxes to that church.

In 1785, through the efforts of Thomas Jefferson, the Virginia Assembly separated church and state, and an earlier statute in Virginia had permitted the public to support the church of their choice. These actions meant that the Episcopal Church was no longer entitled to support from taxes and that religious liberty was available to all citizens. The church immediately declined in membership in the east, and it gained few members west of the mountains.

By 1792 an Episcopal congregation was established at Wellsburg under the direction of the Reverend Joseph Doddridge. Morgantown and Clarksburg also had Episcopal churches.

Yet few Episcopalian ministers were ordered across the mountains, and because this church insisted on a well-educated ministry, a frontiersman could hardly receive the "call for preaching" and minister to the people of that faith. By 1842 the Episcopal Church reported only six Episcopal clergymen in western Virginia. By 1853 there were only thirteen clergymen and 636 communicants of the faith in the west.

Presbyterian Church

Another religious denomination which placed great emphasis upon education and a trained ministry was the Presbyterian Church. The Scotch-Irish were the traditional members of this church, a people who emphasized hard work and simple living as important in finding favor with God. In the early days the Presbyterians disapproved of most amusements, including dancing and card playing.

Presbyterians may well have founded the first church in present West Virginia in 1719. This was the Potomoke Church, near Shepherdstown. On Tuscarora Creek in Berkeley County, a Presbyterian church was erected by the year 1750. Here the Scotch-Irish brought their guns and hung them on pegs in the walls while they sang and prayed. By the 1790's almost every village in the Eastern Panhandle had a Presbyterian church because of the work of the visiting ministers from Presbyterian centers in Maryland and Virginia.

Presbyterians may also have built the first church across the mountains, at Lewisburg in Greenbrier County. This church was replaced by the Old Stone Church in 1796.

chapter fourteen / religion and the three r's

Old Stone Church in Lewisburg Old Stone Church is the oldest Protestant church unrestored and in continuous use west of the Alleghenies. It was built in 1796, when George Washington was President of the United States. During the Civil War the church served as an emergency hospital. *(Photo courtesy of Rev. Robert A. Pfrangle)*

Quakers

Although Episcopalians and Presbyterians demanded special training for ministers, Quakers questioned the need for any minister. They looked upon their fellowmen as "Friends," because in the sight of God all men were equal. Therefore, they could depend on a man's conscience for direction in manners and morals rather than upon preachers. As no man was entitled to more respect than any other man, the Quakers refused to follow the custom of taking their hats off to anyone, including the king and the governor.

Thrift and hard work were fundamental principles of Quaker life. Simplicity was followed in dress and in homes as it was in worship. Opposed to violence, Quakers disapproved of war and refused to pay taxes for war. But they were willing to give their money for the relief of human suffering.

Most Quakers came to western Virginia from Pennsylvania. Earlier the Quakers had come primarily from England and Wales.

In 1734 the Quakers opened a meetinghouse at Hopewell on Opequon Creek. Quakers in Berkeley County erected a church at Arden by 1781.

German Religious Sects

Although the majority of early German settlers belonged to the Lutheran Church and the Reformed Church, there were groups of Germans who formed small religious communities. Such groups in western Virginia were the Mennonites, the Moravians, the Dunkards, and the Seventh Day Baptists. Many of these people, like the Quakers, refused to take oaths or bear arms. In matters of education, some also shared the Quaker belief that girls as well as boys were entitled to schooling.

In western Virginia the Dunkards founded Dunkard Bottom on the Cheat River and made settlements in the South Branch Valley. Along the South Branch and Patterson's Creek, Moravian missionaries held services. Seventh Day Baptists, most of whom came from Shrewsbury, New Jersey, located in the north central section of the state in Harrison, Doddridge, and Ritchie counties. At New Salem they built a church in 1792.

Each of the German sects had unique beliefs and special talents. The Seventh Day Baptists set aside Saturday rather than Sunday as their day of religious observance. In the early Moravian settlements, all settlers shared the land and its products. The Mennonites were highly skilled weavers, and the Moravians were known especially for their musical talents. Many of the Germans were skilled blacksmiths and wagon makers.

These religious sects dressed in plain clothes, and some have continued these costumes to the present day. The men wore broad-brimmed hats, the women wore bonnets, and the children for the most part were dressed exactly like the adults. Because many worshiped in their own homes, they differed from the German Lutherans or members of the German Reformed Church who worshiped in churches.

Although the members of the German Reformed Church followed the teachings of John Calvin and the Lutherans followed the teachings of Martin Luther, the two church groups were remarkably similar. They often used the same church building and shared the same traveling clergyman. At first most sermons in the Lutheran Church were delivered in German, and the sermons in the German Reformed Church were delivered in English. But as time passed, even this

A Rural Church This simple West Virginia church might have copied the lines of earlier places of worship west of the mountains. (Arnout Hyde, Jr., Photo, West Virginia Department of Natural Resources)

difference disappeared because later generations understood only the English language.

In contrast to the smaller German religious bodies in America, the Lutherans made use of solemn ceremonies in their church services. They also emphasized church music. In the early period, most Lutheran churches were in the Eastern Panhandle, and Lutherans did little missionary work beyond the Alleghenies.

Lutheran churches at Shepherdstown in Jefferson County and at Martinsburg in Berkeley County were probably established by 1765, followed by the Propst Church in Pendleton County in 1769.

Catholics

For many years Catholics were forbidden in the Virginia Colony. Although a few entered the colony, most located in nearby Pennsylvania and Maryland. Some priests visited the faithful in Virginia, but it is said that they did so only by night and that they slept beside their horses so that they might speed away at the slightest warning. The archbishop of Baltimore encouraged priests in Pennsylvania to visit the small Catholic group at Wheeling, and on occasion they crossed the mountains to administer the sacraments there.

The earliest record of a Catholic pastor's appointment at Wheeling was in the year 1829. On the eve of the Civil War, the Catholic population was sufficient for the Diocese of Wheeling to be formed from the Diocese of Richmond. In recognition of the change, the bishop of Richmond was made the first bishop of Wheeling.

Christians (Disciples of Christ)

A concern for Christian unity expressed by Barton W. Stone in 1804 was endorsed by Thomas Campbell and his son, Alexander, in 1809. The Disciples of Christ, following the Campbells, formed a church at Brush Run in Pennsylvania, and the Christians, following Stone, formed a congregation at Cane Ridge in Kentucky. By 1832 the Christians of Kentucky and the Disciples of Pennsylvania were united, and a general convention of believers was held in 1849.

Members of the Disciples of Christ Church emphasized the personal religious feelings of the individual. They disapproved of impressive church buildings and elaborate religious ceremony. Reflecting the growing democratic movement of religion on the frontier, the Disciples received many Baptists and Presbyterians into their fold.

The headquarters of the new denomination centered in present West Virginia. Bethany College, growing out of the Buffalo Academy, opened its doors in 1840 and became a training ground for teachers and ministers of the new religion. Bethany College is now the oldest college in existence in West Virginia. It houses the library of the Campbells—in West Virginia the greatest collection of books prior to the Civil War.

Baptists

On the American frontier, the Baptists were one of the most important of the new religious groups. At the time of the Civil War, there were about 10,000 Baptists in the area of present West Virginia. For a long time they had been persecuted in Virginia, and they found western Virginia more tolerant. Across the Alleghenies a Baptist congregation formed Simpson Creek Church at Bridgeport, Harrison County, in 1773; another established the Forks of Cheat Church at Stewartstown in Monongalia County within a few years; and a third built a church at Alderson in Monroe County a little later.

In the period before the American Revolution, a Baptist congregation established itself at Mill Creek, a tributary of Opequon Creek, in 1743. In 1754 on the Opequon in Berkeley County a Baptist church was founded under the ministry of Reverend John Gerard for settlers from New England.

Religious Encampment in the Mountains in 1845 (Photo from "West Virginia, Her Land, Her People, Her Traditions, Her Resources" by Maude A. Rucker. Photo courtesy of West Virginia University Library)

Baptists were opposed to centralized control. They were willing for each congregation to accept the services of a volunteer, self-appointed, and often unpaid, clergy. They attracted many followers through camp meetings. There were open-air revivals where many persons could find self-expression by participating in singing, praying, shouting, and confessing. These meetings in the open fields continued into the early morning hours and lasted as long as a week. The Baptists were also strong on the frontier because their ministers often accompanied settlers to the new lands in the west. Squire Boone, Daniel Boone's brother and Baptist preacher, accompanied settlers who located in Kentucky.

Because the Baptists believed in baptism by total immersion, as also did the Dunkards and Disciples of Christ, persons intolerant of that rite sometimes attempted to drown them. Sometimes they were set upon because they were opposed to slavery. As early as 1789 Baptists urged that every legal measure be used to rid Virginia of the evil of slavery.

Shortly before the Civil War, Baptists of western Virginia bought property at Blue Sulphur Springs, where they opened a school under the name of Allegheny College, but the buildings were destroyed by the Union armies. Dr. W. P. Walker also started Rector College at Pruntytown in Taylor County. For a time Rector College received state aid in the form of free scholarships. But this college also closed before the Civil War.

Methodists

Methodists became significant both numerically and politically in western Virginia. By 1850 the Methodist Episcopal Church in West Virginia listed 54 ministers serving a membership of 14,201 persons. Their strength was due, in part, to their organization and also to the recruiting skill of their officials.

Methodists, under John Wesley, had attempted to reform the Episcopal Church of England. After the Revolutionary War, the Methodists separated from the Episcopal Church and formed the Methodist Episcopal Church. They retained, however, the concept of centralized control through appointment of bishops.

Francis Asbury was appointed the first bishop in America. The Virginia area was of special concern to him. Almost every year from 1789 to 1816 he was in the territory of present West Virginia. During this period he kept a journal which recounts much of his activity in implanting Methodism on the frontier.

To take care of the religious needs of a frontier people, the Methodists established circuits. The circuits provided traveling preachers who conducted religious services for the people in the west.

Circuit riding was lonely and dangerous, and it required good health and great stamina. But, according to Asbury, it was much more disagreeable to preach in the open air at a camp meeting than it was to travel and preach within a circuit where churches and congregations had already been established.

The first Methodist Circuit in western Virginia was in the Eastern Panhandle. It was known as the Berkeley Circuit and was established in 1778. After the completion of a meetinghouse known as the Rehoboth Church in Monroe County in 1786 the Greenbrier Circuit was formed in 1787. The Rehoboth Church, now the oldest remaining church building west of the Alleghenies, was frequently visited by Francis Asbury. As he reported on Sunday, July 6, 1788 in his journal, he always had large congregations at the Rehoboth Chapel which caused him to preach with "some satisfaction."

Other circuits followed in rapid order. In the Greenbrier Valley, the Allegheny Circuit was organized in 1783; in the Monongahela Valley, the Red Stone Circuit was formed in 1784; and at Wheeling, in the Ohio River area, the Ohio Circuit was established in 1787.

Education at the Elementary Levels

Community schools in western Virginia might be in barns or private homes, and some were in rude structures in out-of-the-way locations in abandoned old fields. Those located in such fields were known as "old field" schools.

The early schools were sometimes called subscription schools because parents "subscribed" to them—that is, parents contracted with the schoolmasters to teach their children for a certain sum of money.

Literary Fund. A free public school system was suggested by Thomas Jefferson as early as 1799, and such a system seemed possible about the time of the War of 1812. In 1809, largely through the votes of western counties, the Virginia General Assembly created a Literary Fund to be used for education. The money came from fines and forfeited property belonging to the state. In 1816 new money was added to the Fund when the United States paid sums owed to Virginia for helping to finance the War of 1812.

Rehoboth Church under Its Modern Shelter *(Photo courtesy of Methodist Historical Society)*

Eastern and western counties quarreled as to how the Literary Fund should be spent. The east wanted a large part of the sum used for higher education, the academies, the colleges, and the state university. The west wanted more money spent on elementary schools. By 1818 a compromise was worked out whereby one-fourth of the Fund was given to the university and three-fourths given to the counties on the basis of their white population.

But the money that was used was restricted for the purpose of instructing poor children in reading, writing, and arithmetic, and it was not used for black children. It did not at first create new schools; the money paid the tuition of the poor children at the established subscription schools. The rate of tuition was from two to four cents a day.

Lack of Attendance. Some parents did not send their children to school because they considered the Literary Fund to be charity and were too proud to accept the assistance. Others did not send the children because the children provided valuable labor at home. By 1830 only a little over half of the poor children in western Virginia were estimated to be in attendance at school. However, if there were enough poor children in certain areas, the tuition, with the state's contribution per child, was sufficient to create a new school. By 1850 more than 1,300 schools so aided existed in western Virginia. School periods varied in length from 40 to 80 days.

By 1840 the governor expressed dissatisfaction with the state's system of education. He stated that illiteracy was actually increasing in the state. The figures he published alarmed the citizens. A number of communities held conventions which made recommendations for a state-wide system of free public schools supported by taxes and open to both rich and poor children on equal terms.

Young Pioneers in School   *(Photo courtesy of West Virginia University Library)*

Free Schools. The first county west of the mountains to establish district free schools before the Civil War was Kanawha County. This type of school provided instruction on the elementary level for all white children above the age of six. Such schools were also established in Ohio County and Jefferson County. The Virginia legislature granted permission for such schools in 1829 and in 1846. In 1829 a free school plan had been tried at Sinks Grove in Monroe County, but it did not last very long. The free school plan really began to operate successfully when West Virginia became a state in 1863 and adopted a constitution that required free schools.

Secondary Education

At the secondary-education level, western Virginians created academies. These would compare to present-day junior and senior high schools. The academies taught the literary classics, higher mathematics, and the sciences, but they also gave instruction in elementary subjects. The state gave very little money for their support. They depended largely on tuition fees paid for the students.

Randolph Academy at Clarksburg in Harrison County was the oldest regularly incorporated secondary school in Virginia west of the Alleghenies. The trustees of the academy were prominent men—Benjamin Harrison, Patrick Henry, and Edmund Randolph, for whom it was named. For western Virginia, Randolph Academy was expected to become the equal of William and Mary College in the eastern part of the state.

Before the outbreak of the Revolution, Shepherdstown also had an academy.

Academies into Colleges

Although Randolph Academy failed to become an institution of higher learning, several academies formed the beginnings of later colleges in the state. Marshall Academy at Huntington was the forerunner of Marshall University. West Liberty Academy prepared the way for West Liberty State Normal School, now West Liberty State College. Monongalia Academy with Woodburn Female Seminary provided the start of West Virginia University. Buffalo Academy became Bethany College. Potomac Academy is now Potomac State College of West Virginia University, and Lancastrian Academy at Wheeling became Linsly Institute.

Bethany College in Its Early Years Founded by Alexander Campbell in 1840, Bethany College is the oldest institution of higher learning in West Virginia. Bethany has become one of the leading church colleges in the United States and one of the wealthiest small colleges in the country. *(From "The West Virginia Review," October 1938)*

chapter fourteen / religion and the three r's

By the time of the Civil War, twelve academies had been established in the Eastern Panhandle, seventeen in the Monongahela Valley, and twenty-one along the Ohio River. In the Kanawha Valley, including the Greenbrier area, twelve had been founded. Northwest Virginia, however, was western Virginia's land of academies.

Educational Leadership

In the early days, according to present-day standards, many teachers were not well qualified for their duties. However, before the Civil War, important leadership in education developed. Gordon Battelle, later a presiding elder of the Methodist Episcopal Church, served at Northwestern Academy at Parkersburg in Wood County. Alexander Martin, later president of West Virginia University, served at Preston Academy at Kingwood in Preston County. Reverend John McElhenny, missionary from the Lexington Presbytery, served at Lewisburg Academy in Greenbrier County. William R. White, a minister of the Methodist Episcopal Church and principal of the Fairmont Male and Female Seminary, became the first superintendent of free schools in the state of West Virginia.

Among those who led the fight for free schools were Alexander Campbell, founder of the Church of the Disciples of Christ; Henry Ruffner, president of Washington College, later to become Washington and Lee University; and Governors David Campbell and James McDowell of Virginia. Horace Mann of Massachusetts endorsed the free school movement in western Virginia.

Log Schoolhouse of an Improved Type Early schoolhouses were frequently used for church services. *(Photograph by J. Roy Fuller)*

Libraries

In the census of 1850, eleven libraries in the state reported possession of a little less than 8,000 volumes. The two most important collections were college libraries — one at Bethany College in Brooke County reporting 3,000 volumes, and the other at Rector College in Taylor County reporting 2,500 volumes.

Traveling Preacher

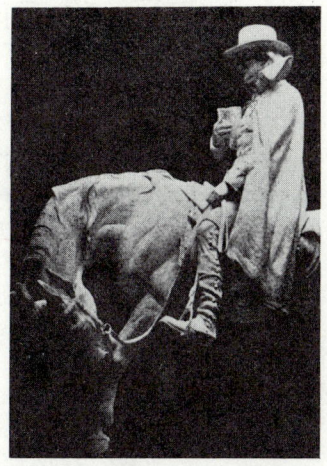

Francis Asbury, Methodist Bishop

Francis Asbury, the first Methodist bishop in America and a frequent visitor to western Virginia, was born in August 1745 near Birmingham, England. Francis grew up under the care of an emotional mother who dreamed her son would be a great religious leader. He had very little formal schooling and is said to have experienced a religious awakening at the age of fourteen. Asbury was soon associated with the Methodists in England and became a preacher. At the age of 21 he went to London, and in 1771 he volunteered to go to America and serve in missionary work.

Other missionaries had preceded Asbury to America, but he felt an unusual sense of responsibility for the land and its people. After serving in New York for a short while, Francis set out to take religion to the inhabitants elsewhere. In October 1772 he was appointed general superintendent of Methodism in America.

In June 1773 Asbury had to subordinate himself to a newly arrived leader and was summoned home in 1775. But Asbury decided to stay in America where revolution seemed imminent. Realizing that England could never subdue the rebellion, he refused in Maryland to take an oath of loyalty to England. He fled to Delaware and became a citizen of that colony.

Asbury was made head of the Methodist organization in America in 1779, being consecrated superintendent, and began to refer to himself as bishop. He now attempted to carry Methodism to the boundaries of America's frontiers. He traveled extensively for his cause and became ill from exhaustion. His arduous activity caused his death in 1816.

Asbury is said to have used two horses always on his travels through frontier America. One was for him to ride upon, and the other to carry his bedding and his teapot. No matter where he found himself in America's wilderness, tea enabled him to preserve one of his English traditions.

Asbury first visited what is now West Virginia in 1776 when he traveled to Berkeley Springs. As the frontier beckoned, he again visited the Eastern Panhandle in 1781, 1782, 1783, and 1784. In 1785 he crossed the Alleghenies and pursued his missionary work in Morgantown. He reached the Northern Panhandle in 1786. By 1815 he had crossed that section no less than fourteen times.

In 1788 he had begun an intensive effort to bring Methodism to the mountain areas, and by 1796 he had crossed the state from north to south several times. His favorite church was said to be Rehoboth Church in present-day Monroe County. He dedicated this church in 1786. Asbury's association with western Virginia was extensive, and his endeavors helped the spread of organized religion to all the frontier settlements.

Chapter 15 INDUSTRIAL EVOLUTION: NEW WAYS TO MAKE A LIVING

The change from pioneer days to an industrial era came slowly in western Virginia as most of the people in the state remained on the farms even into the twentieth century. In 1860 eight out of ten people in the state lived on farms. There were no large cities, and factories were few and far between. In 1830 only six towns had a population which reached or exceeded 1,000 persons. Four of these towns were in the Eastern Panhandle, and two were in the Northern Panhandle. However, from 1800 to 1830 the number of counties in the present state of West Virginia increased from 13 to 23, and by 1860 the counties numbered 50.

Primitive Agriculture

The production of farm crops in quantities large enough to be sold beyond the local communities was of slow growth, too. As late as the year 1850 little advance had been made in the use of labor-saving machinery on the western Virginia farms. Wooden moldboard plows and a few iron plows were the most common implements. Most plows, harrows, axes, rakes, hoes, and other implements of tillage had been made in the local blacksmith shops and had been attached to wooden handles made by the farmers themselves.

Horsepower on an Early West Virginia Farm At one time the farmers in the state employed horses to furnish power for hauling and for operating the few machines that were available then.

The cradle, scythe, and sickle were the tools used to cut the grain and grass, and thrashing machines were not introduced into western Virginia until shortly before 1850. Horses supplied power for the few machines. First, the thrashers did not even separate the grain from the chaff, but tossed both to the side for separation by hand.

The best farms of the state lay along the river valleys, and some of the most prosperous farmers were slave owners. Principal crops were wheat, corn, and buckwheat. At the beginning of the Civil War wheat and corn were still planted by hand in the state.

Mills for Local Manufacture

Marino sheep were brought into western Virginia in 1806, and sheep raising became widespread on the hills. These domesticated animals, of course, provided wool, and numerous carding mills to comb and roll the wool appeared in the west.

With their spinning wheels and hand looms the women worked the wool into yarn and cloth. They also wove linen materials from flax, which had been raised on their home places. Wool and linen, as we know, were used in the making of the common linsey-woolsey.

By the 1830's Wellsburg had a large cotton factory with 1,200 spindles.

Gristmills to grind the wheat and corn and buckwheat into flour served practically every community. Gristmills were located near

An Old-Time Waterpower Mill (West Virginia Department of Commerce Photo)

streams which would provide waterpower to turn the huge mill wheel. The waterwheel turned one millstone against another to grind the grain.

Wheeling and Wellsburg became centers of large milling industries, which sent thousands of barrels of flour to the lower South and to the West Indies. For sale, products from the gristmills in the Eastern Panhandle were sent down the Potomac River to Georgetown.

Sawmills appeared in many places, to use the trees of the forests. At the sawmill the waterwheel caused the saw to cut through the log in a straight up-and-down movement. By the 1830's Wellsburg had a steam-powered sawmill which cut 3,000 feet of plank in twelve hours.

A dozen sawmills were in operation in the Eastern Panhandle by 1776, and 60 more by 1800. In 1810 there were 50 sawmills in Berkeley County. The first sawmill west of the mountains is said to have been the one constructed in 1776 by John Menear near the town of St. George in Tucker County. In 1835 there were 40 or more waterpower sawmills in western Virginia. Most of these mills were on Middle Island Creek and its tributaries in Pleasants, Tyler, and Doddridge counties. In winter these mills were in operation day and night, sawing choice yellow pines for markets in the South.

Lumber mills turned out barrels and casks in which salt and flour and salted meat were shipped to markets. Wood fiber, as well as cotton, linen, and rags, furnished the raw material for pulp and paper mills, which were located in Wheeling by 1839.

chapter fifteen / industrial evolution: new ways to make a living

Log Rafts on the Little Kanawha River Logs, floated down the rivers to the mills, became lumber to be used for boats, buildings, furniture, wagons and for countless other articles.

The wood industries remain very important in West Virginia. We shall learn more about the products of our forests.

Glass

The first glassware made west of the Alleghenies came from a factory established about 1797 by Albert Gallatin on the Monongahela River in Pennsylvania. By 1813 Isaac Duval had built a plant at Wellsburg in western Virginia for the manufacture of flint glass and colored glassware.

By 1820 one glass plant in Wheeling was making window glass and glass bottles, and by 1821 another plant was making pitchers, wine glasses, and tumblers. In 1830 Wheeling had five glass factories and two glass-cutting establishments which gave employment to 193 persons. By the time of the Civil War, Wheeling had a total of eight glass plants.

West Virginia is known today for its production of fine glassware.

Salt

Real industrial development in western Virginia began with the manufacture of salt. Salt is needed universally by animals and man and is essential today in countless manufacturing processes. Salt is found in quantities in the state. In parts of West Virginia salt comes from underground deposits dating back to early geological ages. Salt deposits were produced by a long process of evaporation of water left by oceans and lakes which had covered the area but had receded and disappeared millions of years earlier. In northern West Virginia salt occurs in the solid form of rock salt. In central West Virginia it is recovered from salt springs.

For many years a great salt "lick," known as the Great Buffalo Lick, located on the northern side of the Great Kanawha River six miles above the mouth of the Elk, had attracted buffalo and deer, for here the animals could lick their needed salt. Following the trails of the animals, the Indians found salt for their needs. In 1755 the Indians carried their white captives from the Draper's Meadow settlement at New River to this spot and stopped there to make a supply of salt. They utilized the primitive method of boiling the brines in kettles placed directly over fire, in order to obtain the dry salt. Mrs. Mary Ingles was one of the group of prisoners who was forced to help her captors in their work.

In 1774, members of Andrew Lewis's army stopped here on their way to Point Pleasant to participate in Lord Dunmore's War against the Ohio Indians. This source of salt in the Kanawha Valley became known throughout western Virginia.

Early Salt Manufacture. In 1792 a noted ranger, Adam O'Brien, blazed a trail from his cabin near Sutton, Braxton County, to salt springs at or near Bulltown on the Little Kanawha River. John Haymond, who set up evaporating kettles and a furnace there, transformed the Bulltown salt springs into a commercial operation in 1809. A nearby competitor, John G. Jackson, set up a rival operation on West Fork River near Clarksburg in 1810.

At the mouth of Campbells Creek, near the Great Kanawha salt springs, Elisha Brooks operated a saltworks that produced as much as 150 pounds of salt a day in 1797. About 200 gallons of brine was required to evaporate into one bushel of salt. To increase production, Brooks acquired two dozen kettles and a furnace. He dipped brine from wells that were eight-to-ten-feet deep and lined with hollow gum-tree casings. For fuel, he used from four to five cords of wood per day.

Salt, a Major Industry. It was in 1808, however, that the Great Kanawha River salt industry developed into a nationally known operation. This was largely the enterprise of David and Joseph Ruffner. This operation at first used 64 evaporation kettles. It manufactured 25 to 30 bushels of salt per day. The Ruffner interests, followed by six other major concerns in the valley, produced brine in larger quantities than had been made by individuals, and it was of finer quality from much deeper wells with improved casings.

These manufacturers also quit the primitive methods of their predecessors. They now used grainers and vacuum pans over direct heat from coal. They were now digging to depths of 150 to 450 feet in search of stronger brines. They converted a ten-mile stretch of land along the Kanawha into the largest salt production area in the United States. Their distribution outlets eventually extended throughout Ohio and the upper Mississippi River basins.

Because of the Napoleonic Wars in Europe and the War of 1812 which involved the United States and Great Britain, supplies of salt from abroad, particularly from England, rapidly declined in America. The resulting scarcity produced prosperity for the Kanawha salt makers. By 1814 the Ruffner interests were utilizing 52 furnaces and were manufacturing from 2,500 to 3,000 bushels of salt per day. A total of about 600,000 bushels was produced in 1814. Total employment in the Kanawha salt area increased to 2,500 men and involved the related activities of coal digging, boat building, and barrel making which were necessary to keep the salt-making interests in full production. At its peak, the salt industry resorted to slave labor for its basic work force. Salt industries not only owned many slaves but also leased slaves from eastern Virginia.

In time, salt makers of western Virginia were faced with the problem of overproduction. Their economic difficulties came be-

Scene at the Saltworks on the Kanawha River near Charleston
An industry of considerable size developed at the Kanawha Salines. *(From the Roy Bird Cook Room, Kanawha County Public Library, Charleston)*

cause of competition with one another and with foreign producers, because of inadequate banking facilities in western Virginia, the state taxing system, and state regulation of inspection.

The operators of the salt industries of the Kanawha Valley now joined together to protect their interests. By 1817 they had agreed on production quotas, prices, shipments, and distribution timetables. They also supported a protective tariff to protect themselves from foreign competition.

In combining their interests to discourage competition, the operators formed the first "trust" in the United States. Their cooperation for the next several years permitted the salt industry to reach its greatest volume of sales about the year 1850, when more than 3,000,000 bushels of salt were marketed annually.

Decline of the Industry. After 1850 the salt industry declined rapidly. Nearby Cincinnati, on the Ohio, had been a headquarters for the meat packing industry, which used large quantities of salt. Many of the meat packing plants had now moved farther west, and Chicago displaced Cincinnati as the meat packing center. Meigs County, Ohio, and Mason County in western Virginia now surpassed the Kanawha area in production of salt. Western New York and Michigan also offered serious competition. Railroads were taking freight from the rivers, and the waterways were not so important as they once had been.

The important Ruffner Company dissolved in 1856. Interest shifted from salt to cannel coal, natural gas, and oil. In 1861 the Kanawha Valley was flooded, and some salt furnaces disintegrated under the waters. Others were destroyed during the Civil War. Only the Dickinson furnace at Malden, built in 1832, survived.

Iron

To the well-being of the Virginia frontiersman iron was almost as necessary as salt. In the same way that salt was first imported from the east, some iron was carried across the mountains into western Virginia. In a short time, however, native ores were discovered along the tributaries of the Potomac River and the Monongahela River, and iron makers built small furnaces to develop these resources.

Charcoal was found to be superior to coal as fuel for the furnaces, and surrounding hillsides were stripped of their forests to provide the fuel.

On the lands of Lord Fairfax, at "The Bloomery" near Harpers Ferry, the first iron furnace in present West Virginia was established

Peter Tarr's Iron Foundry as It Onetime Lay in Ruins The historic pioneer furnace, the first iron foundry west of the Alleghenies, has been restored, as the accompanying photograph shows. The man seated at the ruins of the foundry is the great-grandson of the old ironmaster.

in 1760. George Washington is said to have considered the product of this furnace so superior that he used his influence for the establishment of the federal arsenal and gun factory at Harpers Ferry in 1794. This arsenal could manufacture 1,400 muskets a month.

Between 1790 and 1794 Peter Tarr built the first iron furnace west of the Alleghenies on Kings Creek in Hancock County. The Peter Tarr Furnace, with a capacity of less than two tons a day, made cooking pans, pots, skillets, and grates. It also cast the cannonballs used by Commodore Oliver H. Perry in the Battle of Lake Erie in 1813. The site of the furnace is now owned by the city of Weirton.

A few furnaces developed in the Eastern Panhandle. The Hampshire Furnace, about twelve miles south of Romney, manufactured stoves. Moorefield, Greenland Gap, and Wardensville in Hardy County also had furnaces. A few appeared in Preston County. But most were in the Cheat Valley near Ices Ferry and along Deckers Creek near Morgantown and were established around the year 1800. In a short time they were furnishing employment for more than 1,200 persons. The Jackson Iron Works on Cheat River became a very well-known iron establishment.

In 1832 a large iron mill was constructed at Wheeling. With seven machines, this mill turned out about 5,000 pounds of nails a day. Nails were very rare and expensive items in pioneer life. By the time of the Civil War, Wheeling possessed four iron foundries and had gained the nickname the "Nail City."

Peter Tarr's Iron Foundry (Restored) Robert Tarr, great-great-grandson of Peter Tarr, is shown here. He holds a cannonball produced at the original furnace in the early 1800's. *(Photo courtesy of Weirton Steel Division, National Steel Corporation)*

In the southern part of present West Virginia a furnace was built at the mouth of Strange Creek in Clay County, and as late as 1870 a furnace was in operation for a few years at Quinnimont, Fayette County.

About 1880 the making of iron from ore ceased in West Virginia when rich ore beds were found in the Mesabi Range in Minnesota and Michigan. At the outbreak of World War I, the only operating iron mine in West Virginia was located on the Potomac River in Jefferson County four miles above Harpers Ferry at a point named Orebank.

Although most of the iron products produced by the early settlers were used by the settlers themselves, some of the iron products were shipped to Pittsburgh and distributed to markets on the Ohio River and farther west.

Coal

West Virginia coal was probably first used by blacksmiths or by the settlers whose cabins were near outcrops of coal. By 1810 the people of Wheeling obtained coal from a mine discovered near the city and began to use the fuel in their homes. In 1811 the steamboat *New Orleans* burned coal which her captain, Nicholas Roosevelt, had found on the banks of the Ohio in 1809.

In 1817 coal was discovered in the Kanawha Valley. This fuel began to take the place of wood for use in the production of salt at

View inside a Coal Mine Many Years Ago

the Kanawha Salines near Malden above Charleston. A small mine was opened near Mason City in 1819 and another in 1832.

Two early reports on coal which stimulated western Virginians' interest in this natural resource were made before the Civil War. In 1835 Dr. Samuel P. Hildreth of Marietta, Ohio, published a report on the Appalachian coalfield, directing attention to western Virginia. From 1836 to 1840 Professor William Rogers, Virginia geologist, made analyses of coals in Harrison, Monongalia, Taylor, Fayette, Mineral, Grant, Preston, and Kanawha counties.

By 1840 coal produced in western Virginia amounted to 300,000 tons. Two-thirds of this amount was used in Kanawha salt furnaces, and the remainder by factories and homes in Wheeling. Between 1840 and 1860 many coal companies were organized, and corporations were created under the laws of Virginia for the purpose of encouraging the investment of money from foreign countries.

Of particular interest was the discovery of cannel coal (at Cannelton), a coal rich in oil which could be used for lighting purposes. In 1857 the Kanawha Cannel Coal Mining and Manufacturing Company erected buildings at Charleston, and in 1858 the Crowin Cannel Coal Company constructed buildings at Mill Creek seven miles up the Kanawha.

Oil and Natural Gas

Oil was first discovered on the Great Kanawha in 1807 in connection with drilling for salt wells. First, the oil was used as medicine and for lubricating wagon wheels, and by 1826 it was used in lamps. By 1836 oil was discovered at the mouth of the Hughes River.

Not far distant from the Hughes on the Little Kanawha River was Burning Springs, two springs from which natural gas escaped. Thomas Jefferson had mentioned this site as early as 1781. He noted the brilliance the gas produced when a lighted candle was thrust into it. His account may be the first description of a natural gas flame in the United States.

In 1859 the Rathbone brothers, while boring a well in a test for salt brine, struck petroleum at a depth of 200 feet. In 1860 the Rathbone brothers and associates in Parkersburg had wells that were producing from 200 to 1,200 barrels daily.

Other Industries

Small tanneries were established early throughout western Virginia. In the tanyards crude wooden vats contained a fluid made from oak bark to cure animal hides. After the hides were cured as leather, shoemakers, harness makers, and saddlers made their special leather articles.

Trade also existed in animal skins and furs. In autumn a few families would send a caravan of packhorses laden with skins, ginseng, and bears' grease to settlements in the east; there these articles would be exchanged for iron utensils and equipment. Sometimes the caravans consisted of 10 to 15 horses, each horse carrying about 200 pounds.

In the late 1830's and early 1840's an attempt was made in many parts of the state to produce silk through the raising of silkworms. Thousands of mulberry trees were planted to furnish food for the worms. Interest was so widespread that at Brandonville, Preston County, in 1839 and 1840 a magazine was printed called *The Silk Culturist and Farmers' Manual.*

In those same years a small plant was built at Clarksburg to use the cocoons which were created by the silkworms and from which the silk thread is taken. But silkworms did not thrive in western Virginia, and the new industry failed.

Growth of Business

As the towns grew in population, various businesses developed. In 1835 Martinsburg advertised the special services of one confectioner, four tailors, one chair maker, one plough maker, four wagon makers, one hatter, two cabinetmakers, two tin- and coppersmiths, and three blacksmiths. In addition, the town had two printing offices, two tanyards, two saddleries, two boot and shoe factories, two flour mills, one woolen manufactory, one iron and brass foundry, and two druggist shops.

Journalism

Opportunities for success in the professions — that is, in the practice of law, medicine, and the like — were limited but were decidedly on the rise by the time of the Civil War. In addition to a few doctors and lawyers, newspaper editors appeared in increasing numbers in western Virginia. In 1790 Nathaniel Willis, who moved into the state from Boston, was publishing *The Potowmac Guardian and Berkeley Advertiser* at Shepherdstown. His publication was originally printed on paper nine by fifteen inches. Later he moved his business to Martinsburg.

Other papers appeared: at Shepherdstown in 1797 the *Impartial Observer*, and in Charles Town in 1808 the *Farmer's Repository*, the first agricultural journal west of the Blue Ridge Mountains. The *Farmer's Repository* merged with *The Virginia Free Press* in 1827.

Thomas Jefferson was at one time interested in locating the national capital in the South. Jefferson counseled with Alexander Hamilton and with Alexander White of Berkeley County, the first representative of the first district to sit in the first session of Congress. From the interest of these men the possibility existed that Shepherdstown might become the headquarters of the new national government. The headquarters was then in Philadelphia. To some extent this situation explains the early development of many newspapers in the Eastern Panhandle.

The *Monongalia Gazette and Morgantown Advertiser* was published at Morgantown in 1804. Before that time, both Morgantown and Clarksburg depended on the appearance of their news in *The Pittsburgh Gazette*. Wheeling's first newspaper was the *Repository* in 1807, and Clarksburg's first newspaper was the *Bye-Stander* in 1810. In 1820 Charleston published its first newspaper, *The Kenhawa Spectator*, whose first editor also became head of Mercer Academy.

In 1842 Enos W. Newton founded *The Kanawha Republican* in Charleston, and in the same year John G. Jacob founded the *Wellsburg Herald*.

In order to survive, most pioneer newspapers depended upon the advertising placed in the papers. But when the slavery dispute was reaching its climax, newspapers were able to maintain themselves by subscriptions because of public interest in the debate over

  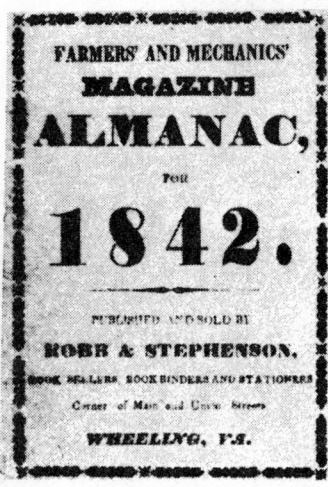

Almanacs, Essential Items in Early Homes These booklet covers show that printers in western Virginia were turning out attractive printing long before West Virginia became a state.

freedom for the blacks. One antislavery newspaper was the *Wheeling Intelligencer*, founded in 1852.

By 1850 there were three daily and twenty-one weekly newspapers in western Virginia. The circulation of these newspapers was confined to fourteen counties. Between 1850 and 1860 forty-three newspapers were circulating in nineteen counties. These consisted of three dailies, two triweeklies, thirty-six weeklies, and three monthlies. Circulation, however, never passed 1,200 for weeklies and 900 for dailies. But *The Millennial Harbinger*, a monthly religious publication edited by Alexander Campbell at Wellsburg, hit an unusually high circulation figure of 8,500.

An important item that issued from the print shops of the day was the annual almanac. It was an essential article in every household. It provided a calendar of the months of the year, gave a long-range weather forecast, and told the sequence of the phases of the moon. It contained an "encyclopedia" of interesting facts, short literary compositions and stories and jokes sometimes illustrated with pen drawings. It was a "doctor book" and a cookbook. Puzzle pages amused the young folk.

Almanacs were often used as textbooks in the pioneer schools, for schoolbooks were hard to obtain, and nearly every home could furnish an almanac for a reader.

A Builder

Leonard Lamb and the Henry Clay Furnace

During the early part of the nineteenth century the mining and smelting of iron ore was a new and developing industry in the northern and eastern parts of present West Virginia. The earliest iron furnace in the state was built in Jefferson County about the middle of the eighteenth century, and a few others were operating by the end of the 1790's.

The great growth in the industry occurred between 1800 and 1870. At least seven furnaces were operating during the period in Monongalia County alone. One of these, the Henry Clay Furnace, provided new employment opportunities for western Virginians.

The Henry Clay Furnace was built in what is now Coopers Rock State Forest between 1834 and 1836 by Leonard Lamb for Tassie Morrison and Company, or, as it was better known, Tassie and Bissell. This was a cold-blast furnace, run by steam. It had a capacity of about four tons of pig iron (crude iron) each twenty-four hours.

The iron was shipped by boat down the river until 1839, when the furnace was sold to new owners.

Wooden-railed tramways connecting the ore pits to the furnace were built and assured more profitable operation. Iron ore, limestone, and charcoal (the latter two necessary to the smelting process) were dumped into the 34-foot stack from wheelbarrows, and along the side of the wall a water pit was placed into which the melted iron was drawn to cool.

At the furnace by about 1840, nearly two hundred men were employed in digging ore and making charcoal and in transportation. The furnace was responsible for creating a community of five hundred people housed in nearly one hundred dwellings. The town also maintained a school, a church, and a store.

The old furnace, with a base about thirty feet square and more than thirty feet high and in the shape of a truncated pyramid, is now being restored.

Chapter 16 INTERNAL IMPROVEMENTS IN WESTERN VIRGINIA

Western Virginia's economic development depended on its ability to market the products of its industries and farms. Therefore an adequate transportation system of roads, navigable rivers and streams, and occasionally a canal must be provided.

For transportation the pioneers at first had used packhorses, and these beasts of burden sometimes carried on their backs goods weighing as much as two hundred pounds, including necessarily their own food, corn and oats, in packsaddles.

Wagons

But the packhorses were soon replaced by Conestoga wagons, covered wagons which could carry four to eight tons of freight. The wagon had broad wheels, six to ten inches wide. The wheels were often rimmed with an iron band, which made travel possible over soft dirt roads, deep mud, and snow.

The wagon bed was shaped similarly to a boat in that it was higher at both ends than it was in the middle. This design kept goods from spilling from the wagon as it went up and down the western Virginia mountains, and it also enabled the wagon to float when streams had to be crossed. Those wagons that were driven too fast for comfort were realistically nicknamed "shakeguts."

The Conestoga wagon was originally built to haul heavy loads from Lancaster, Pennsylvania, to Philadelphia. It got its name

Covered Wagon on the Northwestern Turnpike Covered wagons traveled the roads, carrying goods, passengers, and the United States mail. (From a sketch by J. H. Diss Debar)

from the Conestoga Valley in Lancaster County, Pennsylvania. The massive running gears of the Conestoga wagon were often painted blue, and the box bodies were painted red with scenic panels on the side. Wooden staves were bent over the box bodies to serve as support for canvas coverings. These canvas cloths were tightly secured in both the front and rear by drawstrings. The wagon was made sixteen feet long and four feet wide and required a team of four to six horses to pull it. It also needed roads that were better and wider than those used by packhorses. In time, hard-surfaced or macadamized roads eased travel.

Roads

The first public road in present West Virginia ran from Winchester, Virginia, to the home of Colonel Morgan Morgan near Martinsburg. Morgan Morgan engineered the road under the authority of the county court of Frederick County, Virginia, in 1743. But this road served only the Eastern Panhandle. It did not provide for the marketing or traveling needs of western Virginia. Many years passed before the roads connecting east and west received serious attention.

In 1818 the Cumberland, or National, Road was completed from Cumberland, Maryland, to Wheeling, West Virginia. This road eventually became U.S. Highway 40. In its time it was one of the best-built roads in the nation. It had a cleared space 60 feet wide for a roadbed 20 feet wide. The roadbed was covered with 18 inches of small crushed stone. For many years it was in constant use, perhaps bearing heavier traffic than any other road in America.

Carrying the Mail This mail carrier has stopped for a rest for himself and his horse and her colt. The first mail routes covered long distances, and the mail was delivered not oftener than once a week. *(From a sketch by J. H. Diss Debar)*

The Kanawha Turnpike, or the Midland Trail, reached the navigable waters of the Kanawha River in 1790 and reached the mouth of the Guyandotte River at its confluence with the Ohio in 1800. This turnpike became U.S. Highway 60. The Northwestern Turnpike was built to connect Winchester and Parkersburg, by way of Romney, Grafton, and Clarksburg in 1838. The Northwestern Turnpike became U.S. Highway 50.

The chief engineer for this road was Colonel Claudius Crozet, a French artillery officer in Napoleon Bonaparte's army in the Russian campaign. Crozet had also been a professor of engineering at the United States Military Academy from 1816 to 1823.

Other important roads in the early period between 1786 and 1789 were the State Road from Winchester by way of Romney to Morgantown, with a branch to Clarksburg (which was the first road connecting eastern and western Virginia), and a road from Clarksburg to the Ohio opposite the site of Marietta, Ohio. By legislative decree, these roads were supposed to be at least 30 feet wide.

In 1790 the Lewisburg-Warm Springs road entered the Kanawha Valley. In 1791 the Morgantown-New Martinsville road was constructed. In 1795 the Morgantown-Moundsville road was built. One of the reasons for the Warm Springs-Lewisburg road was the need to transport salt. In 1847 the Staunton-Parkersburg Turnpike was built by Irish workmen, former laborers on the Baltimore and Ohio Railroad.

chapter sixteen / internal improvements in western virginia

Turnpikes. On some improved roads a fee, or toll, was charged. Such a road was called a turnpike because a pike, or pole, blocked the road at a station where tolls were collected. After the traveler paid his toll, the pike was raised or turned so that he could continue on his journey. Some typical toll fees were 25 cents for wagon, team, and driver; 20 cents for a four-wheeled riding carriage; 1/4 cent for one head of cattle; 3 cents for a score (twenty) of sheep or hogs; 5 cents for each person. The tolls were used to keep up the roads.

Stagecoaches were soon traveling the turnpikes. The stagecoach was more comfortable than the heavy Conestoga wagon. It made better time, and it stopped every fifteen miles or so and changed horses. There were several kinds of stagecoaches. The box-shaped ones gave way to egg-shaped ones about 1820.

Persons traveling by stagecoach were likely to meet prominent people who were also passengers. The coaches made rest stops at taverns which provided lodging, dining facilities, and sometimes entertainment. Tavern charges were fixed by county courts, and licenses for taverns cost $18 per year. The horses also received care, and perhaps the cattle, sheep, and hogs that sometimes were brought along.

At the taverns all the passengers and drivers ate at the same long table without regard to social rank, and European observers often commented on the "excessive democracy" of the west. In time, some taverns became social centers and health resorts, such as White Sulphur Springs, where dances and festivals became regularly scheduled events. A popular rest stop was the Ruffner place near Charleston. It became noted for its stage performances and its nearness to a camp-meeting ground.

Prices for food and lodging were regulated by law. The Berkeley County Court, for example, set the following prices: 40 cents for dinner, 28 cents for breakfast, 30 cents for supper, 10 cents for lodging. Space in a stable and hay for a horse were 25 cents for a night. Pasturage per night was 7 cents, and corn and oats per gallon were 12-1/2 cents.

The Wheeling Bridge

Towns along the rivers and canals became more and more important as people and goods moved to the west. The towns became jealous of each other's success and prosperity. Two towns in particular became competitors: Pittsburgh, Pennsylvania, and

Old Stone House, Celebrated Tavern on the Old James River-Kanawha Turnpike This roadhouse, built in 1824, was popular with noted travelers, was headquarters for General Robert E. Lee and other generals in the Civil War, and served as a military hospital. The house is located on State Road 10 near Clifftop. *(Photo courtesy of Rev. C. Shirley Donnelly)*

Wheeling in western Virginia. Wheeling sought to surpass Pittsburgh by building a bridge across the Ohio River to the state of Ohio.

The Wheeling Bridge was completed in 1849 after two years of construction. It cost almost a quarter of a million dollars, a large sum of money for that time. It was designed by Charles Ellet, Jr., and was said to be the largest structure of its kind in the world.

Canals

To ship goods by boat on waterways was cheaper than transportation by wagon. Where the rivers did not flow together, it was thought necessary to build waterways (canals) from one river to the other.

In 1828 President John Quincy Adams lifted the first shovel of dirt in a ceremony at the proposed Chesapeake and Ohio Canal. The idea for this project could be traced back to a plan conceived by George Washington in 1785. Washington was president of the James River and the Potomac companies. His proposal would join eastern and western waters by the construction of canals. Towns along the Potomac in the Eastern Panhandle watched the progress of the Chesapeake and Ohio Canal as it proceeded from Georgetown to Cumberland, Maryland. By 1850 it reached

Flatboat Used by the Pioneers This was a downstream boat, carried by the current. It was steered by an oar fixed at the rear. This type of boat was sometimes called an ark or broadhorn. *(From an old print)*

Cumberland, but it never crossed the mountains. Costs had risen to $11 million, and competition from the Baltimore and Ohio Railroad arose.

Other canal projects which failed to cross the mountains were those designed to connect the James River with the Kanawha River, and to connect the Potomac River with the Monongahela River as a part of the Chesapeake and Ohio Canal.

Boats

Flatboats. Western Virginians first used boats that were dugouts made from hollowed logs, or canoes of birch bark or skins, which the Indians also used. The pioneers learned to rope and chain logs together into simple rafts. They soon devised the flatboat, actually a large raft with sides and similar to a long squared-corner tub. Its boarded sides reached a height of two to three feet. It often had a cabin in the center or at one end. As it was propelled by manpower, progress upstream against the current was difficult and sometimes impossible. Therefore the flatboat was used almost entirely for trips downstream. A long oar at the rear served as its rudder, and it was moored by a large rope called a hawser.

Keelboats. The popular keelboat was a shallow, covered raft that could be rowed or poled along the rivers. The keelboat was usually from thirty to fifty feet long and ten to twelve feet wide. Along the side of the boat was a "running board." The crew walked along this board with long poles extending toward the bottom of the stream and braced against their shoulders. With much pressure upon the poles, they could push the boat upstream against the current.

Keelboat *(Photo courtesy of West Virginia University Library)*

Sometimes the keelboats and flatboats were used as floating forts, as boatmen had to guard against attacks by Indians and river pirates. The keelboat was particularly popular on the Little Kanawha River, and such a boat as this did not disappear from West Virginia rivers and streams until shortly after 1900.

River Traffic. Traffic on the rivers became heavy immediately after the American Revolutionary War. In one yearly count made of boats that passed the mouth of the Little Kanawha River from November 1787 to November 1788, boats passing up and down the Ohio River numbered 967. These boats carried no less than 18,370 persons. In cargo they also transported 7,986 horses, 2,372 cows, 1,110 sheep, as well as 646 wagons to which the river passengers could transfer for land travel when they disembarked.

Vessels Driven by Sails. A few sailboats plied the western rivers. They were designed for ocean travel and were destined for trade on the eastern coast of North America, in the West Indies, and across the Atlantic Ocean. One of these was built at Elizabeth on the Monongahela River in 1793. In 1803 the schooner or vessel *Dorcas and Sally*, capable of carrying seventy tons, was built at Wheeling. Another such boat, named the *Monongahela Farmer*, was launched in 1800. Pittsburgh, Wheeling, and Marietta were important centers for shipbuilding.

Rumsey's Experiments. In 1783 James Rumsey, a 40-year-old blacksmith and mechanic, took up residence at Berkeley

Model of James Rumsey's Steamboat *(From the West Virginia Department of Archives and History)*

Springs. With a friend, he opened a general store and engaged in the building trade. He constructed a house and stables for George Washington at Berkeley Springs in 1783 and 1784. He also experimented with a mechanical boat on the Potomac River.

Encouraged by Washington, Rumsey worked in secret on a boat that might be propelled by steam. He demonstrated his steamboat on the Potomac in 1787. We shall read more about Rumsey later.

But it was Robert Fulton who received credit for building the first fully successful steamboat, the *Clermont*. In 1807 the *Clermont* made the 150-mile trip up the Hudson River from New York to Albany.

Victory of Steam. The success of the *Clermont* made navigation history. The steamboat not only won over all other types of boats but also made serious competition for wagons and stagecoaches. After 1830, steamboats were making trips on the Mississippi River in one-sixth the time a keelboat required and at one-third the cost per ton of freight.

Many river towns experienced a new prosperity through shipbuilding. Around the year 1830 Wheeling boasted of owning, in whole and in part, between 17 and 20 steamboats, worth almost a quarter of a million dollars. Wheeling noted that arrivals and departures of steamboats in one year's time numbered 738. As Wheeling had been declared by Congress to be a port of entry, goods from any port in Europe could be imported directly to Wheeling without payment of duties at New Orleans.

Steamboat on the Kanawha River in 1854 The city in the background is Charleston.

Important Steamboats. In 1809 Nicholas J. Roosevelt surveyed the Ohio and Mississippi rivers to see if the type of boat which Fulton used on the Hudson River could be used in the interior of America. Traveling by flatboat from Pittsburgh to New Orleans, Roosevelt reported to his associates, Robert Fulton and Robert M. Livingston, that the steamboat would work on these waters. A boat called the *New Orleans*, built in Pittsburgh in 1811, was the first steamboat to navigate these waters.

In 1815 a boat called the *Enterprise*, commanded by Captain Henry M. Shreve, came up the Mississippi and Ohio rivers from New Orleans to Louisville in twenty-five days. It was the first boat to navigate upstream the entire distances of these two rivers. In 1816 Captain Shreve, commanding the *Washington*, made a round trip from Louisville to New Orleans in forty-one days.

The *Washington* was built at Wheeling with timbers from old Fort Henry. It was constructed in an original manner. The engines and boilers were placed on the deck instead of in the hold of the ship, and another deck was built above the machinery. This enabled the *Washington* to float upon the surface rather than in water as was customary for oceangoing ships. Most importantly, the arrangement allowed her to move faster. Before Captain Shreve died, the round trip between Louisville and New Orleans was made in five days.

Steamboats helped increase the numbers of immigrants going west. They also increased the volume of the traffic going both up and down the streams. Both passengers and goods reached their destination in shorter time at lower cost. Farmlands increased in

chapter sixteen / internal improvements in western virginia

A Steamboat on the Ohio River *(Courtesy of West Virginia Department of Commerce)*

price along the waterways, and shipbuilding became an important domestic industry. Boatmen now were relieved of the hard labor of poling their way upstream or walking back through the wilderness. They could now make a return trip either as deck or cabin passengers.

As the years passed, the riverboats became more and more luxurious. They became "floating palaces" where all sorts of people mingled: cardplayers, slave traders, land speculators, foreign visitors, preachers, politicians, peddlers, and theatrical companies. In a way, the steamboats were a "melting pot," the scene of American democracy in action.

But both the steamboat and the canal were at a distinct disadvantage when the railroad became the competitor. Just as the steamboat had competed successfully against the stagecoach, the railroad lessened demand for river traffic. However, canoes, flatboats, and keelboats remained on inland waters for many more years, and riverboats still furnish transportation for quantities of freight.

Important Inventor

James Rumsey and His Steamboat

James Rumsey was born in Bohemia Manor, Cecil County, Maryland, in March 1743. He obtained an elementary education, learned blacksmithing, and is said to have served in the Revolutionary War. While living in Baltimore in 1780, he and an acquaintance operated a gristmill at Sleepy Creek, Maryland. Other business ventures followed for Rumsey, and in 1783 he went to Bath, now Berkeley Springs, to open a store and to begin applying his practical knowledge of the building trade in western Virginia.

During his residence at Bath, he began working in secret on a mechanically propelled boat which would use steam to move the vessel against the current. By forcing water through the stern of the boat, the craft was caused to move forward. In October 1783 on the Potomac at the mouth of Sir John's Run, near Bath, Rumsey demonstrated that his boat would move under its own power.

Rumsey immediately faced difficulties in securing money to continue his experiments, and, for the rest of his life, financial limitations became an obstacle to his success. After procuring monopoly rights to build steam-powered boats and to navigate the inland waters of Virginia and Maryland, he reevaluated his designs.

Both Maryland and Virginia allowed him to use his invention on the waters of these states for a period of ten years and reserved the right to purchase his production for a sum of ten thousand pounds if they so desired. In order to finance his efforts, however, he had to accept a position with a canal company. When this position proved inadequate financially and did not allow time for further work on his boat, he sought financial assistance as far away as Philadelphia and England.

By November 1784 Rumsey had tried the principles of the machinery he intended to use for propulsion, and in May 1785 he employed a carpenter to build the boat model. The machinery was fashioned in Baltimore and Frederick, Maryland, and Rumsey assembled all the components of his steamboat for experimentation on western Virginia rivers by the winter of 1785.

When he received word that others were working on similar projects, Rumsey hastened to make trial runs of his craft. He demonstrated a steam-driven boat on the Potomac in 1787, but he needed more money to stage additional exhibitions.

In Philadelphia Rumsey received some financial backing and was urged to go to England to patent his devices and seek further financial support. While abroad, he patented an improved steam boiler necessary to the better operation of the steamboat and actively demonstrated improvements he had made on sawmills and gristmills.

Before he could perfect his main invention, however, he died in England in December 1792. He was buried in St. Margaret's churchyard near Westminster. Nevertheless, the steamboat, which was brought closer to reality through Rumsey's work, soon revolutionized navigation throughout America.

unit five | Sectionalism in Virginia

Chapter 17   THE BALTIMORE AND OHIO RAILROAD

All major cities on the Atlantic Coast were anxious to capture the trade from the American interior. Their ability to do this depended first on road and river transportation and then upon railroads.

The city of Baltimore and the state of Maryland believed they might be most successful in the competition for trade. At first the National Road seemed to give them an advantage. Then, with the growing importance of water transportation, a canal from the Potomac River to the Monongahela River and its connection to the Ohio promised to serve the purpose. But when New York City and Philadelphia began to develop railroad connections to the west, it was obvious that a railroad to the Ohio was the only way for Baltimore to surpass other Eastern cities.

In 1827 the state of Maryland incorporated the Baltimore and Ohio Railroad, and on July 4, 1838 Charles Carroll, then the only surviving signer of the Declaration of Independence, laid the cornerstone of the road.

Restrictions. In order for Maryland to secure a railroad outlet to the Ohio River and farther west, permission must be obtained to cross either the state of Pennsylvania or the state of Virginia. Pennsylvania and Philadelphia were, of course, not interested in helping Maryland and Baltimore. Virginia, while not unfriendly, established

Early Type of B&O Engine, 1850 *(Photo courtesy of West Virginia University Library)*

certain conditions under which the railroad would be permitted to cross the state. First, the railroad could not be built south of the mouth of the Little Kanawha River.

Later, in 1847, Virginia made more restrictions. The legislature determined that the railroad could not touch the Ohio River at any point farther south than the mouth of Fish Creek, eighty miles north of the mouth of the Little Kanawha River. Virginia feared that the trade of the West and of western Virginia would be diverted to Baltimore and that its own coastal cities, such as Norfolk or the capital, Richmond, would be prevented from developing into major commercial centers.

The railroad company had no choice but to accept Virginia's terms and conditions. By 1853 when the Baltimore and Ohio Railroad was completed to Wheeling, three-fourths of its line lay in northern Virginia. Yet the success of the railroad depended on major investments of the city of Baltimore and the state of Maryland.

Branch Lines. Before the Baltimore and Ohio was completed across Virginia, the railroad built branch lines. Its most important branch was between Baltimore and Washington, D.C. As this branch was for a time the only rail route into Washington, it kept communication open between the North and the national capital during the Civil War. For this reason, the Baltimore and Ohio Railroad was sometimes called Abraham Lincoln's "lifeline" in the struggle between the North and the South. Another branch line of the Baltimore and Ohio Railroad went to Frederick, Maryland.

Within the state of Virginia, the most eastern junction of the railroad was at Harpers Ferry, and the most western junction was at Wheeling. Completing this railroad across western Virginia required more than twenty years. Actual construction time was approximately ten years; the remainder of the time was consumed in debate over location and in the raising of the necessary money.

At Grafton there was a connection of the main line of the Baltimore and Ohio with the Northwestern Virginia Railroad. This latter road extended from Grafton by way of Clarksburg to Parkersburg.

Horsepower to Steam Power. From the beginning, the Baltimore and Ohio Railroad was experimental in design, in operation, and in motive power. At first, cars were pulled by horses. Soon the boxcars were rigged with a mast and square sails in the hope that wind would provide the necessary power. In 1830 Peter Cooper built a railroad steam engine called the "Tom Thumb." On its first return trip to Baltimore, the locomotive lost in a race with a horse.

Engineers were soon able to solve the problem of steam power for the engines, and it triumphed over horsepower. The directors of the railroad offered a prize for any engine that was better than Peter Cooper's "Tom Thumb." Five individuals entered the competition with upright, vertical-boiler engines. Phineas Davis of York, Pennsylvania, not only won the prize but also got the job of superintendent of the Baltimore and Ohio engine shops. By 1837 Davis invented the horizontal boiler-type locomotive, and with it the railroad was able to surpass all competition.

"Tom Thumb" Engine

Disputes. By 1832 the railroad had been constructed to Point of Rocks on the Potomac. There it was stopped by a dispute with the Chesapeake and Ohio Canal over the right-of-way in the narrow valley of the Potomac. A compromise was worked out which permitted the railroad to wind its way slowly beside the river. The legislature forced the railroad to purchase some stock of the canal company, and the railroad company agreed to haul its trains by horses through the valley so that the steam engines would not frighten other horses that were pulling the boats along the canal.

Terminus in Western Virginia. By December 1, 1834 the railroad reached Harpers Ferry. Construction was halted for the next three years while disputes continued over the exact route to be followed. It finally reached Cumberland on November 5, 1842. Then more disputes over the location of the next extension between the years 1842 to 1848 halted further extension of the road.

Wheeling and Parkersburg contested for the right to be the Ohio River terminus, and interesting arguments developed over the question of whether the shortest distance from Baltimore to Cincinnati was through Parkersburg or Wheeling. This dispute was resolved by deciding on Wheeling as the terminus in 1848, and by deciding to build the Northwestern Virginia Railroad, the Grafton-Parkersburg branch, with Parkersburg as the terminus in 1851. In actual mileage, the shortest route to Cincinnati was through Parkersburg.

Two Hundred Tortuous Miles. From Cumberland to Wheeling, the railroad progressed approximately two hundred miles through the most mountainous region yet encountered by any railroad builders in America. The road crossed mountains, ravines, and rivers. It climbed to heights of almost 3,000 feet. It executed astonishing curves and passed through tunnels.

The Northwestern Railroad, essentially a branch of the Baltimore and Ohio Railroad, had as many as 23 tunnels. At Tunnelton in Preston County, the main line of the Baltimore and Ohio passed through a tunnel 4,100 feet long, the longest railroad tunnel yet constructed. This was only one of eleven tunnels bored through the mountains between Cumberland and Wheeling.

Near the site of this tunnel a temporary track with a grade of 530 feet per mile was laid to move the necessary construction materials over the mountain. A 650-foot bridge built across the Monongahela was the largest iron bridge yet constructed in America. This bridge was but one of 113 bridges required between Cumberland and Wheeling.

A Farmhouse of the Middle Period   Homes in western Virginia were now more refined, as the one pictured above proves. This was the home of J. H. Diss Debar, designer of the West Virginia state seal and artist who made many of the sketches in this book. The home was built in 1852 on Cove Creek, Doddridge County. *(From a sketch by J. H. Diss Debar)*

Prosperity

The road created both temporary and permanent prosperity through the regions it crossed. In 1850 the railroad required 3,500 laborers and 700 horses for construction work. People who lived along the route obtained employment, as did hundreds of Irish emigrants who, in their quest for work, chose to follow the surveyors of the Baltimore and Ohio.

Irish Emigrants

Many fights developed among the Irish during the construction work, and between the Irish and the first settlers of western Virginia.

During the Cumberland-to-Ohio-River construction, there were many local skirmishes. At Greigsville, near Tunnelton, several factions of workmen numbering well over 500 engaged in an "Irish War" to determine which groups were to make up the labor force of the construction camp. An acting sheriff, Colonel J. A. F. Martin, had to call out a force of 130 men to stop the battle.

Construction workers from Benton's Ferry attacked construction workers at Ice's Mill and pursued them into the town of Fairmont. The citizens of Fairmont, awakened by the gunshots and yells from the mobs, organized themselves into an enforcement agency and jailed 88 of the rioters.

In the earlier period of construction from Harpers Ferry to Cumberland, there was also trouble. Romney residents appealed for aid in 1837 because of raids on the town by laborers on the Chesapeake and Ohio Canal. Hedgesville saw a clash between Germans and Irish at a tunnel construction site in 1839.

Many of the Irish became permanent residents of western Virginia. Following the Civil War, they became active in West Virginia politics.

New Towns. New towns appeared along the railroad. Rowlesburg, Tunnelton, Mannington, and Newburg were established and survived after the construction period. Tunnelton developed a timber and lumber industry, as well as the first circular sawmill. Because of the railroad, Tunnelton began to mine and ship coal to the Eastern cities. Greigsville, near Tunnelton, became a busy town.

"Old Abe" "Old Abe" was captured by the Confederate army at Martinsburg in 1863 and hauled over dirt roads by manpower and horsepower to Winchester, Virginia. It served its captors until the end of the war and then was returned to the Baltimore and Ohio service.

but it disappeared when the railroad and tunnel were completed and the construction crews departed.

Old Towns. In other cases, old towns received new life. Martinsburg became a first-class railway town, possessing a Baltimore and Ohio Railroad engine house and machine shops. Next to Wheeling, Martinsburg became by 1860 the largest city in what is now the state of West Virginia. Grafton provided the location for railroad shops and buildings, became a division stop for the change of engines and crews, and also served as the terminus for the Parkersburg branch.

Near most of the towns through which the railroad passed, timber resources were developed, coal mines were opened, and shipments of cattle increased. Local manufacturing and commercial interests were stimulated, and to accommodate the greater trade the towns constructed turnpikes to outlying regions.

Celebrations. In January 1853 when the Baltimore and Ohio Railroad reached Wheeling, the *Wheeling Intelligencer* reported that thousands of people had come on steamboats, in coaches, on horseback, and on foot from near and far to celebrate the great achievement, "one of the greatest works of the age — the completion of an unbroken link connecting the Chesapeake with the waters of the Ohio."

Coal-burning Locomotive and Oil-burning Diesel
(Courtesy of West Virginia Department of Natural Resources)

In June 1857 the Northwestern Virginia Railroad was opened to Parkersburg. At the same time several other railroads were opened in other states, and so a route "The Great National Route," was provided all the way from Baltimore to St. Louis. This achievement called for the "great railway celebration" of 1857. Railroad cars, moving from Baltimore to St. Louis, stopped for speeches at different points along the road, including Parkersburg and Clarksburg. However, the major points of celebration were Cincinnati, St. Louis, and Baltimore.

Significance of the Railroad. The Baltimore and Ohio Railroad greatly increased travel between the Ohio Valley and the Atlantic Coast. It was the first railroad in the United States to carry both passengers and freight. The passengers made holiday excursions of their trips to the East and to the Middle West.

As for freight, the Baltimore and Ohio Railroad carried vast amounts of raw material from the Ohio Valley to the East. These raw materials were made into manufactured articles, and a quantity of these articles was shipped back to the West. The passenger and freight traffic bound the country closer together. The road gave entrance into Washington, D.C. The existence of the road even determined a part of the military strategy of the Civil War and perhaps determined that West Virginia would remain in the Union.

Railroad Builders

Crozet, Ellet, and Latrobe, Engineers in Western Virginia

Claude Crozet

Claude Crozet, soldier and engineer, was born in France. He fought with Napoleon and, following the French leader's defeat in 1815, migrated to the United States. In October 1816 he joined the faculty at the United States Military Academy at West Point, New York, as an assistant professor of engineering and became head of the department and professor of engineering in March 1817. In 1832 he became state engineer of Virginia. Crozet had a vision of a grand plan for coordinating all roads, canals, and railroads throughout the state.

Although his grand design was never entirely carried out, he gave Virginia one of the best transportation systems in the country at the time.

He urged, though unsuccessfully, the creation of a through route from the seaboard to the West by constructing the James River Canal from the head of navigation at Richmond up to Lynchburg, and from there by a railroad to deep water on the Kanawha River. Such a development would have greatly aided the economy of western Virginia.

Perhaps Crozet's greatest engineering achievement was the location and construction of a railroad through the Blue Ridge Mountains. This railroad later passed into the possession of the Chesapeake and Ohio Company. The Northwestern Turnpike (now U.S. 50) which connected Winchester and Parkersburg was also one of Crozet's engineering triumphs.

Charles Ellet, Jr., was born in Bucks County, Pennsylvania, to a fairly well-to-do family in 1810. His ambition was to be a civil engineer, and after working on several projects, he went to study in France in 1830. In 1836 he became chief engineer of the James River and Kanawha Canal, a work intended to connect Virginia tidewater with the Ohio and to open western Virginia to easier trade with the East.

Ellet completed the suspension bridge which served across the Ohio River at Wheeling in 1849. Across the Blue Ridge Mountains he built a railroad track of curves and grades that were most difficult to design and was in charge of improving the Kanawha River in 1858. During the Civil War, he helped build a ram-fleet for the Union. Ellet was wounded in the federal capture of Memphis, Tennessee, and died shortly afterward.

Benjamin Henry Latrobe was born in Philadelphia in 1806. He later moved to Baltimore with his family, studied mathematics, and then practiced law. In 1831 he obtained a position in the engineer corps of the Baltimore and Ohio Railroad and advanced rapidly to become principal assistant to the chief engineer.

Latrobe directed the survey which located the Baltimore and Ohio Railroad to Harpers Ferry, and in 1836 he was construction engineer when the line was built from Harpers Ferry to Cumberland, Maryland. Latrobe became the railroad's chief engineer in 1842. One of his biggest projects was the extension of the line to Wheeling.

In 1847 he headed the planning group which surveyed and constructed the line across western Virginia. With 5,000 men, drilling and loading by hand, blasting with black powder, and hauling with the aid of 1,250 horses, he directed the building of 200 miles of the railroad, including 113 bridges and 11 tunnels in less than four years. Construction of the masonry wall for the road along the slopes and hills in the Cheat River Valley and the Kingwood Tunnel (4,100 feet) were his most dramatic achievements along the route.

Today's engineers may wonder at the tremendous accomplishments of engineers in western Virginia in the mid-1800's.

Chapter 18   EAST-WEST CONFLICTS

East-West Differences

Eastern Virginians and western Virginians differed in economic, cultural, and political customs and ideals. In the east, there were large plantations on which one cash crop, such as tobacco, was grown. In the west, there were small farms producing many kinds of crops as well as pastures and grazing lands for varieties of livestock. It seemed possible that the west would develop industrially because of the valuable mineral resources which underlay the land.

In the east many of the large estates were served by slaves, but in the west, a man's labor force consisted mainly of members of his own family. In the east, inexpensive transportation outlets were plentiful on the navigable rivers running from the Blue Ridge Mountains to the Atlantic Ocean. In the west, because of the mountains, few rivers and roads had been made passable and only at great cost.

The white people of eastern Virginia were mostly English, and the black population was African. The people of western Virginia were a mixture of many stocks, with very few of them coming from the eastern part of the state. On the eve of the Civil War, only 4 percent of the total population in western Virginia was black, whereas in eastern Virginia at least a third of the people were Negro. Eastern Virginians were likely to conform to religious tradition; western Virginians were more often of dissenting faiths.

Free-Slave Differences. In 1850 the total population of western Virginia was 302,313. Of this number there were 21,736 slaves. Most of the black population was concentrated in the eastern area or the central portion of the state. Only 247 slaves were located in the Northern Panhandle counties of Hancock, Brooke, Ohio, and Marshall. By contrast, Berkeley County in the Eastern Panhandle had 1,956 slaves and 249 free Negroes.

Political Sentiments. Politically, western Virginians were more loyal to the Union than to the state, and eastern Virginians more loyal to the state than to the Union. In 1788 western Virginians had been more in favor of the new Constitution of the United States. Western Virginians had opposed the Virginia-Kentucky resolutions, which were early secession statements.

In contrast to the lukewarm sentiments of the east, the west not only heartily approved of Henry Clay's "American System" of internal improvements, national banking, and protective tariffs but also strongly advocated free schools. In politics, westerners reflected the kind of nationalism advocated by George Washington rather than the spirit of individualism and sectionalism first associated with Thomas Jefferson.

But it was in dissatisfaction with the three constitutions of Virginia, adopted in 1776, in 1829–30, and in 1850–51, that western Virginia displayed attitudes that were strongly at odds with eastern prejudices. About this time (1852) the *Wheeling Intelligencer* was established, and its editor, Archibald W. Campbell, used the influence of this important paper to condemn slavery. Campbell was a nephew of the founder of Bethany College.

Archibald W. Campbell, Editor, Who Used His Influence to Condemn Slavery *(Photo courtesy of West Virginia University Library)*

A Group of "Gentlemen Justices" Under the Virginia county system the justices of the peace of the county composed the county court. This court had great responsibility. It controlled the financial affairs of the county, held trials, and imposed penalties. *(From a sketch by J. H. Diss Debar)*

The Virginia Constitution of 1776

Earlier than the Declaration of Independence, the first constitution of Virginia went into effect on June 29, 1776. There were only two counties in the present state of West Virginia that were involved in the adoption of the Virginia constitution. These were Berkeley County and Hampshire County in the Eastern Panhandle.

Within a few years after adoption of this constitution, individuals living west of the Blue Ridge Mountains felt that there were three provisions that needed to be changed: First, the constitution limited the right to vote to white males who owned 25 acres of improved land or 50 acres of unimproved lands. Second, each county, regardless of size or population, was entitled to two delegates in the House, the lower body of the legislature; the Senate was composed of 24 members chosen from twenty-four districts, without respect to size or population. The House and Senate composed the General Assembly, the legislature of Virginia. Third, after voting for members of the General Assembly of Virginia, those qualified to vote really voted on no other matters. For example, the governor and other high officials were chosen by the two houses of the legislature. County governments were controlled by justices of the peace who made up the county court. When vacancies occurred in the county government, the county court decided who filled the vacancies in such offices as the sheriff, the coroner, and the county clerk.

Reform Efforts. Between 1776 and 1829 several efforts were made to change the original constitution. Thomas Jefferson was aware of western discontent. He had noted that the majority of men in the state who paid taxes and fought in the wars were not fairly represented in the legislature. In 1782, when there had not yet been any great movement across the Allegheny Mountains, he calculated that the more than 12,000 fighting men west of the Blue Ridge Mountains were entitled to only 32 delegates, but 37,840 men east of the Blue Ridge were entitled to 117 delegates.

Bust of John Marshall, Representative to the Virginia Convention of 1829 John Marshall is renowned yet today as a brilliant Chief Justice of the United States Supreme Court from 1801 to 1835. Marshall University in Huntington was named for him, and this bust stands to his memory in front of "Old Main" at Marshall. *(Photo courtesy of Marshall University)*

Constitutional Convention of 1829–1830

On October 5, 1829 at a constitutional convention in Richmond, capital of Virginia, 96 men from the different counties of Virginia met to rewrite the constitution, now more than fifty years old. Only 18 of the 96 men were from counties that were to make up West Virginia in later years. Consequently the chances of securing reforms pleasing to the west were not very good. Yet estimates of the white population of the state in 1829 showed not too great a difference in the number of persons in the east and in the west.

Representatives. Representatives from the east were well-known political figures. There were two former Presidents of the United States, James Madison and James Monroe, and one who would become President, John Tyler. John Marshall, Chief Justice of the United States, the two senators and the governor of the state, and eleven congressmen helped to make the eastern delegation unusually impressive. James Monroe was made president of the convention.

Representatives from the west were excellent debaters, but they were not so widely known. Among them were Alexander Campbell and Philip Doddridge of Brooke County, Charles Morgan and Eugenius M. Wilson of Monongalia County, Edwin Duncan of Harrison County, and Judge Lewis Summers representing the interests of the Kanawha Valley.

Major Issues. The major issue was representation. The west wanted representation determined on the basis of the white population only. The east wanted representation determined on the basis of white population and property which included slaves. The west wanted an extension of the right to vote and reforms in county governments. The east wanted all voting privileges restricted.

The convention finally agreed to broaden the privileges of voting by extending the vote to leaseholders (those who paid rent for a fixed number of years) and to housekeepers (those who were heads of households) who paid taxes, and to make certain reforms in county government. The number of delegates in the Assembly was reduced. The county system of representation was abolished in favor of district apportionment which was more in accord with actual county population.

In the matter of representation in the General Assembly, however, the easterners retained control, and the westerners failed to gain their objective of determining representation on a white-population basis. The state was simply divided into sections, and the number of representatives was determined by a formula. In the House, 31 delegates were allotted to the trans-Allegheny region, 25 delegates to the Valley region, 42 delegates to the Piedmont region, and 36 delegates to the Tidewater. In the Senate, counties to the east were given 19 senators, and counties to the west were given 13 senators.

With the Blue Ridge Mountains as the dividing line between east and west, the west was allotted a total of only 56 legislative delegates; the east was allotted a total of 78 delegates, out of a total of 134. Philip Doddridge put the results in the bluntest terms: As he saw it, although the east and west were equal in population, the west controlled only 41 percent of the total representatives in the legislature.

Western Reaction

The new constitution did not provide for equal representation on a white basis, which the west demanded. Also disturbing over the next several years were the small appropriations of money coming to the west from the General Assembly. Expenditures on internal improvements and public works were confined to eastern Virginia.

Western Virginia's immediate reaction to the 1829-30 convention could be seen in the vote on the new constitution. Although the constitution was approved in April 1830 by a favorable vote of 26,055 for and 15,563 against, many western Virginians were decidedly opposed to it. Within the boundary lines of present West Virginia, 1,383 were for the new constitution, but 8,365 were against it.

For the next several years western newspapers were critical of the convention and of the Virginia Assembly. There was much talk of separation from eastern Virginia. Some citizens of Wheeling considered the possibility of northwestern Virginia's becoming a part of Maryland or of Pennsylvania. Some entertained the idea of joining Ohio. In 1842 representatives of ten western counties met at Clarksburg to discuss separation. *The Kanawha Republican* proposed a new state to be named "Appalachia."

Between 1830 and 1850

Between 1830 and 1840 five new western counties were formed. In the decade 1840 to 1850, fourteen new counties were organized

Typical Western Virginians of This Period Men of western Virginia were hardy, bold, and independent as they looked to be. *(From a sketch by J. H. Diss Debar, 1848, 1849)*

in the western section. The nineteen new counties were Barbour, Boone, Braxton, Doddridge, Fayette, Gilmer, Hancock, Jackson, Marshall, Marion, Mercer, Putnam, Raleigh, Ritchie, Taylor, Wayne, Wetzel, Wirt, and Wyoming.

Better transportation was being developed. The Baltimore and Ohio Railroad was given permission to extend its lines through Virginia territory from Cumberland, Maryland, to Wheeling.

Constitutional Convention of 1850

Eastern Virginia was beginning to recognize the growing discontent in the west. The east approved another convention to consider change in the state's constitution. The second constitutional convention first met on October 14, 1850, but it adjourned to wait until up-to-date census data for 1850 were available. The convention reconvened on January 6, 1851.

Of 135 members elected to the convention, only 35 were from districts within the present state of West Virginia. Only 59 delegates were sympathetic to western interests and 76 delegates to eastern interests. Despite the inequality in numbers, the eastern delegations seemed more willing to compromise than they had been earlier. Many of the suggested reforms that had been rejected earlier now seemed likely to be accepted.

Western Representation. The west was well represented by such able men as Charles J. Faulkner of Berkeley County, Joseph Johnson and Gideon D. Camden of Harrison, John S. Carlile

Waitman T. Willey Willey was a leader in the new-state movement, United States senator under the Restored Government of Virginia, and one of the first United States senators from West Virginia. *(From a sketch by J. H. Diss Debar)*

of Barbour, Waitman T. Willey of Monongalia, and Benjamin Smith and George W. Summers of Kanawha. The west was fortunate in the fact that George W. Summers was made chairman of the committee to consider the problem of representation.

Western Victories. At this convention, the west achieved notable victories. No specific formula of representation was adopted for the entire General Assembly, but the white population as reported in the 1850 census became the principle for the proportion of members in the House. The possibility existed for the adoption of the same formula for the Senate in 1865.

Other important reforms gave the privilege of voting to all white males over 21 years of age and provided for the direct election of judges, local officials, and the governor. Local officials included sheriffs, county clerks, and justices of the peace. The governor's term of office was extended from three to four years. Jurors were to be paid for their services. A capitation tax (head tax) was levied on every voter. Out of these funds would come money to support the schools.

George W. Summers of Kanawha County attempted to become governor of Virginia in 1851 but was defeated. However, on the eve of secession from Virginia, western Virginia secured a major political triumph: Joseph Johnson of Harrison County, a westerner, was chosen governor by the direct vote of the people. He was the first resident living west of the mountains to become governor of the state of Virginia and the first governor to be chosen by the voters of the state. Later Johnson was to cast his political fortunes with the Confederacy.

Tax Loss. In overall count, the western counties now had 83 delegates in the House, and the east had 69 delegates. For the time being, the east had 30 delegates in the Senate and the west had 20. So in the Assembly, the west controlled 51 percent of the total representation.

However, the west did not do so well on the subject of taxes. Although taxes were supposed to be equal and uniform throughout the state, there were no taxes on slaves under twelve years of age. Those over the age of twelve were valued at $300 for tax purposes. Many slaves were worth six or seven times that much; so the eastern owner was receiving a decided tax benefit.

A farmer who was paying taxes on the full value of his calves, colts, lambs, and pigs regardless of their ages was placed at a special disadvantage on property taxes. Complaints on this issue were not limited to the west, but when the western farmer saw taxes used to build and support public works east of the mountains, but not west of the mountains, he knew he was being cheated.

The constitution also forbade the use of state credit to companies or corporations and prohibited lotteries. This was considered a death blow to any chances for internal improvements such as roads, canals, and railroads. It also seemed doubtful if much money would be made available for western schools.

Nevertheless, every county in western Virginia voted in favor of the reform constitution.

Western Virginia Statesman

George W. Summers, Conventioneer

George W. Summers was born March 4, 1804 in Fairfax County, Virginia. He moved with his parents to the Kanawha Valley in 1813. Taught by his older brother, Lewis, George received an excellent education for the day, and for a short period he attended Washington College (later Washington and Lee University in Lexington, Virginia) and Ohio University.

He began practicing law and was elected to the General Assembly of Virginia for the years 1830–31 and 1834–35. After winning a considerable reputation as a trial lawyer and orator, Summers was elected to the United States Congress in 1840 and 1842.

Representing Charleston at the Virginia Constitutional Convention of 1850–51, George Summers sought a better balance between the number of eastern and western representatives. He also advocated the gradual emancipation of slaves by their owners through purchase by the state, the price being paid from the proceeds of public land sales.

Summers returned from the convention a popular leader and was nominated by the Whig party to be governor of Virginia, an office which for the first time would be filled by the vote of the people. He lost the election, however, and his opposition to slavery may have been the chief reason. In May 1852 he was elected a judge in Virginia and served in that capacity until 1858.

As the Civil War approached, Virginia asked for a meeting of the states to solve the issues. Summers served from the state of Virginia at this conference and defended the Union, but the convention dissolved without reaching its goals. When the state called a convention for February 1861, Summers was elected a delegate from Kanawha County. He again upheld the Union, but the convention eventually decided to withdraw from the Union. Summers voted against the Ordinance of Secession.

George Summers took no part in the organization of the Restored Government of Virginia, preferring to remain neutral. He felt the formation of the new state of West Virginia was unnecessary. He looked to settlement of conflicts and to eventual unification of Virginia as a single state. Because of this opinion many looked upon him as disloyal to the federal government.

Summers continued to practice law in the Charleston area, where he died September 19, 1868.

Chapter 19 SLAVERY: "A FIREBELL IN THE NIGHT"

Thomas Jefferson, a most prominent Virginian, had worried over slavery. Unless slavery was ended, he felt that the issue of freedom would break forth "like a firebell in the night" and disrupt the nation. But for many years frontier Virginians were more concerned with their needs for transportation on water and on roads and for better banking facilities, and with ways of making a living.

Western Virginians certainly had no hatred for the black man; if anything, they were more antagonistic toward the "red" man. Eastern Virginians, for the most part, were determined to keep things as they always had been. Little did any of the people of the state suspect that someday western Virginians might engage in a conflict against eastern Virginians.

Convention Issue

The black man had, of course, been a consideration in the Virginia constitutional conventions of 1829–30 and 1850–51. The conventions did not concern themselves with the black man's freedom, however. The conventions were interested in questions of how to count a population in determining representation and how to tax property when slaves were considered as a white man's property. We have seen that decisions made in these conventions put western

Virginia at a disadvantage. The decisions gave western Virginia fewer representatives in the General Assembly because the westerners possessed few slaves, and the black population, both free and slave, was small there.

Black Population

Yet, in the 1860 census returns, all counties in western Virginia but one, McDowell, reported either free or slave Negroes. Counties with less than ten slaves were Calhoun, Hancock, and Webster. Seven counties had from one thousand to three thousand slaves. These were Berkeley, Greenbrier, Hampshire, Hardy, Monroe, Kanawha, and Jefferson. Jefferson had the most blacks, 4,471, of which 3,960 were slaves and 511 were free Negroes. Yet even Jefferson County had a white majority population of 10,064.

How the blacks, without the vote, without any of the privileges of citizenship, and without assistance from the whites, were to secure their freedom was the hardest of questions. Nat Turner, a Negro minister, provided one answer. He advised his people to revolt. He set the date July 4 for the uprising, but the day for black independence had to be postponed because of an illness Turner contracted. When the sun turned a "peculiar greenish blue" on August 13, 1831, Turner interpreted the sign as a clue to set the revolt for one week later.

Within the next two days Nat Turner and about sixty of his followers murdered Nat's master and sixty other whites, including women and children, in Southampton County, Virginia. The murders caused fear among all whites in Virginia and across the South.

Immediately, the advantages and disadvantages of slavery became a part of the debates in the Virginia General Assembly. But within a year or two, all debates ceased in Virginia and throughout the South. White Southerners determined that the issue of slavery was no longer to be discussed and that the slavery system as it existed was beneficial for all.

Before 1830 there were many Southerners, including Virginians as prominent as Thomas Jefferson, who doubted the benefits of slavery. Many public figures endorsed the principles of the American Colonization Society, an organization which had declared that Negroes should be set free. However, the Society imposed two conditions: The blacks could be free if their owners were paid for the loss of their slaves and if freed Negroes were returned to Africa. After Nat Turner's insurrection, however, few white persons were willing to speak out in favor of freedom for the black man. An "iron curtain" on the subject had dropped across the Southern states.

Criticism of the South was growing in the North.

Abolitionists

At approximately the time of the Turner insurrection, those who would abolish slavery, the abolitionists, were slowly organizing themselves into a political body to bring about the freeing of slaves. An important Northern leader was William Lloyd Garrison, editor of the *Liberator*, who issued the first number of his newspaper in Boston on January 1, 1831. To abolitionists like Garrison, slave-owners had no property rights in slaves. Abolitionists did not argue against slavery on legal or constitutional grounds. They spoke against slavery on moral and religious grounds.

Among the abolitionists were such men as Benjamin Lundy, Theodore Weld, James G. Birney, and Arthur and Lewis Tappan. Benjamin Lundy came to Wheeling in 1808 from New Jersey where he was born. He first came in contact with slavery in Wheeling when he witnessed coffles of blacks passing through the city in interstate trade. After learning the saddlemaking trade in Wheeling, Lundy developed a profitable saddlery business in the Upper Ohio Valley. He organized an antislavery group known as the Union Humane Society, and associated with Charles Osborne in publishing a newspaper called *The Philanthropist*. Weld carried his antislavery message to Wheeling and Parkersburg where it fell on fertile ground.

Jefferson's Rock near Harpers Ferry In 1781 Thomas Jefferson wrote that the view at Harpers Ferry is "worthy a trip across the Atlantic." Shenandoah Bridge is seen in the photo above. *(Photo courtesy of Harpers Ferry National Historical Park)*

Henry Ruffner, Advocate of Freedom for the Slaves
(From "The West Virginia Historical Magazine," Vol. 2, 1902. Picture courtesy of West Virginia Department of Archives and History)

Advocates of Slavery

To offset the abolitionist attack, defenders of slavery in the South developed arguments in behalf of slavery. They declared that the Bible sanctioned slavery. They believed history proved that the most advanced civilizations had been a result of slavery. Supporters of the system were keenly aware of the financial investments made in slavery, for much money had been spent in purchasing and providing for slaves. Many cautioned that agricultural commodities such as tobacco, cotton, rice, and sugarcane could be profitable only if the crops were harvested by slave labor.

Defenders of slavery were convinced that, if equality between white and black people were the rule, the two races could not live in harmony together. Among those advocating slavery were Thomas R. Dew, a professor at William and Mary College, and John C. Calhoun, senator from South Carolina and intellectual leader for the entire South.

Western Virginians and Slavery

Western Virginians did not feel so strongly on the issue of slavery as did eastern Virginians. For one thing, the black population in western Virginia was, as we have learned, considerably smaller than in eastern Virginia. Also westerners had had little experience with slave labor, and many felt that slave labor was more suited to large-scale agriculture than it was to the small-scale domestic industry of the west.

Many people in western Virginia believed the future of their part of the state was going to be industrial rather than agricultural. Two prominent western Virginians who questioned the wisdom of supporting the institution of slavery both in the state and in the nation were Henry Ruffner and Alexander Campbell. Both were ministers.

Henry Ruffner. Henry Ruffner, an educator as well as a minister and missionary, had moved from eastern Virginia into the Kanawha Valley when he was a young boy. His father, David Ruffner, had gone to the Kanawha Valley to engage in the production of salt.

In the early period of his life in western Virginia, Henry Ruffner organized two churches, one in Charleston and one in Teays Valley. He also served for a time as director of Mercer Academy in Charleston. Later, he left western Virginia to serve as president and professor of ancient languages at Washington College, later Washington and Lee University. But he soon returned as minister to his father's church at Malden.

Ruffner Pamphlet. In 1847 Henry Ruffner made an important address on the subject of slavery before the Franklin Society in Lexington, Virginia. Although he disapproved of abolitionists as well as of men who wished to leave the Union because of the slavery issue, he felt he had found a satisfactory solution. He spoke in favor of the gradual emancipation of slaves in western Virginia. Ruffner was convinced that the western areas without slavery would be more prosperous than those with slavery. He contrasted the cities of Wheeling and Pittsburgh in order to prove his point. He concluded that Pittsburgh was forging ahead of Wheeling because Wheeling was in a state in which slavery was established by law, and Pittsburgh was in a state which opposed slavery.

Ruffner wanted masters to be required to have the children of emancipated slaves taught reading, writing, and arithmetic. He urged that all children of current slaves be set free by the time they were twenty-five years old. He advocated that there be no further importation of slaves into western Virginia. His thoughts on the matter were put into pamphlet form, and the Ruffner pamphlet was widely read in the period before the Civil War, not only in western Virginia but across the nation.

National Compromises

By 1850 the slavery crisis in the nation was extremely serious. A war between the North and the South seemed near. In the emergency, the Congress of the United States adopted several legislative acts which offered benefits to quiet all sections of the country. These acts were known as the Compromise of 1850. Among these measures was one which permitted the people in the new territories to decide for themselves whether they wished to have slavery or not. Another

Harpers Ferry Today At Harpers Ferry in Jefferson County in 1859 a dramatic episode preceded the Civil War. John Brown was the leader in this event. The name "Harper" derives from Robert Harper, who purchased squatter rights here in 1747, started operating ferries across the Potomac and Shenandoah rivers, and built a mill. *(West Virginia Department of Commerce Photo)*

law, a concession to the South, was the Fugitive Slave Act, which stated that no one was to assist slaves in escaping from their masters. The abolitionists were determined that the Fugitive Slave Act should not be obeyed.

Attitudes of the Churches

With religious ministers taking definite positions on the subject of slavery, churches, perhaps inevitably, became the early battlefields for arguments. The discussions split many of the congregations into opposing sides, and the nation saw many churches dividing into Northern and Southern branches.

Alexander Campbell, leader and one of the founders of the Disciples of Christ Church and president of Bethany College, was called upon to make known his views on the Fugitive Slave Act. This he did in his paper *The Millennial Harbinger*. This periodical had a large circulation and a great influence in western Virginia and across the country. Alexander Campbell regretted the existence of slavery in the United States. Yet he admitted that the Constitution recognized slavery and that the laws of Congress forbade anyone from helping slaves escape from their masters.

But to Campbell, there was nothing wrong in being charitable to a runaway slave. As long as one did not hide the slave, Campbell advised that anyone could most certainly furnish the black man with food, clothing, and lodging. To Campbell, all suffering humanity was entitled to these necessities of life.

To quiet the turmoil in the nation, Campbell suggested that the North permit the South to have slaves. Campbell also believed that criticism of slave-owners was a waste of time and not entirely fair; that one might sympathize with slave-owners for they had inherited the situation rather than originated it. Campbell, as a law-abiding citizen, believed he had no choice under the Constitution but to accept the Compromise of 1850, which permitted new territories to decide the question of slavery for themselves, and also to accept the Fugitive Slave Act.

The Catholic Church, the Disciples of Christ Church, and the German religious denominations had organizations that resisted division over the Civil War, and generally western Virginians disapproved of slavery. But the Episcopal Church in Virginia favored slavery. Many slave-owners who were Methodists, Baptists, and Presbyterians also approved slavery. In the Eastern Panhandle, the Kanawha Valley, and the Greenbrier area there was considerable sentiment for slavery.

In western Virginia, the Methodist Episcopal Church took a stand solidly against slavery. This was due, in large part, to the influence of men like Gordon Battelle and members of the Methodist congregations like Waitman T. Willey and Arthur I. Boreman.

In 1844 Methodists who supported slavery first proposed forming the Methodist Episcopal Church South. This church became a reality the next year. In 1850 the West Virginia Conference of the Methodist Episcopal Church South was organized at Malden. Originally there were the Parkersburg, the Greenbrier, and the Guyandotte districts, and by 1860 this church had a membership of 12,694 members.

There was also a Methodist Protestant Church, organized in 1828, which was more concerned with internal democratic procedures than with slavery itself. Active members in this organization were the Reverend Asa Shinn and Francis H. Pierpont, provisional governor. For the most part, the Methodist Protestant Church withheld its support of slavery.

chapter nineteen / slavery: "a firebell in the night"

Harper House (Restored) Notice the interesting building materials and the simple, attractive lines of the architecture. *(Photo courtesy of Harpers Ferry National Historical Park)*

In 1861 Presbyterians whose sympathy was with the South withdrew from the General Assembly of the Presbyterian Church in order to unite with an organization formed within the Confederate States of America. Presbyterianism in western Virginia had been administered by two synods: the Synod of Virginia, which took care of the southern area, and the Synod of Pittsburgh, which supervised the northern area.

Until 1861 all Baptist churches in western Virginia generally cooperated with the General Association of Virginia and were known as Virginia Baptists. But at the time of the war, most Baptist churches were disorganized due to congregational differences on slavery.

Harpers Ferry

After the Nat Turner revolt in eastern Virginia in 1831, the next exciting event before the Civil War was the John Brown raid at Harpers Ferry in western Virginia in 1859. In the early days Harpers Ferry was known as Shenandoah Falls. In 1733 Peter Stephen and an Indian companion by the name of Gutterman Tom established a home there. In 1747 Robert Harper, an Englishman, bought their log cabin and land and canoe. In 1749 Harper also purchased land from Lord Fairfax. He established a ferry on his lands.

The community was incorporated as Harpers Ferry in 1763. An arsenal and a gun factory were established there by acts of Congress in 1794 and 1799. By 1859 Harpers Ferry had become an industrial town containing about 3,000 inhabitants. To this town came John Brown.

John Brown. John Brown, born at Torrington, Connecticut, in 1800, was the son of Owen Brown, an abolitionist and agent of the underground railroad, by which runaway slaves escaped to Canada, where they were free.

John Brown followed various occupations, such as tanner, land speculator, sheep raiser, and wool merchant. In search of grazing lands, he visited Doddridge and Tyler counties in western Virginia in 1840. Brown lived in many places. He resided for a time in Hudson, Ohio; Richmond, Pennsylvania; North Elba, New York; Akron, Ohio; and Osawatomie, Kansas. For his acts in Kansas in 1855 he became known all over the country.

In the Kansas territory abolitionists and slave-owners were engaged in a civil war. When Lawrence, Kansas, an antislavery center, was under siege by proslavery forces, Brown entered the conflict. With the help of four of his sons, Brown murdered five persons. He claimed that God had directed the attack.

This incident horrified the South. But it convinced Brown that he should strike for the freedom of all Negroes. He now moved to

John Brown *(Pencil sketch by William Morris Stutler from a photo by J. W. Black, Boston, May 1859)*

chapter nineteen / slavery: "a firebell in the night"

Sandy Hook, Maryland, and later to Dr. Booth Kennedy's farm five miles from Harpers Ferry. On the Kennedy farm Brown stored boxes of ammunition, rifles, pistols, bayonets, and a cannon to be used for freeing the slaves. The costs of the equipment had been borne by Northerners. Prominent among them was Gerrit Smith of New York.

During his three months' residence in the vicinity of Harpers Ferry, Brown called himself Isaac Smith. He said he was in the area to look for minerals. He also explained that his many boxes were household goods and that they would be opened when Mrs. Smith joined him.

Capture of Harpers Ferry. On October 16, 1859 Brown and a party of eighteen men took possession of Harpers Ferry. He captured not only the arsenal but also the rifle works about a mile away. He held some residents as prisoners, seized control of the bridges, detained a railroad train, and cut the telegraph wires. In capturing Harpers Ferry he killed only one person, a free Negro who was baggage master at the railroad station.

The Engine House, "John Brown's Fort," at Harpers Ferry (Gerald S. Ratliff Photo, West Virginia Department of Commerce)

Jefferson County Courthouse, Charles Town *(From the Collections of the Library of Congress. Reproduced by permission of Harpers Ferry National Historical Park)*

Among his prisoners was the great-grandnephew of George Washington, Colonel Lewis W. Washington, who lived five miles from Harpers Ferry. After seizing Colonel Washington and freeing his slaves, Brown took the famous Washington sword. This sword had been given to George Washington by Frederick the Great, king of Prussia, with the sentiment: "from the oldest general in the world to the greatest." Brown believed that possessing the sword insured his victory.

Brown's Capture and Trial. The blacks, instead of joining Brown in his fight, spread the word of his seizure of Harpers Ferry. The Charles Town militia surrounded the town and prevented Brown's escape. Brown asked that he and his men be allowed to leave, but his request was refused.

On October 17 the fight began in earnest. The mayor of Harpers Ferry, the Baltimore and Ohio station agent, and three of Brown's followers were killed. The United States Marines, under the command of Colonel Robert E. Lee and Lieutenant J. E. B. Stuart, were sent to Harpers Ferry. On October 18 they seized Brown and some of his men who had taken refuge in the engine house. Brown was arrested and taken to Charles Town, Jefferson County, for trial.

One of the observers of the trial was Porte Crayon, a western Virginian, whose real name was David Hunter Strother. Strother was a resident of nearby Martinsburg in Berkeley County. He had become one of the nation's highest-paid writers. He produced both sketches and travel essays for *Harper's Magazine*. He not only sketched John Brown on his deathbed but acted as the nation's sole reporter at the trial.

Within a week Brown was found guilty. His plans to liberate the Southern slaves and to set up a government of Virginia with himself as its chief executive, were exposed. He was convicted of treason and conspiracy and was sentenced to death by hanging. In the North Brown now became a martyr.

Later History of Harpers Ferry

Harpers Ferry became a strategic fort during the Civil War. The town and its railroad bridge were captured and recaptured many times. Colonel Thomas J. "Stonewall" Jackson of the Confederate army considered Harpers Ferry of major strategic value to the entire Valley of Virginia. But General Joseph E. Johnston and General Robert E. Lee did not assign it so high a priority, and on occasion did not contest its capture by Union forces.

Once the town was burned, with the exception of the engine house, or "John Brown's Fort." In 1892 the fort was dismantled and shipped for display at the World's Columbian Exposition in Chicago. After the world's fair closed, the fort was sold, and its purchaser proposed to use it for a stable. But due to appeals from Negroes throughout the country and with aid from Miss Kate Field, an actress and journalist, sufficient funds were raised to purchase the building and to return it to Harpers Ferry. In 1910 the building was moved there, to the campus of Storer College, where it served as a museum.

Storer College. Storer College was established at Harpers Ferry in 1866 for the education of former slaves and their descendants.

The college was founded by the Freedman's Bureau through the financial aid of John Storer of Stanford, Maine. Upon the withdrawal of state subsidy in 1955, the college was forced to close.

Renowned Citizen of State and Nation

Alexander Campbell, Minister

Alexander Campbell was born in Ireland on September 12, 1788. His parents attended to his religious and moral education devotedly, and by the time he was sixteen Alexander had joined a church and become an instructor at an academy his father had established. At an early age, he was influenced by independent religious sects and contrasted their teachings with what he considered to be the teachings of the Presbyterian Church.

In 1809, after a year of study at the University of Glasgow, he joined his father in America and eventually settled at Washington, Pennsylvania. Here he and his father became members of a congregation known as the Christian Association, a local independent church.

Alexander Campbell resolved to devote himself to the reform of religion. He conscientiously studied the Bible and classical languages and began a consistent program of preaching in 1810. After the organization of a Church of Disciples at Brush Run, Pennsylvania, he was licensed to preach. The church soon joined a Baptist association.

As Campbell's preachings were not acceptable to the Baptists, he moved on to found Buffalo Seminary at Bethany, in the present state of West Virginia, for the education of young people and the training of preachers. After a few years, however, the seminary was discontinued, and Alexander proceeded to preach and to debate religious issues.

Believing in the power of newspapers and journals to influence thought in the United States, Alexander Campbell started the *Christian Baptist* in 1823 and built up a successful journal through which he spread his opinions among the people. By 1827 he had published a new translation of the Bible, and in 1828 he prepared a volume of 125 hymns.

From 1830 his interest in the second coming of Christ led him to publish the very successful *The Millennial Harbinger*. At Wellsburg, in western Virginia, Campbell published more than fifty volumes and pamphlets which were largely concerned with biblical subjects. He began to travel more and participated in western Virginia politics as a delegate to the Virginia constitutional convention in 1829-30.

Campbell's views and opinions eventually helped form the principles upon which the Disciples of Christ Church was founded, and his beliefs spread throughout the West and even to Canada and Britain. He founded Bethany College in 1840 and was active in the teaching of intellectual and moral philosophy, political economy, and the Bible.

In 1847 he went abroad and preached and lectured in leading cities of England and on the European continent.

As to slavery, Campbell saw no sin in the relation of master to servant, but he felt that slavery was not suitable and was not an advantage in modern civilization. This indecisive attitude helped keep the Disciples of Christ Church from dividing during the Civil War.

Alexander Campbell continued to travel widely throughout the North and the South until his death in March 1866. He bequeathed his excellent library to Bethany College.

Chapter 20 VIRGINIA: UNION AND CONFEDERATE

Early Secession Efforts

Between 1776 and 1860 it seemed possible that the United States might not be able to hold together as a single nation. In the time of Aaron Burr and Harman Blennerhassett, the western areas engaged in several plots to leave the Union. Both before and during the War of 1812, the New England section considered withdrawing from the nation. In President Andrew Jackson's administration (1829–1837), the state of South Carolina threatened to secede.

A Critical Decade

The situation from 1850 to 1860 was one of the most critical the nation had faced. In that decade, the Civil War seemed imminent. The major issue seemed to be whether control of the federal government should be exercised by the North or by the South. Up to 1850 the South had been dominant, but the North was about to gain control because of its constantly growing population.

The two sections had different viewpoints on the tariff, on internal improvements, on slavery, and on territorial expansion. The conflict in their attitudes on these matters developed because the South was primarily agricultural and the North believed its future lay in industry. The section that could control the federal government would have advantages on its side.

The West as a section sometimes supported the South and sometimes the North. Always gaining in new lands and people, the West probably held the key to victory in any contest between the North and the South. By 1860 the West had become convinced that a strong national Union was in the West's best interest. Generally in western Virginia, this same sentiment prevailed, and most of the people west of the Alleghenies could be considered as "nationalists" rather than "secessionists."

One test of a belief in nationalism is a people's willingness to engage in battles to preserve the nation. Before the Civil War, western Virginia had contributed more than its share of manpower in all of the American wars. We have already noted western Virginia's special contributions in the American Revolutionary War. It also sent more than its quota of men to the War of 1812 and the Mexican War.

Western Virginia and National Wars

In the War of 1812 (1812–15) western Virginians had made up most of the total membership of 52 companies of the army resisting the British forces. The western area also supplied a 1,000-man brigade which was placed under the command of General William H. Harrison in Ohio. Western Virginians fought on land and sea in all of the major battles of the war.

When eastern Virginia was invaded in 1814, so many volunteers from western Virginia rushed to the defense of the states, as well as to the defense of the national capital, that more than 1,000 men had to be returned home. Volunteers numbered 15,000 men.

For western Virginia the Mexican War held less interest than the previous two wars which had involved American independence from England. Objectives of the Mexican War were, mainly, the addition of more territory to the United States and, especially among influential Southerners, the addition of more slaveholding states. Such a purpose caused the war to be viewed as a military effort more in behalf of Southern interests than of national interests. Nevertheless, more western Virginians than could be used volunteered for military service.

Most of those in service from the present state of West Virginia were from the counties of Berkeley and Jefferson in the Eastern Panhandle. They were placed under the regimental command of

Colonel John F. Hamtramck Colonel Hamtramck, of Shepherdstown, Jefferson County, commanded the Virginia regiment in the War with Mexico, 1846–48, and was military governor of Saltillo, Mexico, in 1848.

John F. Hamtramck of Shepherdstown. However, Monongalia and Cabell counties supplied men to several companies under the command of General Zachary Taylor. Monongalia, Cabell, Kanawha, Ohio, Preston, and Harrison counties each offered complete companies. But as the entire state of Virginia had been asked to contribute only one regiment in this war, the six complete companies were not enrolled.

From the Mexican War came two western Virginia soldiers who were to become heroes of the Civil War. One was Thomas J. "Stonewall" Jackson, destined to become a Confederate officer. Another was Jesse Lee Reno, destined to become a Union officer. Both had been trained at the United States Military Academy at West Point. We shall read later about these outstanding military leaders.

The Slavery Issue

In the growing contest between the North and the South, the most divisive issue was slavery. The West and western Virginia had little investment in slavery and were somewhat neutral on the subject. But most Westerners, like most Easterners, Southerners, and Northerners, were hopeful that a solution could be found and war avoided.

1860 Election

In 1860 Abraham Lincoln was elected President of the United States. Lincoln carried no Southern state in the election. In the

chapter twenty / virginia: union and confederate

state of Virginia he received less than 2,000 votes. Here each of three other candidates for the presidency received more votes than Lincoln did. Most of the votes for Lincoln came from western Virginia.

The Confederate States of America

Following the election of Lincoln, representatives from six of the seven states of the lower South met in convention on February 4, 1861 and drew up a provisional constitution for a new nation. This constitution was adopted by the convention March 11, 1861. The new government was called the Confederate States of America. At first the Confederate States was composed of South Carolina, which had already withdrawn in December; Georgia, Alabama, Florida, Mississippi, and Louisiana, all of which had withdrawn from the Union in January; and Texas, which had withdrawn in February. Jefferson Davis of Mississippi and Alexander H. Stephens of Georgia were chosen President and Vice-President.

Virginia's Decision

The Southern states tended to look to Virginia for leadership. For one reason, Virginia had provided important national leaders. Five Virginians had served as President of the United States: George Washington, Thomas Jefferson, James Madison, James Monroe, and John Tyler; and Virginian John Marshall had served as Chief Justice of the United States Supreme Court. For another reason, from the beginning of the nation, Virginians had questioned the great power exercised by the central government in Washington.

On January 7, 1861 Governor John Letcher called the Virginia General Assembly into extra session in Richmond. Among other matters, the legislature adopted a resolution denying the right of the federal government to coerce, or force, a state into action against its own judgment. The Assembly reorganized the state militia. It also authorized an election on February 4 to choose delegates to a convention which would consider Virginia's position within the Union. Important decisions of the convention were to be referred to a vote of the people for acceptance or rejection.

One hundred and fifty-two delegates, mostly friendly to the Union and opposed to secession, were elected to the Assembly which met in Richmond February 13, 1861. But the events of the next three months changed the pro-Union sentiment of the convention.

President Abraham Lincoln *(J. H. Diss Debar made the sketch of the President in Washington in June 1864)*

Lincoln was inaugurated on March 4. Fort Sumter was fired upon April 12. Lincoln called for military troops from the states April 15. Governor Letcher refused to supply Virginia's quota of men. To him and to others, this call for troops could cause a state to act against its will. The Civil War had begun, and the delegates to the convention in Richmond were deeply concerned about the new situation.

Ordinance of Secession. On April 17 the convention voted 88 to 55 for an Ordinance of Secession. This ordinance was to become effective if approved by a vote of the people on May 23. At the convention, 49 of the 50 counties which were to become West Virginia were represented. McDowell County did not send delegates. The total of delegates from all the western counties was 47 rather than 49 because some counties sent one delegate jointly.

Of the 47 delegates, 11 voted for the Ordinance of Secession; 32 voted against the Ordinance of Secession; and 4 did not vote. After some late voting and switching of votes at the expense of those loyal to the Union, the final vote from the western counties showed only 15 for secession, less than one-third of the western delegation.

Western Virginians who were opposed to secession soon departed for their homes to help defeat the ordinance when the people would vote on it. Prominent among such individuals was John S. Carlile, a convention delegate from Harrison County. Carlile was responsible for a protest meeting in Clarksburg on April 22. In this "convention" Carlile opposed the secession ordinance, and those who were present authorized a convention of the "wisest, best, and discreetest men" of Virginia to meet in Wheeling on May 13.

First Wheeling Convention

In Washington Hall in Wheeling, the convention assembled. The delegates came near to proclaiming the western counties a separate state. But they decided it was wise to await the outcome of the statewide vote by the people. If the state as a whole approved the secession ordinance, the Wheeling Convention proposed that delegates from the western counties be elected to a general convention on July 11, 1861, to decide the matter for themselves.

If Carlile had had his way in the First Wheeling Convention, a new state would then have been proclaimed without authority of the United States. But the United States Constitution did not permit

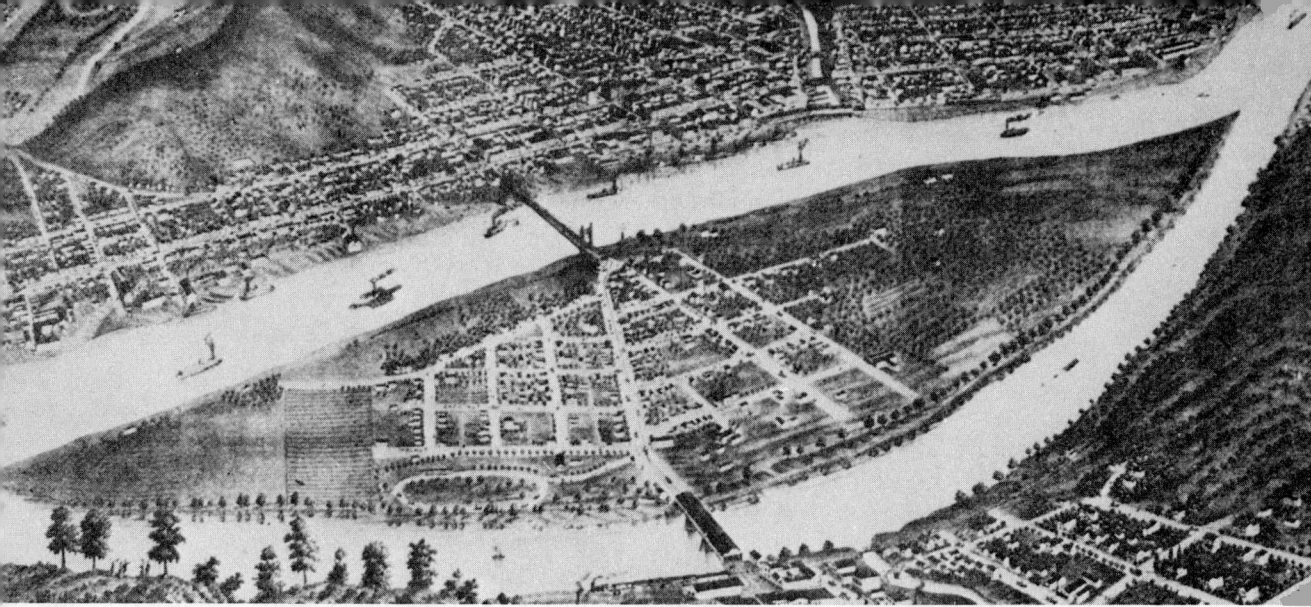

Bird's-Eye View of Wheeling, 1861 The oval appearing in the picture of the Ohio River island is the location of Camp Carlile during the Civil War. *(Photo courtesy of West Virginia University Library)*

the creation of a new state out of an existing state without the existing state's consent.

Second Wheeling Convention

On May 23 the voters of the state of Virginia passed the Ordinance of Secession, but west of the mountains the majority still disapproved. So the stage was set for the Second Wheeling Convention. Chances of success for the western convention were particularly favorable because by this time northwestern Virginia had been occupied by the Union army under the command of General George B. McClellan. On June 11 about 100 delegates from 34 counties of the present state of West Virginia organized the Second Wheeling Convention.

The delegates thanked General McClellan for the protection given to the convention by his troops. The delegates also declared that the secession convention of Virginia was illegal. By means of their own ordinance, they declared themselves the Reorganized Government of Virginia, loyal to the Union. Francis H. Pierpont was elected governor.

The Two States of Virginia

In 1861 there were two Virginias. One, with its capital in Richmond, had joined the Confederate States of America. The other, which called itself the Reorganized, or Restored, Government of

Virginia, had its capital in Wheeling. The Confederate Virginia's governor was John Letcher. Both state governments claimed the other had acted illegally and without authority of the people. Both claimed the entire territory of the original state of Virginia.

A Western Virginian Sent to Congress

John S. Carlile, Undecided Politician

John S. Carlile was born in Winchester, Virginia, on December 16, 1817. He received his early education and his training in morals from his mother. At age fourteen he became a store clerk. After an attempt in a business of his own, which produced only debts, Carlile studied and became a lawyer by 1840. Moving to Clarksburg, he became prominent in the fields of law and politics. Eventually, he served as a state senator, member of the Virginia constitutional convention of 1850–51, and United States senator.

Though defeated as a candidate for Congress in 1857, Carlile faithfully represented the pro-Union sentiment of his people at the secession convention of Virginia held in Richmond in 1861. His extreme views and aggressive conduct made him a target of abuse in the pro-secessionist area of the state, and there were several purported threats against his life.

Carlile returned home with the idea of creating a new state and placing it in the Union which Virginia had forsaken. At the First Wheeling Convention, his proposal of forming a new and separate state had been defeated, but Carlile could not let his proposal die. He was chosen as a United States senator to represent the Reorganized Government of Virginia and was entrusted with the management of a bill to create West Virginia.

Carlile wished to include in the new state the counties of the Shenandoah Valley which were loyal to the old state of Virginia, and this attempt endangered the whole project. Henceforth, Carlile lost his position as leader in the effort to create a new state. He was never again elected to public office.

President Grant nominated Carlile as ambassador to Sweden, but leaders in the United States Senate refused to confirm his appointment. Carlile died in Clarksburg on October 24, 1878.

| unit six | An Old and a New Dominion |

Chapter 21 — THE CIVIL WAR IN WESTERN VIRGINIA

Virginian Against Virginian

The American Civil War brought many personal tragedies in the western part of the state. Sympathies were divided. It was difficult to distinguish friend from foe. Relatives argued and fought against relatives, and neighbors against neighbors.

The John Rogers Cooke family in Martinsburg, West Virginia, affords an example of differences within one family during the Civil War. John Esten Cooke was serving in the Confederate army, while his uncle, Philip St. George Cooke, was an officer in the Union army. The Unionist Cooke was opposed not only by his Confederate nephew but by his famous Confederate son-in-law, J. E. B. Stuart.

Dispute raged in the Jackson family of West Virginia. Thomas J. "Stonewall" Jackson was a great Confederate army officer; his sister, Laura Jackson Arnold, was loyal to the Union and is honored every Memorial Day by an American flag placed over her grave in Buckhannon, West Virginia.

Occasionally, family loyalties were kept secret until the last possible moment. Holmes Conrad knew of the secret loyalties and the nature of the war services of his sons, Holmes and Tucker, and his nephew, Peyton Harrison, only when their bodies were returned to Berkeley County for burial in their Confederate uniforms.

Bitter incidents such as these occurred in many West Virginia families from 1861 to 1865.

Types of West Virginia Volunteers in the Union Army
(Sketched from life by J. H. Diss Debar)

Union Forces. It is difficult to estimate the number of West Virginians who served in the Union forces and in the Confederate forces; some men re-enlisted, some served in other states, and some from other states enlisted in West Virginia. The official estimate is that West Virginia furnished approximately 32,000 regular troops to the Union army. Two hundred and twelve were black soldiers. Enlistments filled 17 regiments of infantry, 7 regiments of cavalry, and a regiment of artillery.

An additional number of men were in the 32 companies of Home Guards, or state militia. The number of men in home defense has been calculated at 2,300. It has also been estimated that more than 3,000 West Virginians in the Union army lost their lives during the Civil War.

Confederate Forces. The number of West Virginians who served in the Confederate army can only be guessed. Adjutant general reports for West Virginia indicate that there were no fewer than 9,000 Confederate enlistments, of which 4,000 probably came from the Eastern Panhandle. Jefferson County alone supplied 1,600 men to the Confederate army.

Another section of the state which was strongly Confederate was the area south of the Kanawha River. Also from the Northern Panhandle and Monongalia County several companies were enlisted in the cause of the Confederate States of America. Twelve companies of West Virginians were in the "Stonewall Brigade," and many West Virginians were found in the Thirty-first and Thirty-sixth Virginia Infantry companies. West Virginians predominated in the Twenty-second Virginia Regiment.

No official estimates of deaths of Confederate soldiers in West Virginia have been provided. It is known that after the war, the adjutant general paroled 5,000 Confederates in and around the Kanawha Valley.

Importance of West Virginia

In the larger strategy of the Civil War, West Virginia was important to both the Unionists and the Confederates for five reasons. First, both sides desired to hold the saltworks in the southern part of the state. Second, in the northern part of the state, control of the Baltimore and Ohio Railroad, the Northwestern Virginia Railroad, and turnpikes leading to the railroads was imperative. Troops and food supplies which passed to the east over the railroads and the turnpikes were vital to the success or failure of the Northern armies. Third, control of the counties in the Eastern Panhandle was essential. Confederate and Union soldiers were brought through these counties to major battles fought in Pennsylvania, Maryland, and Virginia. Fourth, possession of West Virginia as one of the border states (along with Maryland, Delaware, Kentucky, Tennessee, and Missouri) was an objective of Lincoln. By holding border states in the Union the President sought to keep to a minimum the number of states joining the Confederacy.

Fifth, after Virginia withdrew from the Union, breaking this prominent state of the Confederacy into two parts would be a great triumph, both military and political, for the Union.

Action in the Eastern Panhandle

The first year of war, 1861, saw policy changes in Confederate strategy in the Eastern Panhandle. At the time Virginia adopted the Ordinance of Secession in April, the Confederates seized Harpers Ferry and seemed prepared to control the Baltimore and Ohio Railroad in their own interests. But within a month, the Confederate government decided to do everything in its power to destroy the road, and to dismantle the best of its rails, rolling stock, and machinery for use on the railways of the lower South.

In May 1861 Thomas J. "Stonewall" Jackson, who was placed in command of Harpers Ferry for a short period, captured 56 locomotives and hundreds of cars of the Baltimore and Ohio Railroad and transported them into eastern Virginia. On June 20 forty-two engines and approximately 300 cars were thrown into a great fire in the vicinity of Martinsburg.

David Hunter Strother, writing as Porte Crayon, for *Harper's Magazine*, reported the destruction. He also noted the feeling of relief expressed by one of the Negroes regarding the fate of the

Skirmish at the Bridge across the South Branch at Romney June 13, 1861   *(From a contemporary sketch by Gookins, 11th Indiana Infantry, in "Harper's Weekly," July 6, 1861)*

locomotive disintegrating in the heat. The Negro thanked God that the engines were now almost "out of their misery."

For the next four years, the Eastern Panhandle saw a series of raids and counter-raids by Confederates attempting to destroy the railroad and by Federals attempting to put the road back into condition to operate. Martinsburg, a machine-shop center for the Baltimore and Ohio Railroad, changed hands no less than ten times during the war. Five major military operations, including the Battle of Falling Waters, occurred inside Berkeley County. A rough time estimate of occupation shows Martinsburg under supervision of Union forces for about 32 months and under control of Confederate forces for about 16 months, a two-to-one ratio. Romney, the county seat of Hampshire County, was captured and recaptured 56 times during the four years of the Civil War.

Battle of Philippi — 1861

The first year of the war, 1861, saw the development of Union strategy in trans-Allegheny Virginia. The objective was to drive out organized Confederate forces from northwestern Virginia. Success would serve two purposes: (1) protection of the Baltimore and Ohio Railroad and (2) protection of the delegates who were

Brigadier General B. F. Kelley and His Staff General Kelley is seen seated with his private secretary. The general was assigned to the control of Confederate partisans in central West Virginia. *(From "Harper's Weekly")*

Veteran of the Civil War The bridge at Philippi was used by both Northern and Southern troops during the war. This is one of the most celebrated covered bridges in the United States.

planning the new state of West Virginia. To achieve these results, aid was requested of Union General McClellan, who was stationed nearby in Cincinnati, Ohio.

The Confederates began their operations immediately after the First Wheeling Convention. Colonel George A. Porterfield, Confederate officer stationed at Grafton, on May 25 began to destroy bridges and tunnels of the Baltimore and Ohio and the Northwestern Virginia railroads. McClellan responded to the emergency by dispatching troops across the Ohio to Wheeling, Benwood, and Parkersburg. Colonel Benjamin F. Kelley, commander of the 1st West Virginia Infantry, was ordered to proceed by rail from Wheeling toward Grafton, and other Union forces were directed to close in on Porterfield from the south.

On May 28 the Confederate Porterfield, faced with a pincer movement by Federals, withdrew to Philippi, eighteen miles south of Grafton. The move was made too late. On June 3, 1861 Porterfield was routed by Kelley and driven back to Beverly. The retreat of the Confederate forces was so rapid that it was referred to as the "Philippi Races." The Battle of Philippi, also called the first land battle of the Civil War, was a bloodless encounter but a victory important for its psychological effect.

In the Monongahela Valley — 1861

After the defeat at Philippi, the Confederate forces at Beverly were placed under a new commander, Brigadier General Robert S. Garnett. Garnett established strong positions on Rich Mountain

Battle of Rich Mountain *(From an original painting by Chappel. Photo courtesy of West Virginia University Library)*

and Laurel Hill for the purpose of controlling turnpikes leading to the Baltimore and Ohio Railroad. His larger objective was to move against Clarksburg, Grafton, and the Cheat River railroad bridge at Rowlesburg. Because of these Confederate developments, McClellan left his Ohio headquarters and entered western Virginia to assume command in person. He brought with him about 20,000 Union troops.

Rich Mountain. In June McClellan left Clarksburg for Rich Mountain, and General Thomas A. Morris led a force south from Philippi to contain the Confederates under General Garnett on Laurel Hill. On June 30 McClellan's leading brigade, commanded by General William S. Rosecrans, occupied Buckhannon on the Staunton and Parkersburg Turnpike. McClellan's forces joined the main body of forces there on July 1. Nine days later Rosecrans met the Confederates under the command of Colonel John Pegram on Rich Mountain and achieved victory.

The Union forces had been aided by a young boy, David Hart, who showed them a secret pass to Rich Mountain which enabled them to attack Pegram's forces from the rear. The Battle of Rich Mountain was the first important battle of the Civil War after Fort Sumter.

chapter twenty-one / the civil war in western virginia

Camp and Fortification on Cheat Mountain Summit (Contemporary sketch made by a soldier artist of the 2nd West Virginia Infantry)

Corrick's Ford. Garnett, hearing of the defeat at Rich Mountain, attempted to escape from Laurel Hill by way of the Northwestern Turnpike. But on July 13 he was killed in battle at Corrick's Ford, a location which is now the town of Parsons. However, 3,000 of his army managed to retreat behind Confederate lines in the upper South Branch Valley, and the Union victory was not so decisive as it could have been.

Importance of McClellan Victories. Progress toward forming the state of West Virginia had begun at the Wheeling conventions. McClellan, by his control of the Monongahela Valley, aided the formation of the state and influenced its future size. He prevented the disruption of the main line of the Baltimore and Ohio. His victories determined the Confederate boundary line in the state as the Allegheny Mountains rather than the Ohio River. McClellan was soon appointed to supreme command of the Union forces. McClellan's forces had captured 1,000 prisoners including more than 40 officers and had killed 250 of the enemy. He had taken hundreds of arms, baggage, and camp equipage. All this was done, he said, with the loss to the Union army of only 20 killed and 60 wounded.

In the Kanawha Valley — 1861

General Henry A. Wise, a Confederate who had served as governor of Virginia from 1856 to 1860, believed that his Virginia troops could control Charleston and the mouth of the Kanawha River if they went in over the James River and Kanawha Turnpike. If successful, he could then turn the troops north to Parkersburg and to Wheeling. The Kanawha Valley was believed to be sympathetic to the Confederacy, and Wise thought his plan could succeed. Following the passage of the Virginia Ordinance of Secession, he moved his troops from eastern Virginia into the Charleston area and started to the Ohio River.

In July 1861 McClellan's forces invaded the Kanawha Valley to stop the Confederate advance. Jacob D. Cox, a Union general, suffered defeat at Scary Creek on July 17, 1861, but he succeeded in driving the Confederates under command of General Wise back through Charleston to the present site of Gauley Bridge. Cox's forces stopped at Gauley Bridge because Wise had burned the viaduct in his retreat to White Sulphur Springs.

At White Sulphur Springs, Wise was joined by John B. Floyd, also a former governor of Virginia, who assumed command of the combined Confederate forces in western Virginia.

Union General Rosecrans stationed the Seventh Ohio Infantry under Colonel Erastus B. Tyler at Keslers Cross Lanes near Summersville as a defense against Confederates but on August 26, 1861 General Floyd scattered Tyler's forces and occupied the site of Gauley Bridge and the Weston Turnpike at Summersville. Wise held Cox's Union army on Gauley Mountain.

Carnifex Ferry. On September 10 Rosecrans, with reinforcements, was able to drive the Confederates out of Summersville. He also attacked their camp at Carnifex Ferry.

Illness had struck Wise's troops, and Wise did not aid Floyd in the battle at Carnifex Ferry. Floyd was able that day to withstand every assault, but during the night he abandoned his position and crossed the Gauley River. His departure confirmed Union control of the Kanawha Valley. Because of the victories at Philippi and the ousting of Confederates in the Monongahela and Kanawha valleys, the Union forces had had a most successful year.

Generals Thomas J. "Stonewall" Jackson, Joseph E. Johnston, and Robert E. Lee (Copy of a painting. Photo courtesy of West Virginia University Library)

Robert E. Lee in Western Virginia

After General Garnett's death, Robert E. Lee toured northwestern Virginia. Because of Confederate defeats, Lee felt called upon to inspect the Monongahela Valley and to consult with his commanders on new campaign plans. Also by an attack from the direction of Rich Mountain, he hoped to eject General J. J. Reynolds from fortified positions controlling the Huttonsville-Huntersville road and the Parkersburg-Staunton Turnpike.

Despite an advantage of 15,000 troops which he stationed along these roads, Lee encountered the disadvantages of extreme cold, rain, ice, and mud in western Virginia, and his men suffered an epidemic of measles. Subordinates made mistakes in a plan to attack the Union camp at Elkwater, and General W. W. Loring, in command of the Confederate forces, was halfhearted in his aid to Lee. In addition, Lee's friend, Lieutenant Colonel John A. Washington, was killed on an exploratory trip in the Tygart River Valley. Because of the accumulation of misfortunes, Lee gave up all plans of attack in the north and joined Floyd and Wise in the Kanawha Valley.

By uniting the Floyd and the Wise commands, Lee hoped to gain a victory over Rosecrans at Big Sewell Mountain, but Rosecrans avoided the engagement. On October 20 Lee gave up a Confederate offense in western Virginia and ordered General Loring to retreat to Lewisburg. The Confederate pullback gave the Union complete possession of western Virginia.

A few Confederate victories in a year of Union triumphs occurred some months prior to 1862. General H. R. Jackson and his troops turned back a Union invasion in the Battle of Greenbrier River on October 3, 1861. Union armies were also prevented from taking the Staunton and the Virginia Central Railroad in the Battle of Allegheny Mountain on December 13, 1861.

Lee's only satisfaction in western Virginia during the first year of war was his purchase of "Traveller," his famous war horse. Andrew Johnston had bred "Traveller" near Blue Sulphur Springs in Greenbrier County. Johnston had given him to his son, Captain James W. Johnston, who, in turn, sold the horse to Thomas L. Broun. General Lee purchased "Traveller" from Broun for $200. The statue of Lee and "Traveller" is located on Monument Avenue in Richmond, Virginia.

Fremont's Defeat in 1862

The year 1862 opened more favorably for the Confederates when General John C. Fremont was designated commander of the Union forces with headquarters in Wheeling. Fremont attempted to move from Keyser by way of the Baltimore and Ohio Railroad into the Valley of Virginia but was defeated by the Confederate General "Stonewall" Jackson at Harrisonburg. Fremont resigned. General Kelley was, however, able to keep the Baltimore and Ohio Railroad open to Union traffic, although towns along the road changed hands many times during the year.

Jenkins Raid

Without regard to the difficulties experienced by General Wise and General Floyd, General Loring believed that his Confederate forces might be able to recapture the Kanawha Valley. To test the Union strength in the area, he sent Brigadier General Albert G. Jenkins on a raid through counties north of the Kanawha Valley. With 550 cavalrymen, Jenkins left Salt Sulphur Springs in Monroe County on August 24, 1862.

He passed through Beverly, Buckhannon, Weston, Glenville, Spencer, Ripley, and finally reached Ravenswood. From there he crossed the Ohio and entered western Virginia below the mouth of the Kanawha. Traveling by way of the Guyandotte to Raleigh County, he reported to General Loring on the condition of the Union defenses. He was also able to recount his war prizes. At Spencer he had captured 300 prisoners, at Ripley he had seized $5,525 from a Union paymaster, and at Buckhannon he had captured 500 stands of arms.

Loring in Charleston

Jenkins had proved that the Union forces could be damaged. Their defenses had been weakened not only because of the raid but also because 5,000 men had been transferred out of the Kanawha Valley to build up General John Pope's army in eastern Virginia. Loring decided to take advantage of the situation. On September 10, 1862 at Fayetteville, Loring defeated Union General Joseph A. J. Lightburn, who had replaced General Cox.

On September 13, Loring entered Charleston, which he was able to hold until October 8, 1862. During his occupation of Charleston, Loring removed large quantities of salt into Confederate Virginia. But Union troops from Clarksburg and Point Pleasant were able to retake Charleston, and Loring had to fall back to Lewisburg. For failure to hold his position, Loring was removed from command. His troops were assigned to General John Echols, a resident of Monroe County in West Virginia.

Jones-Imboden Raids

The year 1863 was noted for the Jones-Imboden Raid, a month-long Confederate invasion into western Virginia from mid-April to mid-May. The objectives of the raids were the destruction of the Baltimore and Ohio Railroad, the overthrow of the Reorganized Government of Virginia at Wheeling, and ending the West Virginia statehood movement. The raids were also efforts to recruit both men and supplies for Jones and Imboden and for General Lee's invasion of Pennsylvania.

Brigadier General William E. Jones and Brigadier General John D. Imboden spearheaded the attacks. Imboden's forces moved from Staunton through Beverly to Weston. Jones' forces moved from the South Branch of the Potomac to the Monongahela, almost reached the Ohio River, and returned to eastern Virginia by way of the Great Kanawha.

Imboden's forces numbered 3,400 men, with 700 of these mounted. Imboden was able to capture Buckhannon, but he could not defeat Union forces under General Benjamin S. Roberts at Clarksburg or Union forces under Colonel James Mulligan at Grafton.

The northern division of the Imboden forces under command of Brigadier General Jones also failed in efforts to destroy the bridges, trestles, and tunnel at Tunnelton. But Jones' men did destroy a suspension bridge over the Cheat River at Albright as they made their way into Morgantown and Fairmont. At Morgantown, Jones caused Senator Waitman T. Willey to flee by horse and buggy into Pennsylvania, and at Fairmont, Jones burned Governor Francis H. Pierpont's private library.

Between Grafton and Parkersburg, Jones destroyed a large part of the Northwestern Virginia Railroad. On May 9, 1863 he burned over 150,000 barrels of crude oil at Burning Springs in Wirt County. As the burning oil spread out over the Little Kanawha River, the stream became a sheet of fire.

Results of the Raids. Jones reported to Robert E. Lee the official results of his raid. Jones estimated his forces had killed 25 to 30 of the enemy and wounded three times as many. He estimated that his raiders had captured 700 prisoners and their small arms and burned 16 railroad bridges, one tunnel, a large number of boats, tanks, and barrels, and many engines. He catalogued war prizes of about 1,000 cattle and probably 1,200 horses. From his own command, Jones reported 10 killed, 42 wounded, and 15 missing.

Imboden also reported impressive official results to Lee. The Imboden command seized $100,000 worth of horses, mules, wagons, and arms; burned eleven bridges; and brought back 3,100 head of cattle. Imboden estimated that he had enlisted between 400 and 500 recruits along the way.

Minor Battles and Raids

After the Union forces won their important victory at Gettysburg, the war in western Virginia deteriorated into minor battles, skirmishes, and raids. For the most part, control of the Virginia and Tennessee Railroad became the objective. A skirmish occurred at White Sulphur Springs on August 26–27, 1863. Here Confederate troops under General Sam Jones prevented Union troops under General W. W. Averell from capturing the Virginia and Tennessee Railroad and the salt springs in Smyth County, Virginia. On November 6, 1863 Averell forced General Echols to withdraw from Droop Mountain near Hillsboro, in Pocahontas County, with severe losses.

On May 9, 1864, in another attack on the Virginia and Tennessee Railroad, Confederate Generals Jenkins and John McCausland were defeated by Union General George Crook at the Cloyd Farm near Dublin in Pulaski County, Virginia.

On July 30, 1864, General Bradley T. Johnson and General McCausland burned Chambersburg, Pennsylvania, and in retaliation Averell attacked Johnson and McCausland near Moorefield and captured 400 prisoners.

The Averell, or "Big Salem," raid was intended to help General Ambrose E. Burnside defeat General James Longstreet in Knoxville. Averell with 2,500 cavalrymen started from Keyser, December 8, 1863, toward Salem, Virginia. The objective was to capture the Virginia and Tennessee Railroad, which furnished Longstreet with supplies. The raid was successful and was carried out with a total loss of 119 men.

In revenge for Averell's raid, General Fitzhugh Lee invaded the South Branch Valley as far as Romney. The same invasion was repeated in January 1864 by General Jubal A. Early. In May 1864 Captain J. H. McNeill captured Piedmont, taking 100 prisoners and destroying railroad property.

In all, there were several hundred raiding and skirmishing activities in western Virginia.

The Monument Erected on the Gettysburg Battlefield to Commemorate the 7th West Virginia Volunteer Infantry The field of the great Civil War battle at Gettysburg, Pennsylvania, is a National Military Park. It covers 3,277 acres and is visited by thousands of persons each year.

Army General, Diplomat, Artist

David Hunter Strother, "Porte Crayon"

David Hunter Strother, also known as Porte Crayon, was born September 26, 1816 at Martinsburg, now West Virginia. He was educated at the Old Stone Schoolhouse in Martinsburg and at Jefferson College, Canonsburg, Pennsylvania. Strother later studied art in Philadelphia and in France and Italy from 1840 to 1843.

When he returned to America in 1844, he began making drawings for magazines. He illustrated the 1851 edition of *Swallow Barn* and made drawings for *The Blackwater Chronicle* in 1853. In December 1853 Strother contributed to *Harper's New Monthly Magazine* an article entitled "The Virginia Canaan," an account of his visit to the Blackwater region of Randolph County. This was the first of a series of sketches dealing with life in the South which, with numerous pen drawings, appeared from time to time in *Harper's* under Strother's pseudonym, "Porte Crayon."

In 1857 he gathered some of these sketches and 138 pen drawings into a single volume entitled *Virginia Illustrated*.

Strother became one of the highest-paid contributors to *Harper's*, enjoying a commission to travel and write for the magazine. Three characteristic series of articles, appearing at regular intervals, were "North Carolina Illustrated" (1857), "A Winter in the South" (1857-58), and "A Summer in New England" (1860-61).

After having served the Union in the Civil War with the rank of brigadier general, Strother made his home at Berkeley Springs, West Virginia, devoting his time to literature and art. During the years 1866-68, he contributed to *Harper's* a series of articles entitled "Personal Recollections of the War, by a Virginian," based on his diary and pen sketches made on the battlefields.

Between 1872 and 1875, he contributed to the same magazine a series called "The Mountains." By this time, however, a change in the literary taste of the reading public had reduced the demand for writings of the sketchbook and diary type.

Strother was appointed United States consul-general to Mexico City in 1879. He returned to Charles Town where he died in 1888.

Chapter 22 — TWO WESTERN VIRGINIA GENERALS, TWO HEROINES

The two outstanding West Virginians in the Civil War were Jesse Lee Reno and Thomas Jonathan "Stonewall" Jackson. General Reno led Union forces. General Jackson led Confederate forces. General Reno served our country brilliantly. General Jackson has been praised as one of the ablest military leaders of all time. Both gave the country the last full measure of devotion.

Jackson deserved the acclaim he has received; the illustrious Reno has been almost forgotten.

The two were born in nearby cities in what is now West Virginia, Reno in 1823 and Jackson in 1824. At the United States Military Academy at West Point, New York, these two, as young men, marched on the parade ground in their neat cadet uniforms on their graduation day in 1846.

Jesse Lee Reno

Jesse Lee Reno was born June 20, 1823 at Wheeling. We have little record of his childhood. His family moved to Pennsylvania when Jesse was sixteen. A congressman recognized the ability of the boy and appointed him to the Military Academy. Here Reno met Thomas J. Jackson. The young men became friends and were often together at social affairs and on military occasions.

Major General Jesse Lee Reno, United States Army

Reno ranked high in his class and held this rank to the end of his training at the Academy. At his graduation he was commissioned a brevet second lieutenant of ordnance. Ordnance consists of equipment, including weapons, ammunition, combat vehicles, and necessary maintenance and also the obtaining, distributing, and security of supplies.

Jesse Reno soon began his service in the Mexican War. At Chapultepec he was wounded. Here he was promoted to brevet captain.

He became professor of mathematics at West Point. He served as assistant to the Ordnance Board in Washington. He married a Washington girl.

He was sent to serve in engineering in Minnesota; into ordnance service in Pennsylvania; to command at Mount Vernon Arsenal in Alabama; and to command at the Leavenworth Arsenal in Kansas.

In the Civil War Reno commanded a brigade in North Carolina. After an engagement at Camden Reno was made a major general of volunteers. He was a leader in the second Battle of Manassas, or Bull Run, and at Chantilly.

At the Battle of South Mountain, September 14, 1862, Reno was severely wounded while leading an advance. He died from his wounds. He was thirty-nine years old.

"Stonewall" Jackson

"Stonewall" Jackson was born at Clarksburg on January 21, 1824. Misfortunes pursued the boy. His oldest sister and his father died within a few days of each other when Thomas was two years old. The family was left with little money. His mother married again, becoming Mrs. Blake B. Woodson, and thereafter moved to Fayette County. Relatives took the children. Thomas made his home on the old Jackson farm at Jackson's Mill in Lewis County. He lived there for twelve years.

At school Thomas was an honest, well-behaved, and sociable boy. He worked on the farm, caught fish and made maple sugar and sold these products. When thirteen years old, he was a road worker, employed on the Parkersburg and Staunton Turnpike. He read books borrowed from a young lawyer in Weston.

His brother Warren died when Thomas was seventeen.

A Colonel Withers and a Major Bailey helped him to get the position of constable. He took the examination for entrance to the United States Military Academy at West Point, passed the examination, and was admitted to the Academy July 1, 1842. His preparatory education had not been of the best, but young Jackson studied very hard and graduated seventeenth in a class of fifty-nine. He was a brevet second lieutenant.

Thomas J. "Stonewall" Jackson, Confederate States Army

chapter twenty-two / two western virginia generals, two heroines

He was assigned to service in the Mexican War, fought in the Battle of Vera Cruz, and was promoted to first lieutenant. After gallant conduct at Chapultepec he was made a brevet major. Back in the United States after the war, he was engaged in the subduing of the Seminole Indian uprising in Florida.

In 1852 Jackson left the army and became instructor at Virginia Military Institute, Lexington, Virginia. He married a Lexington girl, who died fourteen months after the marriage. Jackson was a devoted member of the Presbyterian Church.

Jackson served in Charles Town during the John Brown trouble. At the beginning of the Civil War, after prayerful consideration, he chose to go into service with the army of the Confederate States of America. He was appointed colonel of Virginia Volunteers and was later promoted to brigadier general. He led a brigade at Bull Run. It was here that General Barnard Elliott Bee said, "See, there stands Jackson like a stone wall," and so came the name "Stonewall."

During the action at Chancellorsville Jackson led the defeat of the right wing of the Union army. He was wounded here by his own men in their error. He lost his left arm. The great commander, General Robert E. Lee, said, "He has lost his left arm, but I have lost my right arm."

"Stonewall" Jackson died of his wounds on May 10, 1863. He was thirty-nine. And so ended the career of one of the most distinguished sons of the upper Monongahela Valley of West Virginia and one of the great military tacticians. Jackson was elected to the Hall of Fame for Great Americans.

Two Civil War Heroines

Two western Virginia girls became famous for their service to the Confederacy. They were Nancy Hart and Belle Boyd.

Nancy Hart. Nancy Hart was born in 1846 in Raleigh, North Carolina, moved with her parents to Tazewell County, Virginia, and then to Harper District in Roane County in western Virginia just as the Civil War began in 1861. When her brother-in-law, William Privee, was killed by Union soldiers, Nancy took to the hills as a girl guerrilla. She joined the Moccasin Rangers, a band of raiders serving the Confederacy. Their headquarters were on the upper reaches of the West Fork of the Little Kanawha River in Calhoun County.

Nancy Hart, the Girl Guerrilla This is the only known picture of Nancy Hart. It is from an ambrotype taken at Summersville. *(From the picture collection of Boyd B. Stutler)*

After a Moccasin Ranger raid into Braxton County in the late fall of 1861, Nancy was taken prisoner by the Braxton Home Guards but was later released. She married Joshua Douglas, a member of the Moccasin Rangers. He enlisted in the regular Virginia forces.

Nancy went into Nicholas County and continued to get information on Union plans and to pass it to the Confederates. But Union forces under Lieutenant Colonel William C. Starr recognized her as the girl guerrilla and imprisoned her at Summersville.

Talking her guard out of his musket on the pretense of comparing it with a rifle, Nancy shot her guard and escaped to a Confederate camp on Greenbrier River. She later returned with 200 Confederate cavalry which drove the Union forces from Summersville.

After Douglas returned from the war, the couple resided at the head of Spring Creek in Greenbrier County. Nancy Hart died in 1902 and was buried on a wild crag of Mannings Knob.

Belle Boyd, Confederate Spy *(From the Collections of the Library of Congress)*

Belle Boyd. Belle Boyd, born May 9, 1844 in Martinsburg, became a well-known Confederate spy. Her father served in a regiment that was part of the "Stonewall Brigade."

When the Confederates were forced to evacuate Martinsburg, a federal soldier insulted Belle's mother, tried to raise the Union flag over the Boyd home, and attempted to burn the home, and Belle shot him.

Later Belle lived in Front Royal, Virginia. There she learned that a Union attack was being prepared against "Stonewall" Jackson. She was able to get the information to Jackson, and Jackson won a victory over the Union army commanded by General Nathaniel Banks at Strasburg. For her daring services to the South, Belle became known as the "Darling of the Confederacy."

Secretary of War Edwin Stanton had Belle Boyd put in prison in Washington, D.C., and later in Fortress Monroe, Virginia. After several thrilling captures and releases, she received permission to go to Canada with the understanding she would not return to the United States.

In 1863 in London she married Lieutenant Sam Wylde Harding, a federal officer who had befriended her during one of her imprisonments.

When Harding returned to the United States, he was imprisoned in Washington, D.C., and was charged with desertion. After the war, the two were united, but the husband was suffering from his years in prison, and he died in a few years.

Belle died June 11, 1900 at Kilbourn, Wisconsin, where she was recounting her adventures on the lecture platform.

Four Soldiers from Ohio

McKinley, Hayes, Cox, Reid

William McKinley

We have seen that many military officers from other states came into western Virginia to give service during the Civil War. Several were especially noteworthy. Of these, four came from Ohio. Two of these men became President of the United States. Three of the four served as governor of Ohio. One was the Republican candidate for Vice-President of the United States.

One future President was William McKinley. McKinley began his service in western Virginia as an eighteen-year-old private. His first duty here was as a picket at Maxwell's Bridge on the Buckhannon Road. He experienced his first fighting at Carnifex Ferry. In time he advanced to commissary sergeant, to second lieutenant at Antietam, to captain after the Battle of Kernstown in the Eastern Panhandle, and ended his western Virginia military service as an assistant adjutant general.

In the fall of 1864 the future President was old enough to vote, and he cast his first vote near Martinsburg. The voting "booth" was an ambulance, and the ballot box was an empty candle case.

McKinley served as governor of Ohio and was President of the United States from 1897 to 1901.

Another who saw service in western Virginia and who became President was Rutherford B. Hayes. Hayes participated in the Battle of Carnifex Ferry. He was promoted to colonel of the 23rd Ohio Infantry and was stationed at Weston, Beverly, and Huttonsville in the early part of the war. He commanded General Jacob Cox's advance guard which occupied Princeton in May 1862. In May 1864 he campaigned under George Crook in the battle for the Virginia and Tennessee Railroad and in June of that year took part in David Hunter's advance to Lynchburg and retreat down the Kanawha.

At the end of the war Hayes concluded his service in the Shenandoah Valley as a brigadier general. He kept a diary of his war years in western Virginia and wrote many letters home, one time saying that "so healthy and so pretty a country is seldom seen." Hayes also predicted that the Kanawha Valley would become the Ruhr of America. The German Ruhr is a great industrial valley.

While Hayes had his headquarters in Charleston, he was visited by Mrs. Hayes and their children. This visit was saddened by the death of their eighteen-month-old son.

Hayes became governor of Ohio and was President of the United States from 1877 to 1881.

Jacob D. Cox, an army general, also became governor of Ohio for the term 1866–68. He supported President Johnson on reconstruction against the radical Republicans and therefore was not renominated for a second term. However, President Grant appointed him secretary of the interior, an act resulting in one of the few good appointments made by Grant. Later Cox served one term in Congress, became dean of the Cincinnati Law School, a position he held for sixteen years, and was president of the University of Cincinnati. General Cox led troops in the capture of Charleston and Gauley Bridge in the early battles for control of the Kanawha Valley.

Whitelaw Reid, also from Ohio, was a war correspondent and aide-de-camp on the staffs of Generals Thomas A. Morris and W. S. Rosecrans in western Virginia. Reid later became editor-in-chief of the *New York Tribune*, United States minister to France, United States ambassador to England, and in 1892 Republican nominee for the Vice-Presidency of the United States.

Chapter 23 THE THIRTY-FIFTH STATE

On June 20, 1861 Francis H. Pierpont delivered his inaugural address as the new governor of the Restored Government of Virginia. He had been unanimously elected chief executive by the convention at Wheeling, and the delegates listened attentively to his remarks.

In Pierpont's view, the men of western Virginia were the loyal citizens who had been forced to reorganize the state for the protection of themselves, their families, and their property. The action the convention had taken to form the new government, he believed, was in accord with the principle that all power resides in the people.

A New State

The next session of the 1861 Wheeling Convention met on August 6 for the purpose of adopting an ordinance which provided for the formation of a new state. This ordinance was adopted by the convention on August 20 and was approved by the voters on October 24. It fixed the boundaries for the new state, and chose a name, "Kanawha." The boundary lines enclosed thirty-nine counties west of the Allegheny Mountains.

Approval of the ordinance was overwhelming. The convention voted 48 to 27 in its favor, and the people ratified it with a vote of 18,408 to 781.

A New Name. The governor called a constitutional convention in Wheeling on November 26, 1861 to draft a constitution for the

West Virginia's Independence Hall, Wheeling In 1861 and 1862 this building, then the Custom House, was the scene of meetings which led to West Virginia's statehood in 1863. In 1963 the West Virginia Legislature authorized the restoration of the building to its former condition. *(Photo courtesy of West Virginia University Library)*

new state. Early in the convention, Delegate Harmon Sinsel of Taylor County made a motion to withdraw the name "Kanawha." The motion carried, and delegates offered many suggestions for the state's name; "Allegheny," "Augusta," "Columbia," "New Virginia," and "Potomac" were proposed. But in the final vote "West Virginia" was the great favorite of the delegates. The chief argument against "Kanawha" was that it was already used in the state as the name of a river and of a county. According to a delegate from Cabell County, nowhere in the United States did a state take its name from one of its political subdivisions.

According to a delegate from Monongalia County, "Kanawha" should be rejected because it was too difficult to spell. This caused laughter at the convention because the residents of Monongalia County had experienced difficulty in spelling the name of the river Monongahela correctly; so their own county's name became permanently Monongalia.

New Boundaries. The constitutional convention also proceeded to redefine the state's boundary lines, adding Greenbrier, Mercer, McDowell, Monroe, and Pocahontas counties to the thirty-nine

Convention Held in the Custom House in Wheeling June 1861 *(From "Harper's Weekly," July 6, 1861. Photo courtesy of West Virginia University Library)*

previously named in the ordinance. If in the future by vote of the citizens the counties of Hardy, Hampshire, Morgan, and Pendleton approved of entering the new state, they would be annexed. If Berkeley, Jefferson, and Frederick approved in the same manner, they would also be added.

Slavery Issue. One of the most difficult matters to resolve in writing the constitution was to define the new state's position on the slavery issue satisfactorily to all delegates. Archibald W. Campbell, editor of the *Wheeling Intelligencer*, and Gordon Battelle, Methodist minister, hoped to reduce the slave population in the state. Battelle, delegate from Ohio County, twice introduced resolutions prohibiting the importation of slaves into West Virginia and providing for gradual emancipation of slaves already residing in West Virginia. Battelle even wanted these resolutions submitted to the voters separately from the constitution.

But a compromise was reached whereby the constitution of West Virginia included the proposition that blacks, either free or slave, could not be brought into the state or permitted to enter for permanent residence. Battelle's idea of gradual emancipation remained alive and was incorporated in West Virginia's constitution in order to make it acceptable to Congress and to the President.

West Virginia Government. In matters of government, the West Virginia constitution was more Northern than Southern. It provided for a township system of government as well as a county system.

The people elected the governor for a two-year term, but the chief executive could be reelected to succeeding terms. A bill of rights was incorporated. A free public school system was instituted. A Supreme Court of Appeals headed the judicial branch of the government.

The constitution provided that taxation should be equal and uniform. It also stated that the state should contract no debt but that it should assume an equitable proportion of the debt of Virginia. Finally West Virginia pledged itself to remain in the United States.

Approval of the Constitution

On April 18, twenty-six counties approved of the constitution by a vote of 14,199 to 368. Counties reporting at a later date finally brought a favorable vote of 18,862 to 514. Few Confederate sympathizers participated, and no elections were conducted in some of the central, southern, and eastern counties.

Restored Government Approves of New State. Following the endorsement of the new constitution by the people, Governor Pierpont called a meeting of the General Assembly of the Restored Government of Virginia on May 6 to consider the creation of a new state from inside the boundaries of an old state. On May 13, the Assembly approved the formation of the state of West Virginia which included 48 counties that had been a part of Virginia. When voters of Berkeley, Jefferson, and Frederick counties would approve the new constitution, they could also be included in the state of West Virginia.

Recall that the Restored Government of Virginia had given its consent, that a new constitution had been approved and was prepared for presentation to Congress. Now the consent of Congress and approval by the President of the United States were required for admission of West Virginia into the Union.

The Willey Amendment

On May 29, 1862 Senator Waitman T. Willey submitted West Virginia's application for statehood to the Senate of the United States. But before the Senate approved, Senator John Carlile of the Restored Government of Virginia and Senator Charles Sumner of Massachusetts almost wrecked the chances for success. Carlile, as a member of the Senate Committee on Territories to which the

Uncertain News — 1863 In the McClure House in Wheeling a group of the founders of the new state listen intently to the news from Washington. *(From a sketch by J. H. Diss Debar)*

statehood bill was referred, wished to add to the new state fifteen counties in the Shenandoah Valley. This addition probably would have prevented Senate approval. Senator Sumner wanted to add an amendment to prevent slavery within West Virginia.

In order to insure Senate acceptance of the original proposal, Senator Willey provided an amendment calling for the gradual abolition of Negro slavery in the new state. An item inserted in the constitution provided that all slaves born in West Virginia after July 4, 1863 would become free when they reached the age of twenty-one.

In July 1862 the United States Senate approved the admission of West Virginia to the Union provided the voters accepted the last-mentioned amendment. On December 10, 1862 the House of Representatives approved the statehood bill.

Lincoln Approves Admission

The bill was forwarded to the President on December 21. Lincoln debated the bill for the next ten days. He asked each member of his cabinet for an opinion. The members were equally divided in their advice on the question. On New Year's Eve Lincoln signed the bill.

Popular Approval Again

Again the state constitutional convention was called into session to consider the Willey amendment guaranteeing gradual emancipa-

PRESIDENT LINCOLN'S PROCLAMATION

By the President of the United States of America.

A Proclamation.

Whereas, by the Act of Congress approved the 31st day of December, last, the State of West Virginia was declared to be one of the United States of America, and was admitted into the Union on an equal footing with the original States in all respects whatever, upon the condition that certain changes should be duly made in the proposed Constitution for that State;

And, whereas, proof of a compliance with that condition as required by the Second Section of the Act aforesaid, has been submitted to me;

Now, therefore, be it known, that I, Abraham Lincoln, President of the United States, do, hereby, in pursuance of the Act of Congress aforesaid, declare and proclaim that the said act shall take effect and be in force, from and after sixty days from the date hereof.

In witness whereof, I have hereunto set my hand and caused the Seal of the United States to be affixed.

Done at the city of Washington, this twentieth day of April, in the year of our Lord one thousand eight hundred and sixty-three, and of the Independence of the United States the eighty-seventh.

Abraham Lincoln

By the President:

*William H. Seward,
Secretary of State.*

tion of slaves. The convention approved the Willey Amendment unanimously on February 17, 1863 and set March 26 as the date for a vote by the people. The people approved by a vote of 27,749 to 572.

Results of the voting were sent to the President on April 16, and on April 20, 1863 President Lincoln issued a proclamation which admitted West Virginia into the Union sixty days after the date of the proclamation. On June 20, 1863 West Virginia became the thirty-fifth state admitted to the Union.

The New Government

On May 28, 1863 the West Virginia voters elected their first governor, Arthur I. Boreman. Before a large crowd in front of the temporary capitol at Linsly Institute in Wheeling, Governor Pierpont of the Restored Government of Virginia reviewed the events which had made the creation of West Virginia necessary. Governor Boreman of the new state then delivered his inaugural message.

In his address he referred to West Virginia's grievances against eastern Virginia. He recounted the heavy taxes, Virginia's refusal to aid in the construction of railroads and canals in the west, and the adoption of the secession ordinance by eastern Virginia. To Bore-

The First Capitol of West Virginia, the Linsly Institute Building at Wheeling (1863 to 1870)
(West Virginia Department of Commerce Photo)

man, West Virginia's "commerce, travel, habits, associations, and interests" had dictated that West Virginia should be severed from the east.

Admitting in his address that West Virginia "is the child of the rebellion," Boreman looked forward to an early end to the war. He promised to assist the federal authorities in every way possible to bring about the conclusion of the conflict.

The first West Virginia Legislature also began its work on June 20, 1863. The Senate was composed of 20 members. The House of Delegates had 51 members. But there was no division into political parties in the state Legislature at this time. All the legislators simply believed in the Union, and this spirit prevailed until the end of the war in 1865.

Departure of the Reorganized Government

It was time for Governor Francis H. Pierpont and the Reorganized Government of Virginia to depart from Wheeling. This government first moved to Alexandria, Virginia, and then to Richmond in December 1865.

The Reorganized Government of Virginia had one more favor to perform for West Virginia. It authorized Berkeley and Jefferson counties to vote on their inclusion in the new state. The two counties voted favorably, and on August 5 and November 2, 1863 the West Virginia Legislature formally included these counties in the state.

All of these actions were reviewed later by both the Congress and the United States Supreme Court and found to be legal.

The Highest Authority

Abraham Lincoln, The Great Emancipator

As president of the United States at the time of West Virginia's admission to the Union, Abraham Lincoln became an essential participant in the creation of the state. Born in 1809 in the neighboring state of Kentucky, he spent his childhood in Indiana and his adult life in Illinois. He had little formal schooling, but he did read the few good books available and learned much through experience.

He served in the Illinois state legislature and the United States Congress, but to Stephen Douglas he lost a race for senator in 1858. The debates with Douglas gained national recognition for Lincoln, however, and he won the Republican nomination for the presidency in 1860.

With the nation divided on major issues, Lincoln came into the office with less than a majority of the popular votes and without a clear-cut mandate on how to preserve the Union. The ensuing war years presented many unusual situations to the new President. Among them was the problem of West Virginia's statehood.

Lincoln's decision to agree to the formation of West Virginia was based upon a long period of discussion and study of the constitutional controversy at a time when the nation was divided in civil war.

After Virginia had passed its Ordinance of Secession on April 17, 1861, the federal government became involved in an effort to preserve Virginia as part of the Union. To prepare for reconstruction of Virginia as a state loyal to the federal government, Lincoln's administration supported the Reorganized Government of Virginia as formed in June 1861.

Within a year a bill was introduced in the United States Congress requesting the formation of a new state in western Virginia. This action was initiated by the Reorganized Government of Virginia, as was required by the Constitution of the United States. The bill passed both houses of Congress and was officially presented to Lincoln on December 22, 1862.

Lincoln asked each member of his cabinet whether the action by Congress was constitutional and whether it was expedient. We have seen that the cabinet members were divided on the question. Chase of Ohio, Stanton of Ohio, and Seward of New York urged Lincoln to approve; Blair of Maryland, Bates of Missouri, and Welles of Connecticut supported a veto by the President.

The President faced a dilemma: The consent of the Virginia General Assembly was necessary for the admission of West Virginia, but was the legislature of the Reorganized Government representative of the state? Without clearly answering the question, Lincoln said, "The admission of West Virginia into the Union is expedient." He signed the bill on December 31, 1862. With the President's approval, West Virginia became a state on June 20, 1863.

Lincoln explained to the nation the need to admit West Virginia to the Union:

> We can scarcely dispense with the aid of West Virginia in this struggle; much less can we afford to have her against us, in Congress and in the field. Her brave and good men regard her admission into the Union as a matter of life and death. They have been true to the Union under very severe trials. We have so acted as to justify their hopes; and we can not fully retain their confidence, and co-operation, if we seem to break faith with them. In fact, they could not do so much for us, if they would.
>
> Again, the admission of the new State turns that much slave soil to free; and thus, is a certain, and irrevocable encroachment upon the cause of rebellion.

Chapter 24 THE OFFICIAL "FIRST FAMILY" OF WEST VIRGINIA

Each new political unit has its founders. Among the founders of West Virginia were Francis Harrison Pierpont, the governor of the Restored Government of Virginia, and Arthur Ingram Boreman, the first governor of West Virginia. West Virginia's first congressional delegation was composed of Waitman Thomas Willey and Peter Godwin Van Winkle as the state's first United States senators, and Jacob Beeson Blair, William G. Brown, and Kellian V. Whaley as the state's first congressmen in the House of Representatives of the United States.

Of the men who made special contributions to the new state, some had been Whigs and some had been Jackson Democrats who, in turn, had become Douglas Democrats. By 1864 almost all were converted to, or already were members of, the Republican-Unionist Party. With a few exceptions, many belonged to the Methodist Episcopal Church. As is true in most revolutions, leaders in the new state of West Virginia, which "was born of rebellion," were, for the most part, ministers, lawyers, teachers, and journalists.

The Governors: Pierpont and Boreman

Francis H. Pierpont was born on his grandfather's plantation at Pierponts, in Monongalia County, then Virginia, now West Virginia,

Francis H. Pierpont   The statue of Francis H. Pierpont stands in National Statuary Hall in the capitol, Washington, D.C., commemorating his great services to the people of West Virginia. His statue, sculptured by Franklin Simmons, was unveiled April 30, 1910. *(From the Collections of the Library of Congress. Photo courtesy of United States Senator Jennings Randolph)*

January 25, 1814. Francis's father later established his family at Fairmont, where his son worked on the farm and in the tanyard. Francis also worked his way through Allegheny College, graduating with honors in 1839. For a short time he taught school in Mississippi, studied law, and began to learn the business of coal mining and brick making. He also served as legal counsel for the Baltimore and Ohio Railroad.

Realizing the western opposition to secession from the Union, Mr. Pierpont planned the Reorganized State of Virginia as an effort to keep Virginia out of the Confederacy. He was an ardent abolitionist, having been influenced against slavery by his wife, the former Julia Augusta Robertson, who came from a Northern family of missionaries.

As governor of the Reorganized Government of Virginia, Mr. Pierpont was responsible for raising and organizing the Union army troops and preparing the way for statehood. He was recognized by President Lincoln as the legitimate governor of Virginia. After the creation of West Virginia, he transferred the Reorganized Government of Virginia to Alexandria, Virginia, and then to Richmond. In 1864 he called the General Assembly of Virginia into session for the purpose of abolishing slavery within the state.

After Congress assumed reconstruction of former Confederate states, Pierpont was removed from the governorship on April 4, 1868 by General John M. Schofield. Pierpont returned to West Virginia and served in its 1870 Legislature.

After the war Pierpont became a Liberal Republican. Later he was appointed collector of internal revenue for the Second West Virginia District by President James A. Garfield. Pierpont died in Pittsburgh on March 24, 1899 and was buried in Woodlawn Cemetery in Fairmont. In 1909 his statue was placed in Statuary Hall in the United States capitol in Washington, D.C., citing Pierpont as one of the two most honored West Virginians.

Arthur Ingram Boreman was born July 24, 1823 at Waynesburg, Pennsylvania. Forsaking the family's merchandising business, Arthur studied law in the office of his brother and brother-in-law in Tyler County and was admitted to the bar in 1845. In 1845 he moved to Parkersburg. From 1855 to 1861, as a member of the Whig Party, Mr. Boreman represented Wood County in the lower house of the Virginia legislature.

Opposed to secession, opposed even to calling the Virginia convention, Arthur Boreman became president of the Second Wheeling Convention and helped reorganize the Virginia government by serving as one of its new circuit court judges. In 1863 he was unanimously elected first governor of West Virginia and was reelected in 1864 and in 1866.

Before his third term expired, he was elected as a Radical Republican to the United States Senate to succeed Peter G. Van Winkle, who was politically more conservative. In Congress Mr. Boreman served as chairman on the important Committee on Terri-

Arthur I. Boreman The picture shows Governor Boreman as he was inaugurated governor of the new state at Wheeling June 20, 1863. *(From a sketch by J. H. Diss Debar)*

chapter twenty-four / the official "first family" of west virginia

tories. In 1888 he was again elected a circuit judge, a position he held until his death on April 19, 1896.

The Senators

Peter Godwin Van Winkle was born September 7, 1807 in New York City and was educated as a lawyer. He married Juliet Rathbone, daughter of Judge W. P. Rathbone, a prominent West Virginian. The couple moved to Parkersburg, and Van Winkle continued his law studies with General John J. Jackson.

For several years Mr. Van Winkle served as secretary and then as president of the Northwestern Virginia Railroad and as president of the Little Kanawha Bridge Company. He served as a delegate to the Virginia convention of 1850-51 and 1861-63 and as mayor of Parkersburg several times. He was a member of the first Legislature of West Virginia. He was elected United States senator. He was one of eleven Republican senators who refused to vote for impeachment of President Johnson.

Formerly a Whig, Mr. Van Winkle joined the Republican Party but did not become a Radical Republican. Although he approved the Thirteenth Amendment to the Constitution, which freed the slaves, he did not approve of the Fourteenth Amendment, which granted citizenship to freedmen. He died in Parkersburg on April 15, 1872.

Waitman T. Willey was born October 18, 1811 in a log cabin near present Farmington in Marion County in present West Virginia. He later moved with his parents to a home on Paw Paw Creek. Willey walked forty-five miles to enter Madison College in Uniontown, Pennsylvania, in 1827. Madison College later merged with Allegheny College, which awarded Willey an honorary degree years later.

Before the Civil War, Willey was a lawyer and Whig politician in Morgantown. He was a Methodist and a temperance crusader. He was elected clerk of Monongalia County and was a member of the Virginia convention of 1850-51.

Willey met two important political defeats: in 1852 when he first ran for Congress and in 1859 when he ran for the lieutenant governorship of Virginia.

As a member of the Virginia convention of 1861, he voted against secession. He opposed Carlile's early effort to declare a new state of Virginia.

A Home of the 1860's The log house was not an uncommon home when West Virginia began its history as a state. *(David P. Cruise Photo, West Virginia Department of Commerce)*

Although he was a member of the First Wheeling Convention, Willey was not a member of the Second Wheeling Convention. He was elected senator of the Reorganized Government of Virginia and in Washington presented West Virginia's application for statehood. He was elected senator from West Virginia in 1863.

Although he had owned slaves, he became a Radical Republican who opposed slavery. He voted for the removal of Andrew Johnson from the office of President. In his later life he served as clerk of the Monongalia circuit court. He died May 2, 1900.

The Congressmen

Jacob B. Blair was born at Parkersburg, Wood County, now in West Virginia, on April 11, 1821. After a common-school education and the private study of law, he was admitted to practice law in 1844. Early in his political career, he advanced the cause of the Union.

When John S. Carlile resigned from the House of Representatives in 1861, Blair was chosen to fill the vacancy. Blair was elected in 1863 as West Virginia's first representative from the First District, and he worked diligently to convince President Lincoln to approve West Virginia's admission to the Union.

Blair was later elected to the West Virginia Legislature and was appointed minister to Costa Rica in 1868. In 1872 Blair was appointed associate justice of the Supreme Court of the Wyoming Territory, and his residence became Laramie City, Wyoming.

William Guy Brown of Kingwood, Virginia, now West Virginia, was one of four sons of James Brown who came from Scotland to Virginia in 1790. William was born September 23, 1800 in Monongalia County, now in West Virginia. After studying with Parkersburg lawyers, he was admitted to the practice of law in Preston County in 1823.

An ardent supporter of President Andrew Jackson and the War with Mexico, Brown served the state of Virginia as prosecuting attorney of his county, as a member of the Virginia Assembly, as a delegate to Virginia's Constitutional Convention of 1850, and as a member of the United States House of Representatives from the Reorganized Government of Virginia in 1861.

He was reelected to Congress as the first member from the Second West Virginia District in 1863. Later, he was a member of the West Virginia convention to revise the constitution in 1872 and a member of the West Virginia Legislature.

Kellian V. Whaley was born May 6, 1821 in Onondaga County, New York. He moved to western Virginia in 1842. At Point Pleasant

Oglebay Mansion, Built at Wheeling in 1832 In contrast to the log home, the Oglebay home is an example of fine western Virginia residences long before West Virginia became a state. The mansion is now Mansion-Museum in Oglebay Park, Wheeling. *(West Virginia Department of Commerce Photo)*

he engaged in the lumber and timber business. He enlisted in the Union army during the Civil War and served as colonel in the Battle of Guyandotte in November 1861. In the battle he was captured, but he made a daring escape.

Like William Guy Brown, he was elected in 1861 as a Union Republican to the House of Representatives of the United States by the Reorganized Government of Virginia. In 1863 he returned to Congress as the first representative from the Third District of West Virginia, becoming a spokesman for the southernmost counties in the state. Like Jacob B. Blair, Mr. Whaley also entered diplomatic service, being appointed collector of customs at Brazos de Santiago, Texas, in 1868.

The Superintendent of Free Schools

William R. White was born November 26, 1820 in Georgetown, in the District of Columbia. He graduated from Dickinson College, Carlisle, Pennsylvania, in 1841. From 1852 to 1855 he was principal of the Olin and Preston Institute at Blacksburg, Virginia, and from 1856 to 1863, principal of the Fairmont Male and Female Seminary (in Fairmont), a Methodist Episcopal School.

Mr. White was the first state superintendent of free schools of West Virginia, serving from 1864 to 1869. He, along with Governor Boreman, persuaded the Legislature of the need for teacher-training schools, then called normal schools. He served as president of Fairmont State Normal School at Fairmont.

As a minister of the Methodist Episcopal Church, Mr. White held pastorates at Morgantown and Wheeling and was presiding elder of the Buckhannon District. In 1886 Allegheny College conferred the honorary Doctor of Divinity degree upon White.

Others in High Position

Other capable and influential men who served with distinction were: J. Edgar Boyer, West Virginia's first secretary of state; Campbell Tarr, the first state treasurer; Daniel Lamb, known as the code maker, delegate to the First Constitutional Convention and chairman of the legislative committee; Granville Davisson Hall, member of the state's new Constitutional Convention, clerk of West Virginia's first House of Delegates, and writer of some note; Gordon Battelle, a minister; and Archibald W. Campbell, a journalist and nephew of an older famous West Virginia Campbell.

Artist and State Official

Joseph H. Diss Debar, Designer of State Seal

Joseph H. Diss Debar is best remembered in West Virginia history as the designer of the state seal. He was born in Strasbourg, France, March 6, 1820. He received a classical and scientific education in some of the best schools in Europe and knew a number of languages, being able to speak French, German, and English well and to translate Latin and Greek. In West Virginia he was known as "an artist of no mean ability as well as a gentleman of faultless manner."

Diss Debar came to America in 1842. On the voyage across the Atlantic he met the famous author Charles Dickens. He landed in Boston, lived a few years in Cincinnati where he married, and later resided in Parkersburg. He became interested in western Virginia lands, was agent for 10,000 acres in Doddridge County, and colonized the land with families from Cincinnati, Baltimore, and Cumberland. He named his colony Saint Clara in honor of his wife.

When West Virginia became a state, Diss Debar ran for a seat in the Legislature. Because of the closeness of the vote, the Legislature had to decide between the two candidates, and Diss Debar lost. He was commissioned to design the state seal. In 1864 he was elected to the Legislature by a great majority. He helped secure the passage of "A Bill for the Encouragement of Foreign Immigration" and started a significant career in gaining immigrants to populate the new state.

In 1864 Governor Boreman appointed Diss Debar commissioner of immigration for the state, a post which Mr. Diss Debar held until 1872. Diss Debar devoted himself diligently to the duties of his commission. He had no less than 20,000 pamphlets and handbills distributed in Europe. In 1870 he published the *West Virginia Handbook and Immigrant's Guide* to introduce the state to prospective settlers. His efforts were vigorous and productive. He was responsible for the Helvetia settlement in Randolph County and has been credited with having brought more than 5,000 immigrants into the state.

Diss Debar spent the last days of his life with his daughter in Philadelphia, but he considered himself a farmer and looked upon West Virginia as his home.

Part Three

The Recent Period

unit seven | **Industrial Evolution**

Chapter 25
FROM "RECONSTRUCTION" TO THE TWENTIETH CENTURY

When the Civil War was over, the President and Congress formulated plans for "reconstruction" of the states that had left the Union and joined the Confederacy. The state of West Virginia had not left the Union and therefore was not subject to this "reconstruction." Unlike Virginia and other Southern states, West Virginia was not reduced to the status of a conquered territory to be administered by Union generals. In some of the Southern states control by the federal army continued from 1865 to 1877.

Governors who served West Virginia in these early years were Arthur Ingram Boreman, Daniel Duane Tompkins Farnsworth, William Erskine Stevenson, and John Jeremiah Jacob.

(Biographical sketches of all West Virginia governors are presented in the appendix to this book.)

For individuals in West Virginia who had favored the Confederacy during the Civil War the situation through "reconstruction" years was difficult. As former Confederates, their lives in West Virginia were heavily restricted and regulated for the next several years.

The Legislature of West Virginia in 1863 had declared that all property lying within the boundaries of the state and belonging to

Confederate soldiers was forfeited to the state. In 1863 this was really a threat to be effective in the future, for the state was then a battleground. The Legislature also passed acts whereby persons found guilty of speaking, writing, or printing anything referring to rebellion or favoring their previous Confederate sympathies would be subject to heavy fines and imprisonment. At this time these measures also were not really enforceable. However, the Unionists who had created the new state were not going to surrender control to Confederates living within the state or returning to the state at the end of the Civil War.

Penalties for Confederates

On February 25, 1865, with Civil War victory in sight, the Unionists of West Virginia prescribed a "test oath." This "test oath" permitted any voter to challenge any other voter as to whether he had borne arms against the United States, against the Reorganized Government of Virginia, or against West Virginia. One voter could challenge another as to whether he had held office in illegal governments and whether he had avoided an oath of loyalty to the constitutions of the United States and of West Virginia. If an individual answered yes to these challenges, he lost his right to vote.

Marshall College as a State Normal School, Huntington In the year 1867 Marshall Academy became a state normal school whose primary purpose was the training of teachers. In succeeding years the normal school has developed into the present imposing Marshall University. See the picture of two of its fine buildings in Chapter 31. *(Photo courtesy of West Virginia University Library)*

By 1866 the state passed a constitutional amendment taking away rights to the vote and to citizenship from all persons who had supported the Confederacy. Between 10,000 and 15,000 persons were thus prevented from voting or holding public office in West Virginia.

By 1866–67 a former Confederate soldier in West Virginia could not hold public office, could not vote, could not practice law, could not serve as a juror, could not teach school, could not sue in court, and in the courts could make no defense for himself in suits brought against him in his absence.

Challenge. Important newspapers in the state advised a "let-up" on former Confederates, and inevitably measures forcing such hardships on Confederates were challenged in the courts. Charles Faulkner, a prominent citizen of Berkeley County, won an important case when the State Supreme Court of Appeals ruled that Faulkner could not be required to take a "test oath" before he could return to the practice of law in West Virginia.

Flick Amendment and Other Concessions. Between the years 1868 and 1871, Republican officeholders themselves began to be more sympathetic to Confederates. In fact, many Republicans either broke with the party and became Liberal Republicans or joined the Democratic Party. The state Legislature of 1871 removed all acts causing hardship for former Confederates. Voter-challenge procedures disappeared, as did "test oaths" and registration of voters. Officers in charge of elections were elected by the people rather than appointed by state officers.

W. H. H. Flick, a state senator from Pendleton County, offered an amendment to the constitution which permitted all male citizens except minors and paupers to vote regardless of race or color. West Virginians favored the Flick Amendment by a vote of 23,546 to 6,323.

Location of the Capital

On April 1, 1870 the legislators changed the location of the state capital from Wheeling to Charleston. Three years later, the Legislature reversed itself and again chose Wheeling as the capital. The move back to Wheeling was made May 21–23, 1875. Because of the three situations of the capital, West Virginia was sometimes said to have "a capital on wheels."

chapter twenty-five / from "reconstruction" to the twentieth century

The Second Capitol of West Virginia (at Charleston) This capitol building served West Virginia from 1870 to 1875.

In February 1877 the Legislature decided that the choice of a permanent state capital should be made by the people and not by the Legislature. It directed that a vote be taken on August 7, 1877 to determine whether the home of the state government should be Charleston, Clarksburg, or Martinsburg.

The Third Capitol of West Virginia (at Wheeling) This capitol building served the people from 1875 to 1885.

In the election, Charleston received 41,243 votes; Clarksburg 29,942; and Martinsburg 8,046. The governor then proclaimed that eight years thereafter, 1885, the state capital would again be Charleston.

Several factors favored Charleston as the state capital. Charleston was more centrally located in the state than Wheeling in the Northern Panhandle or Martinsburg in the Eastern Panhandle. Charleston could be most conveniently reached by people from all over the state. One newspaper noted that Charleston was served by the Chesapeake and Ohio Railroad, which had been completed to the Ohio River in 1873. Charleston also had the Hale House, perhaps the largest and finest hotel in all of West Virginia.

In the first move from Wheeling to Charleston, government personnel and the state documents were transported on a steamboat named *Mountain Boy*. When the capital was moved back to Wheeling from Charleston, two steamboats, the *Emma Graham* and the *Chesapeake*, were required to make the move. In the last move from Wheeling to Charleston, the *Chesapeake* was again used as well as the *Belle Prince*.

The Fourth Capitol of West Virginia (at Charleston) This building in Charleston served from 1885 to 1921, when it was destroyed by fire.

chapter twenty-five / from "reconstruction" to the twentieth century

Convention of 1872

The time was ripe to call another constitutional convention for purposes of rewriting the 1863 constitution which had been drafted by Unionists. Arguments in behalf of such a convention were three in number: Many felt that the township system did not suit West Virginia, that the secret ballot was too expensive to administer, and that possibly suffrage had been extended to too many people.

The vote on calling a convention was close: 30,220 voters approved, and 27,738 disapproved. In October 1871 the delegates to the convention were chosen. Out of 78 delegates, only 12, called the "Twelve Apostles," were Republicans.

The writing of the 1872 constitution took place in the Methodist Episcopal Church at Charleston.

The future seemed brighter for former Confederates in West Virginia when Charles Faulkner was chosen as temporary president of the convention. The constitution incorporated several changes. The qualifications for voting were widened so as not to conflict with the Fifteenth Amendment to the Constitution of the United States which assured the right to vote to all males regardless of race. The constitution stated specifically that a citizen could not be denied the right to vote because his name had not been registered. A voter was given the right to cast his ballot open, secret, or sealed.

The office of lieutenant governor was discontinued. The office of justice of the peace and the county courts were reestablished. Martial law was declared to be unconstitutional.

Fifty-Five Counties

Final determination of the counties to be included in West Virginia was made by the end of the 1800's. On July 22 and September 4, 1863 Berkeley and Jefferson counties voted to become a part of West Virginia. Acts passed by the West Virginia Legislature on August 5 and November 2, 1863 included these counties in the state. By joint resolution on March 6, 1866 the United States Congress confirmed that Berkeley and Jefferson counties were a part of West Virginia.

In 1864, however, the Reorganized Government of Virginia, now in Virginia, assigned seats in the Virginia General Assembly to Berkeley and Jefferson, and in 1865 the Virginia government declared that the acts permitting the two counties to leave the mother state were null and void. The contest between Virginia and West Virginia had to be decided by the United States Supreme Court. In

1871 the Court ruled that Berkeley and Jefferson were West Virginia counties.

Besides Berkeley and Jefferson, five other counties, Grant, Mineral, Lincoln, Summers, and Mingo, created out of counties already included in the state, were added to West Virginia between 1866 and 1895. This addition brought the total number of counties to 55.

Final Boundaries

West Virginia's boundary disputes with Ohio and Maryland after the Civil War had to be resolved. In the dispute with Ohio, West Virginia's western boundary was set at the low watermark on the north side of the Ohio. This decision gave to West Virginia all the islands in the Ohio River between the two states.

Disputes over boundary lines between West Virginia and Maryland went back to the time of Lord Fairfax but became crucial only when Maryland began to form Garrett County shortly before the outbreak of the Civil War. From 1891 to 1910 the dispute was argued in the United States Supreme Court. In the Court's decision West Virginia was denied jurisdiction over the Potomac River beyond the low watermark of the south bank. In another case West Virginia established final control over a part of Preston County that was claimed by Maryland.

Virginia Debt Controversy

At the Second Wheeling Convention, West Virginia promised to pay a just proportion of the public debt of Virginia as it existed in 1861. The West Virginia constitution of 1863 reaffirmed the agreement. Negotiations between the two states regarding the debt were interrupted when Virginia sued West Virginia for the return of Berkeley and Jefferson counties. In 1871 Virginia's General Assembly took action. It determined the amount of the state debt just before the Civil War and assigned one-third of it to West Virginia. The amount Virginia determined as West Virginia's debt in 1861 was approximately $34,000,000.

In 1871 West Virginia argued that the amount due Virginia was a little less than $1,000,000, and a committee in the West Virginia Legislature held that Virginia owed West Virginia a little over $500,000.

Virginia sued in the United States Supreme Court for the money it had assigned as due from West Virginia. The Supreme Court determined that West Virginia's debt was a little more than $7,182,500 as the debt had stood on January 1, 1861.

West Virginia was slow in accepting the decision of the Supreme Court, and through interest charges, by January 1919 the total had grown to $14,562,000.

The Legislature of 1919 provided for a cash payment of $1,062,867.16 and the issuance of 3½ percent bonds due in 1939 to the amount of $13,500,000.

On April 18, 1919 West Virginia made the cash payment to Virginia, and on July 1, 1939 the bonds were redeemed in full.

End of "Reconstruction" and Emergence of "Bourbon" Rule

When "reconstruction" ended, the name "Bourbon" was given to the new political leadership that assumed control in the Southern states. It was a term borrowed from European history, and referred to past monarchies of France, Spain, Naples, and Sicily which clung to the old social and political ideas and refused to accept reform.

When applied to leadership in the South, it meant opposition to Negro suffrage, a refusal by the state to render social services, a belief in the Democratic Party, and a desire by the state to participate in the profits of business and industry while glorifying the rural past.

The West Virginia Bourbons. When applied to West Virginia, the Bourbon leadership meant a belief in business and industry and an allegiance to the Democratic Party. However, there was less evidence that the West Virginia Bourbons were as antagonistic to the Negroes or to the necessity for social services as were their counterparts in the Deep South states.

The Bourbon governors of West Virginia were Henry Mason Mathews, Jacob Beeson Jackson, Emanuel Willis Wilson, A. Brooks Fleming, and William Alexander MacCorkle.

The Governors. The governors tipped the state toward an industrial revolution. Mathews with the use of state troops and the aid of federal troops ended the industrial unrest at Martinsburg in 1877. He also promoted immigration of German and Swiss settlers, the improving of the Ohio River, and the financing of a geological survey of the state. Jackson and Wilson were less Bourbon by their advocacy of tax reforms and antagonism to trusts and monopolies.

"The Castle" at Berkeley Springs "The Castle" was built in 1887, during the "Bourbon" governorship of Emanuel Willis Wilson. The large gray stone residence, which was modeled after the fortified home of a European nobleman, may be seen today. (West Virginia Department of Commerce Photo)

Fleming's and MacCorkle's promotional efforts to bring the natural resources of the state to the attention of industrialists outside the state were more in character with the efforts of industrially oriented politicians of the Deep South.

Courageous Confederate

Charles J. Faulkner, Man for All Seasons

Over a period of years anti-Confederate sentiment softened in West Virginia. The change in attitude was fostered by men of character, such as Charles J. Faulkner. Faulkner was born July 6, 1806 at Martinsburg, Berkeley County in present West Virginia. Orphaned at eight, he worked hard to graduate from Georgetown University, Washington, D.C., in 1822. Afterward he attended law lectures and was admitted to the bar in 1829. Faulkner soon became a successful lawyer in his hometown.

He was first elected to the Virginia House of Delegates in 1829 and served again in that body from 1831 to 1834. In 1832 he urged the gradual abolition of slavery. From 1838 to 1842 Faulkner was a state senator. Elected to the United States Congress in 1850, he served in the House of Representatives from 1851 to 1859.

Prior to the Civil War he was named minister to France by President Buchanan.

Returning to Washington, D.C., after Abraham Lincoln's election, Faulkner submitted his papers to the State Department in 1861. He was detained as a hostage by the War Department and the State Department and was prevented from joining his wife and family in Martinsburg. Secretary of State William Seward informed Faulkner that Faulkner was a political prisoner because he had acknowledged the authority of Virginia which had taken up armed rebellion against the United States.

The secretary of state promised Faulkner release from federal prison if he would swear an oath of allegiance to the United States. Faulkner refused to do so under such bargaining conditions. He later won his freedom in exchange for New York Congressman Alfred Ely's freedom from detention by the Confederates. Faulkner

"Boydville," Home of Charles J. Faulkner "Boydville" is the pride of Martinsburg, Berkeley County. Construction of the home was begun in 1812 by Elisha (or Ellisha) Boyd. His daughter, Mary Wagner Boyd, and her husband, Charles J. Faulkner, moved into the old home in 1840. The home was bequeathed to their son, also Charles J. The fine old place was owned by the family for 146 years. *(Gerald S. Ratliff Photo, West Virginia Department of Commerce)*

returned to the Eastern Panhandle and became an aide of General "Stonewall" Jackson during Jackson's Valley of Virginia campaigns in the Civil War.

After the war Faulkner went back to his Berkeley County home.

Faulkner found himself under the government of the new state of West Virginia. He accepted the change, but he soon ran into the legal blocks thrown up against former Confederates. The anti-Confederacy mood of the postwar period was essentially expressed in laws and regulations, however, and Faulkner was a man of experience in the law.

He founded a newspaper, the *New Era*, in 1865 at Martinsburg to help soothe the enmity against former Confederates.

He applied for permission to resume the practice of law but refused to take a required "test oath." He fought the case in the courts and won. He was admitted to the bar and was hailed as a hero by the oppressed and persecuted Southern men of the state.

His continuing lawsuits did much to calm the mood of vengeance which many held against those who had sided with the South. His success in the suits helped bring the former Southern sympathizers back to a respectable position in the state.

Faulkner also came back politically. In the state constitutional convention of 1872 he served as temporary president and was largely instrumental in having a provision eliminating the "test oath" inserted in the constitution. In 1874 he was again elected to the United States House of Representatives and continued to serve until his death at his Martinsburg home on November 1, 1884.

His son, Charles J. Faulkner, Jr., was later elected to the United States Senate.

Chapter 26 INLAND TRANSPORTATION

By the year 1900 railroads had been widely constructed over the United States. In West Virginia, where construction was difficult, railroad systems were completed somewhat later than in more favorable country. But by 1914 the state had a fairly well-perfected network of railroads.

Railway Growth and Decline

At the conclusion of Woodrow Wilson's first administration, 3,556.98 miles of railroad had been built in West Virginia. For a sixty-year period, dating back to the completion of the Baltimore and Ohio's main line through the state in 1852–53, railroads had grown in West Virginia at a rate of approximately sixty miles a year. The most active period of railroad construction in the state was from 1896 to 1902.

By 1904 railroads had entered fifty-one of the fifty-five counties of the state. In 1912 sixty-four railroad companies of varying mileage and value had been chartered in West Virginia. At the time of World War I, the property of the sixty-four railroad companies in West Virginia was assessed at $181,666,795. The most important in the state were the Baltimore and Ohio, the Chesapeake and Ohio, the Norfolk and Western, the Western Maryland, the Virginian, the Coal and Coke, the Kanawha and Michigan, and the Morgantown and Kingwood. The "Big Three" were the Baltimore and Ohio

Railroad, the Chesapeake and Ohio Railway, and the Norfolk and Western Railway. The primary purpose of the Chesapeake and Ohio and the Baltimore and Ohio was to transport the products of the Middle West to the Eastern markets. The Norfolk and Western and most of the other railroad companies of West Virginia aided in developing the state's natural resources of coal and timber.

The Baltimore and Ohio. The Baltimore and Ohio Railroad was the first major trunk line to cross the state. The road entered the state of West Virginia at Harpers Ferry and proceeded to Grafton, with its main branch leading to Wheeling and on to Chicago, and its auxiliary branch going to Parkersburg and on to Cincinnati. Several branch lines were built from the main line. One branch led from Fairmont to Morgantown, one from Grafton up the Tygart Valley to Belington in Barbour County, and one from the Greenspring Run to Romney in Hampshire County. In addition, two other small branches, from Wheeling to Pittsburgh and from Harpers Ferry to Staunton, Virginia, were constructed.

The Chesapeake and Ohio. The Chesapeake and Ohio Railway was the first of the trunk lines built in West Virginia after the Civil War. In general, the C&O followed the Indian trails and stagecoach routes of an early period. The line entered West Virginia a short distance east of White Sulphur Springs in Greenbrier County, traveled through the canyon of New River, followed the Great Kanawha River for some miles, and then cut across to Huntington on the Ohio River.

Blasting was required along the New River canyon route, and a tunnel had to be dug through the Allegheny Mountains. At a later period the railroad projected itself from Huntington on the Ohio to Cincinnati.

The Chesapeake and Ohio Railway was the successor of the Covington and Ohio Railroad and the Virginia Central which were never completed because of the outbreak of the Civil War. Work on the C&O began in 1868 and was completed in 1873 despite the fact that residents along the way protested its construction. In 1872 the *Greenbrier Independent* carried articles opposing the road, giving as the reasons for opposition that the railroad carried whiskey, killed chickens and cows, scared the horses, and threw the teamsters out of work.

A celebration was held on January 29, 1873 when the last spike was driven on the New River bridge at Hawks Nest. At Huntington

A Modern C&O "Coal Drag" in West Virginia

a barrel of James River water brought from Richmond was poured into the Ohio River, and at Richmond water from the Ohio River was emptied into the James River, signifying that a railroad provided transportation between the two bodies of water.

The first president of the railroad company, General William C. Wickham, made a speech extolling the advantages of the road. These, he declared, were the shortness of the route between the Ohio and Norfolk harbor, the railroad's easy grade and all possible avoidance of curves, the mild climate along the route, and the short distance of the Huntington terminus from Cincinnati.

In its early years the Chesapeake and Ohio suffered from poor management and the prejudices of people along its route. By 1880 the road was extended from Richmond to Newport News on the Atlantic Coast, and later west to Louisville, Kentucky. By working arrangements with other lines, the Chesapeake and Ohio had access to Chicago and other points in the Middle West.

Collis P. Huntington, one of the great railroad builders of the United States, was responsible for extending the line. Mr. Huntington, for whom the onetime western terminus of the C&O in West Virginia was named, first gave financial aid in 1869. By 1878 the road was sold and conveyed to Mr. Huntington. By 1889 he had pro-

Giant Hopper Cars Moving Coal on the N&W Railway

jected the line to Cincinnati and built other branch lines into the coal-mining areas of West Virginia and Kentucky.

As was true of the coming of the railroad generally in West Virginia, the Chesapeake and Ohio Railway brought new prosperity to towns along its route. Particularly Hinton, Ronceverte, Montgomery, Charleston, Saint Albans, and Huntington profited from the rail service.

The Norfolk and Western. The Norfolk and Western Railway marks the year of its origin as 1881. The railroad was originally planned as a narrow-gauge road to connect with the Chesapeake and Ohio at Hinton. But with the discovery of the great Pocahontas coalfield, the N&W was completed as a standard-gauge railroad to serve the coal area. Leaving the New River near Glen Lyn on the Virginia-West Virginia boundary line, the N&W ascended the East River and passed through the Bluestone Valley. The New River division was constructed in 1881–82. The Flat Top Mountain extension down the Bluestone and up its western branches was begun in 1884 and completed in 1886. The Ohio extension was begun in 1890 and completed in 1892. It proceeded from Elkhorn to Tug Fork by way of Pigeon and Laurel Fork, across the divide to Twelve Pole

Creek, and thence to Ceredo and Kenova. The termini were at Columbus and Cincinnati, Ohio.

The original Norfolk and Western line was built with considerable curvature. It was remote from other railways, and during its construction in 1887–88 it passed no villages. Between the Elkhorn tunnel and Welch there were no highways paralleling the tracks.

The Elkhorn tunnel, which followed the famous coal vein through Flat Top Mountain, was begun and finished in 1886. The railroad reached Welch in 1892, the same year that the Ohio extension was completed. Between 1894 and 1911 eleven more branches with their sub-branches were completed.

In a short time many towns appeared along the wilderness route, such as Bluefield, Northfork, Bramwell, Keystone, Welch, Williamson, and Kenova, and they experienced great prosperity.

Projects of Davis and Elkins. Henry Gassaway Davis was a railroad man of great experience, and his son-in-law, Stephen B. Elkins, was an expert railroad financier. The two men made an excellent railroad team.

Davis began his railroad career as a brakeman on the Baltimore and Ohio Railroad in 1842. He rose rapidly to become conductor and supervisor of the line to Cumberland in 1847. He was responsible for the first night trains on the line. Later he assumed the duties of station agent at Piedmont and of division superintendent in charge of trains approaching the summit and crossing over the great Appalachian Divide.

In addition to railroading, Davis extended his interests to farming, banking, timbering, and coal mining. For good measure, he added politics. He served as a United States senator from 1871 to 1883 and in 1904 was the Democratic candidate for Vice-President of the United States.

Davis's son-in-law, Stephen B. Elkins, also enjoyed a political career. From 1891 to 1893 he served as secretary of war in President Benjamin Harrison's cabinet and from 1893 to 1911 as United States senator. Davis and Elkins were railroad statesmen. Davis was appointed to membership on the Intercontinental Railway Commission and served as chairman of the Pan-American Railway Committee. Elkins served as chairman of the Senate Committee on Interstate Commerce and distinguished himself by sponsoring the Elkins Act of 1903. This legislation attempted to outlaw rebates. Elkins jointly authorized the Mann-Elkins Act of 1910, legislation which also regulated railroad rates and rebates.

Cass Scenic Railroad, Pocahontas County *(West Virginia Department of Commerce Photo)*

The three West Virginia railway projects of Davis and Elkins were the Western Maryland Railway, the Coal and Coke Railroad, and the Morgantown and Kingwood Railroad.

The Projects of Henry Gassaway Davis. Henry Gassaway Davis had an interest in the Western Maryland Railroad. After selling his interest in this road, he purchased the Charleston, Clendenin and Sutton Railroad in 1902 and extended it to Elkins where he was developing coal and timber lands. In 1904 he built the road from Elkins to Buckhannon; in 1905 to future Gassaway on Elk River. In that year the road was renamed the Coal and Coke Railroad, and in January 1906 it made its first run into Charleston. Buckhannon, Sutton, and Clendenin enjoyed new prosperity, and the new towns of Elkins (formerly Leadsville), Gormania, Thomas, Davis, Parsons, Hendricks, Durbin, and Gassaway appeared.

The Projects of Camden. In 1884 Johnson N. Camden, a businessman interested in oil, coal, and timber, entered the railroad game by constructing the Ohio River Railroad. The section between Wheeling and Parkersburg was finished in 1884, between Parkersburg and Huntington in 1888, and between Huntington and Kenova in 1893. Branch lines were built from Ravenswood to Spencer and from Millwood to Ripley. In 1890 Camden was responsible for the Monongahela River line, built between Clarksburg and Fairmont with Monongah as its operation center. The railroad lines controlled by Camden as well as those controlled by Davis and Elkins became a part of the Baltimore and Ohio Railroad.

Camden, like Davis and Elkins, became a railroad statesman. At the time of the formation of the important Interstate Commerce Commission in 1887, he argued against major railroad companies, such as the Baltimore and Ohio, charging higher rates for goods hauled a short distance than for goods hauled a long distance. In this instance Camden, a local industrialist, was siding with the farmer against the "outside" corporations taking advantage of West Virginians.

The Projects of H. H. Rogers. H. H. Rogers was responsible for two railway systems in West Virginia. One was the Short Line, and the other was the Virginian. The Short Line connected Clarksburg and New Martinsville and, as its name implied, was a direct route from the coalfields of the Monongahela Valley to the upper

chapter twenty-six / inland transportation

Ohio with a possibility of extension to the Great Lakes. It was completed in 1901.

The Virginian was a more ambitious project. Its modest beginnings in 1894 were as a five-mile coal and timber road from Deepwater on the Kanawha River to Page, a small lumber camp. By 1909, through a combination with the Virginia Tidewater line, Rogers had a low-grade road running east from Deepwater, West Virginia, to Norfolk, Virginia. By way of a bridge over the Kanawha at Deepwater Rogers secured connections with the New York Central which provided outlets to the Great Lakes. The line traversed the southern boundary of Mercer County from Glen Lyn to Ingleside and proceeded due north through the Pocahontas coalfield. It brought prosperity to the towns of Princeton, Matoaka, Herndon, Mullens, and Beckley.

Rogers' concept was to pull heavy freight over the railroads by the force of its own weight toward the Atlantic seaboard in much the same manner that products had floated to market on inland waters. This concept was in line with Rogers' idea of transporting oil through long pipelines. He therefore built his road across streams and tunneled through the hills and mountains to avoid paralleling the streams and ridges. His freight was heavy, and in order to haul 6,000 tons of coal he utilized 150-foot-long locomotives weighing 600 tons.

Although Rogers had been primarily interested in oil, gas, copper, steel, and banking, he had early developed an interest in railroads. For a time he had served as a railroad brakeman and baggageman. The Virginian was his last great venture. It was considered a unique achievement for one man to build a railroad totally with his own resources and credit and to accomplish this during panic years.

The strain of the Virginian project proved fatal to him, and he died suddenly of an apoplectic stroke May 18, 1909, the year the road was completed.

Decline of the Railroad. Automobiles and airplanes have now greatly reduced passenger traffic on the railroads, and most of the railroad lines are in serious financial trouble. To assist the railroads in their difficulties, the federal government inaugurated Amtrak on May 1, 1971. The goal of Amtrak is to "get people back on the trains." Two reminders of an earlier railroad era, however, persist in West Virginia. One is the ballad "John Henry" with its many versions of how the Negro steel driver helped build the Chesapeake and Ohio Railway through the West Virginia mountains. The other

A Coal Tow on the Kanawha River at Charleston *(Gerald S. Ratliff Photo, West Virginia Department of Commerce)*

is the Cass Scenic Railroad in Pocahontas County. On the latter, passengers may ride a logging train pulled by a steam engine, a relic of a bygone era. The train climbs the mountain from Cass to Bald Knob.

River Improvements

When railway traffic was expanding from 1865 to the beginning of World War I, transportation on inland waters almost came to a standstill. But when the United States entered the war in 1917, the railroads could not handle the resulting great volume of freight and passenger traffic, and the need for improved rivers was apparent.

In the 1880's John E. Kenna, congressman from the Kanawha Valley, had been a rather lone fighter for locks and dams on the Ohio and Kanawha rivers to make the rivers navigable for large boats and thus increase means of transportation. By 1922 the federal government made an appropriation to improve navigation on the Ohio River. By 1929 fifty new locks and dams were constructed on that river and its tributaries from Pittsburgh to Cairo, Illinois. These locks and dams provided a nine-foot channel that

Sutton Dam and Lake, Elk River, West Virginia   (U.S. Army Corps of Engineers Photo, Huntington, West Virginia, District)

would accommodate vessels carrying heavy freight. Twenty-one of the dams were in West Virginia, helping create a nine-foot level on the Kanawha River and a seven-to-nine-foot level on the Monongahela.

The Kanawha Valley and the Monongahela Valley thus became a part of an inland navigation system which gave river traffic access to the Great Lakes, since canals connected the waters of the Ohio with those of the Lakes. The valleys now also had access to the Mississippi through the Ohio River and through the Mississippi to the Gulf of Mexico. The Kanawha was allotted three dams with two locks each at Winfield, Marmet, and London with a fourth unit on the Ohio just below Gallipolis.

Reservoirs. Related to the rivers were periodic floods. Droughts in some years also brought difficulties. These recurring problems led to the building of reservoirs. In 1927 a dam was completed across Cheat River near the Pennsylvania-West Virginia boundary line. This dam forms Cheat Lake. In 1938 the Tygart River Reservoir Dam near Grafton was completed. Within the next three decades the Bluestone Reservoir Dam was built near Hinton, the Sutton Dam was built on the Elk River, and the Summersville Dam on the Gauley.

Champion of Charleston

John E. Kenna, Idol of Kanawha

From "reconstruction" days after the Civil War West Virginia began to prosper through the development of its mineral wealth. One reason for the economic advancement was improvement in transportation involving railroad construction and river-channel improvement, which helped speed the minerals and mineral products to the markets.

Among the men who worked for good transportation in West Virginia was John E. Kenna. For the greater part of his life Kenna was identified with the progress of the Kanawha Valley. Kenna was born in Kanawha County on April 10, 1848. After his father died in 1856, the family moved to southern

Missouri. When sixteen, Kenna joined the Confederate army. He was severely wounded in combat.

After the war, Kenna returned to West Virginia. The benevolence of friends here enabled him to study for three years at St. Vincent's College in Wheeling. In 1870 he was admitted to the bar and worked in a Charleston law office.

Riding the rising tide of the Democratic Party in West Virginia, Kenna was elected prosecuting attorney of Kanawha County in 1872 and a member of the United States House of Representatives in 1876. In the Congress he served on the Commerce Committee where he championed railroad legislation and internal improvement.

The development of the resources of West Virginia through improvement in transportation by water was a cherished project for Kenna. His greatest effort was made to secure federal aid for slack-water navigation on the Kanawha River. He was successful in his agitation for making navigable a river which would tap the rich resources of coal, timber, and salt in southern West Virginia. He won widespread popularity in the state and in 1883 was elected to the United States Senate.

In the Senate he continued his work for improved navigation along the Kanawha and its tributaries and became one of the leading advocates of railroad regulation. His sudden death on January 11, 1893, when he was forty-five, cut short a promising career.

In National Statuary Hall in the nation's capitol West Virginia has contributed two statues of distinguished West Virginians judged worthy of national commemoration. One is the statue of Francis H. Pierpont; the other is of John E. Kenna.

Chapter 27 MINERAL FUELS: COAL, OIL, AND GAS

Coal

Before the Civil War, coal mines were opened along the navigable rivers of the west and also along the state's first railroad, the Baltimore and Ohio. After the war the coal industry remained small until in the 1880's and 1890's new railroads were built to carry the fuel to points of sale. In 1870 West Virginia's coal production reached only 600,000 tons. In 1900 coal production in the state surpassed 21,000,000 tons, and on the eve of World War I approximately 67,000,000. Today annual production in West Virginia averages 140,000,000 tons.

It is now certain that West Virginia has proved coal reserves exceeding 62,000,000,000 tons, enough to last from 350 to 400 years. In fact, estimates are that the state actually contains twice 62,000,000,000 tons.

Oil

General Samuel D. Karnes' early oil well near Burning Springs in Wirt County had a daily output of seven barrels of oil in 1860. West Virginia was producing 90,000 barrels of oil in 1884; 120,000 barrels by 1888; and 16,000,000 barrels, the state's peak production, by 1900.

After 1900, production fell at the rate of about 200,000 barrels of oil per year. The decrease was due to exhaustion of the West

Continuous Coal Miner   This massive and costly machine is shown as it moved between working places in a West Virginia coal mine. The machine rips eight tons of coal a minute from the face of the seam. *(Photo courtesy of Joy Manufacturing Co.)*

Virginia fields and competition from oil fields in the Southwest. In 1912, on the eve of World War I, output was approximately 12,000,000 barrels, and forty years later it had dipped to 2,602,000 barrels. From 1960 to 1970 it rose from 2,300,000 barrels to approximately 3,202,000.

The state has reserves of more than 53,000,000 barrels of petroleum.

Gas

In 1906, among all the states in the Union, West Virginia took the lead in the production of natural gas with 120,000 million cubic feet. The state was able to retain the number-one position through the year 1917 with an annual production figure of 308,000 million cubic feet. From 1917 to 1932 the output of gas declined to about 100,000 million cubic feet annually. In the next ten years it climbed back to 252,000 million cubic feet, but in 1950 leveled to about 197,000 million cubic feet. In the twenty-year period from 1950 to 1970 production figures followed a somewhat sustained level but slightly increased. In 1970 West Virginia produced 231,710 million cubic feet.

The state has reserves of approximately 2,500,000,000 cubic feet of natural gas.

Increase in Production

The major reason for the growth of the mineral fuel industries in West Virginia was the enormous natural endowment of the state. In the hundred-year period after the Civil War, the state extracted slightly more than 7,000,000,000 tons of coal from the ground.

In one hundred years, 40,000 oil wells had been drilled and 29,400 gas wells had been sunk in West Virginia. When 14,000 dry oil wells and 600 storage tanks are added for this period, West Virginia had wells with a potential output of over 165,000,000 barrels of oil from 1860 to 1960.

Other important reasons for the dramatic development of the mineral fuels after the Civil War are three in number: Adequate transportation was finally developed so that the products could be marketed throughout the nation; the locations of the mineral resources were scientifically and accurately determined; and the demand for the primary products and their by-products grew in proportion as the needs of an expanding industrialized nation grew. For example, the use of oil for heating purposes, the development of the automobile for both family and business use, the conversion of locomotives and the engines of seagoing vessels to the use of petroleum fuels, the rapid expansion of aviation, and the industrial use of residual and fuel oils helped produce demands for all mineral fuels.

Ten Coalfields

West Virginia may be said to have ten major coalfields. Coal is found in more than sixty minable seams and coalfields lie in forty-four of the fifty-five counties in the state. Twenty-eight counties have more than 1,000,000,000 tons of coal reserves.

The Fairmont Field. One of the larger West Virginia fields is the Fairmont Field, which lies in Monongalia, Marion, Preston, Taylor, Barbour, and Harrison counties. The field developed around the rich Pittsburgh seam. Its production has been favorably affected by service provided by the Baltimore and Ohio Railroad and other rail lines.

On February 14, 1886 the first train from Fairmont to Morgantown traveled over a new extension of the Baltimore and Ohio. This

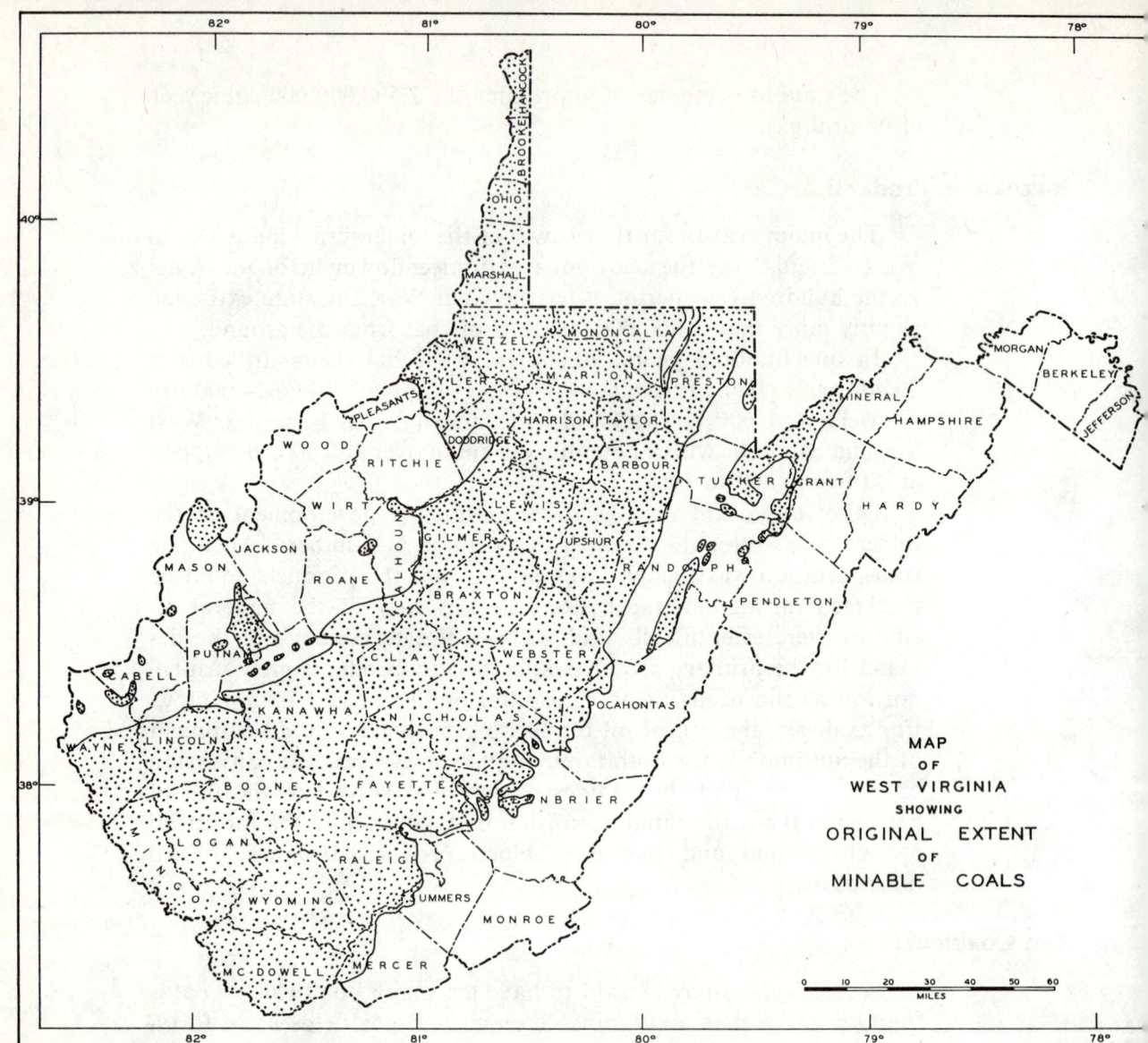

(Source of map: West Virginia Geological and Economic Survey)

road became the foundation for the production and marketing success of the Fairmont Field. By 1900 the Monongah mines near Fairmont were opened, the first beehive coke ovens were developed, and the Monongah mines were electrically equipped and were using cutting machines. The next year the Fairmont Coal Company was formed. It became in a few years the Consolidation Coal Company, one of the great coal-producing companies in the nation. Another major coal company in the area was the Christopher Coal Company.

The Kanawha Field. An earlier great coalfield in West Virginia was the Kanawha Field, which lies in Kanawha, Putnam, Mason, Clay, Boone, Lincoln, and Nicholas counties. In this field the coal industry developed naturally from the salt industry. The great factor in increasing production figures was the Chesapeake and Ohio Railway.

By 1915 thirty-seven companies producing almost 6,000,000 tons of coal had been incorporated in the valley. At the time of World War I the Cabin Creek Consolidation Coal Company and the Paint Creek Collieries Company were the largest of the companies with an investment in twenty-eight mines.

The New River Field. Like the Kanawha Field, the New River Field, lying in Fayette and Raleigh counties, was developed when the Chesapeake and Ohio Railway provided transportation for the coal. One of the most important early coal men was Samuel Dixon, "dean of the coal industry in Fayette County."

Flat Top-Pocahontas Field. The Flat Top-Pocahontas Field lies in Mercer and McDowell counties. Large commercial mines developed in this field when the completion of the lines of the Norfolk and Western Railway made shipping possible. Isaac T. Mann was an important coal developer in Mercer County. The Pocahontas Fuel Company, organized in 1907, dominated the other companies in McDowell, a county which had few other industries. Operations were consolidated into large companies, and mechanical mining was utilized from the beginning of the industry. In the first years of the twentieth century, there was an influx of Negro mine workers from the Deep South into the Flat Top-Pocahontas Field.

The Winding Gulf Field. The Winding Gulf Field lies in parts of Raleigh and Wyoming counties. The field developed when the Virginian Railroad constructed branch lines from its main line to the Chesapeake and Ohio Railway in 1907. Pioneer coal producers in the area were John Laing, G. H. Caperton, and W. Gaston Caperton.

Justus Collins was known as the "baron of the Winding Gulf Field." In 1929 the Collins interests in the Winding Gulf Field and in Mercer and McDowell counties were consolidated as the Winding Gulf Collieries, and their coal was sold under the trade name of "Miltrena."

The Logan Field. The Logan Field lies in Logan and Wyoming counties. Early development in this field was prevented by lack of

chapter twenty-seven / mineral fuels: coal, oil, and gas

First Oil Well in the Sistersville Field, the Polecat No. 1 This well, drilled in 1890, opened one of the richest oil fields in West Virginia. (From "The West Virginia Review")

railroads and by lawsuits involving land titles. In 1904 the Guyandotte Valley Railroad, now a part of the Chesapeake and Ohio system, penetrated the Logan fields. Very quickly Logan became the largest coal-producing county in the state (McDowell the second), and was dominated by the Island Creek Coal Company.

Operators in the smokeless fields played a small role in opening the Logan Field. The Amherst Coal Company became an important producer, as did the Boone County Coal Corporation.

The Southern Coal Producers Association was organized in 1941.

The Williamson Field. The Williamson Field lies in Mingo County. This field became an important producer when the Norfolk and Western Railway entered the area in 1893-94. In Williamson, the county seat, the N&W maintained large railroad shops and yards. The city became the center for coal company offices.

The Elkins Field. The Elkins Field lies in Braxton, Lewis, Webster, Upshur, Randolph, Tucker, Grant, and Mineral counties. Its production of coal increased when shipping facilities were provided by the Baltimore and Ohio Railroad and by the railroad interests of Henry Gassaway Davis and Stephen B. Elkins. A peculiarity of the Elkins Field is that coal is mined in only a small section of each county. The Elkins field has remained primarily agricultural, and here coal mining has never assumed the important place that it has in southern West Virginia.

Labor force is predominantly local native Americans, with Italians making up the remainder. Italians also were the early laborers on the Coal and Coke Railroad.

The Greenbrier and Northern Panhandle Fields. Two other fields are the Greenbrier Field and the Northern Panhandle Field which lies in the counties of Ohio, Brooke, Hancock, and Marshall. The Greenbrier Field, as a recognized producer of coal, is the newest in the state, and the Northern Panhandle Field is probably the oldest. In the Greenbrier Field the Davis and Elkins interests influenced coal production. Major production occurred in 1922 when the Chesapeake and Ohio built extensions into the area.

The Northern Panhandle Field has been for many years a producer for local use. In the area are steel mills, potteries, glass plants, and other industries. These industries would not have prospered had they not been in close proximity to coal mines.

Oil and Gas Fields

Oil and gas fields are found in a broad belt of counties beginning in the Northern Panhandle and along the Pennsylvania border and sweeping in a southwest direction through the length of the state. The width of the belt is from the Allegheny Mountains to the Ohio River. The vast area comprises thirty-three counties. The natural gas field of West Virginia when coupled with that of Pennsylvania is one of the five great gas fields in the United States.

The Burning Springs Oil Field. The first major oil field was at Burning Springs in Wirt County. General Samuel D. Karnes of Pittsburgh drilled a well on land leased from William P. Rathbone. At a depth of 333 feet he struck oil, and the news of his discovery brought 6,000 people to Burning Springs in search of the new wealth. Before the Civil War was concluded, wells were yielding oil in Pleasants and Ritchie counties. In Ritchie County, solid oil, or grahamite, was discovered, and grahamite mines were operated from 1885 to 1909.

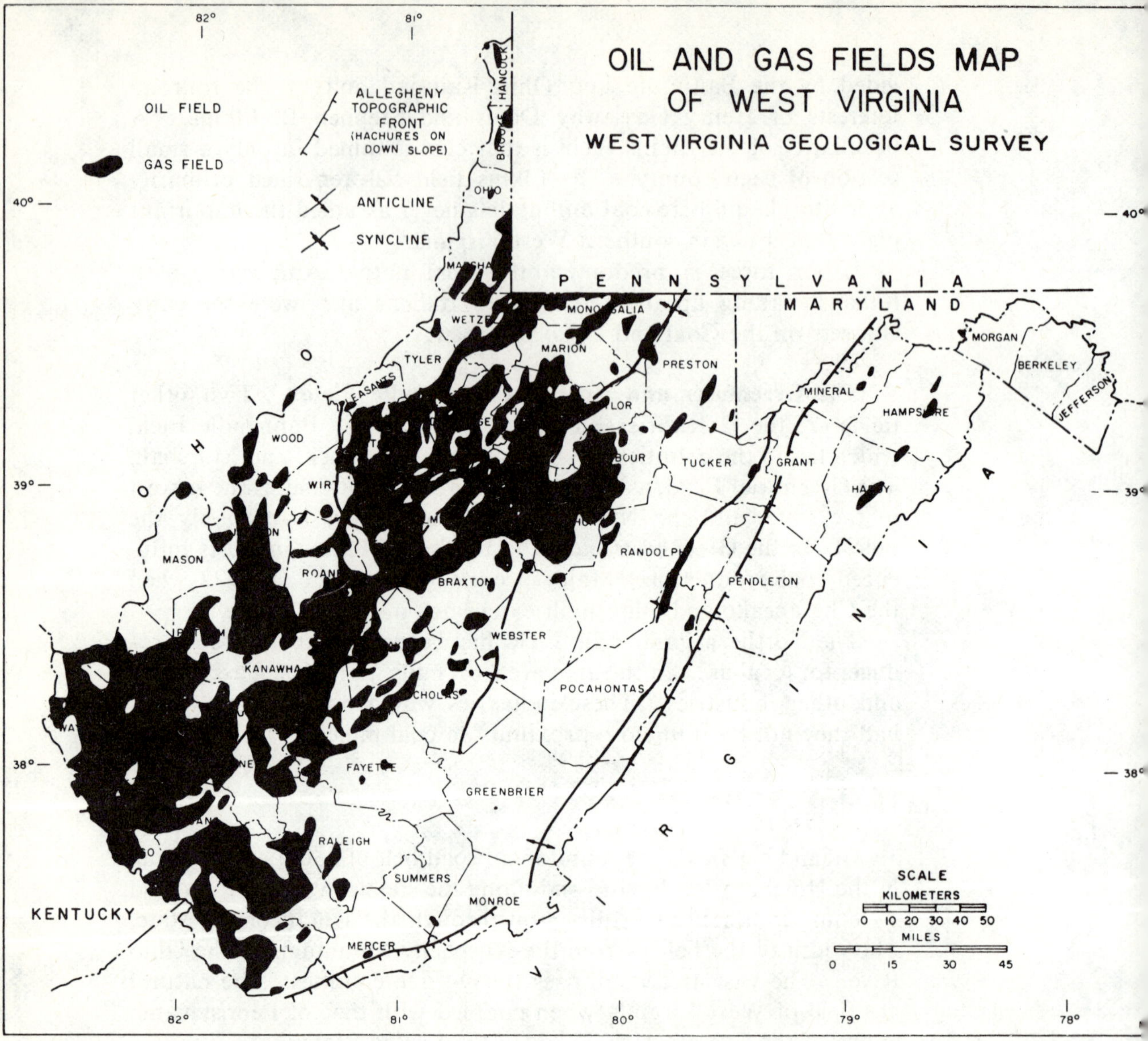

OIL AND GAS FIELDS MAP OF WEST VIRGINIA
WEST VIRGINIA GEOLOGICAL SURVEY

One of the outstanding oil men in West Virginia was Johnson Newlon Camden, who brought in his first successful oil and gas well at the Creel Sand Diggings not far from the Karnes well. During the Civil War Camden and his partners controlled most of the oil fields of the Little Kanawha Valley.

Camden later sold his properties to the Standard Oil Company, and the Camden oil refinery at Parkersburg became the producer of most of the kerosine oil used in the South and West. The Parkersburg refinery operations were later moved to Baltimore, but oil refineries were developed at Cabin Creek, Falling Rock, and St. Marys. (Quaker State)

The Mannington Field and the Sistersville Field. In 1889 the Mannington oil field was opened, largely as a result of Israel C. White's anticlinal theories concerning the location of oil and gas deposits. Next, the opening of an oil field occurred in 1892 at Sistersville in Tyler County. Production from wells sunk in Sistersville totaled 300 barrels on February 27, 1892; 1,800 barrels by March 28; and 4,300 barrels by June 23. On October 17, 1892 Sistersville was producing 16,543 barrels per day from 164 completed wells. By the end of 1892, production was 20,500 barrels a day.

The town's population increased from 600 in 1888 to 7,000 in 1898. Farmers in the town sometimes received as much as $3,000 per day in oil earnings. Many people built fine homes in which much attention was given to trim and decoration, and fine leaded glass was used lavishly. In 1900 Lewis County became the greatest oil-producing county in West Virginia. The Copley well was a partial explanation. In its early stages, it produced more than 7,000 barrels a day.

Natural Gas. In oil operations in the early days a flow of natural gas was only a nuisance. When gas rose from the oil diggings, the well was left unchecked to discharge the gas into the air. The "Big

Oil Field at Sistersville in 1895 The photograph shows mud streets, steam line boxes, old wooden derricks, and oil field shack houses. *(Photo courtesy of Walter W. McCoy)*

chapter twenty-seven / mineral fuels: coal, oil, and gas

Drilling a Gas Well in West Virginia

Moses" well in Tyler County discharged 100,000,000 cubic feet of natural gas a day for almost a year. It was set on fire by lightning, but the flow was so strong that, coupled with the wind, the force of the gas blew out the flames.

In 1904 Dr. I. C. White estimated that West Virginia had lost an appalling amount of natural gas since 1894. He estimated that 500,000,000 cubic feet had been lost into the air daily in the period from 1899 to 1904. In 1908 the West Virginia Conservation Commission on Gas Waste estimated that the value of the natural gas which West Virginia had allowed to go to waste exceeded the value of the coal the state had produced. The committee put a value of at least $1,500,000,000 on the coal.

When the volume of gas produced in West Virginia declined, the West Virginia Legislature attempted to require pipeline companies in the state to satisfy West Virginia consumers with gas before the valuable commodity was exported outside the state. Pennsylvania brought suit to prevent West Virginia from enforcing its act. The United States Supreme Court ruled in 1923 that West Virginia could not obstruct interstate commerce by withholding its gas from Pennsylvania and Ohio consumers.

Yet, despite the increase in natural gas companies in West Virginia natural gas was being imported into the state by 1944. Three pipeline companies bringing gas into West Virginia were the Tennessee Gas Transmission Company, the Texas Eastern Transmission Corporation, and the Columbia Gas System.

By-Products of Coal, Oil, and Gas. One of the most important by-products of West Virginia coal was coke, which in 1880 began to replace charcoal in the manufacture of steel. By-products from coal today make a long list, including saccharin, perfumes, aspirin, lysol, vaseline, vanillin, and dyes. Recent research has discovered certain rare minerals in coal, among them germanium, an element used in the electronics industry.

The most important product from petroleum is gasoline, but the many other by-products from oil include the common benzene, kerosine, naphtha, various greases, paraffin, and many chemicals. The peak oil year in West Virginia was 1929 when 73,000,000 gallons were produced.

An important by-product of natural gas has been carbon black, or lamp black. Carbon black is used in making paints, carbon paper, inks, and automobile tires.

Petroleum and natural gas are now used as raw materials in producing butane and numerous organic chemicals such as olefins, glycol, alcohols, ketons, glycol esters, and others.

West Virginia Philanthropist

Michael L. Benedum, "The Great Wildcatter"

Michael L. Benedum was born July 16, 1869 in Bridgeport, Harrison County, West Virginia. He was the son of a cabinetmaker and former town mayor. After his marriage in 1896, he moved to Cameron, Marshall County. Here his only child, Claude Worthington, was born in 1897.

In 1905 Mr. Benedum and a friend gathered $7,500 and set out to seek a fortune. Michael Benedum found his fortune in oil. His search began in West Virginia and was carried into the states of Pennsylvania, Illinois, Oklahoma, Ohio, Arkansas, Louisiana, and Texas and into Canada, Mexico, Central America, South America, and Eastern Europe. His biggest strike came in

1924 when he tapped the largest petroleum reserve in the country — the Permian Basin in western Texas.

Benedum became as well known for his philanthropy as for his amazing success as an oil "wildcatter." In December 1944 he organized a foundation of which the money was to be used for religious, charitable, scientific, literary, and educational purposes. Funds of the foundation were also to be used in the prevention of cruelty to children or animals. The foundation is the Claude Worthington Benedum Foundation named in honor of Michael Benedum's son who died during World War I.

In setting up the foundation, Mr. Benedum indicated that he expected to leave to it the bulk of his fortune. By the time of his death, his estate was estimated to be between $60,000,000 and $100,000,000.

Besides the foundation, Benedum's gifts during his lifetime totaled many millions of dollars. To his hometown of Bridgeport he gave $4,500,000 to build a civic center and Methodist church. To West Virginia Wesleyan College he gave a student center. Today his name is prominent in his native West Virginia, for, in addition to an airport and the civic center, his name adorns educational buildings, scholarships, and professorships.

After he made his fortune, Michael L. Benedum lived much of his life in Pittsburgh, where he died in 1959 at the age of 90.

Chapter 28 DEVELOPMENTS IN LABOR AND IN THE COAL INDUSTRY

In the development of labor organizations, the earliest activities centered around the railroads and the coal industry in West Virginia. Conditions that called for collective bargaining were wages, hours of work, and better working conditions. The need in West Virginia was apparent. Industrial livelihood exacted its toll, as was seen in the company towns in West Virginia, where individuals worked for the coal company, the railroad, the steel mills, or the company stores. These towns were drab and monotonous, because houses were often built on the same plan, painted the same color, and the streets seldom had sidewalks.

Miners and their families were often required to buy at the company store where prices were often higher than at other stores, and their wages were occasionally in the form of company scrip, rather than in money.

As mining was a particularly dangerous operation, there were many mine tragedies which added to a feeling of doom and frustration. One of the first was an explosion in the Mountain Brook Shaft Mine at Newburg, West Virginia, on January 21, 1886, which resulted in the death of thirty-nine persons.

The Mantrip Miners board the steel-topped mantrip cars to ride to the working face of the mine at the Ireland Mine of Consolidation Coal Co. near Moundsville, West Virginia. *(National Coal Association Photo)*

Mine Disasters

In 1907 at Monongah 361 men were killed in one of the worst disasters in all of coal mining history. At Eccles, 183 men were killed in an explosion on April 28, 1914, and at Layland, 112 men were killed on March 2, 1915. On April 28, 1924 at Benwood, 119 men were killed, and on April 30, 1927 at Everettsville, 97 men were killed. At Bartley, 91 were killed on January 10, 1940; at Dola, 22 were killed on April 25, 1963; and at Mt. Hope, 7 were killed on July 23, 1966. On November 13, 1954 at Farmington 16 men lost their lives, and again on November 20, 1968 at Farmington 78 men lost their lives, a modern disaster that indicated that all troubles of industrial living were not incidents of past history.

Disasters in 1972. When a coal-slag dam burst on February 26, 1972, after three days of torrential rain, a wall of water crashed upon West Virginia's seventeen-mile Buffalo Creek Hollow, leaving at least 118 dead in some sixteen demolished mining camps. The massive dam, which had been formed by coal mine waste of the Buffalo Mining Company, released millions of gallons of silt-laden water which covered the town of Saunders and the homes of over

unit seven / industrial evolution

500 families. To complete the disastrous year, on July 22, 1972 nine coal miners perished in a Blacksville, West Virginia, mine.

Safety Regulations

Disasters such as these called for safety legislation, regulation, and administration. The first mine inspector was authorized in 1883, others were added in 1887 and 1893, and an office of chief mine inspector was created in 1897. A department of mines was added in 1907. In addition, the federal government aided in providing inspectors for federal regulation of safety. For example, special laws passed in 1941 and 1947 permitted federal safety inspection of all coal mines. In 1952 the Federal Bureau of Mines was granted the power to shut down unsafe mines. But the burden in bringing about improvement in living became, in large part, the responsibility of labor organizations.

In West Virginia, the labor organizations were put to a hard test and, after years of struggle, succeeded in their tough assignments. But just as they completed their major organizational efforts, it was discovered that machinery was rapidly replacing men in some of the most difficult industrial tasks.

First National Labor Strike

In the struggle between capital and labor, Berkeley County in West Virginia served as host to the beginning of the first national labor strike in American history. The encounter was a four-day affair in which one brakeman was killed. It sparked the great railway strike of 1877 which swept the entire United States. The fundamental cause was reduction of wages by the major northeastern railroads.

On the Baltimore and Ohio Railroad, workingmen's daily wage had been drastically cut on several occasions. On July 16, 1877 railroad crews struck at Martinsburg, refused passage of the trains, and took possession of the railroad yards. Governor Henry Mason Mathews dispatched the state militia the next day and on July 18 the governor wired President Rutherford B. Hayes for federal troops. By July 19, both state and national troops were in the city; by July 20 the strike was broken in West Virginia.

However, the strikes spread to Pittsburgh, to Cumberland, to Saint Louis, to Baltimore, to Kansas City, and to New York. Before the great railway strikes of 1877 were concluded, President Hayes, at the requests of four state governors, had dispatched federal troops to aid state troops and civil authorities.

Formation of Labor Organizations

In order to provide leadership in the labor strikes that were occurring, national organizations were developed. A major one, which took charge of most of the railroad strikes in the last quarter of the nineteenth century, was the Knights of Labor. It was founded in 1869 by Uriah S. Stephens, a Philadelphia garment-cutter. Its organizational principle was one big union, to which all workers, skilled or unskilled, would belong, regardless of race, color, or occupation.

In the meantime, a rival organization began to make headway among labor groups. It was the American Federation of Labor, founded in 1881 at Pittsburgh. Individuals, as such, were excluded from membership, but labor organizations could belong. Among its goals were the eight-hour day, higher wages, and better working conditions, plus more security in the job and the elimination of child labor. Most of its membership was among the skilled trades, but an important affiliate of the American Federation of Labor was

Coal-cutting Machine Ready for Action

the United Mine Workers which was primarily an industrial union of mostly unskilled membership.

Task of the United Mine Workers. The state union of United Mine Workers of America was organized in 1890 in Wheeling, at the instance of President Samuel Gompers, and it became the dominant labor organization in West Virginia. Aided by the Knights of Labor, the two organizations began unionization of the miners. By 1897 they were given a very special assignment in the thirty-fifth state. Coal operators of western Pennsylvania, Ohio, Indiana, and Illinois, from an area called the "Central Competitive Field," agreed to unionization of their mines in West Virginia and Kentucky. Their purpose was to make sure that West Virginia coal, whose low cost was due in part to low wages, was not sold cheaper on Mid-West and Great Lakes markets. Samuel Gompers, head of the American Federation of Labor, and the presidents of the United Mine Workers and Knights of Labor, held a conference of local and national labor leaders in Wheeling on July 27, 1897 to perfect the strategy in West Virginia.

Success in Northern and Central West Virginia. The labor organizations were not immediately successful. On June 7, 1902 a general strike was called which covered fifteen counties, involved 16,000 miners, and closed about one-fourth of the state's mines. Unsuccessful in the smokeless coalfields in the southern part of the state, the labor leaders nonetheless organized most of the mines in the Kanawha Field. The early effort of "Mother Jones," the "Angel of the Miners," helped in the central Kanawha area, in northern West Virginia, and in the Northern Panhandle counties.

"Mother Jones" was Mary Harris Jones who became an organizer for the United Mine Workers in 1891. In 1902 she entered West Virginia to help organize the Fairmont, Kanawha, New River, and Pocahontas fields. She returned in 1912–13 for the Paint Creek-Cabin Creek strikes and in 1921 for the "March on Logan." Then ninety-one years old, she tried to dissuade miners from entering Logan and Mingo counties.

Born at Cork, Ireland, in 1830, she lived to be one hundred. She taught in a convent at Monroe, Michigan, and in a school in Memphis, Tennessee. She operated a dressmaking shop in Chicago. Her husband and children died from yellow fever, and following the loss of home and family, she dedicated her life to the labor movement.

Coal Tipple   Hopper cars of the Western Maryland Railway stand loaded ready to roll from the tipple of a mine of the Consolidation Coal Co. near Fairmont, West Virginia. *(Photo courtesy of Western Maryland Railway)*

The Breaking of Peace in Central West Virginia

In 1912, operators on Paint Creek, Kanawha County, refused to renew their contracts with the union. The Cabin Creek area miners joined with the Paint Creek miners in a general protest. The miners were demanding the nine-hour day, better housing, and payment in money instead of company store scrip. All strikers were discharged and evicted from their houses. In retaliation, the miners created a tented city and threatened action. In July 1912 the miners marched on Mucklow and in a battle with the company guards, twelve miners and four guards were killed. Governor William E. Glasscock established martial law over Paint Creek and the Cabin Creek districts.

The Hatfield Contract

In 1913, trials were conducted by military courts, and about a hundred persons, including "Mother Jones," were sentenced. But Governor Henry D. Hatfield modified the long terms of imprisonment. He also persuaded the operators to grant the miners the right to organize. He also secured agreement for a nine-hour day, the right to trade at stores other than company stores, and semimonthly pay checks. The Hatfield Contract seemed to settle conditions in the Kanawha Valley.

The Hitchman Case

Trouble then shifted to the Northern Panhandle. The Hitchman Coal and Coke Company mines near Benwood, Marshall County, asked the federal courts to prevent union organizers from interfering with the operations of their mines. The case finally reached the United States Supreme Court in 1917. The court ruled that the operators had a legal right to operate their mines under their own rules and regulations and without interference from the unions. Because World War I demands brought federal controls and regulations to the mines, the implications of the case were nullified for several years.

March on Logan

From the end of World War I to the advent of the Franklin Roosevelt New Deal, labor had a difficult time in West Virginia as it did across the nation. Membership declined in almost all organizations, and strikes were generally unsuccessful and severe. In 1919 coal miners called a general strike, but learned that unionization was being prevented in Logan County. Governor Cornwell promised an investigation of Logan County, but organizers insisted on an invasion of the county.

On September 5, 1919 Cornwell spoke to 5,000 armed bituminous coal miners on Lens Creek, fifteen miles from Charleston. He was able to convince most of them to disband. However, a nucleus of 50 remained, and started toward Logan the next day. Cornwell warned that if they crossed the Coal River, dividing line between Logan and Boone counties, he would call in federal troops. His warning was heeded.

Matewan Massacre

For several years attempts had been made by the United Mine Workers to organize the fields along the Norfolk and Western Railway. The coal companies responded to these efforts by discharging those who joined the union. They also evicted the families of the discharged miners from the company-owned houses.

In Matewan, in Mingo County, company detectives of the Baldwin-Felts Detective Agency clashed with local miners over eviction proceedings. On May 19, 1920, the "Matewan Massacre" occurred in which the leader of the company detectives, six of his

Coal Preparation Plant Modern mines wash and clean the coal before shipping it to markets.

men, the mayor of the town, and two union men were shot to death. During the rest of the year, small battles were fought in "Bloody Mingo." Federal troops had to be called to Mingo by Governor Cornwell and again by Governor Morgan.

Battle of Blair Mountain

When "Two-Gun Sid" Hatfield, who had been charged with murder in the Matewan Massacre, was himself murdered in August 1921 on the courthouse steps in Welch, county seat of McDowell County, thousands of miners assembling at Marmet decided to invade Mingo and Logan counties. At Blair Mountain and at Hewitt's Creek battles took place between the miners and the state police, deputy sheriffs, mine guards, and federal troops from Fort Thomas, Kentucky, and a squadron of bombers from Langley Field, Virginia.

In Governor Ephraim Franklin Morgan's 1923 message to the state Legislature, he noted that the miners, many of whom were veterans of World War I, had arranged the battle with military precision. As he saw it, "the attacking party used modern weapons of warfare, seized railroad trains, confiscated supplies, and were accompanied by physicians and nurses." In the battle, 3 men were killed, 40 were wounded, and the miners were defeated; 543 persons were brought to trial; and 22 leaders were charged with treason against the state of West Virginia. The treason charges were dropped, and those on trial were acquitted.

Labor Gains

During the Franklin Roosevelt era, the National Industrial Recovery Act (NIRA) was passed to help industry and labor during a period of depression. Eight-hour-day and minimum wage provisions were included, and Section 7A guaranteed employees the right to bargain collectively through representatives of their own choosing. Also outlawed was the "yellow dog" contract by which an employee agreed not to join a labor union. Although the NIRA was declared unconstitutional in 1935, most of the industries of West Virginia had been unionized by that time. The state Legislature and the federal government changed their attitudes toward labor.

In 1935 the state abolished the mine-guard system, approved a wage-rate law, aided in the workmen's compensation law, and provided compensation for workmen suffering disability or death from silicosis. By 1939 it prevented the employment of children under sixteen in the mines and under eighteen in hazardous occupations.

From the CIO to Independence

In 1935 John L. Lewis organized the Congress of Industrial Organizations, which incorporated the United Mine Workers. The CIO organized the employees of the steel companies of West Virginia and Ohio. In 1942 the United Mine Workers withdrew from the CIO and became an independent labor organization. In 1946 there was a major strike, during which President Truman seized the mines. In the settlement of this strike, miners procured important welfare and retirement fund clauses and $100 a month pension for retired mine workers. In the 1970's miners procured important compensation benefits for "black lung."

The gains helped offset the fact that a great loss of jobs had occurred in coal mining in West Virginia. In 1950 coal mines provided employment for 119,568 men; in 1970 the mines employed 47,000 men. Much of the decrease came about with the introduction of machinery.

Residential Section of the Coal-mining Town of Kopperston, West Virginia *(Photo courtesy of Eastern Gas & Fuel Associates)*

Changes in Mining Methods

The earliest coal mining in West Virginia had followed simple and even primitive methods. When an outcrop of coal was found, coal was dug by pick and shovel, was placed in sacks, and was carried to the loading area. As mine openings were made larger, coal was carried out by sleds, by wheelbarrows, and by two-wheeled and four-wheeled carts. At the loading tipple (a building constructed over a railroad track or coal-loading area) the coal was dumped into railroad cars, river barges, wagons, or trucks.

Mechanization gradually prevailed. Electrically operated coal cutters were used by 1890, and electric motors supplanted the mules which had hauled the coal. Safety equipment came into use. Rock dusting, electric-battery headlamps, testing of the flow of air and ventilation, installation of telephones in the mines, the use of compressed air in place of explosives to shoot down coal — all these safety measures became standard.

Machinery rather than men became dominant in coal production. The "continuous miner" came into use. This is a huge machine which strikes into the coal with cutting teeth. It can cut eight tons of coal in a minute with a crew of four to seven men. Giant augers, with immense shovels, and draglines surfaced or stripped as much as ninety tons of coal in one swift operation.

Surface mining, or stripping and augering methods, started on a small scale in 1914. In a more recent year this method was used in producing 10 percent of the bituminous coal output in West Virginia. Surface mining, or stripping, devastated the hillsides of West Virginia and polluted the streams, but strip mining increased.

Surface mining was the subject of the 1972 political campaign. Many politicians lined up "pro and con." A young lawyer, Warren McGraw, of Wyoming County, made this issue his chief campaign issue against Senator Tracy W. Hylton whom he defeated in the primary as well as in the general election. Also State Senator "Si" Galperin of Kanawha County and John D. "Jay" Rockefeller IV, Democratic candidate for governor in 1972, put on a vigorous campaign for the abolition of strip mining. As a result of the previous campaign, the state Legislature following the 1970 election passed a stronger strip mining bill.

Up From the Ranks

Walter P. Reuther of the CIO

Walter P. Reuther, a well-known labor leader, was born September 1, 1907, in Wheeling, West Virginia. He followed in his father's footsteps, for Valentine Reuther was president of the Ohio Valley Trades and Labor Assembly and an international organizer of the United Brewery Workers. At fifteen, Walter left high school to work in the Wheeling Steel Corporation plant. He was soon dismissed, however, when he organized the workers in protest against Sunday and holiday work.

In 1926 Reuther went to Detroit where he held a number of jobs until he gained steady employment with Ford Motor Company. He completed high school and attended Wayne University for three years. Even while attending college and holding his job with Ford, his interest in the labor movement continued to grow. But the Ford Motor Company dismissed him for union activity in 1932. For the next three years Reuther toured Europe and the Far East, working and studying labor conditions.

Returning to Detroit in 1935, Reuther organized the United Auto Workers (UAW) West Side Local 174, which in one year

chapter twenty-eight / developments in labor and in the coal industry grew in membership from 78 to 30,000. In 1936 he was elected to the international executive board of the UAW and was reelected until 1942, when he became its vice-president. In 1936–37 he was an active leader in the Detroit and Flint, Michigan, "sitdown" strikes which were largely responsible for the unionization of the entire automobile industry. His activities at General Motors produced numerous benefits for the workers.

After World War II, Reuther led a 113-day strike against General Motors to gain an increase in pay without an increase in prices. This action was the first time a labor union based its fight on the issue of broad national economy, an issue which would be used on innumerable occasions in the future.

In 1946 Reuther was elected president of the UAW, and in 1952 he became head of the Congress of Industrial Organizations (CIO). Later he helped with the merger of the CIO and the American Federation of Labor and became a vice-president of the organization. Not seeing eye-to-eye with its president, Reuther withdrew the UAW from the organization in 1968, but he afterward allied his union with the Teamsters Union to form a 3.6 million member unit. His organizing activities continued until his death in a plane crash in May 1970.

unit eight | Newer Life-Styles

Chapter 29   THE FARMS AND THE FORESTS

Agriculture Before the Civil War

Eighty percent of West Virginia's population lived on farms in 1860. There were no large cities in the state, factories were virtually unknown, and transportation facilities were at a minimum. Almost the only agricultural products that found their way out of West Virginia were cattle, horses, sheep, and hogs. These animals traveled beyond the state's borders on their own feet and were directed by herdsmen. As early as 1800, cattle from the hill counties had been driven across the state to Baltimore and other Eastern cities. As late as 1850 thousands of hogs were driven from the Ohio and Kanawha valleys over the mountains to Richmond.

Prior to 1850 machinery for farm work was virtually unknown in West Virginia. Only during the Civil War did the homemade double plow, known as the "bull tongue," come into use. This crude implement, possibly the first in a long series of mechanical inventions for the benefit of agriculture, threw the soil into rows and covered the corn which had been dropped into the soil by hand. The process which had required the services of three men now needed only one man's labor.

Reconstruction

When the Chesapeake and Ohio Railway and the Baltimore and Ohio Railroad were completed to the Ohio River and secured

A West Virginia Farmstead Today *(Arnout Hyde, Jr., Photo, West Virginia Department of Natural Resources)*

connections to the West, trainloads of corn and other grain poured into West Virginia from the Mid-West and the Great Plains. These products gave West Virginia farms severe competition.

Moreover, the Panic of 1873 had caused prices of agricultural products to fall, the market for farm goods had declined, and the value of the state's farm products in 1880 was $4,000,000 less than in 1870. Farmers had neglected conservation, the soil had deteriorated, and insects and blights had ruined many crops.

Farmers in West Virginia had to turn to science for help. They were compelled to learn and follow scientific methods of farming. They must use mechanical and power equipment, although large machines could not be used on West Virginia farms so economically as on the larger farms of the West.

The row-crop type of small farm tractor replaced horses. Side-delivery rakes, hay loaders, pick-up balers, forage harvesters, corn pickers, corn binders, plows, cultivators, and discs were introduced as soon as they became available. Reapers, mowers, and threshing machines replaced the grain cradles and the scythes in a brief time.

Previous to 1880 no commercial fertilizer had been used in West Virginia. But within a short period thereafter, fertilizers, new sprays, insecticides, and better diet for farm animals became a part of the scientific breakthrough in West Virginia agriculture.

West Virginia University, founded as a land-grant institution, contributed to the betterment of West Virginia farmers. In 1889 the University established the Agricultural Experiment Station and in 1896 established the College of Agriculture. In 1912 the state first employed county agricultural agents, and in 1913 authorized a state commissioner of agriculture.

In 1913 Professor T. C. Atkeson, formerly dean of the College of Agriculture of West Virginia University, analyzed the 15,000,000 or more acres of the state of West Virginia from the standpoint of use for agriculture. He estimated that 5,000,000 acres of West Virginia could never be plowed and that about 5,000,000 additional acres of West Virginia should never be plowed. This, in his account, left only 5,000,000 acres suited to profitable cultivation of farm crops of any kind.

Mr. Atkeson suggested that more land be converted to pasture range for cattle and sheep, that more land be devoted to fruit production, and that farmers practice a more intensive system of cultivation.

In 1914 the Smith-Lever Act provided that the federal government should match the contributions of states in a program of agricultural extension courses. These courses were designed for the

Harvesting Corn for Silage on the West Virginia University Dairy Farm Corn, the main crop of the pioneers, is still important today.

chapter twenty-nine / the farms and the forests

education of farmers through county agents. The Department of Agriculture, working through land-grant colleges, supervised the programs.

Farm Organizations. In 1867 the Grange was founded. This organization was intended to advance the cultural and social lives of farm families and to promote scientific farming. With social meetings, picnics, and fairs the Grange helped West Virginians to overcome the antagonisms caused by the Civil War. Although the Grange did not develop great political power in West Virginia, it elected some of its spokesmen to high office.

Four-H Clubs were organized in West Virginia as early as 1911. The membership was derived in part from boys' and girls' "corn" clubs which had originated in a "corn" contest in Monroe County in 1907. Following the passage of the Smith-Lever Act by Congress in 1914, the Four-H movement became a national organization under the supervision of the United States Department of Agriculture. The 4-H Clubs conceived a fourfold program that dealt with the mental, social, spiritual, and physical phases of life. It adopted as its symbol the four-leaf clover, with an "H" on each leaf to represent the head, the hand, the heart, and health.

Projects were initiated to inform boys and girls of better seeds and better methods of farming. The organization expanded to include a scientific study of corn, potatoes, tomatoes, chickens, and livestock, and advanced to promote a knowledge of better home practices.

The 4-H Camp in West Virginia is at Jackson's Mill in Lewis County, on the West Fork River, seven miles north of Weston, the boyhood home of "Stonewall" Jackson. The Monongahela West Penn Public Service Company presented the site to the state in 1920, and additional acres have been added by state purchases. A dining room in the architectural style of "Mount Vernon" was erected, and a swimming pool was provided. Over the course of several years, counties erected cottages for boys and girls who assembled for training courses. The youth work at Jackson's Mill was described as the "most equally balanced youth program in the United States."

Future Farmers of America, an organization for boys interested in farm life, was nationally incorporated in 1928 and chartered in West Virginia on April 20, 1929. It developed from high school vocational-agricultural clubs. FFA also held annual meetings at Jackson's Mill. Future Homemakers of America for girls became the corresponding organization of FFA.

Raising Cattle in West Virginia Excellent facilities for raising cattle are found on West Virginia farms. *(Arnout Hyde, Jr., Photo, West Virginia Department of Natural Resources)*

The Farm Products

Based on cash income, West Virginia farm products rank in importance as: meat animals (cattle, calves, hogs, sheep, and lambs); poultry and eggs; dairy products; fruit (apples and peaches); and certain field crops.

Livestock and Poultry. Livestock consists of beef cattle, swine, sheep, and goats. Poultry consists of chickens, turkeys, ducks, and geese. Both lines of livestock are produced in largest numbers in Greenbrier, Jefferson, Monroe, Mason, Pendleton, Preston, Harrison, Hardy, Berkeley, and Hampshire counties. Angus, Hereford, and shorthorn beef cattle are found on stock farms in West Virginia. Among the dairy herds are Ayrshire, Holstein, Guernsey, Jersey, and Brown Swiss. Holstein is the predominant breed.

Total cattle numbers in West Virginia fell from 612,000 in 1935 to 461,000 in 1969. This reduction was particularly noticeable in milk cows. Beef cattle in a thirty-five year period, however, rose from 37,000 to 196,000.

Poultry remains a growing industry. Chickens are found in most livestock producing counties, in the South Branch Valley, and in Jackson, Raleigh, Monongalia, and Mineral counties. Turkeys are found in all sections of the state, but ducks and geese are found primarily in the lowlands.

Hydraulically Controlled Tower and Pruner as Used by Up-to-Date Commercial Apple Growers in West Virginia *(Photo courtesy of West Virginia University)*

Horticulture. When George Washington on March 18, 1774 leased to William Bartlett 125 acres of land in Berkeley County for the purpose of growing apple and peach trees, he inaugurated horticulture in West Virginia. However, the true fathers of commercial fruit growing were Jacob Nessly of the Northern Panhandle and W. S. Miller of the Eastern Panhandle. Jacob Nessly moved to Hancock County in 1786 and planted fifty acres of apple and peach trees. He also manufactured fruit brandies. He made the Northern Panhandle famous for its production of winter apples. Nessly lived to see the orchard industry spread south into the Ohio River area as far as Huntington.

W. S. Miller, who first planted sixteen acres of orchards in 1851, established the orchard industry in the Eastern Panhandle. At the time of the Civil War, he set out large numbers of peach, apple, pear, and plum trees which he himself had bedded. At the close of the war, he had 4,000 fruit trees, which in a few more years had increased to 6,500. Miller and his several sons became owners of large commercial orchards.

Of the many varieties of apples in West Virginia, two are native to the state, and one has been transplanted from Missouri to West Virginia with great success. The Grimes Golden originated on the farm of Thomas W. Grimes in Brooke County. The Golden Delicious came from a seedling on A. H. Mullins' farm on Porter's Creek near the boundary of Clay and Kanawha counties.

The owner of the Golden Delicious tree rented it for five years for $5,000; at a later date he sold it for another $5,000. A nursery in Missouri bought the Golden Delicious tree, enclosed it with a high wire cage, and stationed a guard to see that no one cut any of its branches.

William Gano, a descendant of the Gano and Kitchen families of West Virginia, prominent in agriculture, produced the famous Gano apple from a seedling on his Ozark, Missouri, farm. He then adapted the Gano apple tree to the soil of the Eastern Panhandle.

Large commercial orchards led to the development of the fruit-processing industry. National Fruit Product Company began operations in Martinsburg in 1920, and the Musselman Company followed with processing plants at Inwood in 1921. Main varieties of apples produced commercially in West Virginia were Jonathan, Red Delicious, Stayman Winesap, York, and Rome. Most of the apples used for processing were Yorks.

In the old orchards, trees were planted 36 to 40 feet apart and required 10 years to reach bearing age; newer methods changed to smaller trees which were planted closer together and which matured in a much shorter time. Higher yields of fruit were, therefore, produced from smaller acreage.

The apple has been named the state fruit.

Field Crops. In 1970 West Virginia produced 3,599,000 bushels of corn, 924,000 tons of hay, 616,000 bushels of oats, 495,000 bushels of barley, 429,000 bushels of wheat, and, in addition, 2,960,000 pounds of tobacco.

In 1970 corn was the largest crop. It is grown in every county in the state but is produced most abundantly on river bottom lands and on uplands below 1,500 feet above sea level.

Hay was the most important field crop. Hay supports the livestock industry.

The wheat crop is grown in the wider valleys and on the great limestone hills of the state. Buckwheat is generally grown in the mountain counties. Oats do best in the northern counties and on the higher elevations, but they are grown throughout the state. Also grown in the state are timothy, red top, the clovers, and orchard grass. Bluegrass is predominant throughout West Virginia.

The 1970 figures show that most of the tobacco was grown in counties south of the Little Kanawha River. It was collected at a large tobacco warehouse at Huntington, Cabell County, and was shipped to points outside the state for processing.

Experimental Picker Transport for Harvesting Strawberries This transport is seen at an experimental farm operated by West Virginia University.

West Virginia's farm economy had been geared to a livestock-grass enterprise supported by a large commercial poultry and egg industry, with a continuing interest in horticulture.

Number of Farms and Acreage

In 1900 there were 92,874 farms occupying 10,600,000 acres in West Virginia. It was such a large area devoted to farming that Dr. Atkeson had deplored in 1913. The figure he advised as profitable for agriculture in West Virginia was 5,000,000 acres. In 1917 farm acreage approached that figure, with 4,340,554 acres given to farming in the state. The number of farms, likewise, had decreased to 23,142.

The average size of a farm in West Virginia had increased. In 1950 the average size was 100.9 acres. In 1970 it had risen to 187.5 acres. In 1950 West Virginia farms had an average value per acre of $57.90; in 1970 the average value was $135.69 per acre.

Market Value of Farm Products

In 1971 West Virginia received $109,346,000 in cash receipts from farm marketing. Of this amount $81,733,000 came from livestock; $24,978,000 from crops; and $2,645,000 from government payments of various kinds.

As West Virginia agriculture moved into the decade of the 1970's, a few counties in the state had more than 50 percent of their land in farms. Those that remained true to the customs of earlier days when farming was the principal occupation were Barbour, Berkeley, Grant, Hardy, Harrison, Jackson, Jefferson, Lewis, Marshall, Mason, Mineral, Monroe, Pendleton, and Taylor. A few counties had less than 10 percent of their land in farms. These counties were Boone, Logan, McDowell, Mingo, and Webster, which, by and large, depended on coal as their economic mainstay.

The Forests

Originally West Virginia was covered with magnificent forests which stood their ground until the advent of the railroad. In 1870 forests still covered 14,000,000 acres, and, of these, 10,000,000 acres remained primeval. This forest acreage prevailed even when the Baltimore and Ohio Railroad passed twenty to thirty sawmills, each cutting 3,000 feet of lumber a day.

These mills served not only the Eastern cities but also the barrel factories (then producing 150 to 200 barrels daily) and the small ship-building industries along the Ohio River. By 1880 the number of sawmills had increased to 472, but they were still confined to areas along the railroads and the tributaries of the Ohio River, and their production remained small. Before 1880 it has been estimated that only 500,000,000 board feet of lumber was cut in West Virginia.

Between 1880 and 1920 the choice timberlands of the state were purchased by major lumber companies, mostly companies with headquarters in New York, Pennsylvania, Michigan, and Wisconsin. With the use of the bandsaw and with the transportation facilities of an increasing number of railroads, the original forests of West Virginia quickly disappeared.

Peak Production. The peak year for the West Virginia lumber and timber industry was 1909. In that year 1,473,942,000 of feet board measure, valued at $28,758,000, was produced. For the next ten years 900,000,000 board feet was manufactured annually. West

chapter twenty-nine / the farms and the forests

Log Train in West Virginia When Timber Was King (West Virginia Department of Natural Resources Photo)

Virginia was the nation's chief producer of chestnut and yellow poplar lumber. In addition, oak, chestnut, and maple placed the state third in the production of hardwood lumber and seventeenth in the production of all grades of lumber in 1919.

From World War I through the Korean War, West Virginia lumber production steadily declined. In 1953 the state produced only 382,000,000 board feet. But by 1970 production reached 521,000,000 board feet, slightly more than one-third of production in the peak year, 1909. For the lumber industries, conservation of the timber supply had now become the order of the day; more wood was now being grown than was being cut. The new sawtimber volume on commercial lands in West Virginia was estimated at nearly 29,000,000,000 board feet. Oaks made up more than 40 percent of the hardwood volume.

The West Virginia Department of Natural Resources, Oglebay Park in Ohio County, and the Agricultural Experiment Station and the School of Forestry of West Virginia University are intensely interested in conservation. One of the state department's projects is two forest nurseries which are at Parsons and at Lakin. They pro-

Cathedral State Park Cathedral State Park, containing one of the few virgin tracts of timber yet standing in the East, is at Aurora, Preston County, West Virginia. Cross-country U.S. Route 50 bisects the park, but few persons who travel this route realize what a wonder they behold. *(David P. Cruise Photo, West Virginia Department of Commerce)*

vide seedlings for planting and replanting. Another vital conservation project is fighting and preventing forest fires.

West Virginia now has 11,389,000 acres in forest lands, approximately 74 percent of the land area resting in forested acres, a situation not unlike the one prevailing in the state in 1870.

Past Uses of Wood

In the early days lumber was used for residences, barns, boats, and oceangoing vessels. Wooden barrels were needed for packing meat, whiskey, and beer. Staves, headings, and hoop poles were required for the transportation of crude oil. Crossties, used in building the railroads, demanded their share of wood. Tanneries were supplied with "tanbark" stripped from the tree trunks.

With the completion of the railroads and the use of pipelines, metallic storage tanks, tank cars, and drums, much of the demand for wood disappeared. Today most of West Virginia's timber is shipped outside the state and is used primarily in the manufacture of furniture.

State Forests and State Parks

Forest lands remain important to West Virginia. These lands provide water for agriculture, timber for industry, and areas for recreation. When properly managed, forests help prevent erosion and control floods. West Virginia's forest beauty is unexcelled.

The West Virginia state forests total many thousands of acres. The state parks contain great spreads of forest lands. We shall read more about the state forests and state parks later.

National Forests

There are three national forests in West Virginia: Monongahela National Forest, George Washington National Forest, and Jefferson National Forest. Monongahela National Forest, established in 1920, has about 800,000 acres in parts of Grant, Greenbrier, Nicholas, Pendleton, Pocahontas, Preston, Randolph, Tucker, and Webster counties. George Washington National Forest has 157,568 acres in Hampshire, Hardy, and Pendleton counties. Jefferson National Forest includes 29,651 acres in Monroe County. As of June 30, 1973 West Virginia had 947,215 acres of national forest area.

Harvesting Christmas Trees in West Virginia *(West Virginia Department of Agriculture Photo)*

chapter twenty-nine / the farms and the forests

STATE PARKS

PARKS	COUNTY	POST OFFICE	ACRES
Audra	Barbour	Buckhannon	355
Babcock	Fayette	Clifftop	3,637
Beartown	Pocahontas-Greenbrier Border	Droop	107
Berkeley Springs	Morgan	Berkeley Springs	7
Blackwater Falls	Tucker	Davis	1,688
Bluestone	Summers	Hinton	4,977
Cacapon	Morgan	Berkeley Springs	6,115
Canaan Valley	Tucker	Davis	6,015
Carnifex Ferry Battlefield	Nicholas	Keslers Cross Lanes	156
Cathedral	Preston	Aurora	133
Cedar Creek	Gilmer	Glenville	2,034
Chief Logan	Logan	Logan	3,305
Droop Mountain Battlefield	Pocahontas	Droop	288
Grandview	Raleigh	Beaver	878
Hawks Nest	Fayette	Ansted	237
Holly River	Webster	Hacker Valley	7,798
Little Beaver	Raleigh	Beaver	385
Lost River	Hardy	Mathias	3,680
North Bend	Ritchie	Cairo	1,402
Pinnacle Rock	Mercer	Bramwell	245
Pipestem	Summers & Mercer	Pipestem	4,027
Prickett's Fort	Marion	Rt. 3, Fairmont	188
Tomlinson Run	Hancock	New Manchester	1,399
Twin Falls	Wyoming	Mullens	3,776
Tygart Lake	Barbour & Taylor	Grafton	1,376
Valley Falls	Marion & Taylor	Rt. 6, Fairmont	1,034
Watoga	Pocahontas	Marlinton	10,057
Watters Smith Memorial	Harrison	Lost Creek	278
Mont Chateau Lodge	Monongalia	Morgantown	42

STATE FORESTS

FORESTS	COUNTY	POST OFFICE	ACRES
Cabwaylingo	Wayne	Dunlow	8,149
Calvin W. Price	Pocahontas	Dunmore	9,482
Camp Creek	Mercer	Camp Creek	5,897
Coopers Rock	Monongalia & Preston	Bruceton Mills	12,747
Greenbrier	Greenbrier	Caldwell	5,062
Kanawha	Kanawha	Charleston	6,597
Kumbrabow	Randolph	Huttonsville	9,431
Panther	McDowell	Panther	7,810
Seneca	Pocahontas	Dunmore	11,686

An Agrarian Prophet

Thomas C. Atkeson, "Mr. Agriculture"

Thomas C. Atkeson, a well-known West Virginia agricultural expert, was born on his parents' farm near Buffalo, Putnam County, now West Virginia, on February 15, 1852. Though his early schooling was interrupted by the Civil War, he later attended Buffalo Academy. In 1871 he enrolled at West Virginia University with the intention of studying agriculture. The next year, however, when a sister died, he decided to stay on the farm and work.

He began publication of a magazine called *The West Virginia Agriculturist*, which received much local attention. Pursuing his agricultural interest, Atkeson sold the magazine and studied at Kentucky Agricultural and Mechanical College. After another stint as editor, he returned home and began the practice of law.

In 1880 Atkeson joined the Grange movement to help improve farm conditions. He became associate editor of one of the Grange papers. Elected master of the West Virginia State Grange in 1896, he served the state in that position for twenty-four years. He strove in every way possible to spread the gospel of better agricultural practices and better farm life.

Atkeson wrote the law which created the West Virginia State Board of Agriculture in 1891 and became president of the board shortly thereafter. While in that office, he successfully urged the state to subsidize courses in agriculture at West Virginia University. He personally contributed to the project by serving as teacher of agricultural subjects until economy forced abolition of the professorship.

During the mid-1890's Atkeson was appointed a member of the State Board of Regents of West Virginia University, and in this position he worked for the establishment of the College of Agriculture in 1898, serving as dean fourteen years. His program of study was made to suit the needs of the state.

For those unable to attend on the campus, he began the Home Reading Course in Agriculture. His development of agricultural education became so well known that he was awarded honorary degrees by four colleges.

In this chapter we have read of Professor Atkeson's study of the soils and terrain of West Virginia, of his advisory for their use for profitable agriculture, and of eventual reduction of farmland acreage to his recommendations.

After leaving the University in 1914, Dr. Atkeson held a number of national offices in the Grange. In 1918 he was made legislative representative and lobbied for many bills which aided in improving agriculture. He retired as a lobbyist in 1927, but until his death in 1935, Atkeson continued to write about agriculture and its primary place in the life of the country.

Chapter 30   NEW EMPLOYMENT OPPORTUNITIES

Inadequate transportation was one of the important factors which delayed the industrial revolution in West Virginia and prevented the creation of many kinds of new jobs. The advent of the railroads and improvement of the rivers were only partial solutions in changing the nature of the state's economy. For many years the building of highways in the state was neglected. Explanations for the delay in road building were: the necessary experimentations in road construction and the fact that road construction in the Mountain State was difficult, time consuming, and expensive. Then, too, the pressure for better roads had not yet developed. Until the beginning of the 1900's automobiles and trucks were not major carriers of passengers and freight, and air travel was, of course, unknown.

But once the highways and the airports were under construction, employment opportunities never before dreamed of by West Virginians were suddenly opened.

The *Martinsburg Journal* on the eve of 1970 expressed very well the nature of the change brought about by the construction of Interstate Highway 81 through Berkeley County. The same sentiments and hopes for the future, as stated in the *Martinsburg Journal* on December 30, 1969, could be echoed throughout the entire state. The newspaper article said:

Interstate 81 Cloverleaf Interchange, Berkeley County This interchange, West Virginia's only full cloverleaf, provides access to and from W. Va. Feeder Route 9 near Martinsburg. *(West Virginia Department of Highways Photo)*

This modern highway has opened up a whole new outlook for the community. Of course, its primary purpose was to speed up traffic and to eliminate downtown congestion to aid both local and through traffic but its impact is much more far reaching. For example, it is known that neither the General Motors plant nor the Lockheed-Georgia plant would have been located here had it not been for I-81. The highway has also brought new stores, new motels, and other new business enterprises with even more undoubtedly to follow. It has also had much to do with increasing the value of land throughout the section.

Early Period

In the early period the county courts were charged with the duty of building and maintaining roads and bridges, and road work was never taken seriously. In 1897 the Legislature provided for a state highway inspector who could use the facilities of West Virginia University in testing road-building materials, provide supervisory assistance to counties, and conduct a "road school" under the auspices of the University. By 1909 a state road fund was established, and a Commission of Public Roads was created. But in 1911 the county courts resumed their original responsibilities, and the commission and the inspector's office were abolished.

World War I Era

By 1913 it was obvious that the old system would not work. A State Road Bureau was then created, county courts were given permission to increase road levies and to use prison labor for construction and maintenance of roads. In spite of these changes, the bureau still declared that the West Virginia roads were the "worst in the nation."

Financing of Highways. In 1917, however, a breakthrough occurred. A new road commission created a connecting system of about 4,600 miles of inter-county roads and named them "Class A" state highways. The commission allocated to a road fund the revenue from a state tax on motor vehicles. This was for the purpose of obtaining money from the federal government on a matching dollar-for-dollar basis. The legislation was designed to take advantage of the Federal Highways Act of 1916. In determining amounts the states would receive from the federal government, their size, population, and existing mail routes became decisive factors in determining money formulas.

In 1919 the Legislature asked the people to approve a $50,000,000 bond issue to construct a modern state highway system connecting at least the county seats of the state. With the aid of various organizations throughout the state and a telling slogan, "To Help Pull West Virginia Out of the Mud," the voters began their long pattern of approving "good road" amendments.

Primary and Secondary Roads

In 1921 and 1923 further road improvements occurred. Roads were classified as "state" or "county-district," and each county seat received at least one hard-surfaced road. Plans were laid to connect state roads with those of adjoining states, the sale of more bonds was authorized, and a tax was placed upon gasoline in behalf of better roads.

Again from 1923 to 1933 bonds were placed on the market, and gasoline taxes were increased. It was discovered that road work, by providing job opportunities for hundreds of workers, was one way to offset the Great Depression.

In 1933 a single road commissioner was appointed, and county district roads became a part of the roads' secondary system. Municipal streets and bridges became a part of the primary state road system and subject to state maintenance. In 1933 approximately 4,560 miles of state road were designated primary, and 31,166 miles of road were considered secondary.

Between 1933 and 1953 the rural population demanded better maintenance of secondary roads. To satisfy the needs of outlying communities, bond issues were marketed for secondary roads, and an increase in the gasoline tax was earmarked for these rural routes.

East-West and North-South Routes

Primary roads in West Virginia were important historically, particularly those running from east to west. US Route 50, the George Washington Highway, traveled along the old Northwestern Turnpike. US Route 40 was the old Cumberland Road. US Route 60 followed the old Midland Trail, the route over the James River and Kanawha Turnpike. US Route 33 was the Blue and Gray Trail. US Route 52 connected Huntington and Bluefield by following the Big Sandy River and its tributaries.

Those running from north to south, important in producing state unity, were especially needed and also possessed historical significance. US Route 19 was known as the Stonewall Jackson Highway. It was paralleled by Route 119. Farther to the east was US Route 219, known as the Seneca Trail. Route 2 followed the Ohio River from Newell to Huntington.

World War II Era

Because of the ever growing number of automobiles, the increased use of trucks in interstate commerce, and the evidence during World War II that highways were important to defense since they were used to transport war supplies and men in the armed forces over great distances, the federal government increased its contributions to highway construction.

In 1944 the government designated an interstate system; in 1952 it began to provide funds for the system; and in 1956 it provided much larger grants-in-aid to assist states in building a network of interstate highways. These highways ran east to west and north to south, bypassed large cities, and created limited-access routes. "Limited access" allowed few roads to enter the interstate highways

Bender Bridge on the West Virginia Turnpike This bridge rises 284 feet from the bottom of the gorge and is the highest bridge east of the Mississippi River. The turnpike has 76 bridges, an average of almost a bridge per mile. *(West Virginia Turnpike Commission Photo)*

and therefore permitted traffic to travel great distances at high speeds with few stops. The federal share of the costs of the interstate system was set at 90 percent. The states' share was set at 10 percent.

Also originating in 1944 was the ABC program. The ABC, or primary, secondary, and urban highway program, an outgrowth of the Federal Highways Act of 1916, was designed for intrastate construction. These roads were not subject to federal standards, to completion dates, and to limited mileage, and the federal government and the states shared costs of the ABC program on a 50-50 basis.

Between the years 1946 and 1965 West Virginia received $143,123,400 from the ABC program and $258,778,662 from the interstate highway program. West Virginia was originally designated for 531 miles of the interstate system and for 13,128 miles of primary and secondary road systems, by means of a federal formula. The mileage figures changed slightly over the next several years.

The West Virginia Turnpike, advertised as "the miracle of the hills," a superhighway 88 miles in length, was opened to traffic on November 8, 1954. The West Virginia Turnpike Commission had been created in 1947 to plan, oversee, and finance this throughway. The turnpike extends from Charleston to Princeton and cost $133,000,000. The road was considered a notable engineering achievement, as it was in fact. A tunnel was drilled through the mountain between Cabin Creek and Paint Creek. High bridges were constructed over deep ravines and valleys. Mountains and hills were leveled.

Post World War II

President John Kennedy early appointed a task force to consider special programs to stimulate the economies of "lagging" areas in the country. Appalachia was one of those areas. At a later date President Lyndon Johnson recommended a bill calling for flood control and health facilities, vocational training programs, and a 2,850-mile highway system for Appalachia. The bill was passed by Congress the following year. The bill was designated the Appalachian Regional Development Act of 1965.

With help from these various federal programs dating back to 1916, West Virginia experienced a revolution in highway construction. In interstate highway construction, West Virginia shared in three east-west routes. These were Interstate Highways 70, 470, and 64, which paralleled approximately the old US Routes 40 and 60. Three interstate routes running north and south were designated Routes 77, 79, and 81. Interstate Route 77 connected Parkersburg and Bluefield. Interstate Route 79 connected Morgantown and Bluefield. Interstate 81, running through the Shenandoah Valley, provided a commercial revolution in certain Eastern Panhandle counties.

From the Appalachia program the state received six highways designated as Appalachian Corridors. Corridor E connects Morgantown with US Highway 40 at Cumberland; Corridor D proceeds from Cincinnati by way of Parkersburg to Clarksburg; Corridor H links Buckhannon to Highway 66; Corridor L is a north-south route extending from Sutton to Beckley; Corridor G moves south from Charleston to Corridors R and Q in Kentucky and Virginia which

Appalachian Development Highway, Corridor D, US 50 in Doddridge County *(West Virginia Department of Highways Photo)*

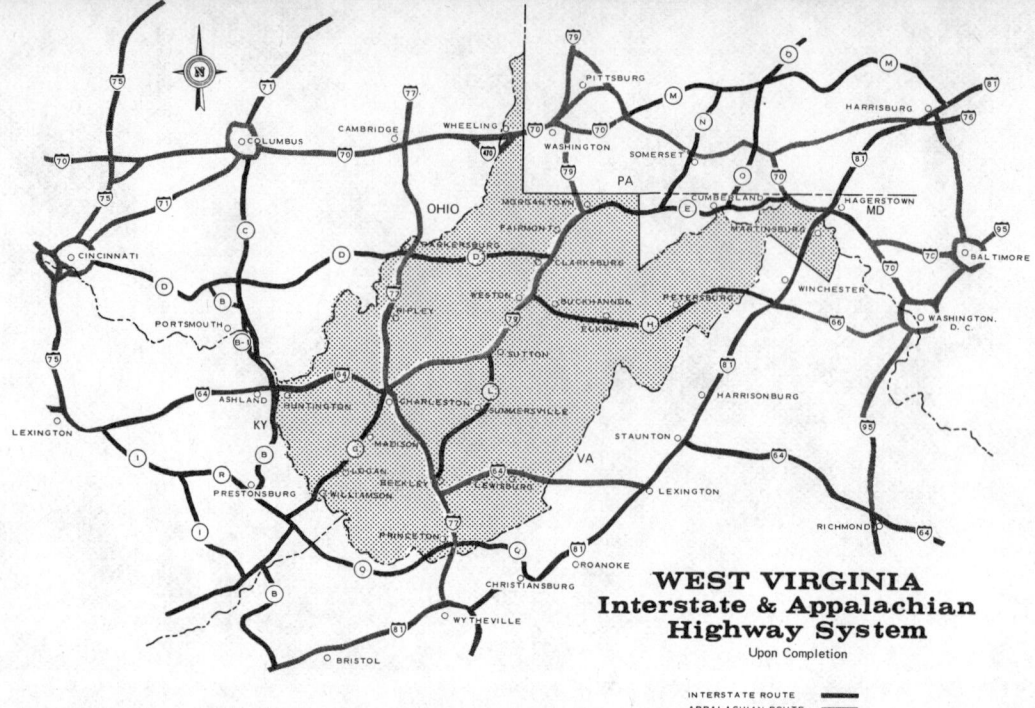

(Reprinted from "1973 West Virginia Economic Profile," West Virginia Department of Commerce, Industrial Development Division)

connect Lexington with Interstate Highway 81; Corridor Q enters West Virginia for a short distance and connects Princeton to Interstate 77. In total figures West Virginia was designated to receive about 518 miles of superhighways known as Interstates and about 425 miles of highways known as Appalachian Routes.

Interstates and Appalachian Corridors therefore represented within the state approximately one thousand miles of new roads costing from one billion to one and a half billion dollars. Such a sum was to be spread over several years in the ranges of annual construction contracts of a quarter of a billion dollars. In addition, West Virginia, at the end of December 1970, had a grand total of 36,355 miles in its state system. Expressways, trunklines, feeder and state local service roads consisted of 31,696 miles. Roads in national and state forests, and toll roads totaled 4,659 miles.

In recent years the public has registered its approval of better roads. In 1920 the state approved a fifty million dollar bond issue; in 1928 a thirty-five million dollar bond issue; in 1942 an amendment limiting to road purposes the use of all revenues derived from motor vehicles and motor fuels; in 1948 a fifty million dollar bond issue; in 1964 a two hundred million dollar bond issue; in 1968 a three hundred and fifty million dollar bond issue; and in 1973 a five hundred million dollar bond issue.

That these roads and bond issues were needed is evident in the 1970-71 statistics for in-state motor registration. Almost three quarters of a million vehicles registered from West Virginia alone, including 611,607 automobiles, 2,355 buses, 47,019 trucks, 51,411 trailers, 643 taxicabs, and 4,342 other vehicles, were on the state roads.

Air Travel

The first airport in West Virginia was constructed in 1910, but no regular aviation passenger service existed in the state until 1933 when federal airport construction funds became available. The Kanawha Airport opened on December 1, 1947 and was completed in 1950. It was a $9,000,000 engineering accomplishment. By 1955 there were seven interstate airway communication stations and thirty-three other licensed airports.

In 1972 there were nine flight service stations in West Virginia: the Mercer County Airport, at Bluefield; the Kanawha Airport at Charleston; the Martinsburg Municipal Airport at Martinsburg; the Wood County Airport at Parkersburg; the Wheeling-Ohio County Airport at Wheeling; the Morgantown Municipal Airport at Morgantown; the Elkins Municipal Airport at Elkins; the Tri-State Airport at Huntington; and Benedum Airport at Bridgeport. Altogether, West Virginia listed 46 licensed airports in 1972.

Only one major disaster marred a generally satisfactory record of safe flying in the state which presents serious topographical difficulties for aircraft. When a Southern Airways DC-9 crashed near Huntington, West Virginia, on November 14, 1970, seventy-five lives were lost. Forty-three of the dead were Marshall University football players and coaches.

Primary-Metal Industries

The primary-metal industry, a development of the iron and steel interests of an earlier era, is principally located in northern West Virginia, in the Northern Panhandle. The area may be considered a part of the Pittsburgh industrial region. Plants also operate farther south along the Ohio River.

In 1970 primary-metal industries employed 25,400 persons in the state, and fabricated metals employed 7,600. These employment figures had remained virtually the same for a ten-year period beginning in 1960.

Entrance to Wheeling Tunnel on Interstate 70 Pictured is the eastern end of the multimillion-dollar Interstate 70 tunnel through Wheeling Hill in Wheeling. *(West Virginia Department of Highways Photo)*

In the Northern Panhandle large numbers of workers are employed by the Weirton Steel Division, at Weirton in Hancock County, and by the Wheeling-Pittsburgh Steel Corporation, at Wheeling in Ohio County. The Weirton Steel Division's "Steel Mill of the Future" became the first fully integrated plant to combine some of the greatest fundamental advances in steel technology. Six primary-metal industries are located at Wheeling, two in Brooke County, and four in Marshall County. The Wheeling Steel Corporation has plants in Marshall, Ohio, and Brooke counties.

Counties on the Ohio River (Cabell, Jackson, Wood, and Mason) also have large primary-metal industries. The International Nickel Company at Huntington in Cabell County is one of three such concerns. International Nickel has the world's largest rolling mill devoted exclusively to the production of high-nickel base alloys. The Kaiser Aluminum and Chemical Corporation, operating at Ravenswood in Jackson County, is a complete integrated aluminum plant. Ingots of electrolytic aluminum produced at the plant are rolled into sheet, plate, and commercial foil.

Amax Specialty Metals, Incorporated, is one of the three primary-metal industries at Parkersburg in Wood County. This company, a consolidation of American Metals Climax, Incorporated, and Carborundum Mills, produces zirconium sponge from zircon sand. Foote Mineral Company at New Haven in Mason County operates a 57,700 KVA three-phase submerged arc furnace, one of the largest in the world.

Other primary-metal industries are scattered throughout West Virginia. Union Carbide Corporation's large ferroalloy plant at Alloy, Fayette County, operates 18 submerged arc electric furnaces. Kanawha, Marion, Marshall, Randolph, Preston, and Mercer also have primary-metal industries.

Chemicals and Allied Products

Shortly before World War I, modern chemical plants had been built at Clarksburg, Moundsville, Huntington, and South Charleston. When the war cut off supplies of German-produced chemicals, attention was directed to the Kanawha and Ohio valleys as domestic

Weirton Steel's Ultramodern Mill   This "Steel Mill of the Future" made possible dramatic improvement in air- and water-pollution control. In the picture the white plume escaping from the stack is steam.

chapter thirty / new employment opportunities

Union Carbide Chemical Complex, South Charleston

sources of supply. By 1936, fifteen chemical plants were operating in the Charleston industrial area. In 1963 the chemical industries provided 29,100 jobs. In 1970 the chemical industries employed 26,900 persons.

By 1972 every county along the Ohio, with the exception of Jackson, had a chemical plant employing at least 25 persons. Brooke, Ohio, and Marshall each had one chemical and allied-product company. Wetzel had two; Tyler had one; Pleasants had one; Wood had four; Mason had three; Cabell had two; and Wayne had one. Major chemical plants also operated in Monongalia, Marion, Nicholas, and Berkeley. But Kanawha County had the largest number, eleven major plants.

The Union Carbide Corporation at Charleston, at Institute, and at South Charleston was one of two major employers; the E. I. du Pont de Nemours & Company, Incorporated, with plants at Parkersburg and Belle, was the other. More than 1,000 persons were employed by the FMC Corporation at Nitro and South Charleston, and a like number by the PPG Industries at New Martins-

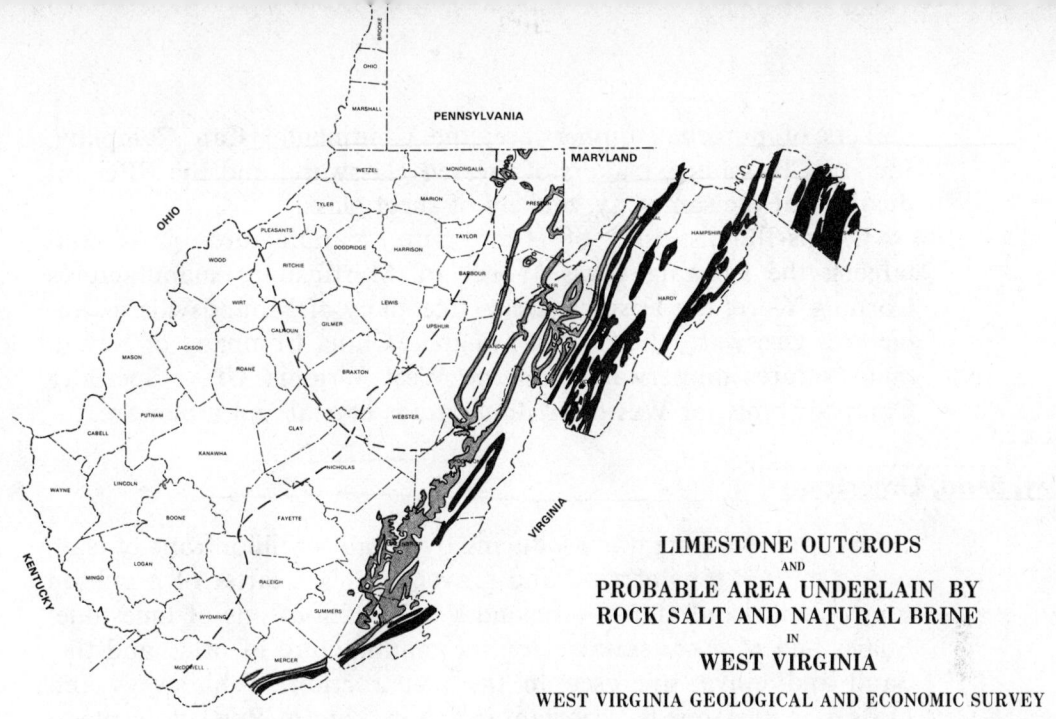

LIMESTONE OUTCROPS
AND
PROBABLE AREA UNDERLAIN BY
ROCK SALT AND NATURAL BRINE
IN
WEST VIRGINIA

WEST VIRGINIA GEOLOGICAL AND ECONOMIC SURVEY

ville. The Holland-Suco Color Company at Huntington, the American Cyanamid Company at Willow Island, and the Mobay Chemical Company at New Martinsville also have had large employment rolls.

Earthenware and Glass

An old industry in West Virginia was the making of pottery and other kinds of earthenware. The industry began in Morgantown as early as 1785. Early pottery plants in the state were in Hancock County, with chinaware centers at Newell and New Cumberland. Early earthenware plants were located at Wheeling, Huntington, Mannington, Paden City, Ravenswood, Grafton, and Parkersburg. Glass factories were established at Huntington, Weston, Williamstown, Morgantown, New Martinsville, Moundsville, and Milton. The Blenko Glass Company, a specialty glass company at Milton, produces fine glassware, some of which was used in restored Williamsburg, Virginia. The colored glass used in the Cathedral of St. John the Divine in New York City and in the National Cathedral in Washington, D. C., was also fashioned by the Blenko Glass Company.

Some of the leading manufacturers of glass in 1970 were the Libbey-Owens-Ford Glass Company, at Charleston, makers of window glass; the Taylor Smith and Taylor Company, at Chester, makers of porcelain dinnerware; the Continental Can Company, Inc., of Clarksburg, makers of pressed glassware; and the PPG Industries, of the same city, makers of sheet glass.

Owens-Illinois, Inc., of Huntington, manufactures glass containers; the Corning Glass Works of Martinsburg manufactures Corning Ware; the Fostoria Glass Company of Moundsville manufactures glassware; the Homer Laughlin China Company of Newell manufactures dinnerware; and the West Virginia Glass Specialty Company, Inc., of Weston, manufactures crystal and tableware.

Clay, Sand, Limestone

By 1968 the state was producing over half a million tons of clay, over a million tons of sand and gravel, over a quarter of a million tons of sand, and almost nine and a half million tons of limestone. Shales and clay are suitable for the manufacture of brick and tile. Sand and gravel are used in the construction of highways and bridges. Limestone is important in the making of Portland cement, insulating materials, fertilizer, and a variety of chemical products. Silica sand and limestone were responsible for the development of the glass industry in West Virginia. In stone, clay, and glass factories in West Virginia 19,300 persons found employment in 1970. In glass manufacture 14,200 were employed; in pottery and related manufacture 2,800 were employed.

Capitol Cement Company Plant at Martinsburg

Textiles

Textile centers in the state were established at Parkersburg, where rayon was manufactured; at Charleston and Parsons, where plants specialized in wool blankets; at Martinsburg, where upholstering goods, men's suits, and hosiery were made; at Wheeling, whose calicoes became famous; and at Huntington, where work clothes were made.

In 1968 the Martinsburg Mills, Inc., at Martinsburg; Corbin, Ltd., and Peoples Company at Huntington; Maidenform, Inc., at Princeton; the Morgan Shirt Company, Inc., of Morgantown; the Harrisville Garment Corporation of Harrisville; the Renmar Manufacturing Company, Inc., of Parkersburg; and the Kellwood Company of Spencer were the largest employers in the production of textiles and apparel.

In the state in 1970 approximately 6,900 persons found employment in textiles, and 1,400 in apparel.

Electric Power

Electric power production in West Virginia set an all-time record of 35.6 billion kilowatt hours in 1970, nine times the total electricity produced in the state in 1940.

In the twenty-year period from 1930 to 1950, West Virginia plants produced 13.6 billion kilowatt hours, and from 1960 through 1970 production reached 186.6 billion kilowatt hours.

The three large producers furnishing electric power to West Virginia and its neighboring states are the American Electric Power System, the Allegheny Power System, and also the Virginia Electric Power Company. Important subsidiaries of American Electric Power are the Appalachian Power Company and the Wheeling Electric Company. Important subsidiaries of the Allegheny Power System are the Monongahela Power Company and the Potomac Edison Company.

Major generating facilities include Vepco's Mt. Storm Generating Station in Grant County, Monongahela's Fort Martin Plant in Monongalia County, and Appalachian's Phillip Sporn Plant in Jackson County and its Kammer-Mitchell Plant in Marshall County. These generating plants have a total capacity of 5,856,480 kilowatts.

Indicative of the newer developments in electric power is the John E. Amos plant on the Kanawha River in Putnam County near Nitro. It is one of the world's largest generating establishments.

John E. Amos Plant in Putnam County
This electric power plant is one of the world's largest generating establishments. *(Photo courtesy of Appalachian Power Company)*

Other Employment Opportunities

In West Virginia there are many ways to make a living in addition to the opportunities we have noted. In 1970, for example, 7,500 persons found employment in plants producing lumber, wood products, furniture, and wood fixtures; 10,100 in the manufacture of machinery; 3,800 in the manufacture of transportation equipment; 6,900 in the food industries; 4,400 in printing and publishing; and 1,700 in the making of leather and leather products.

In manufacturing processes, 126,400 people were employed in the state, and 387,600 were employed in non-manufacturing businesses. Wholesale trade provided positions for 23,000 persons, and retail trade for 68,100 persons. Federal government services employed 51,300 persons, and state and local government services employed 23,600 persons. General services utilized 95,600 persons. Finance, insurance, and real estate had opportunities for 15,700 persons; transportation, communications, and public utilities, 21,800 persons; and contract construction, 27,500 persons.

Communications Media

In 1923 West Virginia had one radio station; by 1928 there were four stations; in 1970 there were 63 AM radio broadcasting stations and 25 FM broadcasting stations.

In 1949 West Virginia had but one television station; in 1953 it had three television stations; in 1955, six; and in 1970, twelve.

In 1970 West Virginia had 33 daily newspapers, 6 Sunday newspapers, 80 weekly newspapers, 47 periodicals and trade papers — a total of 166 publications.

The first telegraph line reached West Virginia in 1847. It tapped a main line on the western side of the Ohio River to furnish service to Wheeling.

Wheeling also obtained the first telephone in the state when a line was installed between the two Behrens grocery stores in 1879. In 1880, only four years after Alexander Graham Bell had invented the telephone, a telephone exchange servicing 52 telephones was installed at Wheeling.

Between 1882 and 1895 telephone exchanges were installed in Parkersburg, Charleston, Huntington, Moundsville, Clarksburg, Martinsburg, Grafton, Bluefield, Fairmont, and Morgantown. The first long-distance line between Wheeling and Pittsburgh was installed in 1883.

As of December 1972 the Chesapeake and Potomac Telephone Company, West Virginia's major telephone company, serviced about 719,583 telephones for 456,180 subscribers. Southern Bell Company, which had consolidated a number of independent companies, transferred its properties in West Virginia to the Chesapeake and Potomac Telephone Company in 1912.

Inventor, Benefactor of All

Michael J. Owens and the Bottle Machine

Michael J. Owens, inventor and manufacturer, son of immigrant parents, was born in Mason County, then Virginia, January 1, 1859. At age ten, Michael was put to work in a Wheeling glass factory where he eventually learned the glassblower's trade. In 1888 he transferred to a Toledo, Ohio, glass company and worked his way into management positions.

As early as 1891 Owens directed his attention to improving the laborious and physically harmful hand-and-lung method of blowing glass. By 1895 he had patented a partially automatic machine for use in making tumblers and light bulbs. The Libbey Glass Company helped finance his ventures, and he eventually became one of its major stockholders.

Encouraged by the success of his tumbler machine, Owens turned his attention to development of a completely automatic bottle-making machine. After securing a patent in 1899, he began working on designs for a commercial machine. In 1905 a satisfactory machine was licensed. The license was valued at several million dollars by 1916 when it was purchased by the Owens Bottle Machine Company.

The Owens bottle machine entirely revolutionized the bottle-making industry. The process made millions of dollars for its inventor. He worked on other glass-producing processes, and by 1916 he helped found the Libbey-Owens Sheet Glass Company which built its first plant at Charleston, West Virginia. This company speedily developed into the world's largest producer of window glass. The firm later combined to form the Libbey-Owens-Ford Company.

Michael Owens, the foremost figure in the glass industry of his day, died at Toledo, Ohio, in 1923.

Chapter 31 EDUCATIONAL DEVELOPMENT

Education in the State

West Virginia's first Legislature established a free public school system on December 10, 1863. The office of state superintendent of schools was created, and a six-month school term was authorized for all the youth of the state.

William Ryland White, who was appointed West Virginia's first state superintendent of schools, reported on the status of education in the state. In January 1866, more than a hundred years ago, there were 133 schoolhouses in West Virginia. The length of the school terms averaged less than three months. The city of Wheeling had eight schools, and the school term there was nine months.

In three years Superintendent White had instituted great changes. When he left office in 1869 there were 2,198 schools and 2,283 teachers in the state. School buildings and lands were valued at nearly a million dollars.

Realizing that many teachers were ill-prepared for their work, Mr. White advocated teacher training. From 1867 to 1875 the West Virginia Legislature responded by establishing six teacher-training institutions: Marshall College and five state normal schools at Fairmont, West Liberty, Glenville, Athens, and Shepherdstown. The state superintendent himself became principal at Fairmont.

In 1867 the Agricultural College of West Virginia was created in order to obtain the aid of federal funds provided by the Morrill Act

Stewart Harold Smith Hall and Evelyn Hollberg Smith Music Hall, Marshall University These two handsome modern buildings have a place on Marshall's campus today. Recall the picture of Marshall College State Normal School in chapter 25.

"Sunrise," One of the Charleston Art Gallery Buildings West Virginia art galleries feature permanent exhibits, traveling exhibits, and current artists' showings. Many young people are introduced to art here.

unit eight / newer life-styles

of 1862. This important federal legislation was for the purpose of encouraging instruction in agriculture, mechanical arts, and military tactics. In 1868 the Agricultural College became West Virginia University.

In 1871 the Legislature abolished the requirement of "test oaths" for teachers. Several southern counties expressed immediate satisfaction because there only the so-called "rebels" had been available for teaching and for service on local school boards.

By 1876 West Virginia enumerated 3,216 schools and 3,879 teachers in its educational system.

After the "Reconstruction" Era

Progress in education in the new state was slow. Alexander L. Wade's system of grades, promotions, and graduations for country schools was a most important innovation. The second most important event was the compulsory school attendance act passed by the 1897 Legislature. This act required children between the ages of eight and fifteen to attend school.

Enrollment Increases. High schools were slow to develop in West Virginia. At the beginning of the 1900's, there were approximately 25 high schools in the state. In 1910, however, there were 50. In that year, State Superintendent of Schools Morris P. Shawkey organized a campaign that carried the slogan "One Hundred High Schools in West Virginia in Four Years." The Legislature responded in 1911 by offering state aid to high schools.

By 1925 there were 233 high schools in the state.

West Virginia's County Unit Law was partly responsible for better schools and larger enrollment. By legislative decree 413 school boards were consolidated into 55 boards, one for each county. Many consolidations of one-room and two-room schools took place. Transportation was provided for students who did not live within walking distance of their schools. Another sign of educational progress was free-textbook legislation (1939 and 1941), which was designed to help needy pupils and to supply textbooks for the elementary grades.

By 1940 West Virginia had 266 high schools, 103 junior high schools, and 15 private and parochial secondary schools. Total high school enrollment had climbed to 136,519. By 1955 there were 383 secondary schools with a total enrollment of 159,600.

In 1970-71 elementary enrollment in West Virginia was 229,693; secondary enrollment was 181,796; total enrollment was 411,489.

For the elementary schools there were 9,833 teachers; for the secondary schools 8,959 teachers; a total of 18,792 instructors. The number of elementary schools was 1,051; the number of secondary schools was 343. Of the total number of secondary schools, 142 were junior high schools, and 201 were high schools. The number of secondary schools, actually less in number than in 1955, had been reduced by consolidations. In 1970-71 there were 59 private and parochial elementary and high schools attended by 11,805 pupils.

Costs of Education

For four decades appropriations for education had increased. Computations for 1971-72 show basic foundation costs of public schools in the state were $179,971,912. These costs include salaries for teachers and other personnel, transportation costs, and expense for current items.

Over the years West Virginia has responded to the need for better schools by supporting amendments to the constitution. In 1972 the voters overwhelmingly approved $200 million for the building of new schools and the rejuvenation of old ones.

Administration of State Schools

Elementary and Secondary. The elementary and secondary educational system of the state is now administered by the West Virginia Board of Education. The board also has control of business

Weir High School, Weirton

and educational affairs of the West Virginia Schools for the Deaf and the Blind at Romney. The board selects the state superintendent of free schools. Acting as the State Board of Vocational Education, the State Board of Education administers and controls state plans for vocational rehabilitation.

Higher Education. In 1969 the West Virginia Board of Regents was created as the governing body for all state colleges and universities. The board is composed of ten members. It controls, supervises, and manages the financial, business, and educational policies of the colleges and universities; submits a budget for the state system of higher education; and allocates specific functions and responsibilities among these institutions.

State Four-Year Colleges. There are eight four-year colleges. Bluefield State College, at Bluefield, and Concord College, at Athens, both in Mercer County, have been recently recommended for merger by the Board of Regents in order to provide students a larger number of academic programs and to effect economies. Fairmont State College, at Fairmont; Glenville State College, at Glenville; Shepherd College, at Shepherdstown; West Liberty State College, at West Liberty; and West Virginia State College, at Institute have become multipurpose undergraduate institutions, with a long tradition of teacher training. West Virginia Institute of Technology, at Montgomery, is unique among the four-year colleges in that it offers baccalaureate degrees in four fields of engineering and also concentrates upon business, scientific, and technological programs.

Bluefield State College and West Virginia State College, prior to 1954, were teacher's colleges for Negroes. Since 1954, in compliance with the United States Supreme Court decision, both of these colleges admit white students. Colleges that once admitted only white students now admit black students.

State Universities and College of Graduate Studies. There are two state universities, West Virginia University and Marshall University. West Virginia University, in Morgantown, is the state's land-grant and comprehensive university, the only institution in the state which confers doctoral degrees and has a law school and a medical center. Marshall University, in Huntington, is considered to have a strong urban orientation and a long tradition of community service.

West Virginia College of Graduate Studies is at Institute. The college was established in 1972 as an institution granting a Master's

The $7.9 Million Creative Arts Center at West Virginia University The Creative Arts Center contains a 1,600-seat concert theater and two art galleries. The Center is considered one of the finest in the nation.

degree. The college primarily serves part-time students through the faculties and facilities of West Virginia Institute of Technology, West Virginia State College, Morris Harvey College, and Marshall University. At present the college has Master's degree programs in business, education, engineering, mathematics, political science, and industrial relations.

Community and Branch Colleges. Soon after the Board of Regents was established, it created in 1971 and 1972 three community colleges from existing branch institutions. (1) Parkersburg Community College at Parkersburg was established in 1971 as West Virginia's first comprehensive community college. Formerly it was a branch college of West Virginia University. (2) Southern West Virginia Community College developed from two branch colleges, one at Logan and one at Williamson, both administered by Marshall University. The college became a dual-campus institution with one campus in Logan and the other in Williamson in 1971. (3) West Virginia Northern Community College is also a dual-campus institution with campuses located at Wheeling and at Weirton. The Wheeling campus was formerly administered by West Liberty College. At these three community colleges, associate degrees, signifying two years of college work, are awarded.

Only one two-year branch college remains in West Virginia. This is Potomac State College, a branch of West Virginia University, located at Keyser. Although the board recommended conversion of

Potomac State College to a community college, local residents raised strong objections to such a change, and the board determined that Potomac State would remain a branch of the University.

In the fall of 1972 the universities had a combined enrollment of 26,044; the graduate college, 1,499; the four-year colleges, 18,920; the community colleges, 4,600; and the two-year branch college, 741. Total enrollment in public institutions of higher learning was 51,804. The board projected that by 1976 and by 1980 the enrollments would reach 60,068 and 67,704, respectively.

Private Colleges

In the state of West Virginia there are eight private four-year colleges and two private two-year colleges. The oldest of these, and the oldest college in the state, is Bethany College at Bethany. Bethany College was chartered by the state of Virginia in 1840, to establish a college of arts and sciences in western Virginia with a program corresponding "to the university [University of Virginia] in Charlottesville." Bethany has been supported by the Disciples of Christ Church.

Alderson-Broaddus College, founded in 1871, at Philippi and affiliated with the Baptist Church, is West Virginia's second-oldest

Old Main, Bethany College Contrast this fine building on the Bethany campus with Bethany College as it appeared in chapter 14.

Morris Harvey College, Charleston Morris Harvey has served the youth of a wide area for many years, both in the original location and in Charleston.

private college. This college has experimented with a year-round calendar of four terms staggered so that there is one term off for vacation for freshmen, another for sophomores, and alternate terms off-campus for special experience for juniors and seniors.

Davis and Elkins College at Elkins, supported by the Presbyterian Church, and Morris Harvey College at Charleston, have also experimented with comparable educational programs. Morris Harvey College was founded at Barboursville in 1888, and was associated with the Methodist Episcopal Church South. It moved to Charleston in 1935, but did not become an independent college until 1942. Salem College at Salem is an independent, private, coeducational college of arts and sciences, granting Bachelor and associate degrees. The college offers preprofessional training in a number of fields and maintains a branch at Clarksburg.

West Virginia Wesleyan College at Buckhannon and Wheeling College at Wheeling provide education with a Christian emphasis. Wesleyan is supported by the United Methodist Church, and Wheeling College by the Jesuits.

Appalachian Bible Institute at Bradley is a private semi-professional institution offering a degree in Bible and theology.

Entrance to Robert F. Kidd Library, Glenville State College This four-story structure contains 30,000 square feet of floor space. The building has a capacity for 125,000 volumes and seats over 300 patrons. This includes open reading and study areas, student carrels, seminar and study rooms, and classrooms.

Wheeling Symphony Orchestra in a Performance in Oglebay Park, Wheeling West Virginia orchestras contribute greatly to cultural advantages in the state. Students enjoy these offerings.

chapter thirty-one / educational development

The two two-year private colleges are Beckley College at Beckley and Ohio Valley College at Parkersburg. Ohio Valley College, not legally bound to any religious organization, is operated by members of the Church of Christ.

In the fall of 1972 the four-year private colleges enrolled 9,421 students, and the two-year private colleges enrolled 1,146 students, for a total enrollment of 10,567. The Board of Regents has projected 1976 and 1980 enrollments for these colleges as 12,461 and 13,630, respectively.

Governor Arch Moore, in his budget address to the 1973 Legislature, proposed awarding $500 to private schools for each West Virginia freshman and sophomore attending such institutions and $700 for each junior and senior. An allocation of $2.2 million to private institutions was included in his budget. However, this measure did not pass.

Enrollment in Higher Education

A grand total of 62,371 students attended institutions of higher education in West Virginia in the 1972-73 academic year. Of these students 83 percent were in public institutions, and 17 percent were in private institutions. The percentage of West Virginia high school graduates enrolling in a college or university was 42.5 percent, a rate of enrollment below the national average. However, note the gain since 1940: In that year only 11.73 percent of the state's young people of college age were attending college.

Vocational Education

Vocational education is designed to develop knowledge, skills, and proper attitudes and work habits needed by workers to enter and succeed in their chosen employment.

Seven major program areas have been developed by the West Virginia Division of Vocational Education: vocational agriculture, business and office education, distributive education (incorporating such subjects as marketing, merchandising), health occupations education, home economics education, vocational industrial education, and technical education. The programs operate at three levels: secondary, post-secondary, and adult education.

From 1961 to 1970 the state of West Virginia provided $66,127,189 for vocational education. With a great increase in vocational programs, vocational enrollment in one decade increased from 31,214

Vo-Ag Lesson in a Greenhouse
Operation of a greenhouse is one of the most intensive types of agriculture. *(West Virginia Department of Agriculture Photo)*

in 1961 to 52,883 in 1970. Secondary vocational education enrollment rose 50 percent. In 1969 post-secondary vocational education enrolled ten times the number of students enrolled in 1961. Adult vocational education enrollment increased 40 percent in a decade. Particularly, enrollment in health occupations education, vocational industrial education, and technical education increased. Data processing, electronics, metallurgy, nurse-aid, and dental-assistant courses became the most popular offerings. More than $23,000,000 was expended on 24 vocational-technical centers in West Virginia.

Nationally Acclaimed Educator

Alexander L. Wade and the Graded School Plan

Alexander L. Wade, author of the graded school plan, was born in Indiana in 1832. When he was five years of age, his parents moved to a farm in Monongalia County, Virginia, now West Virginia. Upon his father's death in 1846, the burden of caring for the family fell to Alexander, the oldest son. At the age of sixteen he was able to help his family by teaching the three-month term of the county schools.

After marrying in 1854, Wade bought a small farm, continued to teach, and was elected clerk of Monongalia County Court. About

chapter thirty-one / educational development

the time of the Civil War, he moved to Morgantown and served as recorder for eight years. He also became a successful realtor.

In 1871 Wade was elected clerk of the County Board of Supervisors as well as school commissioner. In the fall term of 1871 he became principal of the Morgantown Graded School and later served as assistant county superintendent of schools. Wade was shocked to find that Monongalia County did not obey the state school law which provided that each pupil should follow a prescribed course of study. It was then that he decided he must study the problems of the schools and try to remedy their faults.

The problems were many and obvious. In most schools all the students were taught in one room regardless of age or number of years of attendance. There was little opportunity for individual students to advance as successfully as they were able to progress.

Wade began a systematic program to classify each student as a member of a particular class or department. Since state law prescribed a list of courses to be taught in the schools, Wade recommended that each student enroll in a particular course. When the student had finished the course, he would advance to the next course until he completed the entire required list.

Wade advocated that a public examination be held at the end of each school term. Those who passed the prescribed courses were to be recognized publicly through graduation exercises and the receipt of a diploma.

The incentive program, or graduating system, worked so well in Monongalia County that other counties began using it. The state Legislature, however, defeated an 1879 bill to adopt the method over the entire state. But in 1891 the Alexander L. Wade system was adopted throughout West Virginia.

The father of the graduating system died in 1904 with the knowledge that great changes had been made in the country schools and that his recommendations for West Virginia had been accepted as common practice throughout the nation.

Chapter 32 THE BLACKS IN WEST VIRGINIA

The number of Negroes in West Virginia has always been small in comparison with the total population of the state, but blacks have been an important element in the history of West Virginia. Their situation was a critical consideration in the writing of West Virginia's first constitution and in the admission of the state into the Union in 1863. Their status has influenced decisions in certain social, political, and economic matters at the national level of government and at the state level.

Negroes accompanied Governor Spotswood's expedition into western Virginia in 1716. They joined the Blennerhassetts on the island in the Ohio River. During the colonial wars Negroes, Indians, and free mulattoes were employed in the state militia as drummers, trumpeters, and "hatchet men," the last group being those who with hatchets and axes helped to clear the forest for paths and roadways.

In the manufacture of salt, black workers contributed a large share to the industry. Negroes did a great deal of the labor entailed in mining coal. They helped conquer the mountains for the building of highways and railroads.

Like their white fellow citizens, black West Virginians aided on both the Union and the Confederate sides during the Civil War. We have noted earlier that, even among Confederate sympathizers in West Virginia's Eastern Panhandle, a comparatively small number owned slaves.

When Alexander L. Wade was experimenting with his theories in education, he wanted his concept of "graduation" to be as valid for black students as for white. He therefore served as principal of a black school in Morgantown in order to incorporate Negro students in his testing program.

Later, in the twentieth century wars, when energy crises developed, black labor helped to achieve record production of coal, particularly at Cabin Creek and Fairmont. In all the wars of this century entire Negro companies represented West Virginia at the fighting fronts.

White West Virginians have had no enmity against the black race. The freedmen were accepted here in whatever situations they attained.

Percentage of Negro Population

From 1790 to 1830 the Negro population, percentage-wise, was at its peak in West Virginia. During that forty-year period, the percentages of Negroes ranged from a low of 7 percent to a high of 11 percent of the total number of residents in the state. In the years from 1830 through the Civil War and the "reconstruction" era, the percentage of Negro population declined to slightly below and slightly above 4 percent. Just prior to emancipation, the percentage of free Negroes was about 1 percent. Obviously, during the Civil War and "reconstruction" many blacks left the state until they could determine exactly the status of the blacks in the newly created West Virginia.

Centers of Negro Population

In 1888 West Virginia's Negro population was concentrated in McDowell, Mercer, Raleigh, Fayette, Kanawha, Mingo, and Logan counties. Negroes found work in those counties, helping to build the railroads in the southern part of the state, particularly the Chesapeake and Ohio Railway and the Norfolk and Western Railroad, and extracting the great quantities of coal discovered there.

By 1970 the number of blacks in the state was estimated to be 73,931, a loss of 15,447 from the 1960 census. Thus, the percentage of Negroes approximated 4 percent of the total population, a statistic not unlike the one in 1860, with the large number of blacks still in the coal-mining areas.

"Separate but Equal" Schools

Negroes in the mining communities and construction workers along the new railroads began to bring pressure upon the state

View of an Area of West Virginia State College Today Three West Virginia Negroes have served as high officials at West Virginia State: John Warren Davis, Carter Godwin Woodson, and William J. L. Wallace.

Legislature to provide schools for Negro children. Provision for education for black pupils had been omitted from West Virginia's first constitution. In 1866 the Legislature approved the establishment of a Negro school wherever there were 20 or more black children to attend with an average attendance of 16. The law was amended in 1867 to authorize a Negro school wherever there were 15 black children between the ages of six and twenty-one years to attend.

These first laws did not make clear that the two races were to be educated separately. The revised constitution of 1872 stated specifically that white children and black children were not to be taught in the same school.

In 1873 the requirement for the establishment of a school for black children was an enrollment of 24.

West Virginia was the first Southern state whose law provided that Negroes and white children were to be educated in schools that were "separate but equal."

An example of the operation of the "separate but equal" doctrine is the following: In the year 1913 in 353 Negro elementary schools there were libraries containing 46,781 volumes, an average of 132 books for each school. In 5,372 white elementary schools there were libraries containing 696,709 volumes, an average of 111 books for each school. There was not too great a difference in the average number of books in each black and each white school library. So the average was almost "equal."

chapter thirty-two / the blacks in west virginia

Negro Colleges

The demand for Negro colleges grew. West Virginia responded to the need as well as to the demand. In Harpers Ferry, Storer College was founded in 1867, but from a source outside the state. Storer College was an outgrowth of the work of the Freedmen's Bureau, a federal government agency set up at the conclusion of the Civil War to aid freed slaves. The government bureau's assistance provided for education, food, clothing, shelter, and economic help through possible distribution of land. The college also received help from private philanthropy. John Storer of Standford, Maine, contributed financial assistance for the education of former slaves and their descendants.

The first direct response from the state of West Virginia came in 1892 when the West Virginia Colored Institute, now West Virginia State College, was established at Institute in Kanawha County. The college was founded at the time of the building of the Chesapeake and Ohio Railway, and its primary purpose was the training of Negro teachers.

Another reason for its establishment was to enable the state to take advantage of the Second Morrill Act, which concerned instruction of black students in agriculture and mechanic arts. The college curriculum emphasized the dignity of labor. The vocational training programs were in line with Booker T. Washington's philosophy of education at Tuskegee Institute. Throughout the United States, West Virginia State College became a model land-grant institution for Negroes. The college is now integrated.

The second state response came in 1895 when Bluefield Colored Institute, now Bluefield State College, was established. It was founded at the time of the building of the Norfolk and Western Railroad and the opening of the southern West Virginia coalfields. Bluefield State College became a training center for Negro teachers. The college is also now integrated.

Race Relationships

Both Democrats and Republicans elected Negroes to the state Legislature in the twentieth century. In the formulation of their own state educational policies, Negroes created an advisory board of persons of their own race. Within this period, a law was passed that gave Negroes the right to serve as jurors and the right to use public libraries that were not a part of a school plant.

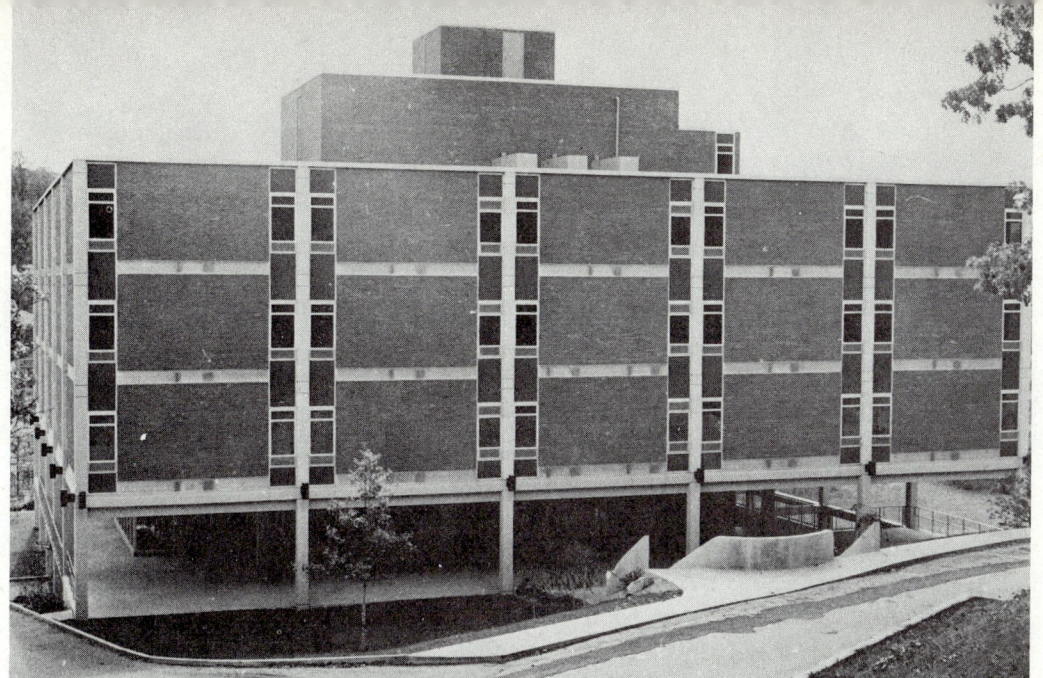

Science Building, Bluefield State College, Bluefield At one time the college was Bluefield Colored Institute. The college is now an integrated institution.

Following Negro participation in World Wars I and II, attitudes toward the Negro, particularly toward the "separate but equal" doctrine, underwent considerable change. The patriotism of blacks and their demonstrated abilities in assuming the duties of citizenship were unquestioned. The executive branch of the federal government responded by ordering integration of the armed forces. The judicial branch responded by its historic decision on May 17, 1954 that the principle of "separate but equal" educational facilities for the races was in conflict with the Constitution of the United States. The legislative branch responded with far-ranging civil rights legislation in the 1960's.

According to William W. Trent, who served as the state superintendent of free schools from 1933 to 1957, West Virginia was more than ready for the integration of the races in all its schools, including the black colleges. Mr. Trent stated that in the 1920's West Virginia University had admitted Negro students to extension classes that had formerly been open only to white students. Educational conferences and workshops held by the State Department of Education during World War II were integrated for meals and planning sessions. In October 1954 the West Virginia Educational Association for white teachers and the West Virginia State Teachers' Association for Negro Teachers united as one organization called the West Virginia Education Association.

chapter thirty-two / the blacks in west virginia

Mr. Trent observed that before the Supreme Court decision of May 17, 1954, Alderson-Broaddus College, Davis and Elkins College, Bethany College, and West Virginia Wesleyan College had voluntarily opened their doors to Negro students. By November 1954 all state colleges had enrolled Negro students, and in one year following the Supreme Court decision well over half the counties of West Virginia had integrated their schools.

At an earlier time, in 1870, the West Virginia Legislature had established at Romney schools for the deaf and the blind white children, and similar schools for black children at Institute in 1921. In 1955 by action of the Legislature, the schools at Institute did not reopen in the fall of 1955; the children from Institute were transferred to the school at Romney, to integrate the student body.

By 1956 all counties in West Virginia had begun or had completed integration of their schools. Mr. Trent was able to affirm that the state had fully complied with the declaration of the United States Supreme Court and had peaceably produced a situation of greater opportunity for the West Virginia Negro.

Notable West Virginia Negroes

Members of the black race have always been numbered among laudable West Virginians. Dick Pointer, Negro slave, helped save Fort Donnally from Indian attack. John Henry, mighty black of song and story, labored in construction crews on the Chesapeake and Ohio Railway in southern West Virginia. Booker T. Washington, who spent his boyhood in West Virginia, was elected to the Hall of Fame for Great Americans, an honor shared by only two other West Virginians, Daniel Boone and "Stonewall" Jackson.

Christopher H. Payne, Negro, Republican from Fayette County, was elected to the West Virginia Legislature in 1896. He was the first Negro elected to that body. Carter G. Woodson became a noteworthy educator and author.

John Warren Davis, president of West Virginia State College from 1919 to 1953 and president emeritus since 1953, was United States director of the Technical Cooperative Administration, Monrovia, Liberia, in 1953-54. He served on the Foreign Service Selection Board and on the committee for UNESCO.

Mrs. Howard H. Harper, Negro, was elected to the state Legislature of 1925-27. Lieutenant Edward Greer, Negro, of Welch, was awarded the Silver Star in World War II. Adolph Hamlin was elected by sportswriters to the West Virginia Hall of Fame in 1969.

John C. Norman, M.D., Distinguished Cardiovascular Surgeon and Pioneer in Organ-Transplant Techniques

John C. Norman, distinguished Negro surgeon and pioneer in organ-transplant techniques, was born in Charleston, West Virginia, in 1930. He received the M.D. degree at Harvard Medical School and was lieutenant commander in the United States Naval Reserve. He has had a career prominent in the field of investigative and clinical cardiovascular surgery and was formerly director of the Cardiovascular Research Division, Sears Surgical Laboratories, Harvard Unit, Boston City Hospital. This famed native West Virginian is now associated with Texas Medical Center, Houston. His writings include two books and more than a hundred scientific articles.

Leon H. Sullivan, Black West Virginian, Prominent in Various Fields

Leon H. Sullivan, a distinguished clergyman, pastor of the Philadelphia Zion Baptist Church for nearly a quarter of a century, was born in Charleston, West Virginia, in 1922. He received the A.B. degree at West Virginia State College, studied at Student Union Theological Seminary and received an M.A. in Religion at Columbia. He has been honored by America's outstanding colleges and universities. He is the founder of Opportunities Industrialization Centers which throughout America have taken hundreds of thousands of deprived people off relief roles and trained and placed them in jobs. He has also headed a black capitalism operation in Philadelphia and is the first black member of the Board of Directors of General Motors Corporation.

Edward G. Carroll, bishop of the United Methodist Church of the Boston Area, was born in Wheeling, West Virginia, in 1910. He received an A.B. degree from Morgan College, a B.D. from Yale University, and an M.A. from Columbia University. He served as chaplain in the Army of the United States during World War II. He has served as pastor in churches in Maryland, Virginia, and West Virginia and in such cities as Baltimore, New York, and Washington. He also has held numerous administrative positions in the United Methodist Church on district, conference, national, and international levels.

13 William J. L. Wallace, although a native North Carolinian, is one of West Virginia's outstanding educators. He received his B.S. degree from the University of Pittsburgh, an A.M. from Columbia, and a Ph.D. from Cornell. He has been associated with West Virginia State College for over forty years as a faculty member and administrator, serving as administrative assistant to the president, acting president and president from 1941 to 1973. He has contributed leadership not only in the academic area but also in local, state, and national civic affairs. He has written numerous articles for professional journals and periodicals, especially in his professional field of chemistry. He has also served as pastor and presiding elder in the AME Zion Church.

Two Eminent Black Citizens

Carter G. Woodson,
Outstanding Negro Leader

Carter G. Woodson was born near New Canton, Virginia, on December 19, 1875. Through self-instruction he mastered the fundamentals of the ordinary elementary school subjects. At seventeen, he went to Fayette County, West Virginia, where he worked as a coal miner for six years. He also attended the Douglass High School at Huntington and enrolled for two years of study at Berea (Kentucky) College.

In 1898 Woodson began his teaching career at Winona, West Virginia. In 1900 he became principal of Douglass High School. During the summer he attended the University of Chicago. From 1903 to 1906 he served as supervisor of schools in the Philippines and spent parts of the years 1906 and 1907 in travel and study in Asia and Europe, including one semester at the prestigious Sorbonne University in Paris.

On his return to the United States he completed his education at the University of Chicago, receiving a Master's degree in 1908. Combining teaching in Washington, D.C., with graduate study at Harvard University in Cambridge, Massachusetts, Woodson utilized the Library of Congress for research for a doctoral dissertation, "The Disruption of Virginia." Harvard University accepted his study and awarded him the Ph.D. degree in 1912. After a year of teaching at Howard University in Washington, Woodson served two years as dean of West Virginia State College.

In 1922 Carter Woodson was able to devote all of his time to research and publication in the field of Negro history. He had prepared diligently to achieve such a scholarly ambition. He organized and founded the Association for the Study of Negro Life and History in 1915. The organization had been aided in research projects by grants from several large foundations as well as by contributions from leading American businessmen. In 1916 Woodson had founded *The Journal of Negro History*, a quarterly review containing articles on Negro history. In 1922 Woodson originated Associated Publishers, Inc., in an effort to publish and circulate valuable books about the Negro, works not then acceptable to most publishers.

To gain attention for the achievements of blacks, he also promoted an annual Negro History Week in the schools, and this in turn led to his establishment of the *Negro History Bulletin* in 1937.

Carter Woodson died in Washington, D.C., in 1950. Before his death, he not only had published numerous books and articles of his own for which he received awards but also had established the Foundation for Negro History in the United States.

Booker T. Washington, Benefactor of His Race

One of the most important representatives of the Negro race in America made West Virginia his boyhood home. He was Booker T. Washington. He was born in slave quarters on a plantation at the village of Hale's Ford, Virginia, in 1858 or 1859, but shortly after emancipation of the slaves the boy Booker came with his family from eastern Virginia to Malden, near Charleston, West Virginia. There with his mother's assistance Booker learned the alphabet from Webster's *Blue-Back Spelling Book*. He learned to read when few black people could read and write. He entered an elementary school for Negroes.

His formal education was interrupted for a time because he had to go to work at the local salt furnace. The boy completed his lessons at night with the help of the schoolteacher. Later he attended

Bust and Monument Erected to the Memory of the Great Negro American Booker T. Washington near His Boyhood Home at Malden, Kanawha County   The monument was unveiled by Booker T. Washington's daughter, Portia Pittman, and was dedicated September 29, 1963. *(From the picture collection of Boyd B. Stutler)*

regular classes, working five hours before school in the morning and returning to the salt furnace after school in the afternoon.

For a year and a half, Booker T. Washington was a servant in the home of General Lewis Ruffner, owner of the salt furnace and mine. Encouraged by Mrs. Ruffner, he studied in the evening and attended school one hour a day. From Mrs. Ruffner he learned lessons in order and neatness in taking care of home, yard, and garden.

From the mine workers he heard of Hampton Institute, a vocational training school for Negroes in Virginia. In 1872 he left his West Virginia home for the Institute, walking a distance of 500 miles. In his autobiography, *Up from Slavery*, Washington gave Mrs. Ruffner credit for inspiring him to secure an education.

At Hampton the young Negro learned the brick mason's trade. After three years at the school, Washington journeyed to Connecticut where he worked as a waiter. He returned to Malden to teach in the Negro school there.

In the campaign to determine the permanent location of the West Virginia state capital, Washington stumped the state in 1877, speaking in behalf of Charleston as the state capital.

He studied at Wayland Seminary in Washington, D.C., in 1878-79. In 1881 he became director of Tuskegee Institute (for Negroes) in Alabama. In 1882 he married Fannie M. Smith of Malden.

Booker T. Washington's educational objective was to prepare Negroes to enter industry and trade. He transformed Tuskegee Institute from a small, poor, and little-known school into a world-famous center for vocational training, the first Negro institution of its kind in the United States.

He offered the suggestion: "In all things that are purely social we [blacks and whites] can be as separate as the fingers, yet one as the hand in all things essential to mutual progress." Another memorable admonition he gave to Negroes was to seek opportunity where they lived; as he phrased it, "Cast down your buckets where you are." These sentiments earned him the respect of white industrialists who were seeking qualified labor.

Today Tuskegee Institute has millions of dollars in endowment, thousands of acres of land, and thousands of students.

Booker T. Washington wrote and lectured in his great effort to advance the status of his race. Both whites and blacks stand in admiration before the figure of Booker T. Washington in the Hall of Fame for Great Americans at New York University. This honor is accorded to two other West Virginians, Daniel Boone and "Stonewall" Jackson.

unit nine | Men to Match the Mountains

Chapter **33** NATIONAL AND INTERNATIONAL SERVICES OF WEST VIRGINIANS

Spanish-American War

Spain once ruled the island of Cuba, and Cuba revolted to obtain its freedom in the late 1890's. The Cubans resorted to guerrilla warfare in order to achieve their independence, and Spain retaliated by imprisoning rebel Cubans in concentration camps.

In their quest for freedom the Cubans obtained supplies from the United States. As a gesture of goodwill the United States dispatched the battleship *Maine* to Havana. On February 15, 1898 the *Maine* was blown up by unknown means with the loss of more than 266 officers and enlisted men and the wounding of at least 60 others. President McKinley then asked Congress for a declaration of war against Spain.

The United States entered the Spanish-American War April 25, 1898 and won a quick victory. The independence of Cuba was recognized, and, according to the peace terms, the Cuban government was organized under the direction of the United States. Also our country assumed authority over the Philippine Islands, and took possession of Puerto Rico and the island of Guam.

World War I Memorial Building at Welch This memorial building was the first in West Virginia and one of the first in the nation to honor the soldiers and sailors of World War I.

World War I

In 1914 the heir apparent to the throne of the European country Austria-Hungary was assassinated. This incident was the first in a series that led to World War I. In the early years of the war the United States attempted to remain neutral. Our country was irritated, however, by the loss of property which the British government seized on the high seas, and the American people became incensed when a German submarine sank the ocean liner *Lusitania* on May 7, 1915 with the loss of many lives.

On April 6, 1917 the United States declared war on Germany. Our country proclaimed, however, that it had no desire to acquire territory in the war. On November 11, 1918 both sides in the war agreed to an armistice, which means an end to the fighting.

President Woodrow Wilson worked in behalf of a newly formed League of Nations which might prevent a future world war. The United States failed to join the league, and other nations' desire for additional territory created the conditions that led to World War II.

World War II

German armies began the conquest of Europe. The United States for a time remained neutral. But on December 7, 1941 the

Japanese attacked Pearl Harbor, and the United States entered the war against the combined powers of Germany and its ally, Italy, and Japan. Again our country published its rejection of any interest in obtaining additional territory. Germany surrendered May 6, 1945, and Japan September 2, 1945.

The United States worked successfully for an international organization, the United Nations, in the hope that through it any future war would be avoided.

USS "West Virginia." The USS *West Virginia*, as tall as an eight-story building, was a "hero" of World War II. The ship was originally commissioned at Norfolk Navy Yard December 1, 1923, was sunk at Pearl Harbor by the Japanese December 7, 1941, was raised in 1942, rebuilt and equipped with modern weapons and returned to combat duty in 1944. After 223 days in battle actions and bringing 7,500 World War II veterans home, she was returned to inactive status at Puget Sound Navy Yard.

Korean Conflict

Twice again the United States made armed intervention to resist Communist expansion in Asia. In conjunction with the United Nations our country protested the invasion of North Korea into South Korea on June 24, 1950. The United States insisted that the North Koreans, representing international Communism, withdraw behind the 38th parallel, the dividing line between the two Koreas. Lasting from June 24, 1950 to the armistice of July 27, 1953, the Korean War, officially termed a police action, prevented North Korea from taking over South Korea. However, total victory over the Communist forces was not won.

Vietnam Conflict

In 1950 the United States government recognized the government of South Vietnam in southeast Asia and concluded that North Vietnam by her aggressive action was attempting to spread international Communism in Asia. During President Eisenhower's administration and President Kennedy's administration advisory groups and American military troops were sent to South Vietnam to aid in preserving that country's existence. From August 4, 1964 President Johnson's administration increased United States forces in Vietnam. However, Congress did not declare war in southeast Asia.

USS "West Virginia," Hero of World War II   *(Official U.S. Navy Photograph)*

By the time of the election of Richard M. Nixon to a second term as President of the United States in 1972, American involvement in the ground war in Vietnam had been ended, although heavy bombing continued. In the early months of 1973 the United States began to withdraw its fighting forces from Vietnam and to secure the release of its prisoners of war.

Eight prisoners of war from West Virginia were released by March 1973. Military victory in the war was not achieved.

West Virginia in the Wars

In the Spanish-American War, although 10,000 West Virginians were ready to volunteer, 3,004 saw actual service in the limited engagement.

In World War I, 323,383 West Virginians registered for military duty, and 45,648 were inducted into the armed forces under selective service. The West Virginia National Guard mustered an additional 2,000 men, approximately 13,000 West Virginians volunteered, and 177 West Virginia women served in the Army Nurse Corps. A grand total of 60,000 West Virginians saw service in World War I.

For West Virginians, the casualty figures were high: 517 were killed in action; 1,047 died of disease and other causes, and 194 died of wounds; 3,000 received battle wounds; and 51 were captured, making a total of approximately 5,000 casualties, or one-twelfth of the entire number of West Virginians in service.

In World War II, 465,688 men registered under selective service, and 151,949 were inducted. Volunteers numbered 66,716, producing a grand total of 218,665 West Virginians in the armed forces. Casualties other than wounded—those killed in action or who died of wounds or injuries or who lost lives as a result of operational movements in war zones—included 4,865 Army personnel, 654 Navy personnel, 302 Marine Corps personnel, and 9 Coast Guard personnel, for a total of 5,830 casualties.

In the Korean Conflict, the West Virginia Department of Veterans Affairs published a casualty list compiled from records furnished by the Department of Defense as of January 1962. The list indicated a total of 899 West Virginia casualties, killed or died or missing, at the end of the Korean War. Total figures included both battle and non-battle dead or missing.

In the Vietnam War, the state Adjutant General's Department reported that, as of June 30, 1969, one out of every 67 United States soldiers killed in southeast Asia as a result of hostile action claimed West Virginia as his home state. This was a death rate of 2.75 per 10,000 population, as against a death rate of 1.80 per 10,000 population for the United States as a whole. As of December 31, 1972 the total unofficial death count of West Virginians in the Vietnam Conflict was approximately 711.

Spanish-American War Military Leaders

In every major military conflict, West Virginia has produced leaders. In the Spanish-American War, French Ensor Chadwick, John H. Hill, Julian Lane Latimer, and Andrew Summers Rowan were outstanding.

French Ensor Chadwick, born in Morgantown, February 29, 1844, was chief-of-staff for Rear Admiral William T. Sampson and commanded the battleship *New York*. After the Spanish-American War, he served as president of the Naval War College and as commander-in-chief of the South Atlantic Squadron. He also served as commander of the *Yorktown* and chief of the Naval Intelligence Office. He became a rear admiral on October 11, 1903 and, after retirement, became a historian. His books, *Causes of the Civil War*,

Captain French Ensor Chadwick In the Spanish-American War, Captain Chadwick of Monongalia County commanded the battleship *New York* in the naval engagements in Cuban waters. He was later promoted to rear admiral.

Volume XIX of *The American Nation* series, and *Relations of the United States and Spain, 1776-1898*, were well received. He died January 27, 1919.

John H. Hill, principal of the then West Virginia Colored Institute, was the outstanding Negro officer in the Spanish-American War. Having served in the Army from 1885 to 1887, he reenlisted in 1898, accompanied by six students from the Institute. After the war, he returned to the Institute as professor of mathematics and commandant of troops in the Military Science Department.

Julian Lane Latimer, born in Shepherdstown, on October 10, 1868, served on the *Winslow* during the Spanish-American War. In World War I, he commanded the *Rhode Island*, later served as commandant of the 4th Naval District and Navy Yard, Philadelphia, and was judge advocate of the United States Navy from 1921 to 1925. Latimer died in 1939.

At the request of President McKinley, Lieutenant Andrew Summers Rowan, who was born at Gap Mills April 23, 1857, was sent to communicate with General Calixto Garcia, commander of the Cuban armies. General Garcia was closely guarded by the Spanish in central Cuba. Lieutenant Rowan landed from an open boat near Turquino Peak April 24, 1898. He successfully executed his mission, bringing to the United States forces full information as to the strength of the insurgent army.

Rowan, the first United States Army officer to enter Cuba, was the subject of Elbert Hubbard's essay "A Message to Garcia," which was widely circulated and translated into a number of foreign languages.

Rowan was awarded the Distinguished Service Cross by his commander in the name of the President of the United States in 1922, and in 1940 the West Virginia Legislature awarded him the Distinguished Service Medal. He was the author of *The Island of Cuba* in 1898 and *How I Carried the Message to Garcia* in 1923. He died January 10, 1943.

World War I Military Leaders

Lieutenant Lewis Bennett, of Weston, was shot down by the Germans while serving with the Royal Air Force of Great Britain at Wavrin, France, in August 1918. In Lieutenant Bennett's memory a window adorns London's Westminster Abbey near the tomb of the British Unknown Soldier, and a church at Wavrin, Nord, France, was erected in his honor.

In World War I John Leonard Hines, born at White Sulphur Springs on May 21, 1868, went to France a major and came back a major general, commanding an Army corps. He assumed a position of great responsibility when he was appointed chief-of-staff, September 13, 1924, replacing General John J. Pershing. Later he served as commander of the 9th Corps Area and as commander of the Philippine Department.

Mason M. Patrick, of Lewisburg, served as chief of the Air Service of the United States Army in France. He, too, became a major general, and following the war retained his place as chief of the Air Service in behalf of national defense.

Major General John L. Hines This Greenbrier County man went to France a major and came back a major general, commanding an Army corps. He succeeded General Pershing as chief-of-staff of the United States Army.

William H. Waldron, born in Huntington, West Virginia, on June 28, 1877, served as chief-of-staff of the 80th Division during World War I and chief-of-staff of the 100th Division of Organized Reserves and the 10th U. S. Infantry Division after the war. He had also served in the Spanish-American War and distinguished himself as a writer on military subjects. He wrote *Scouting and Patrolling, Tactical Walks, Company Administration, Army Physical Training, Terrain Exercises,* and *Platoon Training*. In addition, he was secretary of the United States Infantry Association and editor of its journal. He also commanded the West Virginia District of the Civilian Conservation Corps in 1935 and 1936.

World War II Military Leaders

Delos Carleton Emmons, Charles Philip Snyder, and Richard K. Sutherland ranked high in the Air Force, the Army, and the Navy in World War II.

General Emmons, born in Huntington, January 17, 1888, served as brigadier general, major general, and lieutenant general in the Air Corps from 1936 to 1940. From commanding officer, Air Force Combat Command, Bolling Field, D.C., he was appointed to command of the Hawaiian Department December 17, 1941, ten days after Pearl Harbor. He later served as commander of the Western Theatre of Operations and as commandant of the Armed Forces Staff College.

Charles Philip Snyder, born in Charleston on July 10, 1879, served as chief-of-staff of the United States Fleet in 1933-34, was president of the United States Naval War College, and commanded Battle Force, U. S. Fleet, January 1940. He was appointed Naval Inspector General in May 1942. At various times he commanded the *Argonne, Concord, Tennessee,* and *Oregon* and served as commandant of the Navy Yard at Portsmouth, New Hampshire. He advanced through all officers' ranks to full admiral.

Lieutenant General Richard K. Sutherland, of Elkins, served as chief-of-staff to General Douglas MacArthur from 1939 to 1945.

Post World War II Admirals

From 1953 to 1958 Admiral Felix B. Stump, who was born in Parkersburg, West Virginia, was commander-in-chief, Pacific, commanding all United States ground, sea, and air forces, including 500,000 men, 4,000 military planes, and 500 Navy ships. This

Admiral Felix B. Stump, Commander-in-Chief of All United States Ground, Sea, and Air Forces in the Pacific, 1953–58

command was called "the largest, most turbulent, and most important command in the world."

In September 1957 Rear Admiral Frederick Burdett Warder, who was born in Grafton, West Virginia, reported as commander, Submarine Force, U. S. Atlantic Fleet. In 1960 he became commandant, 8th Naval District, with headquarters on U. S. Naval Station, New Orleans.

Presidential Appointments

Martin Delany was the first Negro appointed (by President Lincoln) to the field rank of major in the Civil War.

The quest for peace was pursued by others than those in uniform. Over the years, West Virginia produced outstanding diplomatic representatives. Dwight Morrow, born at Huntington on January 11, 1873, was appointed ambassador to Mexico in 1927. By 1930 tension between the two countries was reduced. Due to Morrow's diplomatic skill, Mexico's constitutional reforms and nationalization laws were accommodated to the interests of United States citizens.

Morrow also served as delegate to the Naval Conference in London, England, in 1930 and as regent for the Smithsonian Institution in Washington, D.C. General Pershing awarded Morrow the Distinguished Service Medal "for exceptionally meritorious and distinguished service" in connection with military shipping matters and the Military Board of Allied Supply of World War I. Morrow died October 5, 1931.

John William Davis, born in Clarksburg, April 13, 1873, practiced law in Clarksburg from 1897 to 1913; was a member of the West Virginia House of Delegates in 1899; served in the United States Congress from 1911 to 1915, as solicitor general of the United States from 1913 until 1918, and as ambassador to Great Britain from 1918 to 1921. After World War I he was appointed a member of the American delegation for conference with the Germans on treatment and exchange of prisoners of war. Davis was nominated as Democratic candidate for the presidency of the United States in 1924.

Joseph Simpson Farland, born at Clarksburg, West Virginia, was United States ambassador to the Dominican Republic, 1957-60, in the Eisenhower administration; to the Republic of Panama, 1961-63, in the Kennedy administration; and to the Republic of Pakistan, 1969-72, and Iran, 1972-73, in the Nixon administration.

John Barton Payne, born at Pruntytown, January 28, 1855, practiced law at Kingwood, was mayor of that city, and became a

Joseph Simpson Farland, Foreign Service Officer

special judge of the circuit court of Tucker County. He served as United States secretary of interior in President Wilson's cabinet from February 1920 to March 1921. He was also director of railroads from May 1920 to April 1921 and was chairman of the American Red Cross.

Louis A. Johnson, born in Roanoke, Virginia, January 10, 1891, began to practice law at Clarksburg, West Virginia, in 1912 and became a member of the Steptoe and Johnson law firm. He served as assistant United States secretary of war from June 28, 1937 to July 25, 1940. As personal representative of the President, he was sent on a diplomatic mission to India in 1942. After serving as national commander of the American Legion, he was appointed secretary of defense by President Harry Truman. Mr. Johnson served in that position from March 1949 to September 1950.

Lewis L. Strauss, born in Charleston, West Virginia, January 31, 1896, was secretary to Herbert Hoover in 1917-18 when Hoover led vast foreign relief work. Strauss was made special assistant to the President for atomic energy matters in 1953, and was chairman of the Atomic Energy Commission 1953-58. He was secretary of commerce 1958-59. In 1962 he wrote *Men and Decisions*.

Cyrus Roberts Vance, born at Clarksburg, March 27, 1917, served as United States secretary of the Army in 1962-63; as deputy secretary of defense, from 1964 to 1967; as special representative of the President to Cyprus in 1967 and to Korea in 1968. He was special United States negotiator at the Paris Peace Conference on Vietnam in 1968-69.

William Leonhart, United States foreign service officer, was born in Parkersburg, West Virginia. He received the Ph.D. degree from Princeton University. His foreign service began in 1944 and included assignments in the American embassies in Buenos Aires, Belgrade, Rome, Saigon, Phnom Pehn, Vientiane, and Tokyo. He was the first American ambassador to Tanzania, was deputy special assistant to the President at the White House in 1966-69, and in 1969 was appointed ambassador to Yugoslavia.

James E. Allen, native of Elkins, West Virginia, was, on February 3, 1969, appointed by President Richard M. Nixon to be United States commissioner of education and assistant secretary of the Department of Health, Education and Welfare. Allen held graduate degrees from both Harvard and Princeton universities. Before his government service, he had been president of the University of the State of New York and commissioner of education for the state of New York. Leaving his government post in Washington in June 1970, he became visiting lecturer in education and public affairs, Woodrow Wilson School of Public and International Affairs at Princeton University.

Special Missions

In addition to high diplomatic missions abroad and defense service on the home front, special assignments were given to a number of West Virginians. These men made important contributions to the country's welfare.

Lieutenant Leonard J. O'Dell, Charleston, served as copilot on the private plane of Generalissimo Chiang Kai-shek. Brigadier General Charles E. (Chuck) Yeager of Hamlin, Lincoln County, became the flying ace of World War II and the first person to fly faster than the speed of sound. Of three major bridges of the West Virginia Turnpike spanning the Kanawha, one was named the Yeager Bridge.

John Warren Davis, outstanding West Virginia Negro, was president of West Virginia State College from 1919 to 1953 and has been president emeritus since 1953. We have noted that he was United States director of the Technical Cooperative Administration in Monrovia, Liberia, in 1953-54. He served on the Foreign Service Selection Board and on committees for UNESCO.

Colonel Ralph D. Albertazzie, Morgantown, was nominated by chief of staff, Air Force, to be personal pilot for the President of the United States. Immediately after the presidential election

Brigadier General Charles Elwood Yeager, First to Fly Faster than the Speed of Sound

November 1968, he was assigned to President Richard M. Nixon's planes and was the President's pilot on the journeys to China and Russia in 1972.

Various Fields

We have read of Dr. John C. Norman, outstanding Negro surgeon and cardiovascular specialist, and pioneer in organ-transplant techniques.

Dana L. Farnsworth, M.D., was born in Troy, West Virginia, and was reared in this state. He was graduated from Harvard Medical School. He served as director of health at Williams College, as medical director and acting dean of students at Massachusetts Institute of Technology, professor of hygiene and director of the university health services at Harvard University and member of the faculty of Arts and Sciences and of the Harvard School of Public Health; later Henry K. Oliver professor of hygiene emeritus and consultant in social psychiatry at Harvard School of Public Health and vice-chairman of the National Commission on Marihuana and Drug Abuse. The list of his books is extensive and impressive. Many honors have been awarded to him.

Phyllis Curtin, Metropolitan Opera Star

Dana L. Farnsworth, M.D., Recipient of High Honors in the Fields of Health and Psychiatry *(Photo courtesy of Harvard University News Office)*

unit nine / men to match the mountains

Many other West Virginians have achieved national recognition in various creative fields — authors, artists, sportsmen, entertainers. Only a few can be mentioned here. In the literary world have been Rebecca Harding Davis, Frank R. Stockton, Melville Davisson Post, Waitman T. Barbe, Louise McNeill Pease, Alberta Pierson Hannum, Julia Davis, John Knowles, John Peale Bishop. Among historians have been Virgil A. Lewis, Charles Henry Ambler, John P. Hale, Roy Bird Cook, Phil Conley, Boyd B. Stutler, and Festus Paul Summers. Folklorists are John Harrington Cox, Marie Boette, Patrick Gainer, and Ruth Ann Musick.

High-ranking musicians include Eleanor Steber, Phyllis Curtin, Suzanne Fisher, and George H. Crumb. Jerry West, Rod Hundley, Hal Greer, Sam Huff have won fame in sports. Don Knotts, Soupy Sales, and Joanne Dru are well-known dispensers of light entertainment.

Lemuel Chenoweth was the state's distinguished builder of covered bridges. Mrs. Francis Pierpont, of Fairmont, in 1869 originated the movement to establish May 30 as Decoration, or Memorial, Day.

Member of the President's Cabinet

Newton D. Baker, Secretary of War

Among outstanding military leaders and statesmen, one West Virginian qualifies in both categories, although he was a civilian leader of the military. He was Newton D. Baker, who became United States secretary of war. He was born at Martinsburg, West Virginia, December 3, 1871. Baker studied at an Episcopal academy in Alexandria, Virginia, and at Johns Hopkins University in Baltimore. He received a law degree from Washington and Lee University in Lexington, Virginia, in 1894.

After serving as private secretary to the postmaster general of the United States in 1896-97, he began the practice of law at Martinsburg. He later accepted an opportunity to work for a distinguished law firm in Cleveland, Ohio, and became involved in the politics of that city. After a period as city solicitor of Cleveland, he was elected mayor of the city in 1911.

chapter thirty-three / national and international services of west virginians

Interested in national political affairs, Baker strongly supported Woodrow Wilson for the Democratic nomination for President in 1912. President Wilson later offered him the post of secretary of the interior, a position which Baker declined in order to continue his service as mayor of Cleveland. He was reelected mayor in 1913 but did not seek renomination to that office for a third term. President Wilson asked Baker to serve as secretary of war, a position of extreme importance at this time, for World War I was seething in Europe. Accepting that high office in March 1916, the new secretary proceeded to make the United States ready for war even while the administration in Washington tried through negotiation to prevent the nation from becoming involved in the conflict.

When the United States finally entered the war on April 6, 1917, the responsibility for marshaling the manpower and the resources of the country fell to Newton D. Baker. Baker succeeded in the enormous undertaking of directing the mobilization and training of 4,000,000 men in a system of camps and bases.

In meetings of the President's cabinet, Baker's counsel on government problems and policies was most valuable.

Newton D. Baker's outstanding ability and accomplishments brought him honorary degrees from many universities, including one from West Virginia University.

After World War I he advocated United States participation in the League of Nations.

Baker died in Cleveland in 1937. His service to the nation was appropriately recognized in 1944: In Martinsburg, his birthplace, the United States erected Newton D. Baker General Hospital for the care and rehabilitation of sick and disabled servicemen.

Chapter 34 STATE AND NATIONAL POLITICS: 1897 TO THE PRESENT

State Politics

As we have already noted, the end of "reconstruction" brought the end of abolitionist control in West Virginia. By 1897, however, the Democratic Party had run its course in state politics, and the Republicans assumed power. With the exception of the World War I era, the Republicans held sway until 1933, the height of the depression. From 1933 until 1957, the Democrats maintained control. Since 1957, the two major parties have enjoyed much briefer periods of dominance. A Republican governor has been followed by two Democratic governors, who have been followed by a Republican governor.

Throughout its history, West Virginia has divided its loyalties fairly evenly between the two major parties. Since 1863 the state has had 15 Democratic governors and 13 Republican governors. In a total of 112 years, from 1863 to 1975, the chief executive has been a Democrat 62 years; the governor has been a Republican 50 years.

1897-1917. The first period, 1897 to 1917, saw George Wesley Atkinson, Albert Blakeslee White, William M. O. Dawson, William

Viewing Golden Trout at One of West Virginia's State Trout Hatcheries *(David P. Cruise Photo, West Virginia Department of Commerce)*

Ellsworth Glasscock, and Henry Drury Hatfield as governors. All were Republicans, and the first four were closely identified with Stephen B. Elkins, who served as United States senator from 1895 until his death in 1911. (Biographical sketches of all West Virginia governors are presented in the appendix of this book.)

The main accomplishments of the period were reforms in property assessment and taxation laws. Attention was paid to road building and to the prevention of election abuses. The creation of a State Board of Health, State Bureau of Labor, and State Road Bureau were examples of West Virginia's attuning itself to the progressivism of the nation.

During this period, both in the state and the nation, the Democrats were at a disadvantage because they appeared to be far less "progressive" than the Republicans. Within the state the Democrats tried for a constitutional amendment making payment of a poll tax a requirement for voting, adopted a platform plank calling for disfranchisement of Negroes, and advocated the use of "Jim Crow" cars in public conveyances. They were unsuccessful in all of these ventures which called for an imagined return to a past, pre-Civil War era.

unit nine / men to match the mountains

In this "progressive" period, 1897-1917, West Virginia continued to advance its conservation program. Conservation measures had been instituted in the early years of statehood; between 1877 and 1897 the state created a Fish Commission for the purpose of establishing hatcheries, stocking waters, and removing obstructions in streams to permit passage of fish; established the Office of Fish and Game Warden; and prescribed heavy penalties for the violation of the fish and game laws.

Between 1909 and 1919, the Office of Fish and Game Warden became responsible for forest protection, the establishment of license fees, and the implementation of a code of conduct for hunters and fishermen. Game refuges, fire towers, and fire prevention societies were created.

Constitutional Changes, 1897-1917. Between 1897 and 1917 several constitutional changes in the 1872 constitution were approved by West Virginians. In 1902 a registration law amendment was added, as was an executive department amendment, providing for election of and outlining the qualifications of a secretary of state.

In 1902 it was decided by amendment that the Supreme Court of Appeals should contain five members. In 1910 the voters rejected an amendment proposal increasing the number of judges to seven.

A sign of the times was the adoption of the prohibition amendment in 1912 which prohibited the manufacture and sale of "intoxicating malt, vinous or spiritous liquors." Another indication of "modified" progressivism occurred in 1910 when a qualification amendment providing for the appointment of female citizens to certain offices in the state was rejected. This action was followed in 1916 by the rejection of a proposed female suffrage amendment.

1917-33. In the second, or "conservative," period John Jacob Cornwell, Ephraim Franklin Morgan, also Howard Mason Gore, and William Gustavus Conley served as the chief executives. Public safety issues and law-and-order themes predominated as the state searched for ways to cope with crime and industrial turmoil in the period after World War I. The West Virginia State Police (now the Department of Public Safety) was created in 1919. Toward the end of the period attention was given to finding ways to overcome the depression.

From 1921 to 1931 the conservation program received great impetus under the state game protector, A. B. Brooks. The state established game preserves, purchased the first state-owned park

Multipurpose Watershed Dam above the Town of Cameron in Marshall County This dam provides flood prevention and also municipal water supply for Cameron. (*USDA—Soil Conservation Service Photo*)

and the first state forest, and cooperated in the establishment of the Monongahela National Forest. By 1928 the various conservation agencies had been consolidated by the state Legislature into the West Virginia Game, Fish, and Forestry Commission.

In 1933 the state Legislature created the Conservation Commission of West Virginia to report, protect, and develop lands, forests, the state parks, animal life, plant life, waters, and the natural scenic resources of the state. The commission also cooperated with the federal government in projects such as the Civilian Conservation Corps, which provided relief for the unemployed throughout the state.

In 1961 the commission was renamed the West Virginia Department of Natural Resources. Like its predecessors, it works to prevent forest fires, to assist in reforestation, to reclaim lands disturbed by surface mining, and to extend the state's recreational complex.

Constitutional Changes, 1917-33. Two highway amendments were adopted in 1920 and 1928. The proposal for a lieutenant governor was defeated in 1930. Several budget amendments were rejected, but the adoption of a budget system was approved in 1918. An indicator of the depression was the approval in 1932 of the tax limitation amendment, providing for more-refined classification of property for taxation purposes as a means of increasing needed revenues for the state.

Main Corridor of the Main Unit of the West Virginia State Capitol This unit of the capitol was built in the early 1930's. *(Photo courtesy of West Virginia University Library)*

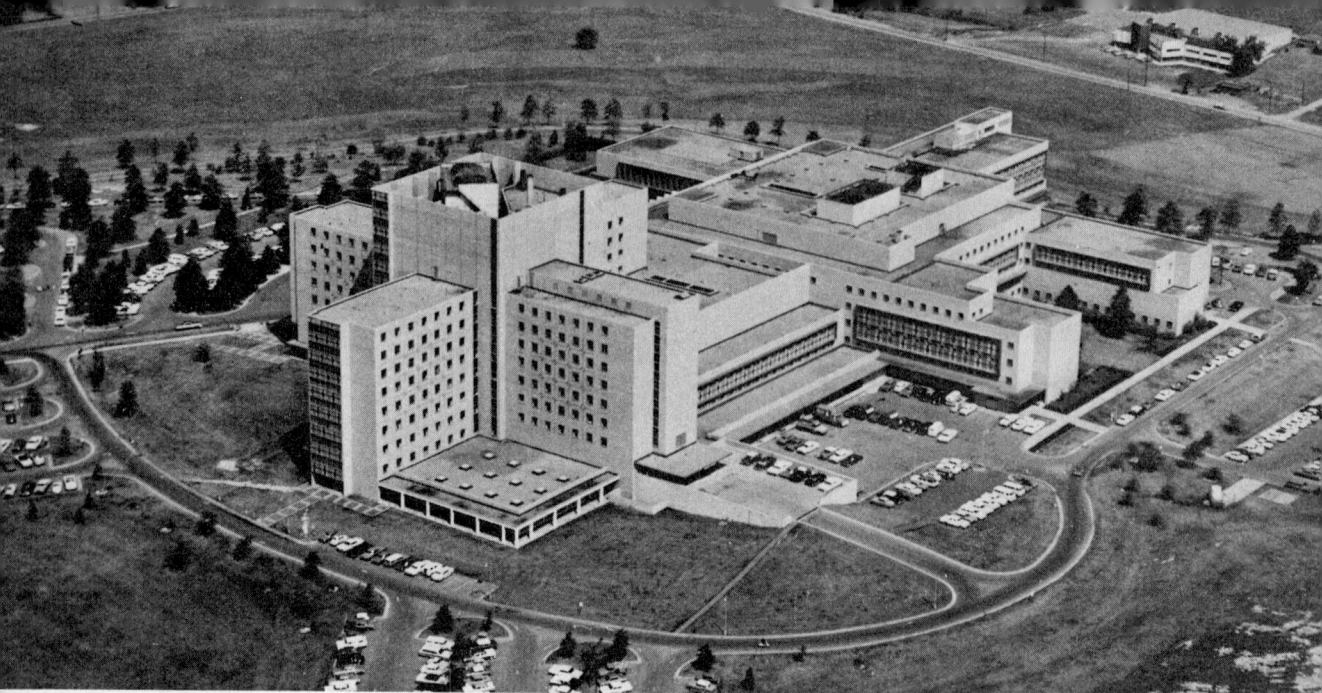

Medical Center at West Virginia University *(Photo courtesy of West Virginia University)*

1933-57. The third period, 1933 to 1957, found the Democrats back in control. Occupying the governor's mansion in succession were Herman Guy Kump, Homer A. Holt, Matthew Mansfield Neely, Clarence W. Meadows, Okey L. Patteson, and William C. Marland. To combat the depression was the first order of business. To see the nation through World War II and the Korean War were other matters of serious concern for the state government. The gross sales tax was increased, and new taxes were imposed upon incomes, chain stores, horseracing, and distributors and retailers of beer, wine, and liquor. Sharing in federal programs, work projects were conducted throughout the state.

In this period decision was made to locate the School of Medicine, Dentistry and Nursing at Morgantown. Financial underpinning of the medical school was to be obtained through taxes on soft drinks. The $27.5 million West Virginia University Medical Center has become one of the finest in the nation.

Constitutional Changes, 1933-57. The old prohibition amendment was repealed in 1934, and the "lame duck" amendment, approved in 1934, provided that the terms of the governor and other members of the executive department begin on the first Monday after the second Wednesday of January instead of the traditional March 4 date.

unit nine / men to match the mountains

In 1936 municipal home rule was permitted for municipalities in excess of two thousand population. Good-road amendments were approved in 1942 and in 1948. Veterans Bonus amendments were passed in 1950 and 1956, and jury service by women was permitted by an amendment ratified in 1956.

1957 to the Present. From 1957 to the present Cecil H. Underwood, William W. Barron, Hulett C. Smith, and Arch Moore, Jr., were governors. First a Republican, then two Democrats, then a Republican thus moved the governor's office from party to party. Education and transportation improvements, increasing tourism in West Virginia, corruption in the state government, and offsetting population loss became the primary concerns of the voters. The federal government's interest in Appalachia and the nation's involvement in Vietnam affected countless citizens of the state.

Constitutional Changes, 1957 to the Present. The office of the state superintendent of free schools was removed from the list of elective offices and made appointive in 1958. Road bond amendments were approved in 1964 and 1968. Although the governor's succession amendment was disapproved in 1966, it was approved in 1970. The Modern Budget Amendment, passed in 1968, increased the governor's powers in that he was the official designated to prepare and submit budgets to the Legislature. Although the annual legislative session of sixty days was proposed and rejected in 1966, it was accepted in 1970.

National Politics at Presidential Levels

1904 National Election. In at least three national elections, the state of West Virginia has figured prominently in the determination and selection of party candidates. In 1904 the Democratic Party, having twice suffered defeat with William Jennings Bryan as a candidate, turned to Judge Alton B. Parker of New York and Henry G. Davis of West Virginia for its presidential and vice-presidential candidates. The Republicans renominated Theodore Roosevelt as the party's presidential candidate, and selected Charles W. Fairbanks of Indiana as vice-presidential candidate. The election was an overwhelming victory for Roosevelt, who carried the nation with 336 electoral votes to Parker's 140. Roosevelt amassed 7,628,834 popular votes, and Parker 5,084,491. In West Virginia, the

Roosevelt-Fairbanks ticket won over the Parker-Davis ticket by a vote of 132,628 to 100,881.

1924 National Election. In 1924 the Democratic Party selected John W. Davis, a leading New York lawyer who was associated with J. P. Morgan, was a former West Virginia congressman and former ambassador to Great Britain, as its presidential candidate. To balance the ticket, the Democrats added Charles W. Bryan, governor of Nebraska and brother of William Jennings Bryan, as vice-presidential candidate. The Republicans selected Calvin Coolidge of Massachusetts and Charles G. Dawes of Chicago as presidential and vice-presidential candidates. Coolidge's electoral vote was 382, and Davis's electoral vote was 136. The popular vote for Coolidge was 15,725,016; for Davis it was 8,385,586. In West Virginia the vote was closer, but Coolidge edged out the native son by a vote of 288,635 to 257,232.

1960 Primary Election. In 1960 when the Democratic presidential primary was held in West Virginia, the principal contenders were Hubert H. Humphrey and John F. Kennedy. This state was regarded as a key testing ground and battleground for Senator Kennedy. It was thought that if Kennedy could win a primary in a predominantly Protestant state, he, as a well-known Catholic, might be able to become President of the United States. In the primary election held on May 10, 1960 in West Virginia, Kennedy decisively defeated Hubert Humphrey by a vote of 236,510 to 152,187. Kennedy went on to capture the Democratic nomination and the presidency of the United States. Kennedy, the thirty-fifth President, acknowledged on several occasions that the action of the thirty-fifth state had been influential in his election.

Senators and Representatives. Senators enjoying two or more terms in the upper chamber of the United States Congress in the twentieth century have been Matthew M. Neely, Harley M. Kilgore, Stephen B. Elkins, Jennings Randolph, and Robert C. Byrd. Since 1940, representatives enjoying long tenure in the House of Representatives have been Robert Mollohan, Harley O. Staggers, Ken Hechler, John Slack, members of the Kee family (John, Elizabeth, and James), Cleveland Bailey, E. H. Hedrick, M. G. Burnside, and Robert Ramsey. Jennings Randolph, Robert Byrd, and Arch A. Moore, Jr., who moved into other political offices, had enjoyed terms in the House of Representatives in the recent time period.

Officials in the President's Cabinet. Eight West Virginians attained positions as cabinet members in the executive branch of the federal government. In the nineteenth century, Nathan Goff served President Rutherford B. Hayes as secretary of the Navy, William L. Wilson served President Grover Cleveland as postmaster general, and Stephen B. Elkins served President Benjamin Harrison as secretary of war.

In the twentieth century Newton D. Baker and John Barton Payne were secretary of war and secretary of the interior in the administration of President Woodrow Wilson. Howard M. Gore served President Calvin Coolidge as secretary of agriculture. Lewis L. Strauss served President Dwight D. Eisenhower as secretary of commerce. Louis A. Johnson served President Harry S. Truman as secretary of defense.

Political Visitor

Eleanor Roosevelt, First Lady

During the 1930's it was not unusual to see Mrs. Eleanor Roosevelt, wife of the President of the United States, traveling about the depressed coal camps of the Monongalia-Preston County area in West Virginia. The reasons for her coming were the circumstances of the Great Depression and the modern welfare projects she helped establish in the state. As a result of her visits and those of the President himself, the Roosevelt name became legendary and influential in West Virginia politics.

The collapse of the stock market in 1929, followed by crippling drought in many parts of the country in 1930, helped bring American industry and agriculture to economic standstills. The West Virginia mining and lumber communities were no exception to the general economic havoc wrought by the Great Depression.

To help alleviate chronic unemployment and lack of income in American society, the federal government initiated many public work programs. One of the first, and of special concern to Eleanor Roosevelt, was the Arthurdale resettlement community established in Preston County in 1933. It was planned for the purpose of relocating and rehabilitating, on small farmsteads, families from abandoned mining communities and lumber camps. At the Arthurdale settlement these families hopefully would have an opportunity to reestablish themselves, both economically and socially.

For this purpose under the auspices of federal administration and the watchful eye of Mrs. Roosevelt, more than 1,100 acres of land were obtained in northern West Virginia. One hundred and sixty-five housing units of four to six rooms were built and maintained by the inhabitants. Each family received, at a nominal rent, a house, combination barn-poultry unit, and about three acres of land. Subsistence gardening and stock raising became family enterprises, and two factories eventually opened for the employment of the settlers.

A cooperative association ran agricultural, industrial, and community service enterprises. The average annual household income was raised to above $1,000 from a level of less than $500 before the project started. Although the effort at the settlement hit many snags and faced much criticism, it did help the families of the area to get back on their feet so that they could earn their own livelihood.

Comparable projects in the Tygart Valley, Randolph County, and at Eleanor near Redhouse in Putnam County, were also begun. All of the settlement projects, each accommodating 170 families, were liquidated after serving their original purpose.

As a memorial to Mrs. Roosevelt, a town in Putnam County, West Virginia, was named Eleanor.

Chapter 35 WEST VIRGINIA GOVERNMENT

A study of West Virginia history must take into account its government. This dictates a study of its constitution, its governmental structure at the state and local levels, and its federal representatives and agents.

We have already noted that the state operates under a constitution adopted in 1872. Various amendments have been submitted since 1880, the more popular ones dealing with good roads and better schools. Rather than rewrite the state constitution, West Virginians have preferred the amendment process as a means of updating their government.

Among the more significant amendments occurring in recent years are the governor's succession amendment, providing that the governor may serve two consecutive terms; the modern budget amendment, providing that the governor be responsible for preparing and submitting the budget to the Legislature; the legislative improvement amendment, providing for a sixty-day session each year; and the Sheriffs Succession Act passed in November 1973.

Like the United States government, West Virginia state government is divided into three major branches: executive, legislative, and judicial. Although the legislative branch and the Board of Public Works have dominated policy changes during most of West Virginia history, there has been a significant swing in recent years toward increasing the executive power of one official, the governor. This internal shift also reflects changes in the balance of power which

West Virginia State Capitol Complex at Charleston *(Gerald S. Ratliff Photo, West Virginia Department of Commerce)*

have occurred in the national government, whereby the President of the United States seems to have increased his authority at the expense of the judicial and legislative branches.

The Executive Branch

The Governor. The governor is the chief executive of the state. He must be at least thirty years old and have been a citizen of the state for five years preceding his election. The governor serves as commander-in-chief of the military forces of the state. In this capacity he may call out the National Guard to enforce laws, suppress insurrection, and repel invasion except when the state militia itself is called into the service of the federal government. He takes care that the laws are faithfully executed. With the advice and consent of the Senate, he appoints many state officers, and he may remove officeholders for cause by declaring their offices vacant. He may remit fines and penalties, commute capital punishment, and grant reprieves and pardons for prisoners after conviction.

Every bill passed by the Legislature is presented to the governor for his approval. The governor may approve and sign the bill, making it a law. Or, if the governor takes no action on the bill within five days of its receipt, the bill can become a law without his signature. Or, he may refuse to sign the bill, which would constitute a veto. But a bill may become a law in spite of the governor's veto if a majority of the members of each house of the Legislature vote to pass it again. A budget bill, or supplementary appropriation bill, disapproved by the governor, requires a vote of two-thirds of the members elected to each house of the Legislature in order to become a law. The voters approved this last provision in 1968.

The governor is expected to deliver a message on the condition of the state at the commencement of each legislative session. He is expected to prepare the budget of the state for submission to the Legislature. This was the substance of an amendment approved by the voters in 1968. In 1970 the voters also approved the governor's succession amendment, providing that a person can serve as governor

The Governor's Mansion West Virginia provides a home for the governor and his family. The residence is near the state capitol. *(Gerald S. Ratliff Photo, West Virginia Department of Commerce)*

for two consecutive terms. In recent years, such action by the voters has considerably strengthened the powers of the governor.

If the governor's office becomes vacant, he is succeeded, first, by the president of the Senate; second, by the speaker of the House of Delegates; and in all other cases by an individual selected by joint vote of the Legislature. The governor can be removed from office if sufficient charges are brought against him by the House of Delegates and if the Senate finds him guilty by a two-thirds vote.

Other Executive Officers. Other elected officers of the executive division, elected for four-year terms by the people, are the secretary of state, attorney general, commissioner of agriculture, auditor, and treasurer. The secretary of state has the care of all state papers and keeps a record of all official acts of the government. He is the chief registration official of the state and, in addition, issues certificates of incorporation for all domestic corporations and certificates of authority to foreign corporations to transact business in the state.

The auditor is the chief bookkeeper of the state and keeps a record of all money paid to the state and money paid out by the state. The state treasurer has charge of the state money. After state money has been placed in banks, it can be drawn out only by a warrant written and signed by the auditor and the treasurer. The attorney general advises the governor and other state officials, boards, and commissions in matters of the law and handles all litigation in behalf of the state.

The commissioner of agriculture promotes agriculture in the state. He is charged with the responsibility of making certain that only wholesome, uncontaminated, and unadulterated agricultural products are offered to the consuming public. He is concerned with preventing the spread of plant and animal diseases and in marketing the farm products of the state. He also gives attention to farm seeds, fertilizers, feeds, and livestock, and assists in establishing official standards and grades of agricultural products.

The Board of Public Works. The six elected members of the executive division with the governor as chairman make up the State Board of Public Works, along with the state superintendent of free schools, who is appointed by the State Board of Education. Until a constitutional amendment in 1958, the state superintendent of free schools was an elected official of this board. The Board of Public Works places a valuation on the property of all public service corporations of the state, and each public service corporation pays taxes according to the valuation. Public service corporations are those that furnish water, natural gas, electricity, telephone service, bus or railroad service, and some freight truck service; these corporations also include power plants, toll bridges, and toll roads.

Other Boards and Administrative Divisions of the Executive Department. The West Virginia Board of Education determines the educational policies of the elementary and secondary schools, has supervision and management of the West Virginia Schools for the Deaf and the Blind, and selects the state superintendent of free schools. The board acts as West Virginia Board of Vocational Education.

The West Virginia Board of Regents, created in 1969, is the governing body for all state colleges and universities. The board submits a budget for higher education and allocates funds to the institutions from the appropriations it receives. It also determines the specific functions and responsibilities of the institutions.

View in Cacapon State Park All West Virginia state parks are under the direction and management of the West Virginia Department of Natural Resources. In the view of Cacapon State Park note the lodge for the accommodation of guests. *(David P. Cruise Photo, West Virginia Department of Commerce)*

Other executives and administrative divisions of the state government are the Adjutant General, the Alcohol Beverage Control Commissioner, the Department of Archives and History, Department of Banking, Nonintoxicating Beer Commissioner, Department of Civil and Defense Mobilization, Civil Service System, Court of Claims, Department of Commerce, Department of Employment Security, Department of Finance and Administration, Geological and Economic Survey, State Department of Health, Department of Highways, Insurance Commissioner, Department of Labor, Library Commission, Department of Mental Health, Department of Mines, Department of Motor Vehicles, Department of Natural Resources, Public Employees Retirement System, Commissioner of Public Institutions, Department of Public Safety, Public Service Commission, State Sinking Fund Commission, State Tax Department, Department of Veterans Affairs, Department of Welfare, and Workmen's Compensation Fund.

Among the many state boards and commissions, the West Virginia Commission on Aging, the Air Pollution Control Commission, the Ohio-West Virginia Interstate Air Pollution Control Commission, the West Virginia Antiquities Commission, the West Virginia Arts and Humanities Council, the Governor's Committee on Employment of the Handicapped, and the Human Rights Commission are examples of agencies undertaking special assignments for state government.

The Legislative Branch

The Legislature of West Virginia is a bicameral body; that is, it consists of two chambers, or houses. The Senate and the House of Delegates constitute, respectively, the upper and the lower house. Senators are elected for terms of four years, and they must be at least 25 years old. Delegates are elected for two-year terms and must be at least 21 years old.

The Senate must have at least 24 members. At present there are 34 members, two sent from each of the seventeen senatorial districts. Each district is made up of from one to six counties, depending upon the population of the counties. The House of Delegates contains 100 members, determined by the 1964 Legislature. For at least one year before they may serve in the Legislature, both state senators and delegates must have been residents of West Virginia and of the county or district from which they are elected. If the senator or delegate moves his residence from the district or county from which he was elected, his seat is declared vacant.

Entrance to Legislative Chamber, West Virginia State Capitol *(From 1972 "West Virginia Blue Book")*

In 1970 the voters approved a legislative improvement amendment which provided for a sixty-day session of the Legislature each year. The Legislature meets each year on the second Wednesday of January. The length of a session may be extended by a two-thirds vote, but no vote is necessary if the budget is under consideration. The Legislature may also meet in special session at the request of the governor, but it may consider only those matters which the governor offers as explanations for the call. If three-fifths of the members of the Legislature petition for a special session, the governor must provide for a legislative session.

How a Bill Becomes a Law. Legislative action is formulated through bills. A bill may be presented by individual or group action, but to be introduced into the state Legislature it must be offered by a delegate or a senator or through a legislative committee. The bill is given a title, a number, and printed copies are made available to members of the Legislature. The bill is then assigned to an appropriate committee for study.

Hearings are usually conducted in which persons or groups may come before the committee to speak for or against the proposed legislation. When the committee concludes its deliberations, it has four possible courses of action. The majority may approve the bill, it may approve the bill with changes, it may disapprove, or it may make no recommendation. The bill is placed on the legislative calendar for further discussion and vote by the house in which it originated.

After debate and vote, the bill, if passed, is sent to the other house for its consideration. If the bill is passed by the second house in its original form, it will go to the governor for his signature. If the bill is changed through amendment, it must go back to the first house, and a conference committee appointed from the Senate and from the House of Delegates will attempt to work out a compromise bill that both branches of the Legislature will approve. If both houses approve the compromise bill, it will go to the governor for his signature.

If the governor signs the legislative act, it becomes the law of the state. If the governor "pocket vetoes" the act, it becomes law within five days without his signature. If he vetoes the bill, it returns to the house that originated the act and is reconsidered.

The Judicial Branch

The state courts make up the judicial division of the government of West Virginia. The highest court is the Supreme Court of Appeals. The Supreme Court is made up of five members who are elected by the people, and the court elects one of its members to be chief justice for a year. Its offices are in the state capitol.

Most cases which come to the Supreme Court of Appeals have been tried in a lower court and are appealed to the Supreme Court. This court also gives an opinion on whether particular laws are contrary to the constitution if in litigated cases the need arises. If the court rules that a law is contrary to the constitution, the law cannot be enforced. In this highest court of the state, no juries are called and no witnesses appear. Lawyers may appear to argue their clients' cases.

In West Virginia there are thirty-three circuit courts. Each court serves from one to three counties. These courts meet in the county

Enjoying the Beauty of His Home State A brook trout stream forms the falls on Seneca Creek in Pendleton County. *(Gerald S. Ratliff Photo, West Virginia Department of Commerce)*

courthouses of the state. All kinds of criminal and civil cases in which the amount involved is not less than fifty dollars are tried before these courts. In criminal cases, grand juries may be called by a circuit judge to decide whether a person should be held for trial. Circuit court judges are elected for eight-year terms.

There are various county courts. A county court is a constitutional body having probate jurisdiction and is largely a ministerial agency without real judicial function.

To provide other services the state Legislature may establish courts of limited jurisdiction within any county with the right of appeal to the circuit court. In some of the larger counties courts of limited jurisdiction have been created. In Kanawha County the intermediate court handles criminal cases, the juvenile court tries persons under eighteen years of age, the domestic relations court acts on divorces and other domestic matters, and the common pleas court tries civil cases.

County Governments

County governments, like the state government, have their own officials. Heading the county government are the county commissioners elected for six-year terms by the people. The commissioners constitute the county court, a body having both executive and judicial responsibilities. The court sets the amount of county taxes, serves as a board to see that no unfair taxes are collected, and appoints election officers. The clerk of the county preserves copies of the orders of the county court, the records of sales of property, tax records, records of finance, records of marriages, births, and deaths, and the wills of persons who have died.

The sheriff is the principal peace officer of the county. He makes arrests and acts as supervisor of the county jail. He also collects taxes and disburses money on orders from the county court and county board of education. The assessor determines the value of property of each individual in the county for purposes of taxation.

The county health officer is responsible for public health standards and regulations. The prosecuting attorney prepares the cases against all persons accused of crime and represents the government in the courts when the persons are tried for breaking the law. The coroner conducts examination into the cause of death when it is suspected that a person has not died of accidental or natural causes.

Notary publics witness the signing of important papers when the signer must have unquestioned proof that he himself has signed his

Jackson County Courthouse at Ripley

name. Notary publics also act as witnesses when a person takes an oath or swears to a statement. County boards of education direct the county school system and appoint a county superintendent who organizes and directs the school work. County surveyors determine boundary lines of property. The clerk of the circuit court maintains the records of the circuit court.

The sheriff, the assessor, and the prosecuting attorney are elected by the people for four-year terms. The members of the board of education and the clerk of the circuit court are elected by the people for six-year terms. Health officers and surveyors are appointed by the county court. Notary publics are appointed by the governor.

City and Town Governments

West Virginia towns and cities are divided into two classes: those with less than two thousand population and those with more than two thousand population. Towns and cities of more than two thousand may have charters of their own choosing and can utilize the mayor-council plan, the commission form, or the city-manager type of government. Those with less than two thousand persons have a charter with the mayor and councilman type of organization. The mayor, the councilmen, the recorder, the city clerk, and the treasurer are elected, and other officers are appointed.

Officers of the Federal Government

West Virginia also has elected federal officials. The state is represented in the United States Senate, the upper house of Congress, by two senators elected for six-year terms. The state is represented in the House of Representatives, the lower house of Congress, by four representatives elected for two-year terms. These officials must be residents of the state, and representatives are expected to reside in the district from which they are elected.

When the population of West Virginia was greater and the overall population of the United States was less, the state once had as many as six representatives in the House of Representatives. The results of the 1970 census, showing population loss in West Virginia, reduced the delegation in the House of Representatives from five to four.

Also within the state are federal officials such as revenue collectors, commissioners, and marshals, law-enforcing agents from Washington, D.C. As the state also falls into federal judicial districts which are supervised by federal judges, four federal judges serve the state. One federal judge is for the northern district, two federal judges for the southern district, and one federal judge is classified as a "roving" judge for the entire state, both north and south. Appeals from the decisions of these judges are heard in the Fourth Federal Circuit Court, which is composed of the states of West Virginia, Virginia, Maryland, North Carolina, and South Carolina.

Consultant to Governors and the Legislature

Carl M. Frasure, Political Scientist

Carl M. Frasure, born at Oakland, Ohio, in 1903, has served the state of West Virginia in numerous capacities since the late 1920's. After receiving a Ph.D. degree from Ohio State University in 1928 and engaging in graduate study at the University of Chicago and Cambridge University, England, Dr. Frasure joined the faculty of West Virginia University, serving that institution for forty-five years.

When he began his teaching career at West Virginia University in 1927, political science was part of the history department. It was made a separate unit in 1930, and Frasure became acting chairman in 1935. In 1940 Dr. Frasure was appointed chairman and in 1961 was appointed dean of the College of Arts and Sciences.

Dr. Frasure has served as a consultant to governors and the state Legislature in various capacities. Under Governors H. G. Kump (1933-37) and M. M. Neely (1941-45), he helped draft considerable legislation of the New Deal era. Under Governor Wallace Barron (1961-65) he advised the Tax Study Commission, a group whose recommendations included a personal income tax which subsequently became state law. During 1940-41 Frasure served as director of a merit-system study which resulted in the setting up of the state's Civil Service System. In 1942-43 Frasure was director of the State Office of Price Administration.

From 1944 to the present, Dr. Frasure has been a member, and since 1962 chairman, of the drafting committee which produces an annual volume on "Suggested State Legislation." He assumed direction of the Office of Price Stabilization for West Virginia in 1951 and the directorship of the West Virginia University Bureau of Government Research in 1949. In 1967 he became a member of the Citizens Advisory Committee on State Legislation and helped prepare a report which became the substance of the Legislative Improvement Amendment endorsed by the voters in 1970.

His work as a consultant to the federal government has been with the Office of Emergency Preparedness, the regional Economic Stabilization Commission, and the National Defense Executive Reserve.

West Virginia University has established an internship program in Dr. Frasure's name in honor of his service to the state. This program allows a select group of students to visit the state Legislature at each year's session and to participate in the processes of government.

A West Virginia Countryside   *(Gerald S. Ratliff Photo, West Virginia Department of Commerce)*

Chapter 36 IN CELEBRATION OF THE MOUNTAIN STATE

State Parks and State Forests

West Virginia's system of state parks and state forests is a celebrated and prideful feature. The state is a national leader in the development of vacation and recreation lands. The first West Virginia state parks were constructed in the 1930's. They featured log cabins with stone fireplaces, swimming pools, riding trails, and game courts. From the first they were immensely popular. The cabins were filled almost from the opening day.

Park facilities have been expanded and improved continuously. Many of the parks have been developed in rugged wilderness. Today, with their great beauty, luxurious lodges, standard and deluxe cabins, golf courses, riding and hiking trails, and, in suitable locations, ski facilities, the West Virginia state parks cater to more than 4,000,000 guests each year. Some parks provide accommodations the year round.

Each of the state forests covers thousands of acres. In them timber is grown and harvested scientifically, and here also game refuges are maintained. In most of the forests cabins, boating, swimming, fishing, riding, hiking, and children's playgrounds are enjoyed.

Overriding attractions at the state parks and forests are the expanse of natural beauty and the refreshing and stimulating atmosphere.

Hiking near Spruce Knob in Monongahela National Forest Spruce Knob is in Spruce Knob-Seneca Rocks National Recreation Area in the National Forest. *(U.S. Forest Service Photo)*

Small wayside parks and picnic areas are found along the highways of the state.

Oglebay Park at Wheeling (not in the system of West Virginia state parks) is a cultural center presenting music, opera, art exhibits, other exhibitions, sports.

Vacation Farms

West Virginia farmers are, perhaps, providing a West Virginia version of the Western ranch vacation. The state Department of Agriculture and Department of Commerce have worked together to develop the Farm Vacation Program. Farmers who subscribe to the program furnish rooms, food, and recreation for paying guests.

Accommodations for Sportsmen

The state Department of Agriculture and Department of Natural Resources together have developed the program that provides accommodations for sportsmen on West Virginia farms. The extensive forests and the contour-plowed and strip-farmed land in West Virginia attract wildlife, and sportsmen most likely find good accommodations at farms within reach of hunting areas. A folder can be obtained which contains a road map showing the location of public hunting grounds in West Virginia, the national forests, the state forests, state parks, and lakes.

West Virginia in the Space Age

West Virginia is the home of the National Radio Astronomy Observatory, a marvelous scientific plant which surpasses all others of its kind in the world. The observatory is at Green Bank in Pocahontas County. The giant telescopes are used to study space, to study the planets that are millions of miles away. The telescopes are also very sensitive radio receivers which bring in sounds from outer space. The observatory was designed with the support of the United States Government and through the National Science Foundation.

The Naval Radio Station Sugar Grove, at Sugar Grove, Pendleton County, West Virginia, about 30 air miles from the National Radio Astronomy Observatory at Green Bank, is a link in the United States

Administration Building at Watoga State Park, Pocahontas County The administration building at Watoga contains lodging rooms and a restaurant. The park lies in one of the wildest natural settings in West Virginia. *(Hal Dillon Photo, West Virginia Department of Natural Resources)*

Ninety-Seven-Foot Diameter Antenna, the Dominant Feature of the Etam, West Virginia, Station for Satellite Communications *(Communications Satellite Corporation Photo, Washington, D.C.)*

Navy's "Voice of Command." The station is in an area informally known as the National Radio Quiet Zone. The zone, which covers about 100 square miles, is relatively free from electromagnetic interference, is unique in the United States and in the free world is the only area so designated.

The Sugar Grove station is the main receiving facility for the Navy's global high-frequency radio communications and also for the Navy-operated Defense Communications System's long-range "point-to-point" circuits destined for Washington, D.C.

Youth Programs

West Virginia programs for youth are known nationally. Outstanding among them is the three-week National Youth Science Camp held annually at Camp Pocahontas, Bartow, West Virginia. The boys who gather there include two top high school senior science students from each of the fifty states. The camp was first conducted in 1963, West Virginia's centennial year, and was sponsored by the West Virginia Centennial Commission. Young scientists have continued to meet at the Science Camp, and the state of West Virginia has assumed sponsorship.

Resident staff members expert in particular fields and visiting authorities lead in the lecture program at the Science Camp. In a series of seminars the campers present their own scientific research projects, and a full schedule of athletic and camping activities is conducted. Visits to installations of scientific interest and to Washington, D.C., are usually included.

We have mentioned the Four-H Camp for boys and girls at Jackson's Mill. This is one of the most beautiful and useful of the state camps. Visitors from every state in the nation and from foreign countries come to observe this fine camp in operation.

Two projects aim to give boys and girls an understanding of the workings of state government. One project is the Mountaineer Boys State sponsored by the American Legion; the other is the Rhododendron Girls State sponsored by the American Legion Auxiliary. Both are conducted at Jackson's Mill. Six hundred boys and girls attend these camps each year.

Fairs and Festivals

In order to exhibit its individuality, not only to its visitors but also to its own citizens, the state has a variety of entertainment and

Competing in White Water Weekend Races *(Arnout Hyde, Jr., Photo, West Virginia Department of Natural Resources)*

county, regional, and state fairs and festivals offered from January through December. In the first month of the year, West Virginians may enjoy the Mountaineer Dinner Theatre on Teays Valley Road in Putnam County (the theatre is open the year round) and in the second month the Alpine Festival and Winter Skiing Carnival at Davis, which features ski and snowmobile events at the Blackwater Falls State Park.

March heralds the beginning of spring in West Virginia, and statewide observances acknowledge the blossoming of the redbud, serviceberry, and dogwood. By April Petersburg is prepared to host the White Water Weekend, featuring canoe and kayak races. Four historic towns in the Eastern Panhandle of the state, Harpers Ferry, Martinsburg, Shepherdstown, and Charles Town, sponsor house-and-garden tours within Jefferson and Berkeley counties. The state forests and the state parks make cabins and picnic facilities available in April.

By May West Virginia opens all its recreation areas, swimming pools, and restaurants at the state parks and forests. Richwood sponsors the Cranberry Mountain Spring Nature Tour and the Spring Nature Tour. Davis hosts the West Virginia Wildflower Pilgrimage at Blackwater Falls State Park. Camp Caesar invites visitors to enjoy the Webster County Nature Tour. A Southern

Coal Show at Bluefield, golf festivals at White Sulphur Springs, and a Mother's Day Ceremony at St. Andrew's Church at Grafton are scheduled.

The West Virginia Strawberry Festival at Buckhannon in June has attracted increasing numbers of persons since its inauguration in 1926. Most of the activities center at West Virginia Wesleyan College, featuring contests, art exhibits, parades, dancing, music, and the coronation of the strawberry king and queen.

In June, aspiring to make West Virginians aware of their cultural heritage, the West Virginia State Folk Festival is held at Glenville.

Tramway at Pipestem State Park Pipestem Resort in Summers and Mercer counties is the most spectacular state park development in West Virginia or anywhere in America. The tram carries guests to one of the lodges which is secluded at the base of Bluestone Gorge. *(David P. Cruise Photo, West Virginia Department of Commerce)*

Centering at Glenville State College, this festival has, since 1950, utilized in its programs such ballads as "John Henry" and "Barbara Allen" and "Sourwood Mountain" to relate traditions of the state. As summer officially begins, the Calhoun County Wood Festival at Grantsville, the Ohio Valley Amateur Golf Championship in Oglebay Park at Wheeling, and the Braxton County Regatta at Sutton attract crowds.

Beckley provides two outdoor musical dramas at Grandview State Park, "Hatfields and McCoys" and "Honey in the Rock," both productions inspired by West Virginia history. The Hatfields were mostly West Virginia Confederates; the McCoys were mostly Kentucky Unionists. Their disputes over boundary lines, encroachment upon each other's properties, elections, romances, and ownership of a razorback hog date from 1882. Their fighting and their feuding attracted nationwide attention, making them natural dramatic figures.

On stage Johnse Hatfield, the mountain Romeo, and Rose Anne McCoy, his Juliet, and bearded Devil Anse, the father of the Hatfield Clan, and Rand'l, leader of the McCoy Clan, present a powerful cast of characters. Both families suffered deaths, and their escapades even provoked rivalries between political personages. Governor Simon Bolivar Buckner of Kentucky and Governor Emanuel Willis Wilson of West Virginia became involved in the family disputes as did the Supreme Court of the United States. "Honey in the Rock," first presented in 1963, commemorates West Virginia's attaining statehood and represents the Civil War period.

In July Fourth of July celebrations are held around the state. Those at Ripley and Alderson are especially noteworthy. Ripley also hosts the Mountain State Art and Craft Fair at Cedar Lakes. The spinning, weaving, and woodcarving of pioneer days are featured, as are the ancient domestic skills of making apple butter and home canning. At Marlinton, pioneer folkways are demonstrated at Pocahontas County Pioneer Days. St. Albans sponsors a fair, and Moorefield plays host to the West Virginia Poultry Festival.

August is a festive month. The Magnolia Fair at Matewan, the Bluestone Valley Fair at Spanishburg, the Tyler County Fair at Middlebourne, the Paw Paw District Fair at Rivesville, the Jackson County Junior Fair at Ripley, the Nicholas County Fair at Summersville, and the Tri-County Fair at Augusta crowd the calendar.

Unusual is the Cherry River Festival at Richwood. This festival has sometimes been concluded with a parade of admirals and one

Spinning Exhibit at Mountain State Art and Craft Fair Spinning and weaving provide two of the most popular exhibits at this fair, which is held at Cedar Lakes. *(West Virginia Department of Agriculture Photo)*

deckhand from the "Cherry River Navy" and its flagship, *The Clothespin*. Lewisburg hosts the State Fair of West Virginia, held annually since 1923. Central features are the horse show and races. Of special interest is the West Virginia Oil and Gas Festival at Sistersville. The State Dairy Cattle Show, exhibiting champion dairy cattle and farm equipment, is held at Jackson's Mill, near Weston.

Since 1941 Kingwood has sponsored the Preston County Buckwheat Festival in September. The various women's groups of the county serve buckwheat cakes, sausages, syrup, apple sauce, and coffee. There are parades, fireworks, and the crowning of "Queen Ceres." Philippi hosts the Barbour County Street Fair; Camp Caesar, the Webster County Fair; Circleville, the Pendleton County Fair; and Hendricks, the Hick Fair.

chapter thirty-six / in celebration of the mountain state

Beckley promotes the Appalachian Arts and Crafts Festival; Hinton, the West Virginia Water Festival. Glenville is the scene of the Gilmer County Farm Show, and Summersville scene of the Nicholas County Potato Festival. New Martinsville sponsors a regatta, as does Huntington. Arnoldsburg supports the Molasses Festival and Fair. Parkersburg has the Annual Harvest Moon Festival, and Franklin, the Treasure Mountain Festival. To complete a perfect month of recreation, the squirrel, mourning dove, and migratory game bird hunting season opens in West Virginia.

In October Elkins sponsors the Mountain State Forest Festival. Held since 1930 on the campus of Davis and Elkins College, the festival witnesses the coronation of "Queen Sylvia" and other forest princesses representing the congressional and state senatorial districts. Richwood opens the annual Autumn Nature Tour. Spencer sponsors the Black Walnut Festival. This festival features foods made with black walnuts and wood items made from the black walnut tree. The grouse, turkey, and raccoon hunting season opens as well as the deer and black bear bow-hunting season.

November signals the deer and black bear firearm hunting season, the rabbit, quail, and ring-necked pheasant hunting season, and the trapping season for raccoon, muskrat, mink, and beaver. The Chrysanthemum Show in Oglebay Park at Wheeling is another event of the eleventh month.

December finds the ski slopes open at Canaan Valley, Chestnut Ridge, Oglebay Park, and Alpine Lake. Special winter rates at the state park lodges at Blackwater Falls, Cacapon, Hawks Nest, Pipestem, and Twin Falls are in effect.

Other Popular Features

To complete the recreational and amusement facilities of West Virginia, the state has endorsed for sportsmen a year-round fishing season for all species of fish.

The Beckley Exhibition Mine provides an opportunity to inspect an actual coal mine and see the machinery used in mining. At French Creek Game Farm visitors may see a live buffalo, rattlesnake, copperhead, and black bear.

The state capitol, an architectural masterpiece, is one of the most beautiful capitols in the United States. It was designed by the famous architect Cass Gilbert and was completed in February 1932. The state museum at Charleston is another important attraction; it incorporates a collection of frontier artifacts.

Canaan Valley State Park Ski Slope The new $2,500,000 winter sports complex at Canaan Valley will be on a par with Vermont and New Hampshire winter sports centers. *(Gerald S. Ratliff Photo, West Virginia Department of Commerce)*

Huntington Galleries in Huntington feature paintings and sculptures, both American and European, as well as prayer rugs, tapestries, and collections of silver and firearms. "Sunrise," once the home of Governor William G. MacCorkle, in Charleston, houses a museum and (in an adjacent building) an art gallery, and offers many special projects and programs. At Oglebay Park in Wheeling is the Mansion Museum.

At Grafton may be viewed the Mother's Day Shrine, in honor of Anna Jarvis, who originated Mother's Day on May 10, 1908.

Racing is enjoyed at the Charles Town Turf Club and at Shenandoah Downs, Charles Town; at Waterford Park, Chester; and at the Wheeling Downs, Wheeling. Jamboree U. S. A. is held every Saturday night at Wheeling.

chapter thirty-six / in celebration of the mountain state

Fishing the South Branch of the Potomac River This is a scene in the Monongahela National Forest in West Virginia. *(U.S. Forest Service Photo)*

The West Virginia Athlete

Jerry West, Super Star

Jerry West, former All-American basketball star at West Virginia University and standout with the Los Angeles Lakers of the National Basketball Association, is representative of West Virginians who have become well known in the area of sports. Jerry, with colorful, flattering, and apt nicknames, like Mr. Clutch and Mr. Consistency, was born on May 28, 1938 at Chelyan, Kanawha County.

Slowly but surely Jerry West climbed the rungs of the basketball ladder. At East Bank High School he scored an average of only three points per game in his sophomore year, but that season he had broken his foot and played only eight games. The next year he averaged 24 points per game, and in his senior year he led his high school to its first state championship. West averaged 34 points per game, and he furnished numerous assists and rebounds in each game he played.

During his outstanding varsity career at West Virginia University, West averaged 24.8 points and 13.3 rebounds per game, shot 50.6 percent from the floor and 73.2 percent from the foul line, and managed 261 assists. He wound up rewriting the record book with the most points, the most rebounds, the most field goals, and the most free throws.

Jerry stole the show on many occasions and received loud and lengthy standing ovations from enthusiastic and appreciative crowds while he led the school into various championships. To top off an excellent college career, West was chosen one of the captains for the 1960 United States Olympic basketball team, and he was singled out by the players themselves in the presentation of the Gold Medal to the team from America. One of the great compliments they paid to West was that he was essentially a team player.

Jerry West inevitably moved into a professional career in basketball. Having played his entire professional career with the Los Angeles Lakers, West became the most dedicated athlete in Los Angeles history. The statistics Jerry has amassed have been phenomenal. He has scored more than 20,000 points, made over 7,000 free throws, and contributed in excess of 5,000 assists. In 1972 he was instrumental in leading his team to the National Basketball Association championship for the first time.

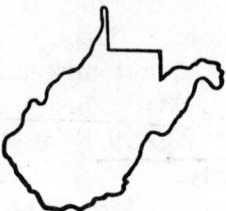

West Virginia has passed from a condition of undisturbed wealth, through a period of exploitation and quick extraction, into a modern period of conservation. The pioneer of an earlier period has simply been replaced by today's pioneer who adopts new methods and techniques for the preservation of the thirty-fifth state.

Each generation finds its own special role to play in history. West Virginia's current generation, with a rich heritage, has a vital assignment. But, despite the new assignments and new roles, the spirit of the state motto, Montani semper liberi—Mountaineers are always free—remains among the people.

Appendix A

West Virginia Governors

APPENDIX A

WEST VIRGINIA GOVERNORS

West Virginia has had twenty-eight governors. All but six of these men were born either in West Virginia or, in the earlier years, in that part of Virginia which became West Virginia. Under the first state constitution, which was adopted in 1863, the governor was elected for a term of two years and could be reelected for any number of terms. The state constitution which was adopted in 1872 limited the governor's term to four years; an amendment adopted in 1970 permits the governor to succeed himself in office.

The First Governor — *Arthur Ingram Boreman*

West Virginia's first governor was born in Waynesburg, Pennsylvania, July 24, 1823, but when he was a child, his parents moved to Tyler County, now in West Virginia. He attended the local schools, studied law, and was licensed to practice law at the age of twenty. Boreman was a member of the Virginia legislature for six years just before the Civil War. Later he was judge of the circuit court in Parkersburg.

He presided over the Wheeling Convention which reorganized the government of Virginia in an effort to retain the state's loyalty to the Union. On June 20, 1863, the day West Virginia was admitted to the Union as a separate state, Boreman became governor. He was reelected to the office twice, serving until February 26, 1869. He was elected to the United States Senate, and five days before the end of his last term as governor, he resigned to begin his duties as United States senator from West Virginia. Completing his term in the Senate in 1875, he returned to his home in Parkersburg, where he died April 19, 1896.

The Second Governor — *Daniel Duane Tompkins Farnsworth*

The second governor was born on Staten Island, New York, December 23, 1819. When he was two years old, his family moved to Buckhannon, Upshur County, now in West Virginia. Farnsworth worked as a tailor, then as a storekeeper, and then as a farmer. In 1861 he was elected a member of the Virginia legislature but, instead of assuming his duties in the legislature, he took part in the Wheeling Convention which reorganized the government of Virginia. He was a member of the first House of Delegates of West Virginia and later of the West Virginia Senate, which he served as president.

When Governor Boreman resigned to begin his duties as a United States senator, Farnsworth, the president of the West Virginia Senate, became governor. He held the office only five days, from February 27 to March 3, when the regularly elected governor took office. Farnsworth was a member of the Second Constitutional Convention in 1872. He died in Buckhannon on December 5, 1892.

The Third Governor — *William Erskine Stevenson*

The third governor was born in Warren, Pennsylvania, March 18, 1820. He was a member of the legislature of Pennsylvania in 1856. The following year he moved to Wood County, now in West Virginia, where he purchased a farm. He was a member of the Constitutional Convention in 1861 and of the West Virginia Senate from 1863 to 1868.

Stevenson was president of the Senate three years. In 1868 he was elected governor of West Virginia and served one term of two years. He died in Parkersburg on November 29, 1883.

The Fourth Governor — *John Jeremiah Jacob*

The fourth governor was born in Hampshire County, now in West Virginia, December 9, 1829. He attended Romney Academy and graduated from Dickinson College. He was a professor at the University of Missouri for seven years but returned to Romney and began the practice of law in 1865. He was elected to the West Virginia House of Delegates in 1869, and the following year was elected governor of West Virginia. During this term of office, the present state constitution was written and adopted.

Jacob ran for a second term as governor and was again elected. He was the first governor to serve a four-year term. When his term of office ended in 1877, he moved to Wheeling. In 1879 he was elected to the West Virginia House of Delegates and later was appointed judge of the circuit court. He died in Wheeling on November 24, 1893.

The Fifth Governor — *Henry Mason Mathews*

The fifth governor was born in Frankfort, Greenbrier County, now in West Virginia, March 29, 1834. He attended Lewisburg Academy, graduated from the University of Virginia, graduated in law from the school of Judge Brockenbrough in Lexington, Virginia, and became a professor in Allegheny College at Blue Sulphur Springs.

Mathews served in the Confederate army and then returned to Lewisburg. He was elected to the West Virginia Senate, but he refused to take the "test oath," and because of his having fought in the Confederate army, he failed to qualify for his seat in the Senate. He was a member of the Constitutional Convention of 1872, served as attorney general of the state, and was elected governor in 1876. At the end of his term, he returned to Lewisburg, where he practiced law until his death on April 28, 1884.

The Sixth Governor — *Jacob Beeson Jackson*

The sixth governor was born in Parkersburg April 6, 1829. He began the practice of law in St. Marys. He served as prosecuting attorney of Pleasants County for nine years, returned to Parkersburg, and served as prosecuting attorney of Wood County, as mayor of Parkersburg, and as a member of the West Virginia House of Delegates.

In 1880 Jackson was elected governor of West Virginia. At the end of his term of office, he returned to Parkersburg, where he died December 11, 1893.

The Seventh Governor — *Emanuel Willis Wilson*

The seventh governor was born at Harpers Ferry August 11, 1844. He was a lawyer. In 1870 he was elected to the West Virginia House of Delegates, and two years later to the West Virginia Senate. In 1884 he was elected governor of West Virginia.

When the result of the next election, in 1888, was questioned, Wilson continued in office until the result was made clear and Governor A. B. Fleming was inaugurated, February 6, 1890. At the end of Wilson's term of office, he practiced law in Charleston, where he died May 28, 1905.

The Eighth Governor — *Aretas Brooks Fleming*

The eighth governor was born in Fairmont October 15, 1839. He studied law at the University of Virginia, began the practice of his profession in 1863, and the same year was elected prosecuting attorney of Marion County. In 1872 and 1875 he served in the West Virginia House of Delegates.

In 1878 Fleming was appointed judge of the circuit court. In 1888 he was nominated for governor, but on election day his opponent, Nathan Goff, appeared to have been elected. The election was contested, however, and in 1890 the Legislature declared Fleming to be the governor. At the end of Governor Fleming's term of office, he returned to his home in Fairmont, resumed the practice of law, and took part in various business activities, including the development of coal mines. He died there on October 13, 1923.

The Ninth Governor — *William Alexander MacCorkle*

The ninth governor was born in Lexington, Virginia, May 7, 1857. He graduated from the College of Law at Washington and Lee University in 1879 and in that same year began the practice of law in Charleston. The following year he was elected prosecuting attorney of Kanawha County.

In 1892, at the age of thirty-five, MacCorkle was elected governor of West Virginia. At the end of his term of office he resumed the practice of law but devoted most of his time to industrial development in the Kanawha Valley. In 1910 he was elected to the West Virginia Senate and served one term. He wrote several books, among which are *The Monroe Doctrine*, *The Book of the White Sulphur Springs*, and *Recollections of Fifty Years in West Virginia*. He died in Charleston on September 24, 1930.

The Tenth Governor — George Wesley Atkinson

The tenth governor was born in Kanawha County June 29, 1845. He graduated from Ohio Wesleyan University in 1870 and later studied law at Columbia University. He began the practice of law in Charleston but soon moved to Wheeling. He was United States internal revenue agent, served one term in the United States Congress, and was elected governor of West Virginia in 1896. At the close of his term, he was appointed United States attorney for the Southern District of West Virginia and later was made associate judge of the court of claims.

Atkinson was the author of a number of books, including *The History of Kanawha County*, *The West Virginia Pulpit*, *After the Moonshiners*, *Political Economy*, *Prominent Men of West Virginia*, *Psychology Simplified*, *Chips and Whetstones*, and *Bench and Bar of West Virginia*. Governor Atkinson was the leading literary man among the governors of this state. He died in Charleston on April 4, 1925.

The Eleventh Governor — Albert Blakeslee White

The eleventh governor was born in Cleveland, Ohio, September 22, 1856. He attended elementary and high schools in Columbus, Ohio, graduated with highest honors from Marietta College in 1878, and in the same year entered the newspaper business in Lafayette, Indiana.

In 1881 White came to Parkersburg, where he owned and published the *State Journal* for eight years. He served three terms as collector of internal revenue for this state. He was president of the National Editorial Association and president of the West Virginia Press Association.

White was elected governor of West Virginia in 1900. At the close of his term of office, he returned to Parkersburg and engaged in banking and other business. In 1907 he was appointed state tax commissioner and served two years. In 1936 he was elected a member of the West Virginia Senate. He died in Parkersburg on July 3, 1941.

The Twelfth Governor — William Mercer Owens Dawson

The twelfth governor was born in Bloomington, Maryland, May 21, 1853. When he was ten years old, his parents moved to West

Virginia. Dawson worked in a cooper shop, clerked in a store, and taught school. When he was twenty years old, he became editor of the *Preston County Journal*. Dawson began the practice of law in 1891, served as a member of the West Virginia Senate from 1881 to 1889, was appointed secretary of state in 1897, and served two terms. He was elected governor of West Virginia in 1904. After his term of office, he made his home in Charleston, where he died March 12, 1916.

The Thirteenth Governor — *William Ellsworth Glasscock*

The thirteenth governor was born on a farm in Monongalia County December 13, 1862. He attended country schools and West Virginia University, taught school for a number of years, and served a term as county superintendent of schools of Monongalia County. In 1902 he began the practice of law with his brother.

Glasscock was collector of internal revenue for a time but resigned to become a candidate for governor. He was elected governor of West Virginia in 1908. At the close of his term of office he returned to Morgantown, where he continued to practice law until his death on April 12, 1925.

The Fourteenth Governor — *Henry Drury Hatfield*

The fourteenth governor was born on Mate Creek, Logan County, September 15, 1875. He attended local schools; graduated from Franklin College, New Athens, Ohio, in 1890; graduated in medicine from the University of Louisville when he was nineteen years old; studied further in New York University, New York Polyclinic Medical School, and Cornell University School of Medicine; and practiced medicine in McDowell County.

Hatfield took an active interest in politics, became a member of the county court and later a member of the West Virginia Senate. He served as president of the Senate in 1911. In 1912 he was elected governor of West Virginia.

In World War I Hatfield served in the medical corps of the United States Army. Later he established hospitals in Huntington and Logan. In 1928 he was elected a member of the United States Senate. At the close of his term as senator, he returned to Huntington to continue the practice of medicine. Dr. Hatfield had a distinguished career both in the field of politics and the field of medicine and surgery. He died on October 25, 1962.

The Fifteenth Governor — *John Jacob Cornwell*

The fifteenth governor was born in Ritchie County, West Virginia, July 11, 1867. When he was a small child, his family moved to Hampshire County. He attended Shepherd College and West Virginia University. In 1890 he became principal owner and publisher of the *Hampshire Review*.

Cornwell was an editor, lawyer, financier, and politician. He was a member of the West Virginia Senate from 1896 to 1906 and was a candidate for governor in 1904. He was elected governor of West Virginia in 1916. At the end of his term of office, Governor Cornwell became attorney for the Baltimore and Ohio Railroad, then chief counsel, then vice-president. Retiring from the company and returning to Romney, he edited the *Hampshire Review*. He died on September 8, 1953.

The Sixteenth Governor — *Ephraim Franklin Morgan*

The sixteenth governor was born in Forksburg, Marion County, January 16, 1869. He attended local schools and Fairmont State Normal School, taught school for some years, graduated in law from West Virginia University in 1897, and the following year began the practice of law in Fairmont.

From 1907 to 1913 Morgan was judge of the intermediate court of Marion County and then was appointed a member of the Public Service Commission. In 1920 he was elected governor of West Virginia. Soon after his term ended, he was appointed solicitor of the United States Department of Commerce. He retired from this position in 1933 and continued to live in Washington until his death on January 15, 1950.

The Seventeenth Governor — *Howard Mason Gore*

The seventeenth governor was born near Clarksburg October 12, 1877, attended rural schools and Clarksburg High School, and graduated from West Virginia University in 1900. He became interested in agriculture and in raising livestock, was assistant secretary of agriculture of the United States, and later was named secretary of agriculture by President Coolidge.

Gore was elected governor of West Virginia in 1924. At the end of his term of office, he returned to his home, where he continued his interest in livestock activities. He was appointed state commissioner of agriculture and served from 1931 to 1933. In 1944 he was appointed a member of the Public Service Commission of West Virginia and served until his death on June 20, 1947.

The Eighteenth Governor — *William Gustavus Conley*

The eighteenth governor was born on a farm near Kingwood in Preston County January 8, 1866. He attended local schools, taught school for five years, served as superintendent of schools in Preston County for one term, graduated in law from West Virginia University in 1893, and began the practice of law in Parsons. He served as councilman and mayor of Parsons and prosecuting attorney of Tucker County. He was one of the founders of the *Parsons Advocate*.

In 1903 Conley returned to Kingwood to practice law. Here he served as a member of the council and as mayor. In 1908 he was appointed attorney general of West Virginia to serve an unexpired term and was then elected for a full term.

In 1913 he began practicing law in Charleston. In 1928 he was elected governor of West Virginia. At the close of his term of office, he resumed his practice in Charleston, where he died October 21, 1940.

The Nineteenth Governor — *Herman Guy Kump*

The nineteenth governor was born October 31, 1877 at Capon Springs, Hampshire County. He attended public schools, was taught by private tutors, graduated in law from the University of Virginia in 1903, and two years later began the practice of law in Elkins. He served as prosecuting attorney of Randolph County for two terms, was elected mayor of Elkins in 1921 and judge of the circuit court in 1928.

Kump was elected governor of West Virginia in 1932. At the close of his term of office, he returned to Elkins and resumed the practice of his profession. He died on February 14, 1962.

The Twentieth Governor — *Homer Adams Holt*

The twentieth governor was born near Lewisburg, Greenbrier County, March 1, 1898. He attended Greenbrier Military Academy and graduated from Washington and Lee University in 1918. He served in the Coast Artillery in World War I and returned to Washington and Lee, where he taught mathematics and studied law. After graduating in law in 1923 and serving as professor of law at the University for two years, he resigned and began the practice of law in Fayetteville.

In 1932 Holt was elected attorney general of West Virginia and four years later was elected governor of the state. At the close of his term, he opened a law office in Charleston.

The Twenty-First Governor — *Matthew Mansfield Neely*

The twenty-first governor was born at Grove, Doddridge County, November 9, 1874. He taught school, attended Salem College and West Virginia University, but left his studies to enlist as a private in the Spanish-American War. He returned to the University, graduated in 1901, and graduated in law the following year. He practiced law in Fairmont and was elected mayor there in 1908.

Two years later Neely was elected to the West Virginia House of Delegates. In 1913 he was elected a member of the Congress of the United States, was reelected four times, served in the United States Senate from 1923 to 1929 and from 1932 to 1941. He resigned from the Senate to become governor of West Virginia in 1941. In 1946 he was elected to the House of Representatives of the United States and in 1948 was again elected to the United States Senate. He died on January 18, 1958.

The Twenty-Second Governor — *Clarence Watson Meadows*

The twenty-second governor was born in Beckley February 11, 1904. He graduated from Georgia Military Academy, attended Washington and Lee University, and graduated in law from the University of Alabama in 1927. He began the practice of law in Beckley, represented Raleigh County in the West Virginia Legislature in 1931-32, served a term as prosecuting attorney of Raleigh County, was elected attorney general of West Virginia in 1936 and reelected in 1940.

Meadows resigned from that position, was appointed judge of the tenth judicial circuit, and was then elected to this office. He was elected governor of West Virginia in 1944. At the close of his term of office, he continued to live in Charleston, where he practiced law and had other business interests. He died on September 12, 1961.

The Twenty-Third Governor — Okey L. Patteson

The twenty-third governor was born in Mingo County September 14, 1898. He attended public schools, graduated from West Virginia Wesleyan College, and continued study at Carnegie Institute of Technology in Pittsburgh. He served as a member of the county court, as sheriff of Fayette County, and as administrative assistant to Governor Meadows.

Patteson was elected governor of West Virginia in 1948. At the end of his term as governor, he made his home in Mount Hope.

The Twenty-Fourth Governor — William C. Marland

The twenty-fourth governor was born in Johnson City, Illinois, March 26, 1918. He attended public schools in Glen Rogers, Wyoming County, West Virginia; received an A.B. degree from the University of Alabama in 1940 and the LL.B. degree from West Virginia University in 1947.

Marland was appointed law clerk to Federal Judge Ben Moore in 1947; appointed assistant attorney general in 1948; appointed attorney general in 1949, and elected attorney general in 1950. Marland was elected governor of West Virginia November 4, 1952. He died in Barrington, Illinois, on November 26, 1965.

The Twenty-Fifth Governor — Cecil H. Underwood

The twenty-fifth governor was born in Joseph's Mills, Tyler County, November 5, 1922. He attended public schools in Tyler County; received the A.B. degree from Salem College in 1943 and the M.A. degree from West Virginia University in 1952. He taught in high school 1943-46; was a member of the staff of Marietta College in 1946-50; and was vice-president of Salem College in 1950-56. In 1944, at twenty-two, he was elected to the West Virginia House of Delegates and was reelected in 1946, 1948, 1950, 1952, 1954.

Underwood was elected governor of West Virginia on November 6, 1956. He was nominated by the Republican Party for United States Senate in 1960. He served as temporary chairman of the Republican National Convention in Chicago, Illinois, July 23-27, 1960. He became director of civic affairs for the northeast region, Monsanto Company, with offices in Nitro, West Virginia. In May 1972 Underwood was selected as president of Bethany College, Bethany, West Virginia.

The Twenty-Sixth Governor — *William Wallace Barron*

The twenty-sixth governor was born December 8, 1911 in Elkins. He attended public schools in Randolph County; received an A.B. degree from Washington and Lee University and the LL.B. degree from West Virginia University. He served a term as mayor of Elkins and held other appointive positions in Randolph County. He was elected to the West Virginia House of Delegates from Randolph County in 1950 and 1952.

Barron was appointed chairman of the West Virginia Liquor Control Commission and served 1953-55. He was elected attorney general of the state in 1956. On November 8, 1960, he was elected governor of West Virginia. At the conclusion of his term as governor, he practiced law in Charleston.

In 1968 Barron was acquitted of federal charges linking him to a bribery conspiracy. In 1971 he was charged with bribing a juror in the federal case, was indicted, pled guilty, was fined and sentenced to prison.

The Twenty-Seventh Governor — *Hulett C. Smith*

The twenty-seventh governor was born at Beckley, Raleigh County, October 21, 1918. He attended Beckley public schools and Beckley College. In 1938 he was graduated with honors from the Wharton School of Finance and Commerce of the University of Pennsylvania, and has received the honorary LL.D. degree from Beckley College, Concord College, West Virginia University, and Marshall University. Bethany College gave him an honorary Doctor of Public Affairs degree.

Active in business and civic affairs in his native city since young manhood, Smith has been chiefly interested in the field of insurance, holding the professional designation of Chartered Property and Casualty Underwriter, which he earned in 1948. He was commissioned ensign, U.S. Navy, March 15, 1942; served in the Atlantic in World War II; was discharged as lieutenant commander. He has been a licensed private air pilot since 1940 and served as chairman or member of the West Virginia Aeronautics Commission from 1947 through 1959.

Smith was chairman of the State Democratic Committee from 1956 until 1961. He was appointed the first commissioner of the West Virginia Department of Commerce in 1961 and served until 1963 when he resigned to enter the campaign for governor. He was elected governor of West Virginia at the general election on November 3, 1964.

The Twenty-Eighth Governor — Arch A. Moore, Jr.

The twenty-eighth governor was born in Moundsville, West Virginia, April 16, 1923. He attended public schools. He served as a combat infantry sergeant in World War II, European Theater; was seriously wounded in Germany; and was awarded the Purple Heart Medal. He studied at Lafayette College, Easton, Pennsylvania, 1943; received the A.B. degree from West Virginia University in 1948 and the LL.B. degree from the same university in 1951.

Moore was a member of the law firm of Moore and Moore in Moundsville. In 1952 he was elected to the West Virginia Legislature and in 1956 to the United States House of Representatives, where he served six consecutive terms. With each election his majority increased. He was the fourth-ranking Republican on the Judiciary Committee; ranking minority member of the Select Committee on Small Business, the Sub-Committee on Immigration, and the Sub-Committee on Interstate Taxation; member of the Joint House-Senate Committee on Immigration and Naturalization Policy of House and Senate; and author of the Criminal Justice Act of 1964, which is considered one of the major accomplishments of the 88th Congress. For his work in Congress in developing understanding among nations he was awarded Italy's "Cross of Commander in the Order to the Merit of the Italian Republic," the highest decoration Italy can bestow upon a non-Italian.

Moore was a delegate to the National Republican Convention in 1964 and member of the Platform Committee; Republican national committeeman from West Virginia. At the general election in November 1968 he was elected governor of West Virginia; was elected chairman of the National Governor's Conference September 1971, was reelected governor of West Virginia November 1972, the first West Virginia governor permitted under the governor's succession amendment to succeed himself in office.

Appendix B

**United States
Senators
From
West Virginia
1863–1974**

APPENDIX B

UNITED STATES SENATORS FROM WEST VIRGINIA

Peter G. Van Winkle 1863-1869
Waitman T. Willey 1863-1871
Arthur I. Boreman 1869-1875

Henry G. Davis 1871-1883
Allen T. Caperton 1875-1876
Samuel Price 1876-1877

Frank Hereford 1877-1881
Johnson N. Camden 1881-1887
John E. Kenna 1883-1893

Charles J. Faulkner 1887-1899
Johnson N. Camden 1893-1895
Stephen B. Elkins 1895-1911

Nathan B. Scott 1899-1911
Davis Elkins 1911-1912
Clarence W. Watson 1911-1913

William E. Chilton 1911-1917
Nathan Goff 1913-1919
Howard Sutherland 1917-1923

Davis Elkins 1919-1925
Matthew M. Neely 1923-1929
Guy D. Goff 1925-1931

Henry D. Hatfield 1929-1935
[1]Matthew M. Neely 1931-1941
Rush D. Holt 1935-1941

Harley M. Kilgore 1941-1956
[2]Joseph Rosier 1941-1942
[3]Hugh Ike Shott, Sr. 1942-1943

Chapman Revercomb 1943-1949
Matthew M. Neely 1949-1958
[4]William R. Laird, III 1956-1956

Chapman Revercomb 1956-1959
[5]Jack D. Hoblitzell, Jr. 1958-1959
Robert C. Byrd 1959-
[6]Jennings Randolph 1959-

---

[1]Resigned to become governor on January 12, 1941.
[2]Appointed by Governor M. M. Neely January 13, 1941 to fill unexpired term of M. M. Neely as U. S. senator. Served until November 3, 1942.
[3]Elected for short term from November 3, 1942 to January 3, 1943.
[4]Appointed March 13, 1956 by Governor W. C. Marland to fill vacancy caused by death of Senator Harley M. Kilgore on February 29, 1956. Served until November 6, 1956.
[5]Appointed January 25, 1958 by Governor Cecil H. Underwood to fill vacancy caused by death of M. M. Neely on January 18, 1958.
[6]Elected November 4, 1958 to fill unexpired term ending January 1961.

ACKNOWLEDGMENTS

For the privilege of reproducing illustrations the authors and publisher are grateful to the following: Agencies of the United States government, the West Virginia University Library, the Kanawha County Public Library, the West Virginia universities and state colleges, the private colleges, the various West Virginia state departments and agencies, the industries, organizations and individuals, and the *Journal of the National Medical Association*, September, 1970.

INDEX

A

Abolitionists, 229
Academies, early, 176-78
Accommodations for sportsmen, 440
Adena culture, 51, 59
Admission to the Union, approved by United States Senate, House of Representatives, President Lincoln, 277; Lincoln's proclamation, 278-79
Agricultural College, 343, 375, 377
Agricultural Experiment Station, 343, 350
Agriculture, early, 181-82; improvement, 341-43; products, 345-49; number, size, value of farms (1900-1970), 348
Airports, 365
Albertazzie, Colonel Ralph D., 410
Albright, town of, 261
Alderson, Rev. John, 134
Alderson, town of, 134, 172, 446
Alderson-Broaddus College, 381, 392
Aliquippa, Queen, 99
Allegheny, the name, 68
Allegheny College, 173
Allegheny Front, 4, 5, 15
Allegheny Highlands, 15-17
Allegheny Mountains, 3, 306
Allegheny Plateau, 4, 5, 8, 15, 16

Allegheny Power System, 371
Allen, James E., 410
Alloy, 367
Almanacs, 193
Alpine Festival and Winter Skiing Carnival, 444
Alpine Lake, 448
Alum Rock, 31
Amax Specialty Metals, Incorporated, 367
Ambler, Charles Henry, 413
American Cyanamid Company, 369
American Electric Power System, 371
American Federation of Labor, 332
American Legion, 443
American Legion Auxiliary, 443
Amtrak, 312
Anglican Church, 166
Animal life, 19-21
Appalachia, 3; map, 4; 39; state of, proposed, 222
"Appalachia," meaning of, 68
Appalachian Arts and Crafts Festival, 448
Appalachian Bible Institute, 382
Appalachian Corridors (highways), 362-64; picture, 363
Appalachian Divide, 309
Appalachian Mountains, 3, 5, 75, 77
Appalachian Power Company, 371

473

Appalachian Redevelopment Act, 362
Apples, 346-47
Arbuckle, Matthew, 69
Archaeological discoveries, 47-55
Archaic Foragers, 59
Arden, 169
Area of state, 5, 37
Arnoldsburg, 448
Art galleries and museums, Charleston, 449, picture, 376; Huntington, 449; Wheeling, 440, 449, picture, 288
Arthur, Gabriel, 77, 78
Arthurdale, 423-24
Articles of Confederation, 137-38
Asbury, Bishop Francis, 173-74, 179-80
Athens, 375, 379
Atkeson, Thomas C., 343, 348, 355-56
Atkinson, Governor George Wesley, 415; *see* 416-17; 459
Atlantic Coastal Plain, 3
Augusta, 446
Autumn Nature Tour, 448
Averell, General W. W., 262

B

Bailey, Anne, 148-49
Bailey, Cleveland, 422
Baker, Newton D., 413-14, 423
Bald Knob, 314
Baltimore and Ohio Railroad, 207-16, 305, 306
Baptist Church, early, 172-73, 233, 234, 381
Barbe, Waitman T., 413
Barbour County, 66; formation of, 223; 349
Barboursville, 382
Barron, Governor William Wallace, 421; *see* two paragraphs; 465
Bartow, 443
Bath, town of, 32, 160, 205
Battelle, Gordon, 178, 233, 275, 289

Battle at Carnifex Ferry, 257
Battle of Allegheny Mountain, 259
Battle of Greenbrier River, 259
Battle of Lake Erie, 188
Battle of Philippi, 254
Battle of Point Pleasant, 120; results, 123; 127
Battle of Rich Mountain, 254-55
Battle of the Monongahela River, 101-2
Battle of The Trough, 103
Battleship *West Virginia*, 401, 402
Batts, Thomas, 75-77
Bears, 20; state animal picture, 20
Beckley, 40, 312, 446, 448
Beckley College, 384
Beckley Exhibition Mine, 448
"Bee line" for Boston, 134
Belington, 66, 306
Belle, 368
Belleville, 134
Benedum, Michael L., 327-28
Benedum Airport, 365
Bennett, Lieutenant Lewis, 405
Bens Run, 48, 54
Benwood, 330
Berkeley, Governor William, 74
Berkeley County, 4, 15, 35, 92, 93, 100, 103; created, 112; 134, 167, 169, 171; slaves, 218; 219, 228, 242, 253, 275, 281; admission to West Virginia, 298-99; 331, 346, 357, 444
Berkeley Springs, 32, 114, 180, 202, 205
Bethany, 172, 381, 392
Bethany College, 172, 177; picture, 177; 179, 381, 392
Beverly, picture, 90
Bienville, Celeron de, 80, 96
"Big Moses" gas well, 325-26
Big Sandy River, 7, 9, 68, 103
Birds, 20-21; state bird picture, 21
Bishop, John Peale, 413
Blacks, 42, 227-29, 238, 277, 312, 321, 379, 387-98; number of Negroes, 388; centers of population, 388; schools,

388-90; integration, 390-92; notable blacks, 392-98; 404, 408
Blacksville, 331
Black Walnut Festival, 448
Blackwater Falls, 28, 29; picture, 29
Blackwater Falls State Park, 444, 448
Blair, Jacob B., 283, 287-88
Bland, Edward, 74, 75
Blenko Glass Company, 369
Blennerhassett, Harman, 156, 157, 162-63, 241
Blennerhassett Island, 47, 156, 163
Blockhouse, 154-55
"Bloody year of the three sevens," 127
"Bloomery," the, 187
Bluefield, 5, 67, 134, 144, 309, 365, 373, 445
Bluefield Colored Institute, 390
Bluefield State College, 379, 390; picture, 391
Bluestone Dam, 315
Bluestone River, 10, 134
Board of Public Works, state, 428-29
Boats, 200-204; flatboat, 200; picture, 200; keelboat, 200; picture, 201; river boats, early, 201, 203-4; picture, 204
Boette, Marie, 413
Boone, Daniel, 81, 141, 149-50
Boone County, 223, 349
Boreman, Governor Arthur Ingram, 233, 279-80, 283, 285-86, 293, 455-56, 469
Borland Springs, 32
Boundaries of state, 6-7
Boundary dispute, Virginia-Pennsylvania, 117-18; with Ohio, 299; with Maryland, 299
Bouquet, Colonel Henry, 108
"Bourbon" rule, 300-2
Boyd, Belle, 268, 270
Boyer, J. Edgar, 289
Bozarth, Mrs. John, 144
Braddock, General Edward, 101-2
Bradley, town of, 382
Bradstreet, Colonel, 108

Bramwell, town of, 309
Brandonville, town of, 191
Braxton County, 147, 185; formation of, 223; 269
Bridgeport, 56, 172, 327, 328, 365
Brooke County, 4, 34, 112, 179, 218, 346, 366, 368
Brooks, Alonzo Beecher, 23-24
Brooks, Elisha, 185
Brown, John, 234-38
Brown, William Guy, 283, 288
Bruceton Mills, 112
Buck, Pearl, 43-44
Buckhannon, 110, 255, 260, 311, 382, 445
Buckwheat, 347
Buckwheat Festival, Preston County, 447
Buffalo, town of, 78; Village, ancient, pictures, 46, 49; 54-55
Buffalo Academy, 172, 177; Seminary, 239
Buffalo Creek Hollow, 330
Bull, Captain, 147
Bullitt, Thomas, 112
Bulltown, 147, 185
Burning Rock, 26, 27
Burning Spring (natural gas, Kanawha County), 106
Burning Springs (gas, Wirt County), 191; oil, 261, 323
Burnside, General Ambrose E., 262
Burr, Aaron, 162, 241
Bushy Run, 108
Bye-Stander, the, 192
Byrd, Robert C., 422, 470
Byrd, William, 83-84

C

Cabell County, 35, 40, 50, 243, 366, 368
Cabin Creek, 321, 325, 362, 388
Cacapon River, 10, 31, 68

Cacapon State Park, 448
Calhoun, John C., 230
Calhoun County, 228, 268
Callahan, James Morton, 13, 14
Camden, Gideon D., 223
Camden, Johnson Newlon, 311, 324, 469
Campbell, Alexander, 172, 177, 178, 193, 221, 230, 232-33, 239-40; picture, 239
Campbell, Archibald W., 218; picture, 218; 275, 289
Campbells Creek, 185
Camp Caesar, 444, 447
Camp Pocahontas, 443
Camp Union, 105, 120
Canaan Valley, 28, 30
Canaan Valley State Park, 30, 448; picture, 449
Canals, 199-200
Cannel coal, 190
Cannelton, 190
Caperton, Allen T., 469
Caperton, G. H., 321
Caperton, W. Gaston, 321
Capitals of West Virginia, 295-97
Capitols of West Virginia, first capitol, picture, 280; second capitol, picture, 296; third capitol, picture, 296; fourth capitol, picture, 297; present state capitol, 448; capitol complex, picture, 426; main corridor, picture, 419; entrance to legislative chamber, picture, 431
Carbon black, 327
Cardinal, state bird, picture, 21
Carlile, John S., 223, 246, 248, 276
Carnifex Ferry, battle at, 257
Carroll, Edward G., 394-95
Cass Scenic Railroad, 310, 314
Castle Rock, 27
Cathedral State Park, 351
Catholic Church, early, 171, 233
Cattle, 345
Cedar Grove, 112
Cedar Lakes, 446

Ceredo, 309
Chadwick, Captain French Ensor, 403-4
Charleston, 40, 41; picture of Civic Center, 41; 112, 131, 134, 150, 260, 308, 365, 368, 369, 371, 373, 449; *see* "Capitals" and "Capitols"
Charleston Art Gallery, "Sunrise," picture, 376; 449
Charles Town, designated a town, 134, 238; pictures, 115, 116; 449
Charles Town Turf Club, 449
Cheat Lake, 315
Cheat Mountain, 66
Cheat River, 8, 9, 66, 68, 315
Chemical industry, 367-69
Chenoweth, Lemuel, 413
Cherry River Festival, 446-47
Chert, 35
Chesapeake and Ohio Canal, 199, 200
Chesapeake and Ohio Railway, 305-8, 388
Chesapeake and Potomac Telephone Company, 374
Chester, town of, 369
Chicago, 306, 307
Chilton, William E., 470
Chinese, 42
Christ Episcopal Church, picture, 92; 94
Christian Baptist, the, 239
Chronicles of Border Warfare, 56
Churches, early, 166-74; first church in West Virginia, 167; attitudes on slavery, 232-34; *see* under "Colleges, private"
Cincinnati, 306, 308
Circleville, 447
Cities, largest, 40-41
City officers, 436
Civil War, east-west differences, 217-25; slavery issue, 227-39; secession of Virginia, 241-48; votes of western Virginians, 246; the conflict in western Virginia, 249-62; Union troops, 250-51; Confederate forces, 251; im-

portance of western Virginia, 251-52; "reconstruction" era, 293-95
Claims to western Virginia lands, early, 96-98
Clark, George Rogers, 133
Clarksburg, 40, 110; designated a town, 134; 147, 167, 177, 209, 214, 222, 246, 311, 367, 370, 373, 382
Clay County, 189, 346
Clays, 35, 370
Clendenin, 311
Clendenin, George, 131, 134
Clermont, the, 202
Climate, 18, 19
Coal, 33, 189-90; cannel coal, 190; 317; coalfields, 317-23; map of coalfields, 320; by-products, 327; mine disasters, 329-31; labor movement, 329-39; black miners, 388
Coal and Coke Railroad, 305, 311
Coal River, 10, 77, 79
Colleges, private, 177, 178, 381-84; state, 177, 375, 379-81; *see under* individual colleges
Collins, Justus, 321
Community colleges, 380
Concord College (Athens), 375, 379
Conestoga wagon, 195-96
Confederate States of America, organization of, 244
Congress of Industrial Organizations, 337, 340
Conley, Phil, 413
Conley, William Gustavus, 417, *see* 417-18, 462
Connolly, John, 118
Conservation measures, 339, 417, 418
Consolidation Coal Company, 320
Constitutional Convention, 273, 277-78, 298
Constitution of West Virginia, 275-76; approval of, 276-77; approval by United States Senate, 277; approval by House of Representatives, 277; approval by President Lincoln, 277; (1872), 298-99

Continental Can Company, 370
Cook, Roy Bird, 413
Cooke family, divided sympathies, 249
Copley Oil Well, 325
Corbin, Ltd., 371
Corn, 347
Corning Glass Works, 370
Cornplanter, Indian, 58
Cornstalk, Chief, 120, 123-24; murder of, 130
Cornwell, Governor John Jacob, 335, 336, 417; *see* 417-18, 461
Corrick's Ford, battle at, 256
County officers, 434-36
County Unit Law, 377
Courts in West Virginia, 432-36
Covington and Ohio Railroad, 306
Cox, General Jacob D., 257, 260, 272
Cox, John Harrington, 413
Cranberry Glades, 28, 30
Crawford, William, 114
Crayon, Porte, *see* Strother, David Hunter
Creel Sand Diggings, 324
Cresap, Michael, 118
Cresap Mound, 54
Cresap's War, 118
Crozet, Claude, 197, 214-15
Crumb, George H., 413
Cumberland Mountains, 15
Cumberland Plateau, 16
Cumberland (National) Road, 196
Curtin, Phyllis, 413; picture, 412

D

Dairy products, 345
Dams, 314-15
Darke, William, 102, 134
"Darling of the Confederacy," 270
Davidson, Mrs. Andrew, 144
Davis, Henry Gassaway, 309, 421, 469
Davis, John Warren, 392, 410
Davis, John William, 408, 422
Davis, Julia, 413
Davis, Rebecca Harding, 413

Davis, town of, 311, 444
Davis and Elkins College, 382, 392, 448
Dawson, Governor William Mercer, 415; *see* 416-17; 459-60
Deckers Creek, 188
Deepwater, 312
Delany, Major Martin, 408
Department of Natural Resources, 350
Departments of state government, 428-34
Dickinson saltworks, 187
Dinwiddie, Governor Robert, 98, 100, 103
Disciples of Christ (Christian Church), 171-72, 232-33, 381
Diss Debar, Joseph H., picture of home, 211; 290
Distances across the state, 5
Dixon, Samuel, 321
Doctors, pioneer, 159
Doddridge, Joseph, 157, 163-64, 167
Doddridge, Philip, 221-22
Doddridge County, 35, 48, 169; formation of, 223
Dolly Sods, 30
Dorcas and Sally, 201
Drainage, 8-11; map, 11
Draper's Meadows, 103, 185
Droop Mountain, 262
Droop Mountain Battlefield State Park, 354
Dru, Joanne, 413
Dunbar, 53
Dunkard Bottom Settlement, 169
Dunkards, 169
Dunmore's War, 118-23
Du Pont Company, 163, 368
Durbin, 311
Dutch settlers, 91
Duval, Isaac, 184

E

Early, General Jubal A., 262

Early man on the American continent, 45-55; origins, 45, 46; migration, 46; in West Virginia, 47-55; time, 47-50
Earthworks by prehistoric man, 51-55
Eastern Panhandle, 4, 17, 34, 48, 60, 62, 68, 89, 178, 180, 233, 251, 253, 297, 346
East Steubenville, 48
East-west conflicts, 217-25
Ebb and Flow Spring, 30
Echols, General John, 260
Eckarly brothers, 90
Education, early, 165, 386; elementary, early, 174-76; secondary, early, 176-77; academies, early, 177-78; free schools established, 375; year 1866, 375; year 1869, 375; year 1871, 377; years 1900-25, 377; years 1940-1972, 377; years 1972-1973, 384; West Virginia Board of Education, 378-79; West Virginia Board of Regents, 379; vocational, 384-85; costs, 378; *see* "separate but equal" schools, 388; legislative provision for Negro schools, 388-89; *see* individual colleges; 388-89; Negro schools, 389-91; integration, 391-92
E. I. du Pont de Nemours & Company, 368
Eisenhower, President Dwight David, 401
Eleanor, town of, 424
Electric power, 371
Elevations of state, 5
Elinipsico, 130
Elizabeth, town of, 201
Elkhorn, 308
Elkins, 66, 67, 311, 365, 448
Elkins, Davis, 469, 470
Elkins, Stephen B., 309-11, 416, 422, 423, 469
Elkins Coalfield, 322-23
Elkins Municipal Airport, 365
Elk River, 8, 10, 68, 141 (*see under* Simon Kenton); 315
Ellet, Charles, Jr., 215

Emmons, General Delos Carleton, 406
Employment, early, 181-93; newer opportunities: 357—; in plants, 373; non-manufacturing, 373; printing and publishing, 373; food industries, 373; leather and leather products, 373; wholesale trade, 373; federal government, 373; state and local government, 373; general services, 373
English claims to the Ohio Valley, 96, 97, 98
English settlers, 91
Enterprise, the, 203
Episcopal Church, 166-67, 233
Etam Station, picture, 442
Evans, Polly, 103
Executive branch of West Virginia government, 426-30
Explorations of western Virginia, 72, 73-82, 89

F

Fairfax, Lord Thomas, 6, 7, 32, 87, 93
Fairfax Stone, 6, 7; picture, 7; 87
Fairmont, 40, 145, 211, 261, 284, 289, 306, 373
Fairmont Coalfield, 319-20
Fairmont State College, 375, 379
Fairs and Festivals, 443-48
Fallam, Robert, 75-77
Falling Rock, 325
Farland, Joseph Simpson, 408
Farmer's Repository, the, 192
Farmington, 286, 330
Farms (the years 1900-1970), number, 348; acreage, 348; size, 348; value per acre, 348
Farnsworth, Dana L., M.D., 412
Farnsworth, Governor Daniel Duane Tompkins, 293, 456
Faulkner, Charles J., 223, 295, 298, 302-4
Faulkner, Charles J., Jr., 469
Fayette County, 25, 48, 54, 112, 189, 190; formation of, 223; 367, 388
Fayetteville, 260
Field crops, 347
Files, Robert, 90
Files Creek, 90
Filipinos, 42
Fish, 21; fishing season, 448
Fish Creek, 208
Fisher, Suzanne, 413
Five Nations (Indian), 59
Flat Top Mountain, 27, 308, 309
Flat Top-Pocahontas Coalfield, 321
Fleming, Governor Aretas Brooks, 300, 302, 458
Flick, W. H. H., 295
Flick Amendment, 295
Floyd, John B., in the Civil War, 257
FMC Corporation, 368
Foote Mineral Company, 367
Forbes, General John, 104
Foreign-born residents, 41, 42
Forests, early, 349; lumber industry, early, 183-84; 349-52; peak lumber production, 349-50; forest nurseries, 350-52; acreage, 352; state forests, 352, 439; list of state forests, 354; national forests, 352; uses of wood, 352
Fort Ashby (restored), picture, 102
Fort Blair, 129
Fort Donnally, 127, 131
Fort Dunmore, 118
Fort Duquesne, 100, 101, 104
Fort Evans, 103
Fort Fincastle, 112
Fort Gower Address, 122
Fort Henry, 77, 78, 112, 128-29
Fort LeBoeuf, 99, 108
Fort Lee, picture, 131; 134, 149
Fort Martin Plant (electric), 371
Fort Morgantown, picture, 130
Fort Necessity, 101
Fort Pitt, 104, 108, 118, 127, 128
Fort Randolph, 127, 129
Forts, early, map, 128
Fort Seybert, 103

Fort Upper Tract, 103
Fostoria Glass Company, 370
Four-H Club, 344, 443
Frankford, designated a town, 134
Franklin, Benjamin, 116
Franklin, town of, 448
Frasure, Carl M., 437-38
Freedman's Bureau, 239
Fremont, General John C., 259, 260
French and Indian War, 95-105
French claims to the Ohio Valley, 80, 96, 97, 98
French Creek Game Farm, 448
Fugitive Slave Act, 232
Fulton, Robert, 202, 203
Furniture, manufacture of, 352
Fur trade, 73, 83
Future Farmers of America, 344
Future Homemakers of America, 344

G

Gainer, Patrick, 413
Gallatin, Albert, 184
Galperin, "Si," 339
Gandy River, 30
Gano apple, 347
Garcia, General Calixto, 404
Garnett, General Robert S., 254, 255
Garrison, William Lloyd, 229
Gas, natural, 33-34, 191, 318, 319, 323; map, 324; 325-26; by-products, 327
Gassaway, town of, 311
Gates, Major General Horatio, 102, 134
Gauley Bridge, 257
Gauley Mountain, 257
Gauley River, 8, 10, 26, 257, 315
Geographical sections of the state, 15-18
Geography, importance of, 11-12
Geological and Economic Survey, 50
George Washington National Forest, 352

German religious sects, 169-71, 233
German settlers, 91, 132-33, 169
Germany, wars with, 400-3, 405-6
Germany Valley, picture, 5
Gettysburg Battlefield monument to West Virginia Civil War soldiers, 263
Gilbert, Cass, 448
Gilmer County, formation of, 223
Girty, Simon, 132
Gist, Christopher, 80, 81, 88, 96, 99
Glass, 34, 184, 369-70
Glasscock, Governor William Ellsworth, 416; see 416-17, 460
Glass sand, 34
Glenville, 379, 445, 448
Glenville State College, 375, 379; picture, 383
Globe Hill Shell Heap, 48
Goff, Guy D., 470
Goff, Nathan, 423, 470
Golden Delicious apple, 346-47
Golden Horseshoe, Order of the, 78, 82
Gompers, Samuel, 333
Gore, Governor Howard Mason, 417; see 417-18; 423, 461-62
Gormania, 311
Government, city and town, 436
Government, county, 434-36
Government, state, governor, 426-28; other executive officers, 428; departments and boards, etc., 428-30; legislative branch, 430-32; judicial branch, 432-34; county government, 434-36; city government, 436
Governor, office of, 425-28
Governor's mansion, picture, 427
Graded school plan, 377, 386
Graffenreid, Baron de, 89
Grafton, 197, 209, 210, 213, 306, 369, 373, 445, 449
Grahamite, 323
Grain mills, 182-83
Grand Ohio Company, 116-17
Grandview State Park, picture, 26; 446
Grange, the, 344

Grant County, 4, 25, 27, 28, 30, 190; admission to state, 299; 349, 352, 371
Grantsville, 446
Grasses, 347
Grave Creek Mound, 48, 51, 52; picture, 52
Gravel, 34
Greathouse, Daniel, 119
Great Kanawha City, 52, 53
Great Lakes, 315
Great Meadows, 100
Green Bank — National Radio Astronomy Observatory, 441
"Greenbrier," the, 32
Greenbrier Coalfield, 323
Greenbrier Company, 88
Greenbrier County, 28, 32, 35, 67, 69; picture, oldest home, 70; 112; formation of county, 134; 167, 228, 233; admission to state, 274; 306, 345
Greenbrier River, 10, 66, 80, 88, 89, 90, 104, 123, 127, 259
Greenland Gap, 188
Greenspring Run, 306
Greer, Hal, 413
Greigsville, 211, 212
Grimes Golden apple, 346
Guyandotte Railroad, 322
Guyandotte River, 9, 68, 197, 260

H

Hackers Creek, 97 (*see* sketch)
"Hair buyer," 127, 133
Hale, John P., 413
"Hale House," hotel, 297
Half-King, 99, 100
Hall, Granville Davisson, 289
Hall of Fame for Great Americans, 268, 392
Hamilton, Alexander, 162, 192
Hamilton Farm Site, 50
Hamlin, 410

Hampshire County, 4, 25, 27, 28, 30, 48, 61; formation of, 86; 100, 219, 228, 253, 275, 306, 345, 352
Hampshire Furnace, 188
Hamtramck, John F., 243
Hancock County, 4, 35, 48, 157, 188, 218; formation of, 223; 228, 346, 366, 369
Hanging Rocks, 28, 61
Hannum, Alberta Pierson, 413
"Happy Retreat," 114; picture, 116
Hardy County, 4, 8, 28, 30, 31, 103; formation of, 134; 188, 228, 275, 345, 349
"Harewood," 114, picture, 115
Harper, Mrs. Howard H., 392
Harper, Robert, 234-35
Harpers Ferry, 5; picture, 17; 187-88, 208, 210, 234-39; incorporated, 235, 238, 252, 306, 444
Harpers Ferry National Historical Park, 17, 18; picture, 17
Harrison, Benjamin, 177
Harrison County, 35, 40, 48, 50, 56; formation of, 134; 172, 177, 190, 223, 243, 345, 349
Harrisville, 371
Harrisville Garment Corporation, 371
Hart, Nancy, 268-69
Hatfield, Governor Henry D., 334, 416; *see* 416-17; 460, 470
Hatfield Contract, 334
Hatfields, the, 446
"Hatfields and McCoys," 446
Hawks Nest, 25, 26, 306, 448
Hawks Nest State Park, 26, 354, 448
Hay, 347
Hayes, Rutherford B., 271, 331, 423
Hechler, Ken, 422
Hedrick, E. H., 422
Helvetia, 290
Hendricks, 311, 447
Henry, Patrick, 129, 130, 177
Henry Clay Furnace, 194
Henshaw, William, 102
Hereford, Frank, 469

Herndon, 312
Heroines, 142-44, 148-49, 268-70
Highways, *see* Roads
Hill, John H., 404
Hines, Major General John Leonard, 405
Hinton, 308, 448
Hite, Joist, 89, 92-93
Hoblitzell, Jack D., Jr., 470
Holland-Suco Color Company, 369
Holt, Governor Homer Adams, 420; *see* 420-21; 462-63
Holt, Rush D., 470
Homer Laughlin China Company, 370
"Honey in the Rock," 446
Hopewell culture, 51, 59
Horse racing, 449
House of Delegates, 430-32
Howard, John, 79
Huff, Sam, 413
Hughes, Jesse, 147
Hughes, Thomas, picture, 97
Hughes River, 190
Humphrey, Hubert H., 422
Hundley, Rod, 413
Hunting, accommodations for sportsmen, 440; season (birds, game animals), 448
Huntington, 40, 41, 177, 306, 307, 308, 347, 365, 366, 367, 369, 370, 371, 373, 449
Huntington, Collis P., 307-8
Huntington Galleries, 449
Hylton, Tracy W., 339

I

Ice Mountain, 30
Ices Ferry, 188
Image Rocks, 27
Imboden, General John D., 261, 262
Impartial Observer, the, 192
Income, per capita of West Virginians, 42, 43

"Independence Hall," West Virginia's, picture, 274
Indian claims to land, 96, 97
Indian place-names, 68
Indians, year 1970: 42; prehistoric, 45-55; historic, 57-68; language families, 57-59; disappearance from western Virginia, 60, 61; appearance, 63; lifestyle, 63; contributions to the white man, 64, 65; trails, 65-68; place-names, 68; 74-80; Monetons, 78; 81, 90; conflict with, 95-104; ceded lands, 96; 107-109, 118, 122; Cornstalk, 123-24; 127-31, 137-38, 142-50
Indian trails, 65-68
Industries, early, 181-93; 365-73
Institute, town of, 368, 379, 390, 392
International Nickel Company, 366
"Irish Wars," 211-12
Iron industry, early, 187-89
Island Creek Coal Company, 322

J

Jackson, Governor Jacob Beeson, 300, 457
Jackson, Thomas J., "Stonewall," 56, 238, 243, 249, 252, 260, 265, 267-68, 270, 344; picture, 258
Jackson County, 223, 345, 349, 366, 368, 371
Jackson's Mill, picture of cabin, 108, 267, 344, 443, 447
Jacob, Governor John Jeremiah, 293, 456-57
James River and Kanawha Turnpike, 257
James River Canal, 215
Japanese residents, 42
Jarvis, Anna, 449
Jay Treaty, 140
Jefferson, President Thomas, 106, 162, 166, 167, 191, 192, 220, 227, 228
Jefferson County, 4, 15, 32, 35, 114, 171, 176, 189, 194, 228, 242, 251, 275, 276,

281; admission to state, 298-99; 345, 349, 444
Jefferson National Forest, 352
Jenkins, General Albert G., 260, 262
Jesuits, 382
John E. Amos Plant, electric, 371
John Henry, 312, 392
Johnson, Joseph, 223, 224
Johnston, General Joseph E., 238; picture, 258
Johnson, Louis A., 409, 423
Johnson, President Lyndon, 362, 401
Johnson, Sir William, 109, 116, 119
"Jones, Mother," 333
Jones, General Sam, 262
Jones, Brigadier General William E., 261
Jones-Imboden raids, 261-62
Journalism, early, 192-93
Judges, state, 432-34

K

Kaiser Aluminum and Chemical Corporation, 366
Kammer-Mitchell Plant, electric, 371
Kanawha Airport, 365
Kanawha and Michigan Railroad, 305
Kanawha Coalfield, 321
Kanawha County, 35, 40, 48, 54, 68, 106, 112, 114; formation of, 134; 141, 150, 176, 190, 224, 228, 243, 334; airport, 365; 367, 368, 388, 390
Kanawha Republican, The, 192
Kanawha River, 9, 10, 26, 68, 77, 79, 81, 127, 190, 314, 315
Kanawha Salines, 190
Kanawha State Forest, 354
Kanawha Turnpike, 197
Kanawha Valley, 47, 48, 54, 77, 178, 233; in Civil War, 251; 257, 314, 315
Karnes, Samuel, 323
Kee, Elizabeth, 422
Kee, James, 422

Kee, John, 422
Kelley, Brigadier General B. F., picture, 253; 254, 260
Kelley, Walter, 112
Kellwood Company, 371
Kenhawa Spectator, The, 192
Kenna, John E., 314-16, 469
Kennedy, President John F., 401, 422
Kenova, 309
Kenton, Simon, picture, 141; 142
Keslers Cross Lanes, 257
Keyser, 4, 259, 380
Keystone, 309
Kilgore, Harley M., 422, 470
Killbuck, Indian chief, 103
Kingwood, 178, 447
Kinnan, Mary Lewis, 142
Knights of Labor, 332, 333
Knights of the Golden Horseshoe, 78, 82
Knotts, Don, 413
Knowles, John, 413
Korean Conflict, 401
Kump, Governor Herman Guy, 420; *see* 420-21; 462

L

Labor organizations, need for, 329-31; Knights of Labor, 332-33; American Federation of Labor, 332-33; United Mine Workers, 333; violence, 331, 334-37; Congress of Industrial Organizations, 337, 340
Laing, John, 321
Laird, William R., III, 470
Lakes, 8, 315
Lakin, 350
Lamb, Daniel, 289
Lamb, Leonard, 194
Lancastrian Academy, 177
Land divisions of United States, 3
La Salle, Robert Cavelier de, 72, 96
Late Prehistoric Period, 49
Latimer, Captain Julian Lane, 404

Latrobe, Benjamin Henry, 215
Laurel Hill, 255
Lead plates, 80
Lederer, John, 74, 75
Lee, General Charles, 102, 134
Lee, General Fitzhugh, 262
Lee, Richard Henry "Light Horse Harry," 31, picture, 132
Lee, General Robert E., 31, 132, 238, 258-59, 261, 268
Lee's White Sulphur Springs, 31
Length of state, 5
Leonhart, William, 410
Letcher, John, 244, 246, 248
Lewis, Andrew, 88, 89, 103, 105, 106, 108, 120, 121, 185
Lewis, John L., 337
Lewis, Virgil A., 413
Lewisburg, 18, 28, 67, 105, 112, 120; designated a town, 134; 149, 167, 259, 260, 447
Lewisburg Academy, 178
Lewisburg Warm Springs road, 197
Lewis County, 35, 97, 134, 267, 322, 344, 349
Libbey-Owens-Ford Glass Company, 369
Libraries, early, 179
Lightburn, General Joseph A. J., 260
Limestone, 34, 370
Lincoln, President Abraham, 243-44; picture, 245; 246, 251, 252, 277-79, 281, 282
Lincoln County, admission to state, 299; 321, 410
Linsly Institute, 177, 279
Literary Fund, 174-75
Little Kanawha River, 9, 67, 185, 191, 201, 208, 261, 268
Little Kanawha Trail, 67
Livestock, 345
Location of state, central, 5, 38; map, 38
Logan, Indian chief, 58; murder of family, 119; 121-22; address, 122
Logan, town of, 335, 380

Logan Coalfield, 321-22
Logan County, 68, 321-22, 333, 335, 349, 388
Logstown Treaty, 96, 97
London Company, 72, 73
Loop Creek, 54
Loring, General W. W., 259, 260
Lost River, 30
Lost River State Park, 31, 354
Loyalists, 132-33
Loyal Land Company, 79, 88
Lumber industry, early, 183-84, 349-52; peak production, 349-50; uses of wood, 352
Lusitania, the, 400
Lutherans, 169-71

M

MacCorkle, Governor William Alexander, 300, 302, 458
McCausland, General John, 262
McClellan, General George B., 247, 254, 255, 256
McCoys, the, 446
McCulloch, Major Samuel, 129
McDonald, Major Angus, 119
McDonald's expedition, 119
McDowell County, 40, 228, 246, 274, 336, 349, 388
McElhenny, Rev. John, 178
McGraw, Warren, 339
McKinley, President William, 271
McWhortersville, 134

Maidenform, Inc., 371
Malden, 106, 141, 190, 233, 396
Mann, Horace, 178
Mann, Isaac T., 321
Mannington, 212, 369
Mannington oil field, 325
Manufacturing, varied, 373; *see under* particular manufacturing; employment, 373

Marion County, 35, 40, 110; formation of, 223; 367, 368
Marital status of West Virginians, 42
Marland, Governor William C., 420; see 420-21; 464
Marlin, Jacob, 90
Marlinton, 67, 90, 446
Marshall, John, 26, 220-21
Marshall Academy, 177
Marshall County, 4, 54, 218; formation of, 223, 349, 366, 367, 368, 371
Marshall University, college, 177; 375, 380; pictures, 220, 294, 376
Martinsburg, 18, 43, 171, 191, 196, 213, 252, 253, 296, 297, 300, 331, 347, 357, 365, 370, 371, 373, 414, 444
Martinsburg Mills, Inc., 371
Martinsburg Municipal Airport, 365
Mason and Dixon Line, 6, 118, 317–18
Mason County, 35, 48, 114, 187, 345, 349, 366, 367, 368
Matewan, 446
Mathews, Governor Henry Mason, 300, 331, 457
Matoaka, 312
Meadows, Governor Clarence Watson, 420; see 420-21; 463
Medical Center, West Virginia University, 420; picture, 420
Medical School, West Virginia University, 420
Memoirs of Indian Wars and Other Occurrences, 69, 70
Memorial Day, establishment of, 413
Mennonites, 169
Mercer, John, 103
Mercer County, 25, 27, 35, 40, 67, 134; formation of, 223; 274; airport, 365, 367, 379, 388
Mercer County Airport, 365
"Message to Garcia," 404-5
Methodist Church, 173-74, 233, 382
Mexican War, 242-43
Michel, Louis, 89
Middlebourne, 446
Midland Trail, map, 67; 197

Military leaders, 403-8
Millennial Harbinger, The, 193, 232, 240
Mills, early, 182-84
Milton, 369
Mineral County, 4, 190; admission to state, 299; 322, 345, 349
Mineral resources, 33-35
Mineral springs, 31, 32
Mingo County, 68; admission to state, 299; 322, 333, 335-36, 349, 388
Mingo Flats, 67, 68
Minority groups, 41, 42
Mississippi River, 315
Mobay Chemical Company, 369
Moccasin Rangers, 268-69
Mollohan, Robert, 422
Moneton Indians, 78
Monongahela National Forest, 30, 352
Monongahela Power Company, 371
Monongahela River, 8, 9, 68, 81, 127, 315; Battle of, 101-2
Monongahela Valley, 67, 178, 254-55
Monongalia Academy, 177
Monongalia County, 35, 40, 48, 50, 68, 110; formed, 112; 134, 144, 190, 194, 243, 251, 345, 368, 371, 386, 423
Monongalia Gazette and Morgantown Advertiser, the, 192
Monroe County, 10, 27, 28, 32, 48, 112, 134, 172, 176, 180, 228, 274, 344, 345, 349
Montgomery, 54, 112, 308
Moore, Governor Arch A., Jr., 384, 421 (*see* 2 paragraphs), 422, 466
Moorefield, 103, 188, 446
Moravian sect, 169
Morgan, Daniel, 102, 132; picture, 133; 134
Morgan, David, 145
Morgan, Governor Ephraim Franklin, 336, 417; *see* 417-18; 461
Morgan, Levi, 145
Morgan, Morgan, 89, 92, 93, 94, 166, 196
Morgan, Zackquill, 110, 112, 132

index 485

Morgan County, 4, 32, 34, 275
Morgan's Chapel, picture, 92; 94, 166
Morgan Shirt Company, Inc., 371
Morgantown, 40, 110; designated a town, 134; 167, 188, 192, 197, 306, 365, 369, 371, 373
Morgantown and Kingwood Railroad, 305, 311
Morgantown-Moundsville Road, 197
Morgantown Municipal Airport, 365
Morris, Levi, 112
Morris, William, 112
Morris Harvey College, 380, 382; picture, 382
Morrow, Dwight, 408
"Mother Jones," 333
Mother's Day, originator of, 449; shrine, 449
Mound Builders, 51-55, 59, 60
Mounds and other earthworks, 51-55
Moundsville, 51, 114, 129, 367, 369, 370, 373
Mountaineer Boys State, 443
Mountaineer Dinner Theatre, 444
"Mountain State," 3
Mountain State Art and Craft Fair, 446
Mountain State Forest Festival, 448
Mount Carbon, 48, 54
Mt. Storm Generating Station, 371
Mullens, 312
Music, Olgebay Park, 440; picture, 383
Musicians, 413
Musick, Ruth Ann, 413

N

"Nail City," 188
Name for the new state, 273-74
National Computer Center, picture, 43
National forests in West Virginia, 352
National Radio Astronomy Observatory, 441
National Road, 196
National Youth Science Camp, 443

Natural gas, 191, 323-27; map, 324
Nature tours, Cranberry Mountain Spring, 444; Webster County, 444
Naval Radio Station, Sugar Grove, 441-43
Navigation, 10, 11, 314, 315
Needham, James, 77
Neely, Governor Matthew Mansfield, 420; *see* 420-21; 422, 463, 470
Negroes, *see* Blacks
Nemacolin's Path, 66, 99, 100, 101
Nessly, Jacob, 157, 346
Newburg, 212
New Cumberland, 369
Newell, 369, 370
New Haven, 367
New Martinsville, 68, 311, 368-69, 448
New Orleans, the, 189, 203
Newport, Christopher, 73
New River, 8, 9, 10, 25, 26; picture, 26; 47, 77, 79, 103, 104, 185, 306, 308
New River Coalfield, 321
New Salem, 169
Newspapers, early, 192-93; 373
Newton D. Baker General Hospital, 414
Nicholas County, 48, 269, 321, 368
Nitro, 368, 371
Nixon, President Richard M., 402, 408, 410-12
Nonhelema, 130, 131
Norfolk and Western Railway, 305, 306, 308, 309, 322, 388
Norman, John C., M.D., 393, 412
Norris, Professor P. W., 52, 53
North American Plain, 3
North Branch of the Potomac, 6, 10, 28
Northern Neck Proprietary, 87
Northern Panhandle, 4, 15, 34, 48, 62, 118, 180, 218, 251, 297, 346, 365-66
Northern Panhandle Coalfield, 323
Northfork, 309
Northwestern Academy, 178
Northwestern Turnpike, 197, 215, 256
Nurseries, forestry, 350-52

O

Oats, 347
O'Dell, Lieutenant Leonard, 410
Officers of the new state, 283-89
Officers of the United States government, 436
Oglebay Park, Wheeling, 23, 24; picture, 288, 383; 350, 440, 446, 448, 449
Ohio County, 4, 34, 40, 48, 50, 68; formation of, 112; 134, 176, 214, 218, 243; airport, 365; 366, 368
Ohio Land Company, 80, 88, 116
Ohio River, 4, 6, 8, 9, 10, 15, 34, 35, 47, 48, 61, 62, 66, 68, 77, 79, 80, 81, 88, 95, 96, 98, 99, 110, 134, 140, 156, 178, 186, 197, 201, 203, 210, 297, 299, 306, 314, 315, 323, 346, 349, 365, 366, 368
Ohio Valley Amateur Golf Championship, 446
Ohio Valley College, 384
Ohio Valley Section, 15, 16
Oil, 33, 34, 190-91, 317-19, 323-27; map of oil fields, 324
Oil fields, 323-25; map, 324
Old Stone Church, 167; picture, 168
Old Sweet Springs, 32
Opequon River, 68, 92, 169, 172
Orchestra, 383
Ordinance of Secession, 246
Organ Cave, 28
Owens, Michael J., 374
Owens-Illinois, Inc., 370

P

Packhorse Ford, 61, 68
Paden City, 369
Page, town of, 312
Paleo-Indian Period, 47, 51
"Panhandle State," 3
Parkersburg, 9, 40, 41, 134, 178, 191, 197, 209, 210, 213, 214, 306, 324, 365, 367, 368, 369, 371, 373, 380, 384, 448
Parkersburg Community College, 380
Parsons, 66, 311, 350, 371
Patrick, Major General Mason M., 405
Patterson's Creek, 10
Patteson, Governor Okey L., 420; see 420-21; 464
Pauley, Margaret Hanley, 142-44
Payne, Christopher H., 392
Payne, John Barton, 408-9, 423
Pease, Louise McNeill, 413
Pendleton County, 4, 5, 25, 27, 28, 66, 103; formation of, 134; 171, 275, 345, 349, 352, 441
Peoples Company, 371
Petersburg, 30, 444
Peter's Mountain, 27
Peterstown, 112, 134
Peter Tarr's iron furnace, 188; pictures, 188, 189
Petroglyphs, 50
Petroleum, see Oil
Philippi, see under Civil War; 447
Philippi, Battle of, 254; picture of bridge, 254; see under Civil War
Phillip Sporn Plant, electric, 371
Piedmont, 262
Piedmont Plateau, 3
Pierpont, Francis H., 233, 247, 261, 273, 279, 280, 283-85
Pierpont, Mrs. Francis H., 413
Pinckney Treaty, 140
Pinnacle Rocks, 27; picture, 27
Pioneer home life, 153-61; buildings, 153-56; food, 157; furnishings, 156-57; clothing, 158-59; health, 159-60; social affairs, 160-61; punishments, 161-62
Pipestem State Park, 30; picture, 445; 448
Pittsburgh Plate Glass (PPG Industries), 368-69, 370
Place-names, Indian, 68
Plant life, 21-23
Pleasants County, 32, 34, 183, 323, 368
Pocahontas County, 28, 30, 67, 68, 262, 274, 314, 352, 441

Pocahontas Coalfield, 321
Pocahontas Fuel Company, 321
Pocatalico River, 68
Poe family, 145
Pointer, Dick, 392
Point Pleasant, 9, 80, 117, 120, 124, 127, 129; Second Battle of, 131; 134, 150
Polecat oil well, picture, 322
Politics, state, years 1897-1917, 415-17; years 1917-33, 417-18; years 1933-57, 420-21; years 1957-70, 421; national, 421-23
Pontiac's War, 108, 109
Population of state, 37, 38; density, 38, 39; urban-rural, 39, 40; concentration areas, 40, 41; minorities, 41, 42; sex, 42; marital status, 42; income, 42; welfare statistics, 42, 43
Porterfield, Colonel George A., 254
Position of state, 5
Post, Melville Davisson, 413
Potomac Academy, 177
Potomac Edison Company, 371
Potomac River, 6; 10, 61, 68, 87, 89, 90, 101, 183, 187, 189, 199, 200, 202, 205, 207, 210, 299; *see* North Branch of the Potomac River *and* South Branch of the Potomac River
Potomac Section, 15, 17, 18
Potomac State College of West Virginia University, 177, 380-81
Potomoke Church, 167
Potowmac Guardian and Berkeley Advertiser, The, 192
Pottery, 35, 369
Poultry, 345
PPG Industries, 368-69, 370
Pratt, 54
Prehistoric man, 45-55
Presbyterian Church, 167; picture, 168; 233, 234, 382
Presidential appointments, 408-10
Preston Academy, 178
Preston County, 35, 90, 112, 178, 188, 190, 191, 210, 243, 299, 345, 352, 367, 423

Price, Samuel, 469
Primary-metal industries, 365-66
Princeton, 134, 312, 371
Pringle, John and Samuel, 110-11
Proclamation of 1763, 109, 110
Propst Church, 171
Protestant Episcopal Church, 166-67
Pruntytown, 173, 408
Putnam County, 54, 114, 115; formation of, 223; 355, 371, 424, 444

Q

Quakers, settlers, 91, 92, 141, 168-69
Quartz, 35
Quinnimont, 189

R

Radio stations, 373
Railroads, 207-16; Baltimore and Ohio, 207-16; restrictions, 207-8; "Irish War," 211-12; longest tunnel, 210; 305-14; Chesapeake and Ohio, 305-8; Norfolk and Western, 305, 308-9; Virginian, 311-12; decline, 312; Amtrak, 312
Rainfall, 18-19
Raleigh County, 40, 54; formation of, 223; 345, 388
Ramsey, Robert, 422
Randolph, Edmund, 177
Randolph, Jennings, 422, 470
Randolph, Peyton, 130
Randolph Academy, 177
Randolph County, 30, 48, 66, 67; formation of, 134; 142, 290, 352, 367, 424
Rathbone brothers, 191
Ravenswood, 114, 260, 366, 369
"Reconstruction," 293; hardships for former Confederates, 293-95; end of, 300, 315; 377, 388

Rector College, 173, 179
Redhouse, 424
Red Jacket, Indian chief, picture, 58
Red Sulphur Springs, 32
Rehoboth Church, pictures, 166 *and* 175; 174, 180
Reid, Whitelaw, 272
Religion, early, 165-74; *see under* various denominations
Renmar Manufacturing Company, 371
Reno, Jesse Lee, 243, 265-66
Reorganized (or Restored) Government of Virginia, declaration of, 247-48; 261, 273; approves new state, 276; departure of, 280-81
Repository, the, 192
Reservoirs, 8, 315
Restored Government of Virginia, *see* Reorganized Government of Virginia
Reuther, Walter P., 339-40
Revercomb, Chapman, 470
Revolutionary War, 123, 125-36
Rhododendron, 19
Rhododendron Girls State, 443
Rhor Rock Shelter, 48
Rich Mountain, 255
Richwood, 444, 446, 448
Ripley, 260, 446
Ritchie County, 169; formation of, 223; 323
River improvement, 314-15
River systems, 8-11
River traffic, years 1700's, 200, 201; years 1800's, 202-4; year 1929, 314-15
Rivesville, 446
Roads, early, first public, 196-98; National Road, 196; Cumberland Road, 196; Kanawha Turnpike, 197; Midland Trail, 197; Northwestern Turnpike, 197; State Road, 197; Lewisburg-Warm Springs Road, 197; Morgantown-New Martinsville Road, 197; Staunton-Parkersburg Turnpike, 197; Morgantown-Moundsville Road, 197; road-building programs, 358-64; 421

Rockefeller, John D. "Jay," 339
Rock formations, 25-28
Rocky Mountains, 3, 46
Rogers, H. H., 311-12
Romney, incorporated, 112; 134, 188, 197; picture of bridge, 252; 253, 306, 379, 392
Ronceverte, 308
Roosevelt, Mrs. Eleanor, 423-24
Rosecrans, William S., 255, 257, 259
Rosier, Joseph, 470
Rowan, Lieutenant Andrew Summers, 404-5
Rowlesburg, 212, 255
Ruffner, Henry, 178, 231; Pamphlet, 231
Ruffner place (tavern), 198
Ruffner saltworks, 186, 187
Rumsey, James, 201-2, 205-6

S

St. Albans, 48, 78, 308, 446
St. Andrew's Church, 445
Saint Clara, 290
St. George, 183
St. Marys, 325
Salem College, 382
Sales, Soupy, 413
Salley, John Peter, *see* Salling, John Peter
Salling (*or* Salley), John Peter, 79
Salt, 16, 31, 35, 184-87, 316
Salt Sulphur Springs, 32, 260
Sand, 34
Scary Creek, battle at, 257
Scenic wonders, 28-31
Schools, *see* Education
Scotch-Irish settlers, 91
Scott, Nathan B., 469
Seal of West Virginia, 12, 13
Second Battle of Point Pleasant, the, 131
Secretary of state, 428

Seneca Caverns, 28
Seneca Rock, 27, 66
Settlement, incentives, 84, 85; location, 89-93; nationalities, 91, 92
Settlement rights to property, 110
Settlers, origin of first, 41; Dutch, 91; English, 91; Germans, 91; Quakers, 91; Scotch-Irish, 91; Welsh, 91
Seventh Day Baptists, 169
Sewell, Stephen, 90
Sex of West Virginians, 42
Shannondale Springs, 32
Shawkey, Morris P., 377
Shenandoah Downs, 449
Shenandoah River, 10, 68, 82, 89
Shenandoah Valley, 15, 75, 133, 141, 248
Shepherd College, 379
Shepherdstown, 112, 134, 166, 167, 171, 177, 192, 243, 379, 444
Shott, Hugh Ike, Sr., 470
Shreve, Captain Henry M., 203
Shrubs, 23
Silk, production of, 191
Sinks of Gandy, 30
Sistersville, 325, 447
Sistersville oil field, 325
Skiing, 444, 448
Slack, John, 422
Slavery, 186, 218-; tax on slaves, 224-25; 227-39, 243, 275
Smith, Benjamin, 224
Smith, Governor Hulett C., 421, *see* two paragraphs; 465
Smith-Lever Act, 343-44
Smoke Hole, picture, 16; 28
Smoke Hole Caverns, 28
Snowfall, 19
Snyder, Charles Philip, 406
South Branch of the Potomac River, 10, 27, 66, 79, 90, 104, 146, 169, 256, 262, 345
South Carolina, secession, 241, 244
South Charleston, 40, 52, 53, 367, 368
South Charleston Mound, 48, 52, 53, 63

Southern Coal Producers Association, 322
Southern Coal Show, 444-45
Southern West Virginia Community College, 380
Space Age, West Virginia in, 441-43
Spanish-American War, 399, 402, 403-5
Spanishburg, 446
Spencer, 260, 371, 448
Sportsmen, accommodations for, 440
Spotswood, Governor Alexander, 78; picture, 79; 81-82, 387
Spruce Knob, 5; pictures, 5, 76
Stagecoaches, 198
Staggers, Harley O., 422
Standard Metropolitan Statistical Area, 40, 41
State animal, 20
State attorney general, 428
State auditor, 428
State bird, 21
State Board of Public Works, 425, 428-29
State Board of Vocational Education, 379
State boards and commissions, various, list, 430
State commissioner of agriculture, 428
State Dairy Cattle Show, 447
State departments, government, 428-30
State Fair of West Virginia, 447
State flag, *frontispiece*
State flower, 19
State forests, 352; list of, 354; 418
State motto, 12
State museum, 448
State parks, 352; list of, 354; 417, 439-40, 448
State Road, the, 197
State seal, 12, 13
State superintendent of schools, 375, 379, 421, 428
State treasurer, 428
State tree, picture, 22
Statuary Hall, West Virginians honored, picture, 284; 285, 316

490   index

Staunton-Parkersburg Turnpike, 197, 255, 259, 267
Steber, Eleanor, 413
Steel, 365-66
Stephen, General Adam, 102, 108, 120, 135-36
Stephenson, Hugh, 133, 134
Stevenson, Governor William Erskine, 293, 456
Stockade, picture, 155
Stockton, Frank R., 413
Stockton, Isabella, 144
Stone, 35
Storer College, 238-39, 390
Strange Creek, 189
Strauss, Lewis L., 409, 423
Strip mining, 54, 339
Strother, David Hunter "Porte Crayon," 238, 252, 264
Stuart, John, 69, 70, 109, 110, 120, 130
Stump, Admiral Felix B., 406-8
Stutler, Boyd B., 413
Sugar Grove, Radio Station at, 441-43
Sullivan, Leon H., 394
Summers, Festus Paul, 413
Summers, George W., 224, 225-26
Summers, Judge Lewis, 221
Summers County, 90, 134; admission to state, 299
Summersville, 257, 446, 448
Summersville Dam, 315
"Sunrise," art gallery, 449
Sutherland, Howard, 470
Sutherland, Lieutenant General Richard K., 406
Sutton, 185, 311, 446
Sutton Dam, picture, 314; 315

T

Tarr, Campbell, 289
Tarr, Peter, 188
Taverns, 198
Taylor County, 35, 173, 179, 190; formation of, 223; 319, 349

Taylor Smith and Taylor Company, 369
Tecumseh, Indian, 57
Telegraph, 373
Telephone, 373-74
Television stations, 373
Temperatures, 18
"Test oath," 294-95, 304, 377
Textiles, 371
Thomas, town of, 311
Timber, 349-52
Title to property, how obtained in early years, 110
Tobacco, 158, 347
Tomahawk rights to property, 110
"Tom Thumb" engine, 209
Tories, 132
Transportation, early, 195-204; pack-horse, 195; wagon, 195-96; B&O, 207-16; railroads, general, years 1852-1912, 305-14; river, 314-15; 357-65; early period, 357, 358; modern highways, 359-65; interstate highways, 362-64; Appalachian Corridors, 362-64; air travel, 365
"Traveller," 259
Treason, 162
Treaty of Camp Charlotte, 120-21
Treaty of Fort Finney, 137
Treaty of Fort McIntosh, 137
Treaty of Fort Stanwix, 105, 109, 137
Treaty of Greenville, 140
Treaty of Hard Labour, 109
Treaty of Logstown, 96
Treaty of Paris, 107
Treaty of Pittsburgh, 127
Trees, 21-23; state tree picture, 22
Trent, Captain William, 100, 116
Trent, William W., 391-92
Tri-State Airport (Huntington), 365
Trough, The, 28
Trout Pond, 8; picture, 8; 30
Trust, first commercial, 187
Tucker County, 30, 66, 112, 183, 322, 352
Tu-Endie-Wei Park, picture, 121; 149

Tug Fork River, 7, 9, 79, 308
Tunnelton, 210, 212, 261
Turner, Nat, 228
Turnpike, the West Virginia, picture, 361; 362, 410
Turnpikes, 198
Tuscarora Mountains, 68
"Twelve Apostles," 298
Twin Falls State Park, 354, 448
Tygart, David, 90
Tygart River, 8, 9, 90, 142, 315
Tygart River Reservoir Dam, 315
Tygart Valley, 112, 259, 306, 424
Tyler County, 48, 54, 183, 235, 325, 326, 368

U

Underwood, Governor Cecil H., 421, *see* two paragraphs; 464
Union Carbide Corporation, 367, 368
United Auto Workers (UAW), 339
United Mine Workers, 333, 337
Up from Slavery, 398
Upshur County, 47, 110, 322
USS *West Virginia*, 401; picture, 402

V

Vacation farms, 440
Valley and Ridge Province, 4
Valley of Virginia, 15, 61, 78, 89, 96, 238, 260
Vance, Cyrus Roberts, 409
Vandalia, 116-17
Van Meter, Isaac, 89
Van Meter, John, 89
Van Winkle, Peter Godwin, 283, 286, 469
Vietnam conflict, 401-2
Vines, 23
Virginia debt, 299-300
Virginia Electric Power Company, 371

Virginian Railway, 305, 311-12
Vocational education, 384-85

W

Wade, Alexander L., 377, 385-87
Waldron, William H., 406
Walker, Thomas, 79-80, 127
Wallace, William J. L., 395
Wardensville, 188
Warder, Rear Admiral Frederick Burdett, 408
Warm Springs, 32, 160
War of 1812, 174, 186, 242
Warrior Path, 68; Trail, 68
Wars, 1898-1973, Spanish-American War, 399, 402, 403-5; World War I, 400, 402-3, 405-6; World War II, 400-1, 403, 406; Korean conflict, 401; Vietnam conflict, 401-2
Washington, the, 203
Washington, Booker T., 392, 396-98
Washington, Charles, 114; picture of home, 116
Washington, George, 87, 98-104; picture, 99; 113-15, 133-34, 137-40; picture, 139; 140, 157, 158, 160, 166, 188, 199, 202, 244, 346
Washington, Lieutenant Colonel John A., 259
Washington, Lawrence Augustine, 115
Washington, Colonel Lewis W., 237
Washington, Samuel, 114; picture of home, 115
Washington Hall, 246
Water area, 7
Waterford Park, 449
Waterways, 199-; canals, 199-200
Watson, Clarence W., 469
Wayne, General Anthony, 140
Wayne County, 5, 35, 48; formation of, 223; 368
Ways to make a living, early, 181-93; 357-74

Webster County, 32, 228, 322, 349, 352
Webster Springs, 32
Weirton, 40, 41, 188, 366; picture of high school, 378; 380
Weirton Steel Division, 366
Welch, 309, 336, 392; picture, 400
Wellsburg, 163, 167, 182, 183, 184, 192, 240
Wellsburg Herald, the, 192
Welsh settlers, 41, 91
West, Jerry, 413, 451-52
Western Maryland Railway, 305, 311
West Fork River, 9, 185, 344
West Liberty, designated a town, 134; 379
West Liberty Academy, 177
West Liberty State College, 177, 375, 379
Westminster Abbey, London, 405
Weston, 134, 261, 267, 344, 369, 370, 405, 447
West Virginia Agriculturist, The, 355
West Virginia Board of Education, 378-79, 429
West Virginia Board of Public Works, 425, 428
West Virginia Board of Regents, 379, 380, 381, 384, 429
West Virginia Board of Vocational Education, 379, 429
West Virginia College of Graduate Studies, 379-80
West Virginia Colored Institute, 390, 404
West Virginia Conservation Commission, 418
West Virginia County Unit Law, 377
West Virginia Department of Agriculture, 440
West Virginia Department of Commerce, 440
West Virginia Department of Natural Resources, 20, 350; forerunners, 417-18; 429, 440
West Virginia Division of Vocational Education, 384

West Virginia Game, Fish, and Forestry Commission, 418
West Virginia Geological and Economic Survey, 50, 430
West Virginia Glass Specialty Company, Inc., 370
West Virginia Hall of Fame, 392
West Virginia Institute of Technology, 379, 380
West Virginia Legislature, 425, 430-32; Senate, 430-32; House of Delegates, 430-32
West Virginia University Medical Center, 420; picture, 420
West Virginia Northern Community College, 380
West Virginia School of Medicine, Dentistry, and Nursing, 420
West Virginia Schools for the Deaf and the Blind, 378-79, 392
West Virginia State College, 379-80, 389-90; picture, 389; 392
West Virginia State Flag, *frontispiece*
West Virginia State Folk Festival, 445
West Virginia Strawberry Festival, 445
West Virginia Supreme Court of Appeals, 432
West Virginia Turnpike, picture, 361; 362, 410
West Virginia University, 177; Agricultural Experiment Station, 350; School of Forestry, 350; Agricultural College, 375-77; 379; picture, 380; 391; Medical School, 420; Medical Center, 420; picture, 420
West Virginia Water Festival, 448
West Virginia Wesleyan College, 382, 392
Wetzel, Lewis, picture of parents' home, 88; 147-48
Wetzel County, 34; formation of, 223; 368
Whaley, Kellian V., 283, 288-89
Wheat, 347
Wheeling, 40, 41, 110, 115, 118, 120, 127, 128, 129, 146, 147, 171, 174, 177,

183, 184, 188, 189, 190, 193, 196, 199, 202, 203, 208, 210, 213, 222, 231, 246, 247, 254, 259, 261, 265, 273, 279, 280, 295, 297, 306, 333, 365, 366, 369, 371, 373, 375, 380, 382, 440, 446, 448, 449
Wheeling Bridge, 199, 215
Wheeling College, 382
Wheeling Convention, First, 246-47; Second, 247, 253-54; 256, 273, 299
Wheeling Creek, 80, 110
Wheeling Downs, 449
Wheeling Electric Company, 371
Wheeling Intelligencer, the, 193, 218, 275
Wheeling-Ohio County Airport, 365
Wheeling-Pittsburgh Steel Corporation, 366
Whiskey, 158
White, Governor Albert Blakeslee, 415; see 416-17; 459
White, Israel Charles, 33, 36, 325, 326
White, William R., 178, 289, 375
White Sulphur Springs, 32, 198, 257, 262, 306, 445
White Water Weekend, 444
Width of state, 5
Willey, Waitman T., picture, 223; 224, 233, 261, 276-77, 283, 286-87, 469
Willey Amendment, 276-77; approval by state convention, 279; approval by popular vote, 279
Williamson, 309, 322, 380
Williamson Coalfield, 322
Williamstown, 369
Willow Island, 369
Wilson, Governor Emanuel Willis, 300, 446, 458
Wilson, Eugenius M., 221
Wilson, William L., 423
Wilson, President Woodrow, 305, 400, 409, 414
Winding Gulf Coalfield, 321
Winds, 18
Winfield, 315
Winter sports, 30, 444, 448
Wirt County, formation of, 223; 317, 323
Wise, General Henry A., 257, 259, 260
Withers, Alexander Scott, 55-56
Wood, Abraham, 73-78
Woodburn Female Seminary, 177
Wood County, 34, 40, 162, 178; airport, 365; 366, 367, 368
Woodland Periods, 48, 49, 51
Woods family settlement, 112
Woodson, Carter G., 392, 395-96
World War I, 400, 402-3, 405-6
World War II, 400-1, 403, 406
Writers, modern, 413
Wyoming County, 27, 35; formation of, 223; 321

Y

Yeager, Brigadier General Charles E. "Chuck," 410; picture, 411
Yeager Bridge, 410
Youth programs, 443

Z

Zane, Ebenezer, 110, 129, 146
Zane, Elizabeth "Betty," 129, 146; picture, 146
Zane family, 110, 146

WEST VIRGINIA HISTORY was designed, composed, printed, and bound by the C. J. Krehbiel Company, Cincinnati, Ohio. It is set in Times Roman, with display in Chelmsford. The book is printed on Finch Title Opaque paper and bound in Columbia Riverside Linen cloth.